Study Guide

to Accompany

WEST'S
BUSINESS LAW
Alternate UCC
Comprehensive Edition

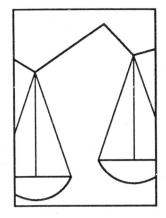

Fourth Edition

GAYLORD A. JENTZ
ROGER LeROY MILLER
FRANK B. CROSS
KENNETH W. CLARKSON

Prepared by
Barbara E. Behr
Professor
Department of Finance and Business Law
Bloomsburg University, Pennsylvania

West Publishing Company
St Paul New York Los Angeles San Francisco

ISBN 0-314-69764-0

CONTENTS

PREFACE

The function of this *Study Guide* is to assist you in your efforts to grasp the fundamental principles of law developed in *West's Business Law: Alternate UCC Comprehensive Edition*, Fourth Edition, by Gaylord A. Jentz, Roger LeRoy Miller, Frank B. Cross and Kenneth W. Clarkson.

Students approaching the subject of business law tend to be overwhelmed because of the unfamiliar terms used and the apparently countless number of legal rules which they are expected to understand. This *Study Guide* highlights important concepts and terminology and provides a framework for organizing your studying. It is hoped that this structured approach will reduce anxiety and eliminate confusion. With this in mind, the materials in the *Study Guide* have been developed in order to give you a variety of learning tools so that you can do your studying in an organized fashion. It is assumed, of course, that you will be reading, studying and referring to the text and relevant appendices while using these supplementary materials.

In the *Study Guide* you will find the following:

1. **Unit Summaries**—Brief overviews of the areas of law covered in each of the nine units.

2. **Chapter Introductions**—Short summaries of the topics covered in each of the 58 chapters. The introductions preview and tie together the concepts presented in more detail both in the text and the chapter outlines provided in this *Study Guide*.

3. **Things to Keep in Mind**—Reminders of important principles. A difficult concept may be clarified or reiterated; relevant principles, developed in earlier chapters, may be recalled; explanations may be given for terminology or items, the significance of which may have been overlooked.

4. **Chapter Outlines**—Detailed systematic reviews of legal principles presented in the text.

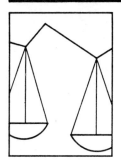

THE LEGAL ENVIRONMENT OF BUSINESS

The purpose of the chapters in this unit is to furnish you with a foundation for your continued study of business law and to introduce you to what have become traditional topics for students in business law courses, such as contracts (covered in Unit Two) and commercial transactions (covered in Unit Three).

The first chapter is devoted to material dealing with philosophies and approaches to the law, sources and classifications of law. The second chapter gives an overview of the legal and court systems in the United States. These chapters are followed by one in which the focus is upon the constitutional bases for the regulation of business in this country. The remaining chapters deal with torts and criminal law, areas of substantive law of importance to most people, including businesspersons.

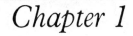

Chapter 1

Introduction to Law
and Legal Reasoning

This introductory chapter will give you some insight into various approaches and philosophies concerning the concept of the law. It provides background, dealing with sources and origins of law in the United States, and contains explanations of some frequently used classifications of law.

THINGS TO KEEP IN MIND

Business law is a category of law, which includes a number of areas of substantive, private, civil law, dealing with relationships among parties engaging in commercial transactions.

An important function of law is that it provides certainty. Knowledge of legal principles is an aid in business decision making for, with such knowledge of existing rules of conduct, one can predict how others will behave in the future.

OUTLINE

I. What is "The Law"? — Enforceable rules governing relationships among people and between people and their society.

II. Schools of legal, or jurisprudential, thought — Custom, history, logic and ideals have influenced the development of legal thought and decision making.

    A. Traditional or historical approach — Body of principles and rules that courts apply in deciding disputes. Emphasis is on the evolutionary process and the function of law to provide stability and certainty.

    B. Sociological or legal realism approach — Instrument of social control and means of serving desirable social needs in order to promote justice and stability.

Emphasis is on the function of law to provide an orderly process for social change and adaptability.

III. Sources of American law.

    A. Historical sources.

        1. Much of law in the United States is derived from the English common law system, rules developed by judges, based upon general principles established in previously decided cases.

        2. Doctrine of *stare decisis* — To stand by or adhere to decisions in previously determined cases.

            a. Courts will use past decisions as precedents in adjudicating cases before them if they are based on similar fact situations.

            b. Results in stability and predictability.

            c. Occasionally, a previous decision will not be adhered to by a court.
                1) Legislation changed the prior rule.
                2) Changes in technology, business practices, society's attitudes, etc.
                3) Error made in prior case.
                4) Conflicting precedents.

    B. Legal reasoning.

        1. Court's opinion in the form of a syllogism relying upon deductive reasoning.

            a. Major premise.

            b. Minor premise.

            c. Conclusion.

        2. Court's opinion in the form of a logical progression of connected points.

            a. Examine a set of circumstances.

            b. Apply legal principles to the circumstances.

        3. Reasoning by analogy — Compare facts in the case at hand to facts in similar cases.

        4. Determining appropriate rules and policies to apply.

    C. More recent sources of the law.

        1. Constitutions.

            a. Federal Constitution.
                1) Supreme law of the land. Any statutory or common law rule that is contrary to the Constitution will not be enforced.

      2) Defines the powers and limitations of the federal government and the rights of the states and people.

      3) Establishes three branches of government with system of checks and balance among them.

        a) Legislature — Congress is mandated power to pass laws in a number of areas. (For example, interstate commerce or business conducted by people or entities residing in different states.)

        b) Judicial — Courts have power to make determinations in disputes (Judicial Review), including power to determine whether or not statutes enacted by Congress are constitutional.

        c) Executive — President is empowered to carry out laws of the U.S.

  b. State constitutions — Are supreme within the jurisdiction of the state, if not in conflict with U.S. Constitution.

2. Codified law — Statutes and local ordinances that have been enacted by legislative bodies.

3. Case law.

  a. Judge-made law, which includes interpretation of constitutions and legislation, in addition to decisions in disputes, in which there is no relevant codified law.

  b. Common law.

    1) Derived from principles of law established by English court decisions.

    2) Decisions that are based upon custom and usage rather than codified law.

4. Administrative agency regulations — Rulings issued by state and federal commissions, boards, etc., having legislative, executive and/or judicial power.

IV. Sources of commercial (or business) law.

  A. The Law Merchant — Rules, based on commercial customs, developed before common law in England and incorporated into both common law and codified law in the United States.

  B. Codification of commercial law.

    1. National Conference of Commissioners on Uniform State Laws drafts proposals for uniform laws, which the state legislative bodies may adopt.

    2. Uniform Commercial Code.

      a. A statute that has been adopted, at least in part, by all the states in the United States.

      b. A major source of law relating to business.

      c. It does not change basic principles, but provides an internally consistent, modern body of clearly stated uniform rules relating to business transactions.

V. Classifications of law.

   A. Substantive versus procedural law.

      1. Substantive law — Defines legal relationships, rights and obligations.

      2. Procedural law — Method and means of enforcing substantive, legal rights.

      3. May be further classified, according to subject matter; for example, substantive law may be divided into agency, commercial paper, contracts, etc.

   B. Public versus private law.

      1. Public law — Law that affects relationships between people and their government and affects the interests of society. Substantive public law includes:

         a. Constitutional law.

         b. Criminal law.

         c. Administrative law.

         d. Tax law.

      2. Private law — Involves legal relationships among people.

   C. Civil versus criminal law.

      1. Civil law — Rules dealing with rights and duties between individuals and other persons.

      2. Criminal law — Wrongs committed against the public as a whole and proscribed by statute.

   D. Remedies at law versus remedies in equity.

      1. Legal remedies provided historically by courts of law.

         a. Possession of land.

         b. Possession of items of value.

         c. Money as compensation.

      2. Equitable relief when remedy at law in inadequate or unavailable or will result in hardship.

         a. Specific performance — A decree ordering a party to perform a particular act.

    b. Injunction — An order requiring a party to refrain from doing something.

    c. Rescission and restitution.

        1) A court may rescind (cancel) or abolish duties created by an agreement and return the parties to the positions that they would have been in if they had not entered the agreement.

        2) If either or both of the parties had given the other something of value, the court will direct that it be returned. This is referred to as restitution.

    d. Reformation — A court may correct an inadvertent error in a writing.

    3. The merging of courts of law and equity.

KEY WORDS AND PHRASES IN TEXT

Schools of jurisprudential thought
Traditional (historical) approach to law
Sociological (legal realism) approach
   to law
Justice
Legal reasoning
Syllogism
Common law
Legal precedent
Codified law
Statutory law
United States Constitution
Judicial review
Statutes
Uniform Commercial Code
Ordinances
Judicial process
Administrative process
Procedural law
Administrative law
Substantive law
Public law
Private law

Civil law
Criminal law
Remedies at law
Equity
Equitable remedies
Equitable principles and maxims
Statute of limitations
Laches
Specific performance
Injunction
Rescission
Stare decisis
Writ of certiorari
Citation
Court decision
Unanimous opinion
Majority opinion
Concurring opinion
Dissenting opinion
Judges and justices
Appellant
Petitioner
Appellee
Respondent

FILL-IN QUESTIONS

1. The ___traditional___ approach to law fulfills the function of law of providing stability, predictability, continuity and certainty; the ___sociological___ approach emphasizes the flexibility of law.

2. Common law refers to rules of law that have been developed over time by _judges in deciding cases based on general principles of law established in_ ___. _previously decided cases_

3. If a court bases its decision on precedents that have been established in earlier cases, it is following the doctrine of _stare decisis_.

4. ___Judicial___ process involves administration of law by courts, which are

judicial bodies; administration of law by nonjudicial government agencies is referred to as _administrative process_

5. The _Universal Commercial Code_ is a model statute which states uniform rules relating to business transactions. It has been adopted in whole or in part by the legislative bodies in the District of Columbia, the Virgin Islands and _____all_____ of the states.

6. The body of law, which pertains to the relationship between individuals in an organized society, is termed _private law_ ; the body of law, which pertains to the relationship between individuals and the government, is termed _public law_ .

7. Today, in the United States, sources of law would include ___#4 below___

_____ .

MULTIPLE CHOICE QUESTIONS

1. Generally speaking, precedents are rules of law established by:
    a. federal and state constitutions.
    b. legislatures.
    c. courts, in deciding cases arising in common law subjects.
    d. legislatures and courts.

2. A basic characteristic of case law is:
    a. statutes are derived from it.
    b. it establishes precedents for other courts to follow when a similar controversy is litigated.
    c. it eliminates the need to apply antiquated doctrines, such as *stare decisis*.
    d. all case law is codified.

3. The classification "private law" includes:
    a. criminal law.
    b. administrative law.
    c. constitutional law.
    d. contract law.

4. A source of law in the legal system of the United States would include:
    a. the federal Constitution.
    b. state statutes.
    c. town ordinances.
    d. court decisions.
    e. all of the above.

5. Current principles of business law:
    a. are derived from the Law Merchant.
    b. are codified in the Uniform Commercial Code.
    c. have been developed in cases decided by state courts.
    d. all of the above.

6. Public law as contrasted with private law:
    a. involves legal relationships between individuals.
    b. involves legal relationships between society and individuals.

    c. includes only criminal law.
    d. includes procedural law and agency law.

7.   Private law includes:
    a. constitutional and administrative law.
    b. contracts and property law.
    c. criminal and civil law.
    d. criminal and tort law.

8.   In regard to actions in equity:
    a. the remedy that will be given may be an injunction.
    b. the remedy that will be given will be compensatory money damages.
    c. the distinction between law and equity has no relevance today.
    d. the court will not apply the doctrine of *stare decisis*.

The following information is given for questions 9, 10, 11 and 12. Note that you will need to use logic and reasoning skills in order to answer the questions.

The United States brought a civil action against Container Corp. of America, and others, asserting that the corporation violated Sec. 1 of the Sherman Act, a federal antitrust law. The lower court's decision was appealed to the United States Supreme Court by the United States. Justices Marshall, Harlan and Stewart agreed with the lower court, but five justices disagreed with the lower court decision. Justice Fortas agreed with the result of the Supreme Court's decision, but he wrote a separate opinion in which he emphasized a particular point. The opinion of the court was written by Justice Douglas and is found in volume 438 of the United States Supreme Court Reports at page 422. It is a 1978 case.

9.   The case can be classified as one involving:
    a. substantive, criminal and public law.
    b. public administrative law.
    c. codified statutory law.
    d. legal realism.

10. Container Corp. of America was:
    a. the plaintiff in the original case and the defendant in the appeal to the United States Supreme Court.
    b. the respondent in the original case and the defendant in the appeal to the United States Supreme Court.
    c. the defendant in the original case and the appellant in the appeal to the United States Supreme Court.
    d. the defendant in the original case and the appellee in the appeal to the United States Supreme Court.

11. The citation for the case is:
    a. U.S. v. Container Corp. of America, et al., 422 U.S.S.Ct. Decisions 438 (1978).
    b. U.S. v. Container Corp. of America, et al., 438 U.S. 422 (1978).
    c. Container Corp. of America, et al. v. U.S., 438 U.S. 422 (1978).
    d. Container Corp. of America, et al. v. U.S., 438 1978 S.Ct. Rep. 422.

12. The following statement is false:
    a. The decision of the lower court was reversed.

b. Justice Douglas wrote the majority opinion and Justice Fortas the dissenting opinion.
c. Justice Fortas wrote the concurring opinion and was a member of the majority.
d. The dissenting justices were Marshall, Harlan and Stewart.

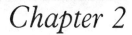

Chapter 2

Courts and Civil Dispute Resolution

An important source of law in the United States is case law—the rules of conduct which are determined by judges when they make decisions in cases that have been brought before them by parties who are involved in controversies. How cases get to appropriate courts so that the disputes can be adjudicated is the subject matter of this chapter. Usually the legal principles that become part of the body of law with which businesspersons will be concerned, have been established by appellate courts. Material in the chapter deals with the federal and state court systems, requirements for jurisdiction, judicial procedure and alternative methods of resolving disputes.

THINGS TO KEEP IN MIND

Usually people recognize and properly perform their legal obligations. In those instances in which a controversy arises between parties, one of the parties (the plaintiff in a civil action) may initiate a case in a court. Frequently, however, the issues between parties are settled or solved without recourse to the courts.

OUTLINE

I. Jurisdiction — Power of a court to decide a case. A court must have jurisdiction over the subject matter and the person and/or property involved in the dispute. In addition, the controversy must have arisen within the territory, over which the court has jurisdiction, and/or the parties to the litigation must be available within that geographic area.

   A. General and special jurisdiction over the subject matter.

      1. General jurisdiction — A court with general jurisdiction has the power to hear all kinds of controversies.

      2. Special or limited jurisdiction — A court is limited in the types of cases which it may hear and decide.

  B. Jurisdiction over the person or the property that is involved in a case.

      1. *In personam* jurisdiction over the parties involved in the lawsuit.

          a. The plaintiff submits to the court's jurisdiction by commencing his or her lawsuit.

          b. The court has jurisdiction over the defendant if the defendant is a resident of the state and/or can be served within the territorial jurisdiction of the court.

          c. A corporate defendant is considered to be a resident of a state if it is incorporated in the state or has an office in the state or does intrastate business within the state.

      2. *In rem* jurisdiction over property, which is the subject matter of the lawsuit.

      3. *Quasi in rem* jurisdiction — A court may have jurisdiction to reach a defendant's interest in property, when the property is within the territorial boundaries of the court.

      4. Long arm statutes enable state courts to obtain jurisdiction over a person who has committed a wrong even if he or she is outside the state.

  C. Venue — A particular court has power to hear and decide a case only within a specified geographic area.

  D. Original and appellate jurisdiction.

      1. Appellate jurisdiction — Court has power to review decisions rendered in other courts, based upon the record.

      2. Original jurisdiction — Court has power to hear controversy when it is first brought for adjudication. (Trial court)

II. Typical state court system.

  A. Inferior trial courts with original, specialized, limited subject matter jurisdiction in criminal and/or civil cases.

  B. Trial courts having general jurisdiction.

  C. Appellate courts with jurisdiction to review decisions of inferior courts and determine whether or not trial court made an error as to law or procedure, based only upon the record of the case.

      1. Intermediate appellate courts.

      2. Courts of final appeal.

D. Judicial review — Courts have the power to determine the constitutionality of actions taken by the legislative and executive branches of government.

III. The federal court system.

A. Specialized courts with limited jurisdiction, created by Congress in accordance with power granted in the United States Constitution, such as the U.S. Claims Court (which hears cases brought against the United States), Tax Court, etc.

B. District Courts with general original jurisdiction.

C. Circuit Courts of Appeal with intermediate general appellate jurisdiction to review cases decided in District Courts and some inferior courts and administrative agencies.

D. The United States Supreme Court is a constitutionally created court (Article III).

1. In a few rare instances, it has original jurisdiction.

2. The Supreme Court has limited appellate jurisdiction.

IV. Jurisdiction of federal courts.

A. Established by Article III of the United States Constitution.

B. Controversies involving federal questions.

1. Federal courts may have exclusive jurisdiction as provided in the Constitution — Federal crimes, admiralty, bankruptcy, patents, copyrights, trademarks, etc.

2. Violations of rights protected by Constitution.

3. Federal courts may have concurrent jurisdiction with state courts in civil suits.

   a. Amount in controversy exceeds $50,000.

   b. There is diversity of citizenship. For example, one or more of the parties is an individual, residing in a different state, or a corporation, incorporated or having its principal office, in a state which is different than that of another party to the controversy.

C. Cases which reach the Supreme Court.

1. Formerly, those in which a party had an absolute right to appeal. (For example, a case involving the constitutionality of a statute.)

2. Those which the Supreme Court determines it will hear following granting of *writ of certiorari.*

3. Rare instances in which Supreme Court has original jurisdiction.

V.   Judicial procedures: following a civil case through the courts.

A. Adversary nature of proceedings.

B. Parties — Litigants.

    1. Plaintiff — Initiates proceedings.

    2. Defendant — Party against whom action is brought and upon whom summons is served.

C. Pleadings.

    1. Complaint — Filed by plaintiff.

      a. May be called a petition or declaration.

      b. States facts:
        1) Explanation of jurisdiction of the court.
        2) The bases for the plaintiff's cause of action.
        3) The remedy that plaintiff seeks.

      c. Filed with clerk of court and copy served on defendant.

    2. Answer — Filed by defendant.

      a. Defendant admits, denies or otherwise challenges the legal validity of the plaintiff's claim.

      b. Choices available to defendant after receipt of summons and complaint:
        1) Default—not respond—in which case the court will enter a judgment against the defendant.
        2) Make motion to dismiss (demurrer) — Defendant claims, as a matter of law, that the plaintiff has not stated a claim upon which relief can be granted.
        3) Counterclaim (or cross-complaint) — Defendant sets forth his or her own claim and cause of action.
        4) Raise affirmative defense — Defendant gives a reason why plaintiff's action should be dismissed.

      c. Filed with clerk of court and copy served on plaintiff.

    3. Reply — Plaintiff may respond to issues raised in answer by filing reply with clerk of court and serving copy on defendant.

D. Pretrial procedures.

    1. Motion to dismiss — Defendant asserts that the plaintiff has not stated a claim upon which relief can be granted.

    2. Motion for judgment on the pleadings — Either plaintiff or defendant claims that, based upon the pleadings, there is no issue requiring a trial.

    3. Motion for summary judgment — May be made by either party. No issue exists regarding the facts and the issue of law should, therefore, be decided by the judge.

4. Discovery — Procedural devices to obtain information.

    a. Depositions — Sworn testimony given before and recorded by court official.

    b. Interrogatories — Answers to questions submitted in writing by one party, involved in the litigation, to the other party.

5. Requests for admissions (written requests for admissions by one party to the other relating to matters involved in the case), documents, objects, etc.

6. Physical and mental examinations — Subject to individual's right of privacy.

7. Pretrial hearing or conference may be initiated by a party or the court.

E. Right to jury.

1. Jurors are triers of facts; judge is trier of law.

2. One's right to have a jury is limited.

    a. Case is one that is not based upon an equitable cause of action.

    b. States may limit right to jury.

    c. In federal courts, one has a right to a jury trial in an action at law when the amount in controversy is more than $20.

3. The right to a jury trial may be waived.

F. The trial.

1. Opening statements by attorneys or parties.

2. Examination of witnesses — Direct, cross, redirect and recross examination.

3. Motion for directed verdict — Judge is requested to enter verdict.

4. Charges to jury — Judge instructs jury regarding matters of law.

5. Judgment notwithstanding the verdict may be entered following motion made by party if decision is contrary to evidence.

G. Appeal.

1. Either or both parties may appeal to court having appellate jurisdiction.

    a. Notice of appeal is filed with trial court.

    b. Record on appeal (including copies of pleadings, transcript, rulings on motions, arguments of attorneys, instructions or charge to jury, verdict, posttrial motions and order for judgment) is filed with an abstract of the record, a brief and arguments, prepared by the attorney, with the appellate court.

2. Appellant — Party initiating appeal.

3. Appellee — Other party.

4. Reviewing court bases its decision on the record and the arguments of the party. It may affirm the lower court's decision, reverse it or remand the case, by returning it to the trial court for a new trial or entry of an appropriate judgment.

VI. Alternative dispute resolution.

A. Mediation.

1. Parties meet voluntarily with third party, a mediator.

2. Mediator facilitates discussion about disagreement by parties.

B. Arbitration.

1. Parties, who have a controversy, may voluntarily agree to have their dispute arbitrated by a third person, or a panel of three people.

2. Parties, who submit to arbitration, agree to adhere to the decision of the arbitrator. In general, arbitrators' decisions are enforceable in the courts.

3. Decisions, which have been made by arbitrators as to matters relating to law, may be reviewed by the courts.

4. Arbitration is a less formal, speedier, and less expensive alternative to having controversies resolved through the court system.

5. In some jurisdictions, arbitration is an integrated part of the judicial procedure for settling civil disputes.

KEY WORDS AND PHRASES IN TEXT

Jurisdiction
In personum jurisdiction
In rem jurisdiction
Quasi in rem jurisdiction
Long arm statute
Subject matter jurisdiction
General jurisdiction
Special, or limited, jurisdiction
Original jurisdiction
Appellate jurisdiction
Venue
Trial courts
Judicial review

Federal District Courts
Federal Circuit Courts of Appeal
Supreme Court of the United States
Diversity of citizenship
Concurrent jurisdiction
Exclusive jurisdiction
Writ of certiorari
Adversary system of justice
Plaintiff
Defendant
Summons
Complaint
Answer

Counterclaim	Cross examination
Reply	Rules of evidence
Pleadings	*Prima facie* case
Motion to dismiss (or demurrer)	Motion for directed verdict
Affirmative defenses	Rebuttal
Motion for judgment on the pleadings	Rejoinder
Motion for summary judgment	Closing arguments
Discovery	Motion for new trial
Depositions	Judgment notwithstanding the verdict
Interrogatories	Notice of appeal
Admissions	Briefs
Pretrial hearing	Oral argument
Jury	Alternative dispute resolution (ADR)
Trial	Mediation
Direct examination	Arbitration

FILL-IN QUESTIONS

1. The power of a court to hear and decide a case is termed _jurisdiction_

2. In order for its decision to be effective with regard to the parties to a controversy, a court must have _in personum_ jurisdiction.

3. Courts, which have power to hear most kinds of controversies, without regard to the subject matter, have _general_ jurisdiction. A federal court, having such jurisdiction is _US Dist. Court_. A federal court, such as _US Supreme Ct ,etc_ has limited or _special_ jurisdiction, because it may hear only cases dealing with particular subject matters.

4. A court, having the power to review decisions rendered by other courts that have original jurisdiction, has _appellate_ jurisdiction. A federal court, having such power is _Supreme Ct._. In the federal court system, the _District Court_ is a court with original, general jurisdiction.

5. The power of a court to determine the constitutionality of a statute, that was passed by the _legislative_ branch of government, or action that was taken by the executive branch, is referred to as the power of _judicial review_.

6. The party initiating a legal proceeding is called the _plaintiff_. He or she commences the action by _filing a complaint + serving notice on defendant_

7. A civil case is commenced when a _complaint_ is filed with the court by the plaintiff. After the defendant is served with a summons and a copy of the _complaint_, the defendant has a period of time within which to respond by filing an _answer_, a copy of which is delivered to the defendant or the defendant's attorney.

8. In order to limit the issues of a case and to save time, the parties in a case may use pretrial procedures. For example, the defendant, who claims that the plaintiff has not stated a cause of action upon which relief can be granted, will make a motion _to dismiss_. Either party, desiring to preserve the testimony of a witness, who will be unable to appear in court, may request that _a deposition be taken_.

9.   Rather than resort to the courts for resolution of a civil dispute, parties may turn to ~~alternative dispute resolution~~ (ADR). The parties may agree to discuss the dispute in the presence of a third person, a ~~mediator~~, who will informally assist them in settling their disagreement, or they may agree to submit their dispute to ~~arbitration~~, in which case one or more experts, called ~~arbitrator~~, will hear the dispute and render a legally binding decision.

MULTIPLE CHOICE QUESTIONS

1.   A court, having original jurisdiction, would be the appropriate court in which to commence an action involving:
     a. the commission of a crime.
     b. a contract.
     c. a corporation.
     d. all of the above.

2.   A court, having appellate jurisdiction, would be the appropriate court in which to commence an action involving:
     a. the commission of a crime.
     b. a contract.
     c. both of the above.
     d. none of the above.

3.   A case, involving a resident of Pennsylvania and a resident of New York, may be commenced in:
     a. an appropriate Pennsylvania or New York court and then appealed as of right to the U.S. Circuit Court of Appeals.
     b. a federal district court, since there is diversity of citizenship.
     c. a federal district court if the amount in controversy exceeds $10,000.
     d. a federal Court of Appeals if the amount in controversy exceeds $10,000.

4.   The United States Claims Court is:
     a. a general trial court.
     b. a specialized court having limited jurisdiction.
     c. a court having jurisdiction over bankruptcy matters.
     d. an appellate court.

5.   Nora York, a resident of the state of New York, has obtained a $1,000 judgment against Sam Dakota, who resides in South Dakota. Sam Dakota's only asset in New York is a $1,000 bank account, which Nora York is attempting to seize in order to satisfy the judgment. This is an example of an action:
     a. *in certiorari.*
     b. *in personum.*
     c. *in rem.*
     d. N.O.V. (not withstanding the verdict).

6.   Today, the power of the United States Supreme Court to review the constitutionality of Acts of Congress:
     a. is well established.
     b. has been successfully challenged because it was based upon the old decision of the Supreme Court in *Marbury v. Madison.*

c. does not exist because the doctrine of judicial review gives courts power to review only judicial decisions and actions of the executive branch.
d. is no longer available because of the 1981 Federal Reorganization Act that was passed by Congress.

7. A litigant has a right to appeal from a decision rendered by a trial court:
a. to a court having original jurisdiction.
b. and on appeal he may cross examine witnesses.
c. when an error as to a fact has been made.
d. when an error as to law has been made.

8. In connection with a controversy brought to court, the term, "legal pleadings," refers to:
a. the complaint filed by the plaintiff and the answer filed by the defendant.
b. the reply filed by the defendant and complaint filed by the plaintiff.
c. the trial of a case in court, with or without a jury.
d. the procedure required in order to appeal a case after a trial.

Chapter 3

Constitutional Authority to Regulate Business

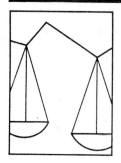

The Constitution of the United States of America is the supreme, or highest, law in this country (Article VI, Paragraph 2). At the time of its ratification in 1788, the existing states delegated a portion of their sovereignty (the powers that nations possess) to the newly created national government. In this chapter, the focus of the authors of the text is only upon some of the constitutional provisions which have an effect upon the legal environment in which business and commerce is conducted.

The chapter first provides an introduction to the Constitution and constitutional law. Thus, there are sections relating to the concepts of federalism, the separation of powers among the three branches of government and the supremacy of federal law. The discussion in the remainder of the chapter is limited to only a few sections of the Constitution and relevant amendments that have significance for the conduct and regulation of business.

THINGS TO KEEP IN MIND

The meanings of various provisions in the Constitution have been interpreted by the courts in tens of thousands of cases. (Samples of some of these decisions are presented in the text.)

Each of the states has a constitution which provides for similar branches of government. Many provisions that are found in the United States Constitution are also found in state constitutions.

OUTLINE

I.   Basic constitutional concepts.

A. Federalism — The relationships, that were created by the Constitution, between the United States government and the states and among the states.

   1. The federal government has only those powers which are conferred upon it by the Constitution.

   2. Any powers that are neither delegated to the national government nor prohibited by the Constitution are retained by the states or the people (Tenth Amendment).

   3. Any rights which are not enumerated in the Constitution are reserved to the people (Ninth Amendment).

B. Delegated powers.

   1. The Constitution is a grant of power or authority from the states to the federal government which they established.

   2. The national government can exercise only those powers which are expressly or impliedly delegated to it because they are necessary and proper for carrying out express enumerated powers.

C. The Bill of Rights — The first ten amendments protect the rights of individuals against intrusion by the federal government.

D. Separation of powers.

   1. The Constitution provides for a government that is composed of three branches.

      a. The legislative branch (Article I) — Congress is empowered to make laws by passing legislation (United States statutes).

      b. The executive branch (Article II) — The President has the duty of executing or carrying out the laws of the United States.

      c. The judicial branch (Article III) — The power to hear and determine controversies, arising out of the laws of the United States, is vested in the United States Supreme Court and the inferior courts that are established by Congress.

   2. One branch may not exercise power that has been conferred upon another branch of government.

   3. Each branch has power, however, to check (or limit) the action of the other two branches.

   4. Checks and balances system — Governmental functions are balanced (or distributed) among the three branches, each of which has checks on the other two.

E. The supremacy clause (Article VI).

1. State laws that conflict with the U.S. Constitution or federal statutes will not be enforced.

2. Sometimes, the federal government and the states have concurrent or shared powers. If Congress has chosen to act exclusively in regulating certain activities, the federal statute preempts, or takes precedence over, the state law.

II. The power of Congress to legislate in areas that have importance for business (Article I, Sec. 8).

A. Congress has express power to make laws dealing with certain enumerated matters (Article I, Sec. 9, Paragraphs 1 through 17).

B. Congress has implied power "to make all Laws which shall be necessary and proper for carrying into Execution" its express powers (Article I, Sec. 8, Paragraph 18).

C. The commerce clause — Congress may regulate commerce with other countries (and the Indian tribes) and among the states (Article I, Sec. 8, Paragraph 3).

1. Commerce among the states means interstate commerce.

2. Congress is not empowered to pass statutes regulating intrastate commerce (business that is conducted purely within a state).

3. The Supreme Court has held that intrastate activities which affect interstate commerce are subject to provisions in federal statutes.

4. States possess police powers in order to protect the public health, safety, morals and general welfare of their citizens.

   a. If a state statute imposes a substantial burden on interstate commerce, it may be held to be unconstitutional.

   b. If the application of a state regulation discriminates against interstate commerce, it may be treated as an unconstitutional exercise of the police power by the state.

D. The power to tax — Congress has the "power to impose and collect taxes, duties, imposts and excises" in order to raise revenue (Article I, Sec. 8, Paragraph 1).

1. Duties, imposts and excises must be apportioned uniformly throughout the United States.

2. Congress cannot tax exports (Article I, Sec. 9).

3. The power of Congress to impose other than a uniform direct or individual tax was originally restricted in the Constitution (Article I, Secs. 1 and 9). The Sixteenth Amendment gave Congress authority to impose an income tax without apportionment among the states.

4. Congress may not indirectly regulate by taxation an activity which it is not authorized to regulate directly.

E. The spending power — Congress has the power to spend revenues (collected by the federal government) in order to pay "debts and provide for the common defense and general welfare" (Article I, Sec. 8, Paragraph 1).

   1. A taxpayer can challenge an exercise by Congress of the spending power only if the taxpayer has standing to sue. The taxpayer must show that he, she or it will incur a direct and immediate personal injury as a result of the allocation of federal funds.

   2. Federal funds can be spent in order to carry out the enumerated powers of Congress and other worthwhile objectives.

III. The Bill of Rights (Amendments I through X).

A. Many of the constitutionally protected rights, which are provided for in the Bill of Rights, apply to legal entities, such as corporations, as well as to natural persons.

B. The Fourteenth Amendment provides that the states "shall not deprive any person of life, liberty, or property, without due process of law." In general, this has been interpreted to mean that the rights guaranteed by the Bill of Rights must also be protected by the states.

C. The First Amendment protects the freedom of religion, speech and the press and the rights to assembly and to petition the government.

   1. Freedom of speech.

      a. Freedom of speech is not absolute.

      b. The First Amendment does not protect defamation.

      c. A defendant in a defamation case, which is based upon statements concerning public officials in the execution of their official duties or statements which disparage a competitor's product, may assert certain defenses.
      1) Honest error.
      2) Lack of actual malice.

   2. Freedom of religion.

      a. Government is prohibited from establishing any one religion or prohibiting the free exercise of religious practices.

      b. A government regulation which places a significant burden on religion is unconstitutional.

D. The Fourth Amendment prohibits unreasonable searches and seizures.

1. Federal, state and local officers may not stop, search or seize a person or his or her property without justification.

2. Federal, state and local officers are required to obtain warrants in order to search or seize a person or property.

   a. Warrants may not be issued without showing that probable cause exists to believe that a crime has been or is being committed.

   b. A warrant must fully describe the person or place to be searched and/or the person or property to be seized.

E. The Fifth Amendment prohibits self-incrimination.

1. A person cannot be compelled to give evidence which may subject himself or herself to prosecution for a crime.

2. The guarantee against self-incrimination does not extend to legal entities which are not natural persons.

IV. Other Constitutional guarantees.

A. Due process — No person may be deprived "of life, liberty, or property, without due process of law" (Fifth and Fourteenth Amendments).

1. Procedural due process — Any governmental action, which amounts to a taking of life, liberty or property, must be conducted in a fair, nonarbitrary and nondiscriminatory manner.

2. Substantive due process — The content, or substance, of legislation must be in harmony with the Constitution.

B. Equal protection — A person may not be denied "the equal protection of the laws" (Fourteenth Amendment).

1. Because the Fifth Amendment due process clause has been interpreted as including the concept of equal protection of the laws, the prohibition against denial of this protection extends to the federal government as well as the state governments.

2. Governments cannot impose burdens or legal obligations on some people and not on others unless there is a rational reason to distinguish between different groups of people.

KEY WORDS AND PHRASES IN TEXT

Federalism
United States Supreme Court
Delegated powers
The Bill of Rights
Separation of powers
Executive branch

Legislative branch
Judicial branch
Checks and balances
Enumerated powers of Congress
Commerce clause
Interstate commerce

Intrastate commerce
Police powers
Supremacy clause
Taxing power
Spending power
Standing to sue
Freedom of speech
Freedom of religion

Protection against unreasonable search
   and seizure
Protection against self-incrimination
Due process of law
Procedural due process
Substantive due process
Equal protection of the laws

FILL-IN QUESTIONS

1. The structure of government in the United States is based upon the concept of federalism. As a result, some governmental __powers__ are exercised by the United States government and others by the __states__.

2. The Tenth Amendment provides that those powers, which have not been delegated to the United States government, nor prohibited by the Constitution, are retained by the __states__ or the people.

3. The United States Constitution provides for the division of governmental functions among three branches of government. The power to enact statutes is given to the __legislative__ branch, composed of the Senate and __House of Representatives__. The executive branch is responsible for executing the laws of the United States. The functions of the executive branch are performed by the __President__. The third branch is the __Judicial Branch__ composed of the courts.

4. The first ten amendments to the Constitution are known as the __Bill of Rights__.

5. The enumerated powers of Congress are set forth in Article I, Section 8 of the United States Constitution. They include the power to regulate __commerce__ with foreign countries, with the Indian tribes and among the several __States__, and the power to raise revenue through taxation. Import taxes, duties and excise taxes must be __uniform__ throughout the United States.

6. The right to be free from __unreasonable__ searches and seizures is protected by the Fourth Amendment. This amendment also provides that search warrants and arrest orders shall only be issued after law enforcement officials establish that there is __probable__ cause to believe that the search or arrest is justified. It also provides that the premises to be searched or the __person__ or __property__ to be seized must be fully described.

7. The Fifth Amendment prohibits double jeopardy and guarantees that a __natural person__ cannot be compelled to testify against himself or herself. This privilege against self-incrimination does not extend to artificial organizations or entities, such as __corporations__ and __partnerships__.

MULTIPLE CHOICE QUESTIONS

1. The Constitution of the United States was a delegation of power by the states to the federal government. As a result:
    a. all governmental powers are exercised by the federal government.

    b. only the federal government has the power to impose an income tax.

    c. the states delegated their "police powers" to the national government.

    d. the states retain some sovereignty.

2. The President of the United States cannot establish a law which regulates interstate commerce because:

    a. the power to legislate is vested in Congress.

    b. of the concept of separation of powers among the branches of government.

    c. Congress has been given the express power to regulate commerce among the several states.

    d. all of the above.

3. The executive branch of government has certain "checks" on the other branches of government. For this reason, the President has the power to:

    a. veto an Act of Congress.

    b. remove a congressman from his position.

    c. overrule a decision of a federal court.

    d. enter into a treaty with a foreign nation.

4. The power to hear and determine controversies arising out of the laws of the United States is conferred upon the United States Supreme Court and other federal courts which may be established by Congress. The Constitution provides that:

    a. the Justices of the Supreme Court are elected by the people.

    b. federal judges are appointed by the Senate with the advice and consent of the President.

    c. federal judges are appointed by the President with the advice and consent of the Senate.

    d. federal judges are uniformly apportioned among the several states.

5. Because of the interstate commerce clause found in Article I, Section 8 of the Constitution, Congress has the power to regulate:

    a. the weight of trucks on interstate highways.

    b. the manufacture of automobiles with specified safety features.

    c. the activities of real estate brokers who are licensed in the state of Louisiana, if their activities substantially affect interstate commerce.

    d. all of the above.

6. When Congress passes a statute relating to a subject over which the states and the federal government have concurrent power:

    a. an existing state law that contains similar provisions is automatically invalid.

    b. a state law is invalid only if Congress has expressly stated in the legislation that the federal statute is meant to preempt state laws relating to the same subject matter.

    c. the federal law preempts state statutes if Congress indicated that it intended that the federal law was to supercede state law.

    d. Congressional action cannot supercede state statutes when both the federal and state governments have concurrent power.

7. A state statute prohibits restaurants from employing people with contagious diseases as food handlers. If a case involving the statute arises, the court is likely to rule that:

    a. the state has power to enact such a statute and its enforcement does not violate the interstate commerce clause of the United States Constitution.

    b. a federal statute to similar effect does not necessarily preempt the state law.

    c. the state statute is unconstitutional because enforcement of the law results in a substantial burden on interstate commerce.

    d. the state statute is contrary to the due process clause in the Fourteenth Amendment of the United States Constitution.

8.   A newspaper has published an article concerning a public official. Which of the following statements is false?

    a. The newspaper does not have an absolute right to freely make statements about the public official.

    b. The newspaper is liable to the public official if its statement was defamatory, even though it made an honest mistake.

    c. The newspaper is liable to the public official if the statement was made with knowledge that it was false or with reckless disregard for whether it was true or false.

    d. The newspaper is not protected by the Fifth Amendment guarantee against self-incrimination and may be required to produce evidence indicating its guilt if it is criminally prosecuted for libel.

9.   The Fifth Amendment to the Constitution of the United States provides that no person shall "be deprived of life, liberty, or property, without due process of law." This provision:

    a. also is contained in the Fourteenth Amendment, which protects people from actions by state governments that violate the rights specified in the Bill of Rights.

    b. is superceded by the Fourteenth Amendment.

    c. means that, as long as a statute is procedurally fair, it can be enforced even though it is substantively unfair.

    d. means that Congress cannot impose an excise tax.

Chapter 4

Torts

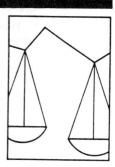

Torts are civil wrongs committed against the person or property of another. All torts involve a breach of duty, owed by the defendant to the plaintiff, which is the proximate cause of an injury incurred by the plaintiff. Conduct may be tortious because of an intentional act or because of a failure to exercise reasonable care. In some instances, strict tort liability is imposed without regard to fault.

THINGS TO KEEP IN MIND

If a plaintiff is alleging that a defendant was negligent, it is not necessary to show that the defendant's conduct was intentional. If liability is imposed because of strict liability, it is not necessary to establish the wrongful intent or negligence of the defendant.

OUTLINE

I. The scope of tort law.

    A. Unreasonable, wrongful conduct by one individual, resulting in injury to the person or property of another, for which the wrongdoer (tortfeasor) should compensate the injured party.

    B. Remedies for torts are obtained in civil actions. If a defendant's conduct is also criminally wrong, he or she may be prosecuted by the state for a crime as well.

    C. Elements of a tort — As a result of the defendant's breach of duty not to harm the plaintiff, the plaintiff is injured.

        1. A duty was owed by defendant.

      a. Private obligation, other than an obligation arising out of contract.

      b. Defendant owed duty of not unreasonably causing harm to the person or property of the plaintiff.

      c. Plaintiff has a reciprocal right not to be wrongfully injured.

   2. Breach of duty — Defendant violated the duty owed to plaintiff because of some act or omission, which was intentional or careless or abnormally dangerous.

   3. Injury to plaintiff.

      a. Plaintiff incurred some loss, harm, wrong to or invasion of a protected interest.

      b. It is not necessary that plaintiff be financially or physically harmed.

   4. Proximate causation — Plaintiff's injury was caused by defendant's breach of duty.

      a. Factual cause.
         1) Injury would not have occurred without the defendant's wrongful act or omission.
         2) Defendant's conduct was a substantial factor in causing the injury.

      b. Proximate or legal cause — Defendant's conduct was the immediate, foreseeable, direct, rather than remote cause of plaintiff's injury.

II.   Intentional torts.

  A. Defendant consciously intended to perform an act which results in an injury to plaintiff or plaintiff's property.

   1. One is assumed to intend the normal consequences of one's acts.

   2. It is, therefore, not necessary to show that defendant actually intended to harm plaintiff or his or her property.

  B. Wrongs against the person.

   1. Battery.

      a. Intentional act which brings about harmful or offensive contact.

      b. Defenses.
         1) Privilege or consent.
         2) Reasonable force to defend oneself, other persons or one's property.

   2. Assault.

      a. Threat by defendant to inflict immediate bodily harm to plaintiff, which creates a reasonable apprehension of harmful or offensive contact.

b. Defenses — Privilege, self-defense, defense of others and defense of property.

3. False imprisonment (false arrest).

    a. Unreasonable, intentional confinement of plaintiff without justification.

    b. Present interference with freedom to move without restraint.

    c. Merchant protection statutes permit reasonable detention of suspected shoplifter, if there is justified or probable cause to believe that the suspect is taking or interfering with the merchant's property.

    d. Injury may be harm to reputation and mental distress.

4. Infliction of mental distress — Extreme, outrageous conduct, resulting in severe emotional stress.

5. Defamation — Harm to reputation and good name.

    a. Publication of statement to or within hearing of others, which holds plaintiff up to contempt, ridicule or hatred.

    b. Slander — False oral statement.

    c. Libel — False written statement.

    d. Defenses — Truth or privilege.

6. Invasion of the right to privacy.

    a. Use of plaintiff's name, picture or other likeness without permission for commercial purposes.

    b. Intrusion upon plaintiff's affairs or seclusion.

    c. Public disclosure of information placing plaintiff in a false light.

    d. Public disclosure of private facts about plaintiff that an ordinary person would find objectionable.

7. Misrepresentation (fraud or deceit).

    a. False representation of fact.

    b. Representation made by the defendant with knowledge of its falsity or reckless disregard for the truth.

    c. Defendant intended to induce plaintiff to change his or her position.

    d. Plaintiff reasonably relied on the representation.

    e. As a result of the misrepresentation, the plaintiff was damaged.

       f. Seller's talk or puffing is distinguishable from actionable misrepresentation.

  C. Wrongs against property.

    1. Trespass to land — Wrongful interference with another person's real property rights, even though there is no actual harm to the land.

    2. Trespass to personal property — Defendant unlawfully injures or interferes with plaintiff's right to exclusive possession and enjoyment of personal property.

    3. Conversion — A wrongful taking and keeping of personal property to which one has no right.

III. Nuisance — Improper use by defendant of his or her property so as to unreasonably interfere with the health, safety, comfort or right of another to enjoy his or her own property.

IV. Negligence.

  A. Unintentional failure to exercise reasonable care under the circumstances, so that a foreseeable risk to another person is created, resulting in an injury to plaintiff.

  B. Elements.

    1. Defendant owed a duty of exercising reasonable care.

    2. Defendant failed to exercise reasonable care (breach of duty).

    3. Plaintiff was injured.

    4. Plaintiff's injury was caused by defendant's failure to exercise reasonable care.

      a. Causation in fact.

      b. Proximate cause.

  C. Defenses.

    1. Supervening or intervening unforeseen force was the cause of plaintiff's injury.

      a. Intervening force breaks the causal connection between defendant's carelessness and plaintiff's injury.

      b. A defendant is not relieved of liability if an intervening occurrence is foreseeable. It is considered to be foreseeable that:
        1) One, who is tortiously personally injured, may develop a reaction or subsequent illness or accident or receive improper medical care.

2) One, whose property is endangered, may be injured in an attempt to protect the property.

3) One, who is personally endangered, may take defensive action.

4) Rescuers may attempt to aid an imperiled victim and be harmed.

2. Assumption of the risk — Plaintiff, expressly or impliedly, knowingly and voluntarily placed himself or herself in a situation involving risk.

3. Contributory and comparative negligence — Plaintiff's own negligence contributed to his or her own injury.

    a. Common law doctrine of contributory negligence — Plaintiff cannot recover from defendant at all.

    b. Comparative negligence doctrine has been adopted in more than forty states. The amount of damages is apportioned between the plaintiff and defendant, based upon the relative fault of each of the parties.

    c. A negligent plaintiff may be able to recover if negligent defendant had the "last clear chance" to prevent injury to the plaintiff.

V. Strict liability — Liability without fault and without regard to defendant's intent or exercise of reasonable care.

A. Abnormally dangerous activities.

1. The activity involves a high degree of risk, which cannot be completely guarded against even with the exercise of reasonable or extraordinary care.

2. The risk is one that involves potentially serious harm.

3. The activity is one that is not commonly performed in the geographic area.

B. Employers are strictly liable to their employees for injuries sustained in the ordinary course of their employment under the workers' compensation statutes. See Chapter 32 and 49.

C. Employers and principals are strictly liable for torts committed by employees and agents, acting within the ordinary course of their employment. See Chapter 33.

D. Manufacturers of products are held strictly liable for damages caused by their products in many states. See Chapter 21.

KEY WORDS AND PHRASES IN TEXT

Tort	Defense of others
Intentional torts	Defense of property
Assault	False imprisonment
Battery	Probable cause
Defense of consent	Infliction of mental distress
Self-defense	Defamation

Libel	Breach of duty of exercising care
Slander	Injury
Truth as an absolute defense	Causation in fact
Privileged communications	Proximate cause
Invasion of the right to privacy	Foreseeability
Misrepresentation (fraud and deceit)	Supervening intervening forces
Seller's talk or puffing	Assumption of risk
Trespass to land	Contributory negligence
Trespass to personal property	Comparative negligence
Conversion	Last clear chance
Nuisance	Strict tort liability
Negligence	Abnormally dangerous activities
Duty of exercising reasonable care	Product liability

FILL-IN QUESTIONS

1. In order to recover in an action based on tort, a plaintiff must establish that the elements of a tort were present. In other words, plaintiff must show that _____ *defendant breached a duty, that was owed* _____.

2. A _*tort*_ is a civil wrong for which an injured party may recover from a person who has caused a personal physical injury or who has harmed another person's property interests.

3. Some torts are intentional torts because the defendant intended to commit a particular act. Intentional torts, such as defamation and battery are wrongs against the _*person*_ ; others, such as trespass and conversion, are wrongs against _*property*_ .

4. An _*assault*_ occurs if one person threatens to inflict immediate bodily harm on another person who, therefore, becomes reasonably fearful or apprehensive that he or she will incur physical harm. If the threatened act is intentionally performed and results in harmful or offensive physical contact, the tort of _*battery*_ has been committed. In either or both instances, it is possible that the defendant may raise a defense, such as: _*consent*_ , self-defense, _*defense of others*_ or _*defense of property*_ .

5. _*False imprisonment*_ is the unjustified intentional restraint or confinement of another. A merchant, who suspects that a customer is shoplifting, may detain the customer without liability if there is probable cause for believing that the customer has taken the merchant's goods and the detention is conducted in a _*reasonable manner*_ and for a _*reasonable*_ period of time.

6. One who makes false and defamatory statements about another person may be liable for the tort of libel, if the statement is _*in writing*_ , or slander, if the statement is made _*orally*_ . In an action based upon defamation, _*truth*_ usually is an absolute defense.

7. A person is liable for the tort of negligence, if he or she causes an injury to the person or property of another because of a failure to exercise the care that a reasonable person would exercise. There are, however, defenses, which can be

raised by a defendant in an action based on negligence. Such defenses include
_____.

MULTIPLE CHOICE QUESTIONS

1. A tort action may be based upon:
    a. negligence.
    b. an intentionally caused injury.
    c. strict liability.
    d. all of the above.

2. The following is a tort:
    a. a breach of duty owed by one person to another, which produces an injury when the one who breaches the duty did not actually know that he or she owed a duty.
    b. a breach of duty owed by one person to another, which was provided for by a contract so that he or she knew that a duty was owed to the other party.
    c. a crime that results in no injury to another party, such as "running a stop sign" when no other car or person is in the vicinity.
    d. all of the above.

3. If John punches Tim without provocation, John has committed:
    a. an assault.
    b. an assault and a battery.
    c. a nuisance.
    d. negligence.

4. A store owner observed that a woman in a black coat took merchandise from a shelf and placed it into a shopping bag that she was carrying. The store owner did not see the woman's face. At the time, there were in the store five female customers who were wearing black coats and carrying shopping bags. The store owner will not be liable for false imprisonment:
    a. if he detains and questions all five women, who were wearing black coats and carrying shopping bags, in his office for three hours because he has probable cause to believe that one of them has taken the merchandise.
    b. if he stops and detains one woman for five minutes after she has left the store and she admits to taking the merchandise and not paying for it.
    c. if he locks the doors to the store and detains all the customers for ten minutes because he is justified in believing that one of them has been shoplifting.
    d. if he locks the doors to the store and detains all the customers for ten minutes in a state that has enacted a merchant protection statute.

5. A person commits the tort of trespass to real property without a defense when she:
    a. parks her car in another person's driveway in order to attend a party at the owner's home.
    b. recovers her car which she left on the owner's property after attending a party at the owner's home.
    c. loses control of her car after skidding on ice, causing her to drive into another person's driveway.
    d. parks her car in a neighbor's driveway because there is no room in her own driveway.

6. Mr. House's home was destroyed by a fire that had been caused by Pyro when he knocked over a kerosene heater that House had placed in front of the entrance to his home.
   a. Pyro can successfully raise the defense of contributory or comparative negligence if he is sued for negligence.
   b. Pyro can successfully raise the defense of assumption of the risk if he is sued for an intentional tort.
   c. Pyro is strictly liable for the tort of arson.
   d. Pyro is not liable for the tort of trespass if House invited him into his home and House did not incur a personal injury.

Questions 7 and 8 are based on the following fact situation: Donna was driving in an erratic manner on an interstate highway at a speed of 76 miles per hour when observed by State policemen, who put on their siren and sped after her. Donna became flustered when she realized that the police were trying to stop her. She carelessly put pressure on the accelerator, rather than the brake, causing her car to collide with that of Victoria. As a result, Victoria's property was damaged and Victoria suffered personal injuries.

7. Victoria may successfully sue:
   a. the policemen, who are strictly liable for the personal injuries suffered by Victoria.
   b. both the policemen and Donna for false imprisonment because Victoria was unable to extricate herself from the wreckage for ten minutes.
   c. Donna, who as a result of her failure to exercise reasonable care, caused both property damage and personal injuries.
   d. Donna, who as a result of her failure to exercise reasonable care, is liable for the property damage but not personal injuries.

8. If Victoria sues Donna, Donna may:
   a. successfully raise the defense of comparative negligence (or contributory negligence) if Victoria was also speeding and driving in an erratic manner.
   b. successfully raise the defense of supervening cause because it was foreseeable that if she was speeding, she would be apprehended by the police.
   c. successfully raise the defense of assumption of the risk because one who drives on an interstate highway assumes the risk of injury.
   d. not raise any defenses because her conduct was the basis for Victoria's suit based on an intentional tort.

9. In a state following the comparative negligence doctrine, a plaintiff, who incurred $10,000 in damages but is found to have been ten percent contributorily negligent, would be entitled to:
   a. recover $9,000 in a civil suit.
   b. recover $10,000 in a civil suit.
   c. recover $1,000 in a civil suit.
   d. no recovery in a civil suit.

10. Sterling, in order to induce Luton to lend him $1,000, which he promised to repay, told Luton that he was the owner of a money making machine but needed funds to purchase paper. Luton has not been repaid and brings a lawsuit against Sterling based on tort.
    a. Luton's contributory negligence will prevent him from recovery for an intentional tort.

b. Luton will not be able to recover for the tort of fraud because his reliance on the representation made by Sterling was unreasonable.

c. Luton will not be able to recover for the tort of fraud because Sterling's representation did not result in any injury to Luton.

d. Luton will be able to recover for the tort of interference with a contractual relationship.

11. In order to put in a foundation for a new store on Main Street, a building contractor used a small amount of dynamite in order to blast a large rock formation. Ingersoll's car, which was parked a block away, was demolished by a large boulder that was catapulted through the air by the blast. Which of the following statements is correct?

a. The building contractor is relieved of liability to Ingersoll because it used extraordinary care in order to prevent harm to property in the vicinity.

b. Because Ingersoll saw that the building contractor was using dynamite when she parked her car, she assumed the risk of its being damaged.

c. The contractor is liable to Ingersoll for the tort of trespass to property.

d. The building contractor is strictly liable to Ingersoll for the damage to the car even though no personal physical injury was incurred by Ingersoll.

Chapter 5

Torts Related to Business

There is a strong public policy favoring the free enterprise system and competition in business in the United States. Competition, however, must be fairly conducted. For this reason, certain intentional conduct of business firms is treated as being tortious if it is contrary to accepted ideas as to what are fair methods of competing and doing business. The business torts discussed in this chapter include interference with business relationships, infringement of protected rights in inventions (patents), creative works (copyrights), trademarks, trade names and trade secrets and other forms of unfair competition. Provisions in the federal Racketeer Influenced and Corrupt Organization Act (RICO) relating to civil liability are also introduced.

THINGS TO KEEP IN MIND

Certain unfair practices, such as restraints of trade, price discrimination and unfair labor practices are also prohibited by statutes and are covered in subsequent chapters.

OUTLINE

I.   Wrongful interference with a contractual obligation — Elements:

    A. A valid, enforceable contract must have existed between two parties.

    B. A third person must have known that the contract existed.

    C. The third person (the tortfeasor) must have intentionally induced or caused one of the parties to the contract not to perform his or her contractual duties in order to advance the pecuniary or financial interests of the third person.

II. Wrongful interference with a business relationship.

A. Use of abusive business practices, not for the purpose of making a profit or advancing a fair legitimate business interest, but in order to interfere with or injure another's business relationships.

B. Elements:

   1. A business relationship must have existed between the plaintiff and others. It need not be based upon a contract.

   2. The defendant, without justification, must have intentionally interfered with the relationship in a manner that was unfair according to contemporary business standards.

   3. The plaintiff must have been damaged as a result of the defendant's interference with the relationship.

C. Permissive activities include:

   1. Fair competitive attempts to attract customers, such as aggressive marketing and advertising strategies.

   2. Labor unions' encouragement of strikes.

III. Wrongfully entering into business.

A. Entering regulated business, trade or profession in violation of a statute or local ordinance. See Chapter 11.

B. Predatory competitive activity that is engaged in solely for the purpose of driving another firm out of business.

IV. Infringement of trademarks, patents and copyrights.

A. A form of unfair competition consists of "passing off" or "palming off" products by making it appear that the goods are made or marketed by a better known producer or distributor. Often this is accomplished by copying or infringing on a trademark, service mark or trade name of a competitor.

B. Trademarks.

   1. Distinctive marks, symbols, designs, devices, etc. which are imprinted or affixed to goods and identify them in the market because the marks are recognized by consumers.

   2. A service mark is used in order to distinguish the services of one person from those of another.

   3. The tort of trademark or service mark infringement occurs when a person copies, uses or imitates another's trademark or service mark without permission and, therefore, misleads potential purchasers as to the origin of the goods or services.

   4. Trademarks and service marks are protected from infringement at common law and by federal statutes, which provide for registration of marks.

5. Certification marks are used in connection with the products or services of one or more people, other than the owner, in order to certify the region, materials used, manufacture, quality or accuracy of the goods or services.

6. Collective marks are used by cooperatives and other organizations for the same purposes as are certification marks.

C. Trade names — It is tortious to use a name that is the same as or deceptively similar to a trade name used by another business enterprise.

D. Patents.

1. A natural person, who has obtained a patent on an invention from the United States Patent Office, has the exclusive right to make, use and sell the invention for 17 years.

2. Infringement occurs when one copies the invention without being licensed (given the right) to do so by the patent holder.

E. Copyrights.

1. A copyright is an exclusive right granted to an author or originator of a literary or other creative work in accordance with the federal copyright laws.

2. Protection against infringement of a copyright is given for the life of the author plus 50 years to the holder of the copyright, or, in the case of a corporation, 75 years.

3. Infringement occurs when a work is copied or a substantial part of it reproduced without the permission of the copyright holder.

E. Theft of trade secrets — Thefts or appropriations of business secrets relating to processes, products, information, etc., which are not necessarily protected by patents, copyrights or contracts, are actionable torts.

V. Disparagement of property or reputation.

A. Disparagement of product — Unprivileged publication of false information concerning another's products or goods (slander of quality, trade libel) or title to property (slander of title).

B. Disparagement of reputation — Unprivileged publication of false information which injures another's profession, trade, business, credit rating or dealings.

C. Defamation by computer — Providing erroneous information relating to another's business reputation, credit rating, etc.

VI. Racketeer Influenced and Corrupt Organization Act (RICO).

A. Federal statute, the purpose of which was to curb entry of organized crime into legitimate businesses.

B. Civil liability.

    1. United States government may seek civil penalties.

    2. Individuals who have been injured may bring civil suits and recover treble damages, costs and reasonable attorney's fees.

    3. Because of the broad language in RICO, business fraud may be treated as a racketeering activity.

C. More than twenty states have enacted similar legislation.

KEY WORDS AND PHRASES IN TEXT

Wrongful interference with a contractual relationship	Registration of marks
Wrongful interference with a business relationship	Infringement of trademarks, trade names, service marks, certification and collective marks
Predatory behavior	Patents
Wrongfully entering into business	Patent infringement
Regulated economic activities	Copyrights
Occupational licensing statutes	Copyright infringement
Trademarks	Fair use doctrine
Service marks	Trade secrets
Trade names	Appropriation
Certification marks	Disparagement of product
Collective marks	Disparagement of reputation
	RICO

FILL-IN QUESTIONS

1. Business torts are usually intentional torts and include disparagement of goods which means _false statements about products_ and unfair competition, such as _malicious injury to business_ .

2. A person is liable in _tort_ for wrongfully interfering with a contractual relationship between other people when he, she or it knew that a valid, enforceable contract existed between them, and he, she or it _intentionally_ caused or induced one of the parties to the contract to violate the terms of the contractual agreement.

3. Super Sales Inc. knew that Everett had a two year contract of employment with IT Corp. when it willfully induced Everett to resign from his position as sales manager for the IT Corp. in order to assume a similar position (at a higher salary) with Super Sales Inc. IT Corp. may successfully sue Everett for breach of the employment contract. IT Corp. may also recover from Super Sales Inc. for the tort of _wrongful interference in a contract_ because (a) it knew that a valid enforceable _contract_ existed between Everett and _IT Corp._ , and (b) it induced Everett to repudiate the terms of his contract with his employer in order to advance its own pecuniary interests.

4. A businessperson, who does not actually interfere with a contractual relationship between a competitor and other people may be liable to an injured competitor if he, she or it intentionally and maliciously engages in _predatory_ behavior or unfair business practices. Engaging in such activities may constitute the tort of wrongful _interference with business practirelations_ or the tort of wrongfully entering into business.

5. A person who, without authorization, copies a distinctive mark, design or symbol used to identify a manufacturer's product may be liable for the tort of _____ _infrigement of trademark_

6. The tort of patent infringement occurs when one copies an invention of a product or process that has been properly registered with _US Patent Office_ . The patent holder's exclusive right to make, use and sell his or her invention is protected for _17_ years.

7. If one copies an unpatented invention without being licensed to do so, he or she may be liable in tort for _theft of trade secrets_ .

8. Unprivileged publication of false statements relating to another person's goods is referred to as _disparagement, slander or libel_ ; publication of false information about another person's business dealings or credit is referred to as _libel if written_ .

MULTIPLE CHOICE QUESTIONS

1. On January 3, 1988 Sanders entered into a valid, enforceable contract with the owners of the Bumblebees, a professional soccer team and agreed to act as coach for two years. New State University had a soccer team that had a record of one win and 12 losses in the past two seasons. As a result, attendance at its games was poor and gate receipts were almost zero. In October 1988, New State University offered Sanders a position as head soccer coach at a salary that was triple what he was receiving from the Bumblebees. Sanders accepted the offer and subsequently refused to perform his coaching duties for the Bumblebees. The Bumblebees may recover from:
   a. Sanders for the tort of failing to carry out his contractual duties.
   b. Sanders because of strict liability.
   c. New State University because it wrongfully interfered with a contractual relationship.
   d. New State University in tort only if it had exercised bad faith or acted with malice.

Questions 2 and 3 are based on the following fact situation: Archibald was the only practicing architect in a town having a population of 19,000. Reginald, a local businessman, employed Archibald to prepare plans for a new building. Reginald was dissatisfied with the plans. Shortly thereafter, Reginald, who was not a licensed architect, established an office for the practice of architecture. Reginald employed Arabelle, a duly licensed architect to work in the office. The name of the firm was R and A Associates, Architects. Reginald circulated false reports that buildings planned by Archibald were unsafe and that Archibald was not properly licensed. He also told customers that if they needed the services of an architect they should contact R and A Associates.

2. Which of the following statements is correct?
   a. Reginald's activities are permissible because, without competition from R and A Associates, Archibald has a monopoly.
   b. If there is a state statute requiring that a person obtain a license from a state board in order to practice as an architect, Reginald is prohibited from engaging in that occupation.
   c. Arabelle has committed a tort because she is engaging in unfair competition.
   d. Archibald can recover from both Reginald and Arabelle for the tort of disparaging his reputation.

3. Archibald can successfully sue Reginald for the tort of:
   a. wrongfully disparaging his reputation.
   b. slander.
   c. maliciously interfering with business relationships.
   d. All of the above.

4. Strictland manufactures and sells security alarm devices that she invented but has not patented.
   a. Strictland cannot recover in tort from E, an employee, who copied and sold devices to buyers because Strictland failed to obtain a patent on her invention.
   b. Strictland cannot recover in tort from F, one of her salesmen, who gave a copy of Strictland's list of customers to Security Plus, Inc., a competitor of Strictland's, for $20,000.
   c. Strictland can recover from Security Plus, Inc., a competitor, which induced G, a key employee of Strictland, to leave Strictland's employment and work for it because Security Plus has tortiously interfered with a contractual relationship.
   d. Strictland can recover from Security Plus, Inc., a competitor, for copyright infringement if it has reproduced security alarm devices that are exact replicas of those produced by Strictland.

5. The D Corp. manufactures chewing gum which is packaged in a wrapper that is an exact copy of the wrapper which P Gum Inc. uses for its product and contains a replica of P Gum Inc.'s trademark. Today, P Gum Inc. will probably be successful if it sues the D Corp.:
   a. whether or not it can prove that D Corp. consciously and fraudulently intended to deceive potential customers.
   b. because customer confusion can easily be shown since the two wrappers are exactly the same.
   c. for trademark infringement.
   d. All of the above are correct.

6. Copy Kat makes multiple copies of five chapters of a book. Which of the following statements is correct?
   a. If Copy Kat is a professor, who distributes the copies to his students for educational purposes, he probably will not be liable to the copyright holder for copyright infringement.
   b. If Copy Kat is a professor, who sells the copies to his students, but clearly indicates the name of the author and publisher, he probably will not be liable to the copyright holder for copyright infringement.
   c. If Copy Kat makes fewer than one hundred copies, reproduction of the material is permitted because of the doctrine of "fair use."
   d. If the book was published thirty years ago, Copy Kat will probably not be liable to the copyright holder for copyright infringement.

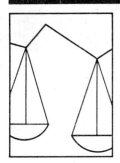

Chapter 6

Criminal Law

Crimes are wrongful acts committed against society and prosecuted by the government. In the United States, a person, who is accused of having committed a crime, is presumed to be innocent until he or she has been proven to be guilty beyond a reasonable doubt. The elements of each specific crime are defined by statute. Usually, a crime consists of an act, or omission, in conjunction with criminal intent. In some instances, a person, having a valid defense, may be excused from or relieved of criminal responsibility. Under our system of laws too, one accused of a crime is afforded certain safeguards by the federal and state constitutions.

THINGS TO KEEP IN MIND

One act may be both criminally and civilly wrongful. The state is a party in the criminal prosecution; the injured party is the plaintiff in the civil action based on tort. If the accused is found guilty of the crime beyond a reasonable doubt, he or she will be punished. If a defendant is found, by a preponderance of evidence, to have committed a tort, he or she will be required to compensate the plaintiff, who was injured by the tortious conduct.

OUTLINE

I. Nature of crime.

    A. Crimes are public wrongs that are defined by statute and prosecuted by the government on behalf of society. Those, who are found guilty of committing crimes, are punished normally by imprisonment and/or a fine, in accordance with the criminal statutes.

    B. Classification of crimes based upon their seriousness.

1. Treason — See U.S. Constitution, Article III, Section 3.

2. Felonies — Punishable by death or imprisonment for more than one year. Felonies can be divided into different degrees based upon the seriousness of the offenses.

3. Misdemeanors — Punishable by imprisonment for less than one year and/or a fine.

4. Offenses (violations that sometimes are referred to as petty offenses) — Punishable by a fine and/or possible brief imprisonment.

5. Attempt to commit a crime usually is considered to be a misdemeanor.

6. A conspiracy exists when two or more people agree to jointly engage in an unlawful act.

C. Most crimes are violations of state criminal statutes.

D. Federal crimes are defined in federal statutes.

E. Classification of crimes based upon the nature of the wrongful conduct:

1. Crimes against property.

2. Crimes against a person.

3. Crimes against the government.

II. Essentials of criminal liability — Most crimes consist of a combination of performance of a prohibited act and specific criminal intent.

A. Prohibited act — The particular criminal behavior for each crime is defined by statute. It may be an act or omission.

B. State of mind — Criminal intent or state of mind is required for most crimes. It may be based upon purpose, knowledge and awareness, recklessness or negligence, or be inferred, for one is presumed to intend the proximate and natural consequences of his or her own acts.

III. Defenses to criminal liability — Conditions that relieve a defendant of liability may exist. A criminal defendant may show that he or she did not commit the crime of which he or she has been accused because he or she did not commit the specific act or did not have the requisite intent. Some other defenses are:

A. Infancy — Most states have statutes providing that certain minors are treated as lacking the necessary moral sense to be capable of knowing right from wrong. There is, however, great variety among the states.

B. Intoxication.

1. Involuntary intoxication is a defense to a crime, if the perpetrator was unable to understand that the act committed was wrong.

2. Voluntary intoxication is a defense only if it prevented the perpetrator from having the necessary intent.

C. Insanity — Different standards are applied among the states.

    1. Perpetrator lacked capacity to "appreciate the wrongfulness" of his or her conduct or to conform his or her "conduct to the requirements of the law."

    2. The person accused of a crime did not appreciate the nature of the act or know that it was wrong.

    3. The person committed the criminal act because of an "irresistible impulse."

D. Mistake — Generally ignorance or mistake of law is no excuse.

E. Consent.

    1. If the presence of consent cancels the harm that is intended to be prevented, consent is a defense.

    2. Some crimes are forbidden without regard to a victim's consent, in which case, consent is not a defense.

F. Duress — Threat of imminent serious bodily harm, which is greater than the harm committed by the person accused of a crime.

G. Justifiable use of reasonably necessary force.

    1. Self-defense.

    2. Defense of dwelling or other property.

    3. Prevention of serious crime.

H. Entrapment — Law enforcement officer encouraged or induced criminal acts in order to apprehend criminal.

I. Statute of limitations — Statutes restrict prosecution after expiration of a stated period of time.

J. Immunity or agreement to prosecute for a less serious offense may be given by the state in exchange for information.

IV. Criminal procedure.

A. Constitutional safeguards — Most of the guarantees, found in Amendments to the United States Constitution, apply to the states as well as the federal government by virtue of the Fourteenth Amendment. State constitutions contain similar provisions.

    1. Fourth Amendment — Protection against unreasonable searches and seizures and prohibition against issuance of warrants without probable cause.

2. Fifth Amendment — Prohibits self-incrimination and double jeopardy; guarantees due process.

3. Sixth Amendment — Guarantees speedy, public trial by jury, right to be informed of charges, confront the accused, subpoena witnesses and assistance of an attorney.

4. Eighth Amendment — Prohibits excessive bail and fine, and cruel and unusual punishment.

B. Criminal process.

1. Arrest — A warrant, based upon a showing of probable cause that the accused committed the crime, is required unless probable cause reasonably justifies an immediate arrest.

2. Indictment issued by a grand jury or an information issued by a magistrate — The effect is to formally charge a defendant with a specified crime or crimes.

3. Trial — The state must prove guilt beyond a reasonable doubt.

V. Crimes affecting business.

A. Forgery — Fraudulent making or material alteration of an instrument or document so as to change the liability of another.

B. Robbery — Unlawful taking of personal property with force.

C. Burglary — Breaking and entering a dwelling or other structure with intent to commit a felony.

D. Larceny — Unlawful taking of personal property without force.

E. Theft of services or intangible property.

F. Embezzlement — Fraudulent conversion of property or money by person to whom it was entrusted.

G. Arson — Willful, malicious burning of a building (and in some states, personal property) of another.

H. Obtaining goods by false pretenses.

I. Receiving stolen goods.

J. Use of mails to defraud — Federal crime.

K. Falsifying measures, labels and weights.

L. Theft of services.

VI. White-collar crimes — Nonviolent crimes, often committed in the course of a legitimate occupation.

   A. Computer crimes — A number of states have enacted specific computer crime statutes. See Chapter 55.

   B. Bribery.

      1. Commercial bribery — "Kickbacks", "payoffs" and other forms of industrial espionage.

      2. Bribery of public officials — Tender of something of value in order to influence governmental official to act in a manner that serves a private interest.

      3. Bribery of foreign officials — The Foreign Corrupt Practices Act of 1977.

   C. Bankruptcy crimes — See Chapter 31.

      1. Submission of false claims by creditors.

      2. Fraudulent transfers of property by debtor.

      3. "Scam bankruptcy".

   D. Corporate crimes — A corporation is liable for a crime if the penalty provided by statute is a fine and intent is not an element of the crime or intent may be inferred.

   E. Criminal provisions in Racketeer Influenced and Corrupt Organizations Act (RICO).

KEY WORDS AND PHRASES IN TEXT

Crimes
Felonies
Capital offenses
Misdemeanors
Petty offenses or violations
Federal crimes
Crimes against property
Crimes against the person
Crimes against the government
Elements of a crime
Commission of a prohibited act
Omission of an act
Wrongful mental state (*mens rea*)
Defense of infancy
Defense of intoxication (voluntary and involuntary)
Defense of insanity (or mental incompetency)

Defense of mistake of law
Defense of mistake of fact
Defense of consent
Defense of duress
Defense of justifiable use of force
Defense of entrapment
Statute of limitations for crimes
Immunity
Presumption of innocence
Unreasonable searches and seizures
Warrants for searches and arrests
Due process of law
Double jeopardy
Speedy public trial
Trial by jury
Right to confront witnesses
Right to counsel
Excessive bail or fine

Cruel and unusual punishment
Criminal prosecution
Arrest
Indictment
Information
Guilt beyond a reasonable doubt
Forgery
Robbery
Burglary
Larceny

Obtaining goods by false pretenses
Receiving stolen goods
Embezzlement
Misapplication of trust funds
Arson
Use of mails to defraud
White-collar crimes
Computer crimes
Bribery
RICO—criminal violations

FILL-IN QUESTIONS

1. A crime is a public ___wrong___, which is defined by statute and prosecuted by ___state___.

2. In order to be found guilty of a specific crime, one must have _committed a wrong_ _____ with the requisite specified criminal state of mind or intent. Criminal intent may be based upon _purpose, knowledge, recklessness or negligence_.

3. If an accused person can show that he or she committed a criminal act while insane or because of duress, he or she has a valid ___defense___, which relieves him or her of criminal responsibility.

4. One, who is accused of having committed a crime, is presumed to be _innocent_ until he or she has been found ___guilty___ beyond a reasonable doubt.

5. An accused person is protected against _unreasonable search + seizure_ by the Fourth Amendment and against _cruel + unusual punishment_ by the Eighth Amendment of the United States Constitution.

6. Prohibitions against the issuance of a warrant without probable cause are provided by the Fourth Amendment and prohibitions against _self incrimination + double jeapardy_ by the Fifth Amendment.

7. The Sixth Amendment guarantees one accused of a crime _a speedy trial, right to be informed of charge, subpoena witnesses + getting attorney_.

8. Crimes involving the theft of property include burglary (breaking and entering into a dwelling, building or other structure with the intention of committing a crime), robbery (_forceful unlawful taking of property_) and _larceny_ (wrongful taking of property without force with the intention of depriving the owner of the possession or use of the property).

MULTIPLE CHOICE QUESTIONS

1. A crime is considered to be a felony if it is:
   a. a federal offense.
   b. punishable by death or imprisonment for more than a year.
   c. punishable by a fine or imprisonment for less than a year.
   d. so stated by the grand jury in its indictment.

2. Least serious crimes are referred to as:
    a. felonies.
    b. misdemeanors.
    c. civil wrongs.
    d. torts.

3. A person who is accused of having committed a crime must be proven guilty:
    a. beyond a reasonable doubt.
    b. by substantially reasonable evidence.
    c. with a preponderance of evidence.
    d. by a majority of the jurors.

4. C. P. Desprite has been subtly altering a client's books of account and as a result has been able to add about $400 a month to his own income. When it is discovered that he has taken and used the money, he probably will be prosecuted for the crime of:
    a. forgery.
    b. conversion.
    c. entrapment.
    d. embezzlement.

5. A defendant, who is being prosecuted for the crime of assault having hit another person with a baseball bat, would most likely be successful in defending against the charge by showing that:
    a. she had to strike the other person in order to prevent what she thought was a deadly threat to her life.
    b. she honestly believed that the law allowed her to strike another person under the circumstances.
    c. she felt morally justified in striking another person, even though she knew that society objected to such conduct.
    d. because of the actions of undercover police officers, she felt trapped and, therefore, struck one of them.
    e. All of the above would be good defenses.

6. One act may be the basis for prosecution for commission of more than one crime. For example, if C breaks into V's home, while V is away, and steals a television set, C may be found guilty of the crimes of:
    a. burglary and robbery.
    b. arson and misrepresentation.
    c. burglary and larceny.
    d. arson and larceny.

7. One act may be the basis for a criminal prosecution by the state and a civil lawsuit by the victim. For example, if an employee takes $600 from his employer's cash register, without the knowledge or permission of his employer, he may be sued by the employer for the tort of:
    a. conversion and prosecuted for the crime of embezzlement.
    b. conversion and prosecuted for the crime of robbery.
    c. larceny and prosecuted for the crime of burglary.
    d. fraud and prosecuted for the crime of deceit.

8. Jones shot and wounded Smith. Jones may:
    a. be charged with homicide or murder if her mental state was such that she

premeditatedly intended to kill Smith.
b. be charged with a crime but not sued civilly by Smith.
c. not be found guilty of a crime if she establishes that she had reasonable justification.
d. not be found guilty of a crime if she establishes that Smith consented to be shot.

9. A policeman stopped a college student, who was running down the street with a smoking revolver in his hand, searched and arrested him without first having obtained a warrant:
   a. The absolute right to be free from a search and seizure has been violated.
   b. The right to be free from an unreasonable search and seizure has been violated if an indictment had not been previously issued by a grand jury or an information issued by a magistrate.
   c. The right to be free from an unreasonable search and seizure has been violated.
   d. The right to be free from an unreasonable search and seizure has not been violated even if a warrant had not been previously obtained from a court.

10. The Foreign Corrupt Practices Act:
    a. prohibits United States companies and their officers, directors, shareholders and agents from making wrongful payments in cash or other benefits to officials of foreign governments for the purpose of obtaining or retaining business.
    b. requires that the financial records of companies, which engage in foreign commerce, accurately and fairly reflect its financial activities.
    c. prohibits making false statements to accountants or false entries in records and accounts of companies engaging in foreign commerce.
    d. All of the above.

Unit Two

CONTRACTS

The objective of Unit Two is to help you understand concepts of contract law, which is the foundation upon which other areas of law relating to business are superimposed. The law of contracts deals with promises that have been made by parties who voluntarily have entered into private agreements, or contracts. Contracts create expectations that the parties to them will act in an agreed-upon manner. Contract law provides the framework for assuring that those expectations will be realized or remedies provided if they are not.

In the chapters in this unit you will be learning about the rules that have been adopted relating to the rights and duties of the parties to such agreements, how contracts are formed and discharged and what happens when parties fail to carry out the promises that they have made.

Chapter 7

Nature and Terminology

Rights and duties of parties to agreements are created when the parties make promises in contracts. Usually contractual promises are executed by the parties so that recourse to the courts is not necessary. Contract law is the body of legal rules that relate to the formation, discharge and breach of legally enforceable promises. In order to understand contract law, it is important that you become familiar with some basic concepts and terminology.

THINGS TO KEEP IN MIND

1. Not all promises that are made will be enforced by the courts.
2. Contracts may be oral, written or inferred from conduct.

OUTLINE

I. The function of contract law in business.

    A. Provides legal framework for reasonably assured expectations within which to plan and venture.

    B. Ensures that the promisor (the person who makes a contractual promise) either will comply with the promise or entitle the nonbreaching promisee (the person to whom a contractual promise is made) to receive some form of relief or remedy.

    C. Provides a major part of the foundation upon which more specialized areas of the law have been built.

II. Basic concepts underlying contract law.

A. Freedom of contract and freedom from contract — In general, one may freely enter into any contract unless it is contrary to law or public policy.

B. Elements of contracts — In order to have a contract, certain requisites must be present.

1. Agreement — The mutual assent and agreement of the parties must be evidenced by an offer and an acceptance.

2. Consideration — Legally sufficient and bargained for consideration must be exchanged for contractual promises.

3. Contractual capacity — There must be two or more parties who have contractual capacity.

4. Legality — The purpose and subject matter of the contract must not be contrary to law or public policy.

5. Genuineness of assent — The assent of the parties must be real, genuine and voluntarily given.

6. Form — The agreement must be in the form that is required by law if one is prescribed.

III. Nature and types of contracts.

A. Definition of a contract — An agreement made by two or more parties, containing a promise or set of promises to perform or refrain from performing some act or acts, which will be enforced by a court.

B. Types of contracts and distinctions between them.

1. Based upon the manner in which the assent of the parties is given.

a. Express contract — The terms of the agreement are stated in words used by the parties.

b. Implied in fact contract — The terms of the agreement are inferred from the conduct of the parties.

c. The parties must objectively have the intention of entering into a contract.

2. Note that quasi contracts (sometimes called contracts implied in law) are not contracts. Equity imposes a duty to pay the reasonable value for a benefit received in order to avoid unjust enrichment. It is an equitable principle.

3. Based upon the nature of the promises made.

a. Bilateral contract — Reciprocal promises are exchanged by the parties, i.e., the promise of one party is exchanged for the promise of the other.

b. Unilateral contract — One party makes a promise in exchange for the other party's actually performing some act (performance) or refraining from performing some act (forbearance).

4. Based upon compliance with a statute requiring a special formality.

    a. Formal contracts — Some formality is prescribed for their creation.
      1) Contracts under seal.
      2) Recognizances.
      3) Negotiable instruments and letters of credit.

    b. Informal contracts — Simple contracts for which no special form or formality is required.

5. Based upon the stage of performance of the contractual promises.

    a. Executed contract — Contract that has been completely performed by all parties.

    b. Executory contract — Contract that has not been fully performed by one or more of the parties.

6. Based upon legal validity and enforceability.

    a. Valid and enforceable contract — All elements of a contract are present.

    b. Void contract — Agreement has no legal effect. (It is really not a contract.)

    c. Voidable contract — One of the parties has the option of avoiding his or her contractual obligations.

    d. Unenforceable contract — Contract that cannot be proven in the manner required by law.

KEY WORDS AND PHRASES IN TEXT

Restatement of the Law of Contracts
Promisor
Promisee
Freedom of contract
Basic requirements of a contract
Agreement (includes an offer and acceptance)
Legally sufficient consideration
Contractual capacity
Legality
Reality of assent
Form
Contract
Contractual promise
Express contract

Implied in fact contract
Objective theory of contracts
Quasi contract (or contract implied in law)
Quantum meruit
Unjust enrichment
Bilateral contract
Unilateral contract
Formal contract
Contract under seal
Recognizance
Negotiable instrument
Letter of credit
Informal contract
Executed contract

Executory contract   Voidable contract
Valid contract   Unenforceable contract
Void contract

FILL-IN QUESTIONS

1. A contract is a legal relationship created when _____ competent, consenting parties agree to perform or refrain from performing a legal act.

2. The elements of a contract are _____
    _____
    _____
    _____ .

3. When words are used to create and define the terms of a contract, the parties have formed _____ contract; when the parties have used conduct, rather than words, they have entered into _____ contract.

4. A _____ contract consists of reciprocal promises; a unilateral contract consists of an exchange of a promise for _____ .

5. Contracts under seal, recognizances and negotiable instruments are characterized as _____ contracts. Other contracts are referred to as simple or _____ contracts. Most contracts are _____ .

6. If all the parties to a contract have completely performed their contractual promises, the contract is referred to as an _____ contract. If one or more of the parties has not completed his or her performance, the contract is said to be an _____ contract.

MULTIPLE CHOICE QUESTIONS

1. An implied in fact contract can be defined as one:
    a. which lacks one or more elements of a true contract, but which may nevertheless be enforced by the courts if it is in the best interests of the parties to do so.
    b. which is formed entirely without the use of words.
    c. in which the intentions of the contracting parties are inferred by the courts in large part from their conduct and surrounding circumstances.
    d. in which the intentions of the contracting parties are expressed with the use of words.

2. A unilateral contract:
    a. is a promise to perform an act.
    b. consists of mutual promises to act.
    c. consists of a promise to act exchanged for performance of an act.
    d. is one that is binding on one of the parties only.

3. A bilateral contract exists if:
    a. a promise to perform is exchanged for performance.
    b. a promise to forbear is exchanged for performance.

    c. a promise to perform is exchanged for a promise to forbear.

    d. performance is exchanged for forbearance.

4. A says to B, "I will pay you $10 if you change the flat tire on my car." B changes the flat tire.

    a. A unilateral contract is created so that A must pay B $10.

    b. A bilateral contract is created so that A must pay B $10.

    c. A formal contract is created so that A must pay B $10.

    d. No enforceable contract results.

5. G says to H, "If you promise to paint my car, I promise to pay you $100." H says, "It's a deal; I promise to paint the car." This creates:

    a. an express unilateral contract.

    b. an express bilateral contract.

    c. an implied in fact unilateral contract.

    d. an implied in fact bilateral contract.

6. An executed contract:

    a. involves more than two parties.

    b. will be enforced unless one of the parties elects to disaffirm it.

    c. is yet to be completely performed.

    d. has been completely performed.

7. An executory contract:

    a. has been completely performed.

    b. is yet to be completely performed.

    c. will not be recognized as enforceable by the courts.

    d. is illegal and will not be enforced by the courts.

8. An agreement to commit arson by burning down a building is an example of a:

    a. valid, enforceable contract.

    b. voidable express contract.

    c. voidable implied in law contract.

    d. void, unenforceable contract.

9. V requests and accepts the services of A, an accountant, without agreeing to pay a specified fee therefor. As to the compensation which A is to receive, there is:

    a. a formal contract.

    b. an express contract.

    c. an implied in fact contract.

    d. an implied in law contract.

10. An implied in law contract can be defined as one:

    a. that is the same as an implied in fact contract.

    b. in which one of the parties would be unjustly enriched even though he or she had not consented to the conferring of a benefit.

    c. in which the intentions of one or all of the parties is inferred from their conduct and surrounding circumstances rather than words.

    d. which has been fully performed by all of the parties.

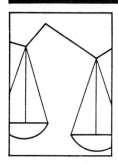

Chapter 8

Agreement

In order to have a contract there must be an agreement. The parties, the offeror and the offeree, must indicate their present, objective willingness and intention to assent to the same terms regarding their respective rights and duties. Their assent is evidenced by the process of offer and acceptance. An offer must have been made by the offeror and an acceptance given by the offeree.

THINGS TO KEEP IN MIND

The parties may contemplate either:

1. A unilateral contract — Actual performance of an act or actual forbearance is exchanged for a promise to act or refrain from acting; OR

2. A bilateral contract — A promise to act or a promise to refrain from acting is given in exchange for a promise to act or forbear.

OUTLINE

I. Manifestation of apparent mutual assent by parties to agreement.

   A. Objective assent — Only present, objective intent of the parties, which they have manifested by such words or conduct as would indicate to a reasonable person an intention to be bound by the same terms, is recognized in law.

   B. Terms.

      1. Material, essential terms — Identification of the parties, the subject matter, the consideration or price to be paid and the quantity (if appropriate).

  2. Incidental terms.

II. The offer — The offeror shows his or her assent when he or she communicates a proposal, the offer, to the offeree, setting forth with reasonable clarity, definiteness and certainty the material terms to which he is presently, objectively agreeing and intending to be bound.

 A. Objective intent manifested by offeror.

  1. The words and/or conduct used by the offeror must be such that a reasonable person would be warranted, under the cirumstances, in believing that a real agreement was intended by the offeror.

  2. It is necessary to distinguish offers from:

   a. Expressions of opinion.

   b. Preliminary negotiations and invitations soliciting offers.

   c. Statements of intention.

   d. Advertisements, catalogues, circulars, price lists.

   e. Offers that are made in jest or under emotional stress.

   f. Other non-offer situations.
    1) Requests for bids.
    2) Requests of auctioneer for bids at auctions.
    3) Social invitations.
    4) Agreements to agree.
    5) Sham transactions.

 B. Definiteness and clarity of material terms — All of the material, essential terms must be indicated in the offer with clarity, definiteness and certainty or a method stated by which the terms will be made certain.

  1. The offeror may provide that one or more of the terms will be made more definite by reference to an outside standard or third person.

  2. Material terms.

   a. The subject matter.
    1) Property to be sold.
    2) Services to be performed.
    3) Sum of money to be borrowed.

   b. The price.
    1) Reasonable price if price is not fixed but a party fully performs.
    2) Refer to outside standard or appraiser.
    3) Open price terms (U.C.C. Sec. 2-305).

   c. The quantity.

       1) Requirements and output contracts (U.C.C. Sec. 2-306).
       2) Exclusive dealings contracts.

C. Communication of offer — The terms of the offer must be received by the offeree.

   1. Offeree must have knowledge of all the material terms of the offer.

   2. An offer may be made to a specific offeree to whom it is communicated.

   3. A public offer, such as an offer for a reward, is treated as communicated to those people who have knowledge of it.

D. Termination of offer.

   1. By actions of the parties.

     a. Revocation by offeror.
       1) Revocation must be communicated to offeree. (It must, therefore, be received by the offeree prior to acceptance.)
       2) An offer to a specific offeree is effectively terminated when it is received by the offeree.
       3) A public offer is effectively terminated when revocation is given in the same manner and for the same period of time as had been used in order to make the offer.
       4) Irrevocable offers.
         a) Common law option contracts — Consideration must be given to offeror by offeree.
         b) Statutory "firm offers" — A writing signed by the offeror is necessary (U.C.C. Sec. 2-205).
         c) Distinguish from provisions in offer that acceptance is to be given prior to a specified date.
       5) Offer to enter into a unilateral contract.
         a) Traditional view — Offer to enter into a unilateral contract may be revoked even though the offeree has begun performance.
         b) Modern view applies doctrine of promissory estoppel — Offeror is barred (estopped) from revoking offer when the offeree has changed position in justifiable reliance on the offer.

     b. Rejection by offeree.
       1) Offeree demonstrates his or her intention not to accept offer.
       2) Rejection must be communicated to offeror.
       3) A counteroffer constitutes a rejection.
       4) An inquiry by offeree is distinguishable from a rejection.
       5) Merchants' variations in terms (U.C.C. Sec. 2-207).

   2. Because of lapse of time.

     a. If duration is stated in offer, offer terminates after expiration of the stated period of time.

     b. If duration is not stated in offer, offer lapses after a reasonable period of time.

3. By operation of law.

    a. Destruction of the subject matter.

    b. Death or adjudication of insanity of a party.

    c. Supervening illegality.

III. Acceptance — The offeree accepts the offer when he, she or it unequivocally manifests his, her or its assent to the terms of the offer.

A. Requisites.

    1. Offeree has knowledge of the terms of the offer.

    2. Offeree's overt conduct manifests willingness and intention to be bound.

    3. Offeree complies with conditions, if any, stated in offer. (Acceptance must be in the proper manner, at the proper place and at the proper time.)

    4. Acceptance must be by the party to whom the offer was directed.

    5. Acceptance must positively, unequivocally accord to the terms of the offer.

B. Manner of acceptance.

    1. If bilateral contract contemplated, offeree makes a promise.

    2. If unilateral contract contemplated, offeree performs required act or forbears from acting.

    3. Silence generally will not be considered to be an acceptance unless:

        a. There was a similar prior course of dealings, or

        b. The offeree accepted the benefits, or

        c. The offeree exercised dominion over the subject matter.

C. Effective moment of acceptance.

    1. If a unilateral contract is contemplated, acceptance is effective when performance or forbearance is completed.

    2. If a bilateral contract is contemplated, acceptance is effective when offeree gives the requisite promise. (Usually this is when the acceptance is sent so that it is out of the offeree's control, even if the acceptance is not received by the offeror.)

        a. If the manner of acceptance is specified by the offeror:
            1) Acceptance is effective when sent in the manner authorized by the offeror.

2) Acceptance is not effective until received by the offeror if the acceptance is sent in an unauthorized manner.

b. If the manner of acceptance is not specified by the offeror, acceptance is effective when sent, if it is sent by the same means of communication as was used for communicating the offer or any customary or reasonable means of communicating.

3. Offeror may include a condition in the offer that acceptance will not be effective until it is received by the offeror.

4. A contract is created at the moment that the acceptance is effective.

KEY WORDS AND PHRASES IN TEXT

Agreement
Manifestation of mutual assent
Offer
Offeror
Offeree
Objective intent to be bound by terms
    of offer
Offers distinguished from expressions of
    opinion, statements of intentions,
    preliminary negotiations, advertise-
    ments, catalogues, circulars,
    agreements to agree and sham
    transactions
Auctions
Definiteness of material terms of offer
    (and contract)
Relaxation of requirement of definiteness
    of terms under the Uniform
    Commercial Code
Partial performance
Communication of offer to offeree
Offers for rewards
Termination of the offer by action of the
    parties
Revocation of offer by the offeror
Irrevocable offers

Option contracts
Merchant's firm offer
Detrimental reliance on the offer
    (promissory estoppel)
Rejection of offer by the offeree
Counteroffer by the offeree
"Mirror image rule"
Termination of offer by operation of law
Termination of offer because of lapse
    of time
Termination of offer because of
    destruction of the subject matter
Termination of offer because of death or
    incompetency of the offeror or
    offeree
Termination of offer because of
    supervening illegality of the
    proposed contract
Acceptance
Acceptance must be unequivocally given
    by person to whom offer was
    directed (offeree)
Silence generally does not operate as
    an acceptance
Communication of acceptance
Mode and timeliness of acceptance to
    offer for bilateral contract

FILL-IN QUESTIONS

1. An essential element of a contract is mutual assent of the parties to the same terms of the agreement, which is evidenced when the offeror communicates _____ to the offeree, who _____ the offeror's terms.

2. Material terms, which must be clearly stated in an offer, include _____

_____
_____.

3. If an offeror has the power to terminate an offer before it has been accepted, one may say that the offeror has the power of _____.

4. A communication from the offeree to the offeror, setting forth different terms than those contained in the original offer, is considered to be a _____.

5. An offer is terminated at the expiration of the period of time that is specified by the offeror in the offer or, if the duration of the offer is not explicitly specified in the offer, after a _____.
   An offer is also terminated by operation of law if _____
   _____
   _____.

MULTIPLE CHOICE QUESTIONS

1. The following advertisement appeared in a newspaper:

   "Brand new bicycles. Worth up to $100. Our price $25. Limited number available."

   This would be considered to be:
   a. an invitation to make an offer.
   b. an offer to a unilateral contract.
   c. an offer to a bilateral contract.
   d. an offer in the alternative.

2. In order for an offer to be effective, the following requirement(s) must be met:
   a. the terms of the offer must be communicated to the offeree.
   b. the material terms of the offer must be reasonably definite, clear and certain.
   c. the offeror must objectively show that he or she intends to be bound by the terms of the offer.
   d. a and b above.
   e. All of the above.

3. The ABC Auto Sales Co. sent the following telegram to Ford Motor Company:

   "We need ten automobiles as soon as possible. Ship to ABC Auto Sales Co."

   a. The telegram contains an offer.
   b. Acceptance by Ford Motor Company will not take place until receipt of the automobiles by ABC Auto Sales Co.
   c. The telegram is too indefinite and uncertain to constitute an offer.
   d. The telegram creates a contract.

4. When goods are placed on sale at an ordinary auction, a contract is formed at the moment that:
   a. the auctioneer shows the goods.
   b. the highest bid is made.
   c. the auctioneer brings down his hammer.
   d. the highest bidder pays for the goods.

5. A communication by the offeree setting forth terms that are different than those contained in the original offer is considered to:
   a. be a counteroffer and, therefore, a rejection.
   b. result in a binding contract.
   c. keep the original offer open.
   d. create a unilateral contract.

6. An outstanding offer to sell a tract of real property is terminated at the time the:
   a. buyer mails a rejection of the offer if the original offer was sent by mail.
   b. buyer learns of the sale of the property to a third person.
   c. buyer learns of the seller's death.
   d. seller mails a revocation of the original offer if the offer was sent by mail.

7. John writes a letter to Bill in which he offers to sell his motorcycle to Bill for $1,000. John may revoke his offer:
   a. after the expiration of one week.
   b. at any time before Bill sends an acceptance to John.
   c. at any time before John receives an acceptance from Bill.
   d. at no time because the offer is in writing.

8. If no time is specified by the offeror as to when an offer will terminate, the offer lapses after the expiration of a reasonable period of time, which depends on:
   a. the nature of the subject matter.
   b. the period of time within which the offeror's purpose can be effected.
   c. the prior course of dealings of the parties.
   d. all of the above.

9. An offer is terminated:
   a. by the expiration of a reasonable period of time although a specified period of duration is stated in the offer.
   b. by the expiration of a reasonable period of time when no specified period of duration is stated in the offer.
   c. when it is not rejected by the offeree.
   d. within a reasonable period of time after the offeror and offeree separate if the offer had been oral.

10. In order to be effective, if the United States mails are used:
    a. an offer must be received by an offeree and a rejection sent by an offeree.
    b. an offer must be received by an offeree and a revocation received by an offeror.
    c. an acceptance must be received by an offeror and a revocation received by an offeree.
    d. an acceptance must be sent by an offeree and a revocation received by an offeree.

Chapter 9

Consideration

In order for a contractual promise to be legally enforceable, it must be supported by sufficient legal consideration so that there is a bargained-for exchange. In general, the party making the promise, the promisor, must be receiving a legal benefit (something which he or she does not already have a right to receive) or the promisee, the party to whom the promise is made, must be incurring a legal detriment (giving up something which he or she has a right to keep) or both, so that something of legal value is given in exchange for the promise.

THINGS TO KEEP IN MIND

The issue of lack of consideration arises when a promisee sues a promisor, who has failed to carry out a promise and who raises the defense that the promise was unenforceable because he or she received nothing in exchange for the promise.

OUTLINE

I.   The concept of legally sufficient consideration.

    A. Parties to a contract.

        1. Promisor — The party who makes a promise to do or refrain from doing something.

        2. Promisee — The party who receives a promise.

        3. If, as in the diagram below, a unilateral contract is contemplated, only one party (A) is the promisor. The other party (B) is the promisee.

A —————promise————> B

4. If, as in the diagram below, a bilateral contract is contemplated, promises are exchanged by the parties. Each party is, therefore, a promisor as to the promise which he or she makes and a promisee as to the promise which he or she receives. Each promise must be supported by consideration.

A ——————promise made by A——————> B
  <—————promise made by B—————

B. There must be a presently bargained-for exchange between the parties. Consideration may be thought of as the "price" paid by the promisee for a promise so that mutual obligations are present.

A ——————————promise——————————> B
  <————bargained for "price" = consideration——

C. Legally sufficient consideration exists when either the promisee incurs a legal detriment or the promisor receives a legal benefit or both.

1. A legal detriment is incurred by a promisee if the promisee does one of the following:

a. Actually gives up something that he or she has a legal right to keep in the case of a unilateral contract, as in the diagram below, or

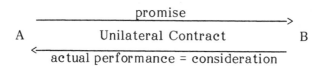

b. Actually refrains or forbears from doing something that he or she has a legal right to do in the case of a unilateral contract, as in the diagram below, or

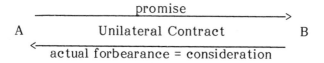

c. Promises to surrender something that he or she has a right to retain as in the bilateral contract diagrammed below, or

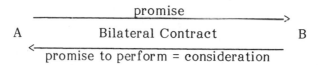

d. Promises to forbear from doing something that he or she has a right to do as in the bilateral contract diagrammed below.

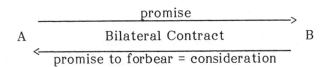

promise

A   Bilateral Contract   B

promise to forbear = consideration

2. A legal benefit is received by a promisor if the promisor received something to which he or she is not entitled, but for the contract.

3. It is not necessary that an economic or material loss be incurred by the promisee or benefit received by the promisor. All that is necessary is a surrender or receipt of a legal right.

II. Adequacy of consideration — Because of the doctrine of freedom of contract, the relative value of consideration given by contracting parties is not examined by courts unless:

A. It is evidence that assent of one party was not genuine.

B. The consideration received by one party was grossly inadequate (equitable principle).

C. No consideration was given.

1. Past or moral consideration, "love and affection."

2. Performance of a preexisting duty that is imposed by law or owed because of an existing contract.

    a. Mutual rescission by parties to contract.
      1) If contract is executory (neither party has performed), parties may agree to rescind or cancel the contract. (Thereafter the same parties are free to enter into a new contract which may have the same or different terms.)
      2) If contract is executed in full or in part by one of the parties:
        a) Parties may modify terms if the party who had not performed gives consideration.
        b) Some courts will enforce modification, even if new consideration is not given, under special circumstances.
        c) U.C.C. Sec. 2-209 provides that a modification of a contract for the sale of goods is enforceable without new consideration.
        d) Some states have enacted statutes providing that if the modification is a signed writing, it will be enforceable without new consideration.

    b. Unforeseen difficulties exception — A promise to pay additional compensation for construction is sometimes enforceable if unknown, unanticipated, unforeseen difficulties arise which greatly increase the burden of performance.

3. Performance of an illegal act.

4. Illusory promise — A promise that appears to be a promise but is not really an undertaking to do anything.

III. Problem areas in business concerning consideration.

    A. Methods for dealing with uncertainty as to future market conditions.

        1. Requirements contracts.

            a. Consideration is given if buyer agrees to purchase and seller agrees to sell all or up to a specified amount that buyer *needs* or *requires*.

            b. Contract is illusory if buyer agrees to purchase only the goods that he, she or it may wish, want or desire.

        2. Output contracts.

            a. Seller agrees to sell and buyer agrees to purchase all or up to a specified amount of seller's output.

            b. Contract is illusory if terms permit seller to sell to other purchasers or if seller's obligation to produce is based upon seller's wish, want or desire.

        3. Exclusive dealings contracts.

            a. One party has sole or exclusive right to deal in or with the products or property of the other.

            b. Parties have obligations to use best efforts to promote subsequent sale, supply sufficient quantity, etc.

        4. Option to cancel clauses.

            a. If right to cancel is absolute and unconditional, contract is illusory.

            b. If right to cancel is conditioned upon the happening of some event, contract is enforceable.

    B. Settlement of claims or debts.

        1. A promise to pay or actual payment of part of a mature, liquidated, undisputed debt is not consideration for creditor's release of debtor's obligation to pay the remaining balance.

        2. Parties may settle by entering into an accord (new agreement) and satisfaction (performance of new terms) if:

            a. The obligation to pay or the amount of the debt is disputed.

            b. The obligation to pay is not yet due — The debt is not a mature one.

            c. The amount owed is not liquidated — The amount is not a definite, certain or exact sum of money or a sum that is capable of being made definite by computation.

            d. Other or additional consideration is given.

       e. Creditor's promise to release debtor is in a signed writing.
         1) U.C.C. Sec. 1-107.
         2) Model Written Obligations Act.

   3. Composition with creditors.

       a. An agreement between a debtor and two or more of his, her or its creditors who agree to accept lesser payments in satisfaction of the debts which are owed to each of them.

       b. Each creditor's promise to accept the smaller sum in lieu of full payment is consideration for the other creditors' similar promises.

   4. Release and/or covenant not to sue.

       a. A release is a relinquishment of a right or discharge of an obligation or claim that one has against another person. It must be supported by consideration.

       b. A covenant not to sue is a promise by one who has a right to bring an action that he, she or it will not sue in order to enforce such right of action. It must be supported by consideration.

IV. Promises enforceable without consideration.

  A. In the past, consideration was not necessary if instrument was under seal.

  B. New promise to pay debt barred by the statute of limitations.

  C. New written promise or reaffirmation of promise to pay debt that will otherwise be barred by discharge in bankruptcy. (Filing with Bankruptcy Court is required. See Chapter 31.)

  D. Doctrine of promissory estoppel or detrimental reliance — In those states in which the doctrine has been adopted, the promisor will not be able to plead lack of consideration if:

    1. A promise is made to induce a promisee to act in a particular way,

    2. The promisor can foresee that the promisee will justifiably rely upon the promise,

    3. The promisee substantially changes his or her position in the foreseeable manner and incurs damage because of reasonably relying upon the promise, and

    4. It is grossly unfair not to enforce the promise.

  E. Charitable subscriptions.

  F. Uniform Commercial Code provisions.

    1. Signed, written firm offer by merchant (Sec. 2-205).

2. Signed, written waiver or renunciation of a claim (Sec. 1-107).

3. Commercial paper (Art. 3).

4. Modifications of existing contract for sale of goods (Sec. 2-209).

G. Model Written Obligations Act and other state statutes.

KEY WORDS AND PHRASES IN TEXT

Legally sufficient consideration
Promise exchanged for something having
   legal value
Bargained-for exchange
Performance of an act
Forbearance (refraining from doing
   something)
Creation, modification or destruction of
   legal relationships
Promisor
Promisee
Legal detriment incurred by promisee
Legal benefit received by promisor
Promise to perform or performance of
   a moral obligation is not legally
   sufficient consideration
Adequacy of consideration ("fairness" of
   bargain is usually not relevant)
Performance of a preexisting duty is not
   sufficient consideration
Mutual rescission and new contract

Modification of contract for sale of goods
Unforeseen difficulties
Requirements, output and exclusive
   dealings contracts distinguishable
   from illusory promises
Illusory promises
Option to cancel clauses
Settlement of claims or debts
Accord and satisfaction
Mature, liquidated, undisputed debts
Release
Signed written waiver or renunciation
Covenant not to sue
Past consideration (giving something of
   value in the past) is not legally
   sufficient consideration
Composition of creditors
Doctrine of promissory estoppel (based
   upon promisee's detrimental reliance
   on a promise)
Enforceability of charitable subscriptions

FILL-IN QUESTIONS

1. Sufficient legal consideration exists if the promisor receives a legal _____ or the promisee incurs a legal _____ in exchange for a contractual promise.

2. At common law, the payment of a lesser sum of money could not be consideration for a promise of a creditor to release the balance of a _____, _____, _____ debt in a greater sum.

3. A promise to buy all the widgets one wishes in exchange for a promise to sell all such widgets is _____ and not supported by legal _____; a promise to buy all the widgets one may require or need in exchange for a promise to sell all such widgets is supported by legal _____ and is termed a _____ contract.

4. _____ means refraining from doing something and may be the bargained-for price (that which is exchanged) for a contractual promise and, therefore, sufficient legal _____.

5. If Johnson promises to pay ABC Video Games $500 if it promises to close its video arcade before 7:00 p.m. every day for one year, ABC Video Games has given _____ legal consideration for Johnson's promise because promising to _____ from doing something, which one has a legal right to do, is consideration for a contractual promise.

6. In general, past consideration is not sufficient consideration to support a present promise. There are, however, exceptions to this rule. For example, _____ _____ _____ _____ _____ .

MULTIPLE CHOICE QUESTIONS

1. The common law doctrine of consideration:
   a. recognizes that forbearance from doing something that one has a legal right to do constitutes consideration.
   b. requires a roughly equal exchange of something that has legal value by the parties to a contract.
   c. requires only that the promisee receive something of value.
   d. has been completely abrogated by statutes in a majority of states.

2. Consideration for a promise must be either a detriment to the:
   a. offeror or a legal benefit to the offeree.
   b. offeree or a legal benefit to the offeror.
   c. promisee or a legal benefit to the promisor.
   d. promisor or a legal benefit to the promisee.

3. The following is an example of a binding promise:
   a. an agreement by a manufacturer to agree to make a contract in the future with a retailer.
   b. a promise by a grandparent to give a grandchild a $10,000 bequest in his/her will.
   c. a promise to obtain free tickets for a friend for a rock concert.
   d. none of the above.

4. Aunt told Nephew, "If you go to Europe and spend the summer there, I will reimburse you for all the expenses that you incur." Nephew went to Europe for the summer but Aunt refused to reimburse him for his expenses. If Nephew sues Aunt, the court will probably hold that Nephew may:
   a. recover because Aunt made a promise to make a gift.
   b. recover because Nephew incurred a legal detriment.
   c. not recover because Aunt received no legal benefit.
   d. not recover because Nephew received a legal benefit.

5. As a general rule, when a creditor accepts a payment of money from a debtor and promises to release the debtor from any further liability, the creditor is legally bound by his/her promise to release the debtor:
   a. only if the debtor can clearly prove that the promise was made (regardless of other circumstances).
   b. only if the original debt was a mature, liquidated, undisputed debt.
   c. only if the original debt was neither mature, liquidated nor undisputed.

d. as long as the statute of limitations had not run before the payment was made (regardless of other circumstances).

6. The doctrine of promissory estoppel:
   a. requires legal consideration in order to be effective.
   b. results in an irrevocable offer.
   c. applies to the sale of goods when one of the parties is a merchant.
   d. allows enforcement of a promise in the absence of consideration.

7. A promise to buy such quantity of goods as one may wish is:
   a. an illusory promise.
   b. a valid contract.
   c. sufficient consideration for a promise to sell such quantity.
   d. sufficient consideration because the promisee is incurring a detriment.

8. Which of the following agreements is not enforceable?
   a. An agreement between a seller of goods and a buyer to alter the place of delivery prior to performance of the contract.
   b. An agreement by a seller to supply to a buyer all the flour the buyer needs to run his bakery for one year at a set price per pound although the total amount is not precisely established at the time the agreement is entered.
   c. An agreement between a buyer and seller for delivery of specified goods in six months which gives the buyer the right to cancel at any time within the six months.
   d. None of the above.

9. Best Buy Sneaker Co. has entered into a contract to purchase all of the shoe laces it may require at a price of 25¢ each for six months from the Last Lace Corp.; and Last Lace Corp. has agreed to sell all of the shoe laces that Best Buy might require during that time at 25¢. The contract is:
   a. void because of illegality.
   b. valid and enforceable.
   c. voidable because no place of delivery is stated.
   d. enforceable by Last Lace Corp. only.

10. Two armed men robbed the First National Bank of Metropolis. A reward of $10,000 was offered by the bank to anyone who gave information leading to the arrest and conviction of the perpetrators of the robbery. Based upon information furnished by a bank employee, a local policeman and a bank customer, the robbers were apprehended and convicted. The employee, policeman and customer applied for the reward. The reward should be given to:
    a. the bank employee.
    b. the local policeman.
    c. the bank customer.
    d. the bank employee, the local policeman and the bank customer.

11. Today in most states, although no consideration is given, a written promise will be enforceable when:
    a. the promise is to pay a debt that is mature and for an undisputed, stated amount.
    b. the promise is to pay a debt that is barred by the statute of limitations.
    c. the promise is to pay a debt that will be barred by a discharge in bankruptcy and

is filed with the Bankruptcy Court.
d. all of the above.

12. Cochran purchased a television set from the Acme Appliance Store. One of the terms of sale was that the Acme Appliance Store would service the television set without charge within 24 hours after Cochran advised it that there was improper functioning of the set during the first year following the purchase. Two months after the sale there was a loss of sound. Cochran called the store promptly but was advised that a service man could not be sent to Cochran's home for a week. Cochran promised to pay $25 if a service man were sent the next day because he desperately wanted to watch the World Series. A service man was sent and the difficulty was corrected. Acme Appliance Store sent Cochran a bill for $25.
  a. Cochran will not have to pay the bill because the store was obligated to send the service man.
  b. Cochran will not have to pay the bill but will have to pay the reasonable value for the services rendered.
  c. Cochran will have to pay the bill because the store can show that the cost of sending the service man was $25.
  d. Cochran will have to pay the bill because it was the fifth time Cochran called the store in order to request service.

Chapter 10

Capacity and
Genuineness of Assent

As explained in the first portion of this chapter, people are presumed to be sufficiently competent to enter into contracts unless they are considered to be at a disadvantage when dealing with others because of their minority, mental impairment, intoxication or another disability that is recognized by law.

The second part of the chapter deals with the reality of the assent of parties to a contract. The issue of genuineness of assent arises because, even though objectively the parties to a contract may have agreed to the same terms, the subjective assent of one or both of them may not have been real, genuine or voluntarily given because of mistake, fraud, misrepresentation, undue influence or duress. If a party was coerced or induced to assent to the terms of a contract to which he or she would not have agreed had he or she known the true circumstances, ordinarily, the contract is voidable.

THINGS TO KEEP IN MIND

Contracts that are made by a person who lacks contractual capacity or was prevented from freely exercising his or her own will when assenting to the agreement may be void. Usually, however, they are considered to be voidable contracts. As a result, the one who lacks contractual capacity or whose assent was not real, genuine or voluntarily given has a number of options. He or she may:

1. Enforce the contract by suing on it, or

2. Avoid the contract by bringing an action for rescission (cancellation of the contract) or, in some instances, sue for damages for the wrongful conduct of the other contracting party, or

3. When sued on the contract by the other party, raise the defense that the contract is voidable because of lack of capacity or lack of real, genuine, voluntary assent.

OUTLINE

I. Contractual capacity.

    A. Minors.

        1. Statutes prescribe the age of majority. In most states, it is 18.

        2. Minors' rights to disaffirm.

            a. Words or conduct may be used.

            b. Minors may disaffirm contracts during minority and for a reasonable period of time after attaining age of majority.

            c. Minors may not disaffirm if a contract has been approved by a court or, in some states because of statute, if contract is for:
               1) Life or medical insurance.
               2) Educational loan.
               3) Medical care.
               4) Marriage.
               5) Enlistment in armed forces.
               6) Transportation by common carrier.

            d. Conveyances of real property cannot be disaffirmed until minor reaches age of majority.

            e. Contract is voidable by minor but not by adult. If minor disaffirms, each party must make restitution by returning consideration received from other party.

            f. Executory contracts.
               1) Minor may disaffirm contract — As the minor received nothing from the other party, there is no need to make restitution.
               2) Majority rule — Continued silence after reaching majority is treated as disaffirmance of executory contract.

            g. Executed contracts — Minor may disaffirm contract.
               1) The adult with whom a minor has contracted must make restitution (return any consideration received from minor).
               2) If personal property was sold by minor to an adult, who resold it to an innocent good faith purchaser, the purchaser will not be required to return the property to the minor.
               3) The minor must return consideration received from adult.
                   a) The majority rule is that he or she must make restitution only if he or she is able to do so.
                   b) In some states:
                       (1) By statute, a deduction is made for deterioration, depreciation and damage.
                       (2) Minor must pay reasonable value for benefit conferred.

            h. Contracts for necessaries.

   1) Necessaries include food, clothing, shelter and services rendered for minor's protection.
   2) Minor may disaffirm contract for necessaries, not provided by parent or guardian, but is liable in quasi contract for reasonable value of necessaries that were furnished to him or her.

3. Ratification.

   a. Contract will be enforceable if minor indicates an intention to be bound (ratification) after reaching age of majority.

   b. Express written or oral ratification.

   c. Implied ratification by conduct indicating satisfaction with contract, such as retaining consideration or accepting benefits.

4. Tort liability of minors.

   a. Minors are liable for all torts unless:
      1) They are very young, or
      2) Enforcement of tort liability has the indirect effect of also enforcing a contract which the minor has disaffirmed.

   b. In most states, if minor has misrepresented his or her age in order to induce another to enter a contract, the minor may still disaffirm the contract.
      1) Other party may also disaffirm contract.
      2) Other states.
         a) Contract is not voidable by minor because of statutes.
         b) Contract is voidable but minor must pay reasonable value for benefits conferred.
         c) Minor will be estopped from showing lack of capacity.

B. Intoxicated persons.

   1. Contracts made by one, who is so intoxicated that his or her judgment is impaired so that he or she does not comprehend the legal consequences of entering into a contract, are voidable.

   2. Contracts may be disaffirmed while intoxicated or within a reasonable time after becoming sober.

      a. Restitution must be made.

      b. Intoxicated person cannot disaffirm if a third person would be injured.

      c. Intoxicated person must pay the reasonable value for necessaries that were furnished.

C. Mentally incompetent persons.

   1. One is considered mentally incompetent or insane if his or her judgment is impaired because he or she cannot understand or comprehend the nature and effect of a particular transaction.

2. If a person is declared judicially incompetent, his or her contracts are void.

3. A contract which is made by a person, who is mentally incompetent but has not been so adjudicated, is voidable by the mentally incompetent person while he or she is mentally incompetent or within a reasonable time after regaining sanity, or by his or her guardian or other representative.

4. Contracts for necessaries may be disaffirmed, but mentally incompetent party is liable for reasonable value of necessaries furnished.

D. Others who may be treated as lacking capacity.

1. Convicts — In some states, those who have been convicted of major felonies do not have full capacity to make contracts.

2. Aliens.

a. Citizens of other countries, who are legally in the United States, generally have contractual capacity and their contracts are valid.

b. Enemy aliens and illegal aliens have limited contractual capacity.

II. Genuineness of Assent.

A. Mistake.

1. A mistake is an error or unconscious ignorance or forgetfulness of a past or present fact that is material, or very important or essential, to the contract.

2. Mistake as to material facts should be distinguished from mistakes of judgment as to value or quality.

3. Unilateral mistake — In general, if only one party to a contract has made a mistake, he or she cannot avoid the contract unless:

a. the other party was responsible for the mistake being made or knew of it or should have known of it and failed to correct it, or

b. in some states, the mistake was made because of an inadvertent mathematical error and the mistaken party was not grossly negligent.

4. Mutual or bilateral mistake concerning material facts — In general, if both parties have made a mistake as to a material fact, the contract is voidable at the option of either party.

a. Mistake as to a past or present material or essential fact.
   1) Mistake as to the existence of the subject matter essential for performance of the contract. Often, courts find that there is no objective mutual assent and the contract is, therefore, void and unenforceable by either party.
   2) Mistake as to identity or nature of the subject matter of the contract.

b. Mistake as to value or a future contingency does not result in a voidable contract.

c. Mistakes as to law.

B. Fraudulent misrepresentation.

1. Fraud in the execution — If a party has been led to believe that an act, which he or she is performing, is something other than executing a contract, his or her assent is not real and any contract that appears to have been formed is void.

2. Fraud in the inducement — A contract is voidable if a party was damaged by being induced to enter the contract because he or she reasonably relied upon a false representation of a material fact.

   a. Elements of fraud in the inducement.
      1) A misrepresentation of material fact was made.
         a) Representation of past or present fact.
         b) Words or conduct may have been used.
         c) Not promises, "puffing," prediction or opinion (unless made by an expert).
         d) Misrepresentation of law.
            (1) Not fraudulent if domestic (local) law misrepresented.
            (2) May be fraudulent if made:
               (a) To one who is not a resident of state whose law was misrepresented, or
               (b) By lawyer or one who, because of his occupation, is presumed to know the law.
      2) Misrepresentation was made by one who had knowledge that it was false.
         a) Knowledge of falsity may be inferred from circumstances surrounding the transaction.
         b) If misrepresentation was made by one with reckless disregard or indifference to its truth or falsity, he or she may be treated as having had knowledge that it was false.
      3) Misrepresentation was made with intent to deceive — The evidence that the representation was made to induce the deceived party to enter into the contract is the fact that the contract was actually formed.
      4) Reliance on representation — Reliance must have been such that a reasonable person would have been justified in relying on the representation.
      5) Injury to the deceived innocent party — The contract would not have been formed or would have been more valuable if the representation had been true.
         a) In some states, in an action for rescission, actual damages need not be established.
         b) In an action for damages, proof of injury is required. Court may award exemplary or punitive damages in addition to compensatory damages.

   b. Fraud because of silence or concealment.

        1) There is no duty to inform contracting party of facts.
        2) Exceptions.
           a) Seller must disclose latent defects, which are not ordinarily discoverable but which cause an object to be dangerous.
           b) Seller, with superior knowledge, may not conceal facts, knowing that other party lacks knowledge.
           c) When a party has previously misstated a material fact and later realizes that he or she made a misstatement, he or she is then required to make a correction.
           d) When parties have a fiduciary or confidential relationship, the party with knowledge of relevant facts has an obligation to disclose them to the other party.
           e) Statutes, such as the Truth in Lending Act, require disclosure of certain relevant facts.

    3. Innocent misrepresentation — If a party unintentionally makes a representation, without knowledge of its falsity, the other party, who relied upon the representation and was damaged, may rescind the contract.

C. Undue influence.

    1. When a party, who is in a dominant position, because of a confidential relationship, secures an unfair advantage in a contract with a weaker, dominated party, the contract is voidable and may be disaffirmed by the dominated party.

    2. There is a rebuttable presumption of undue influence:

        a. When the parties are in a familial or fiduciary relationship based upon trust and confidence, and

        b. The contract is extremely unfair to the dominated party.

    3. Presumption may be rebutted by showing:

        a. Full disclosure was made.

        b. Consideration that was received was adequate.

        c. Independent advice received by weaker party.

D. Duress.

    1. If a party is coerced into entering a contract because of the wrongful use of force or a threat of force, the contract is voidable.

    2. Assent may have been induced by fear of:

        a. Bodily injury to party or a relative.

        b. Criminal (but not civil) prosecution of party or relative.

        c. Harm to property or business under unusual circumstances.

E. Adhesion contracts and unconscionability.

   1. Adhesion contract arises when one party, with overwhelming bargaining power, takes such unfair advantage of other party that the latter has no choice but to adhere to dictated terms or do without a particular good or service.

   2. Resulting contract may be held to be unenforceable because of unconscionability (U.C.C. Sec. 2-302).

KEY WORDS AND PHRASES IN TEXT

Contractual capacity (or competency)
Minors (those who have not reached the age of majority)
Voidable contracts of minors
Minors' rights to disaffirm voidable contracts
Party who lacks contractual capacity has option of disaffirming or ratifying voidable contract
Duty of restitution (restoration)
Bona fide purchaser for value
Misrepresentation of age by minor
Quasi contract liability for necessaries
Express ratification of contract
Implied ratification of contract
Nonvoidable contracts
Liability of minors for torts
Parents' liability for contracts made by minor children
Voluntary intoxication
Involuntary intoxication
Mental incompetency
Contracts made by people who have been adjudicated to be incompetent are void
Contracts made by people who are mentally incompetent, but have not been so adjudicated, are voidable
Capacity of illegal and enemy aliens

Genuine assent
Mistake as to facts
Unilateral mistake as to material facts
Mutual mistakes of material facts
Mutual mistake as to identity of subject matter
Mutual mistake as to value or quality of subject matter
Fraudulent misrepresentation
Elements of fraud
Misrepresentation of a material fact
Statements of opinion
Seller's talk or sales puffing
Misrepresentation of law
Silence as misrepresentation
Fiduciary relationship
Knowledge of falsity of representation of facts
Scienter
Justifiable reliance on misrepresentation
Injury to the innocent party
Innocent misrepresentation
Negligent misrepresentation
Undue influence
Duress
Economic duress
Adhesion contracts
Unconscionability

FILL-IN QUESTIONS

1. If a minor or mentally incompetent person or intoxicated person makes a contract with another person, who does not have a contractual disability, the contract is _____. The one who lacks capacity may _____ the contract, but the other party may not do so.

2. During minority, a minor may _____ a contract to which he was a party.

3. A minor, who has been furnished with necessaries, such as _____
_____ ,
must make restitution if he or she is rescinding the contract, by paying _____
_____ for the benefits received.

4. A minor may not ratify a contract that he or she has entered into until he attains
the age of _____ or within a reasonable period of time thereafter.

5. A person who is mentally incompetent because _____
_____
may disaffirm his or her contract. If such a person is adjudicated to be incompetent, his or her contracts are _____.

6. One whose assent was not real or genuine when he or she entered a contract may
enforce the contract against the other party or he or she may _____ the
contract because the contract is usually treated as being _____ rather
than void.

7. A contract may be rescinded if there has been a _____ mistake concerning a material fact rather than a _____ mistake.

8. If a party to a contract makes a misrepresentation of a material fact with
knowledge that it is false, and the other party to the contract incurs an
_____ because of his or her reasonable and justifiable _____
upon the representation, the contract may be disaffirmed by the innocent party
because of fraud in the inducement.

9. A statement of _____ is usually not treated as a representation of fact
unless it is made by an expert or one who, because of his profession or occupation,
has superior knowledge.

10. Joan agreed to sell and Mary agreed to buy a painting valued at $10,000 for $100.
Joan, who is 100 years of age, may be able to disaffirm the contract if she can
show that mental coercion was employed by Mary, who was a relative or a
fiduciary. In other words, _____ was used to obtain Joan's assent.

MULTIPLE CHOICE QUESTIONS

1. The following best describes a contract entered into by a minor:
   a. illegal.
   b. void.
   c. voidable.
   d. unenforceable.

2. A contract between a minor and an adult may be disaffirmed by:
   a. the minor only.
   b. the adult only.
   c. the minor's parent or guardian only.
   d. either party.

3. When she was 17 years of age, Mary purchased an automobile for $5,000, to be paid
for in 36 monthly installments, from AAA Car Sales. Two years later the car was

totally demolished in an accident and Mary failed to make the last 11 payments. AAA Car Sales sued to recover these 11 payments. In a state in which the age of majority is 18, a court will probably hold for:
   a. Mary because Mary was a minor at the time of the purchase and may disaffirm contracts made when she was a minor.
   b. Mary because the contract was nullified when the automobile was demolished.
   c. AAA Car Sales because Mary ratified the contract by making several payments after turning 18.
   d. AAA Car Sales but recovery will be limited because the automobile was demolished.

4. An item which would be considered to be a necessary if purchased by a minor is:
   a. a winter jacket.
   b. a pizzaburger.
   c. a filling in a tooth.
   d. all of the above.

5. A minor may disaffirm a contract entered into with an adult:
   a. for the furnishing of goods only if they are not necessaries.
   b. for the furnishing of goods even if they are necessaries.
   c. before the minor reaches the age of 18 because, as a result of a federal statute, the age of majority has been established at 18 years of age.
   d. before he has reached the age of majority as may the adult with whom he has contracted even if the goods, which are the subject matter of the contract, are necessaries.

6. Courts of equity may deny relief to a minor, who is a party to a contract, if the minor has:
   a. disaffirmed the contract.
   b. purchased necessaries.
   c. misrepresented his or her age.
   d. all of the above.

7. Civil liability arising out of a tort committed by a minor:
   a. may be disaffirmed much like contractual liability because of common law principles.
   b. may be disaffirmed much like contractual liability because of statutory law.
   c. may be disaffirmed under common law principles, but only if the wrongful act (the tort) was not a crime.
   d. may not, as a general rule, be disaffirmed at all.

8. The Uniform Commercial Code:
   a. does not alter the law with regard to minors' contracts.
   b. does not allow a minor to avoid a contract for the purchase of necessaries.
   c. permits a minor to recover goods originally sold by the minor to an adult if the adult has sold the goods to a good faith purchaser.
   d. prevents a minor from recovering goods originally sold by the minor to an adult if the adult has sold the goods to a good faith purchaser.

9. The contracts of one who is in fact mentally incompetent, but not so adjudicated by a court, may be ratified by:
   a. the mentally incompetent person when he or she is competent.

b. the mentally incompetent person when he or she is competent or mentally incompetent.

c. the other party to the contract so as to bind the mentally incompetent person.

d. the mentally incompetent person only if the contract is for the furnishing of necessaries.

10. If after a person is adjudicated to be mentally incompetent, that person agrees to purchase a CB radio from the Radio Palace for $700, the contract of sale is:
a. enforceable.
b. void.
c. voidable.
d. illegal.

11. When courts decide that one should not be required to perform a contract that was involuntarily entered into, they may be referring to:
a. duress.
b. duress or undue influence.
c. a felony.
d. mistake of law.

12. A fiduciary is one occupying a confidential relationship with another. If a fiduciary uses the relationship to induce the other person to enter into a contract, the fiduciary:
a. will be considered as having used duress.
b. will be considered as having used duress if the resulting contract is grossly unfair.
c. will be considered as having used undue influence if the resulting contract is grossly unfair.
d. will be considered as having used duress if he has made an intentional misrepresentation of a material fact.

13. F claimed that G owed him $100. G insisted that he did not owe F any money. F told G, "If you don't pay me $100, I'll beat you up!" G immediately wrote a check for $100, payable to F, and gave it to F. Soon after leaving F, G stopped payment on the check, and the bank upon which it was drawn refused to honor it.
a. F will not be successful in a suit to make G pay because F used fraud in order to obtain G's assent.
b. F will not be successful in a suit to make G pay because F used duress in order to obtain G's assent.
c. F will be successful in a suit to make G pay because G objectively manifested his assent to the agreement.
d. F will be successful in a suit to make G pay because G's apparent assent was manifested.

14. A court will rescind a contract if:
a. there is a mistake between the parties concerning the existence of the subject matter.
b. there is a mistake between the parties concerning the value of the subject matter.
c. there is a misrepresentation concerning the value of the subject matter.
d. all of the above.

15. S was the owner of a sailboat, which he offered to sell to B for $300. The day before B accepted the offer by telegram the boat was stolen.
    a. There is no contract between S and B because there was a mistake as to the existence of the subject matter.
    b. There is no contract between S and B because there was a mistake as to the identity of the subject matter.
    c. There is a contract between S and B but it may be disaffirmed by S.
    d. There is a contract between S and B but it may be disaffirmed by B.

16. If fraud in the inducement is to be used as the basis for rescission of a contract, the defendant must have made a misrepresentation relating to some material past or existing fact:
    a. with knowledge that the misrepresentation was not true.
    b. in order to induce the plaintiff to enter the contract.
    c. upon which the plaintiff reasonably relied.
    d. all of the above.

17. A necessary element to be shown in an action brought to recover damages for fraud in the inducement is that the defendant:
    a. misrepresented a material fact.
    b. innocently misrepresented a material fact.
    c. intentionally misrepresented a material fact.
    d. any of the above.

18. A seller is obligated to disclose to the buyer:
    a. all defects concerning the subject matter of the sale.
    b. latent defects concerning the subject matter of the sale.
    c. obvious defects concerning the subject matter of the sale.
    d. no defects concerning the subject matter of the sale.

19. Ellen painted over a number of damaged areas in furniture she sold to Van. Such conduct might be the basis for an action for fraud:
    a. in the inducement even though Ellen made no verbal misstatements with regard to the furniture.
    b. in the inducement only if Ellen made a verbal misstatement with regard to the furniture.
    c. in the execution even though Ellen made no verbal misstatements with regard to the furniture.
    d. in the execution only if Ellen made a verbal misstatement with regard to the furniture.

20. A contract induced by misrepresentation is:
    a. voidable.
    b. void.
    c. implied by conduct.
    d. all of the above.

Chapter 11

Legality

If an act to be performed or the purpose of an agreement is criminal, tortious or contrary to public policy, the agreement is void.

THINGS TO KEEP IN MIND

1. Illegal bargains are usually considered to be void and, therefore, really not contracts. In general, courts will neither enforce illegal bargains nor give remedies for their breach.

2. Public morality and ideas, as to what is considered to be wrongful conduct, are reflected in statutes and policies and vary over time and from place to place.

OUTLINE

I. Agreements that are contrary to statutes.

   A. Usury.

      1. Statutes fix the maximum lawful rate of interest that can be charged for a loan of money.

      2. Exceptions.

         a. Prohibitions against usury do not apply if the borrower is a corporation.

         b. Statutes often allow higher rates of interest for small loans.

         c. Usury laws generally do not apply to sales of goods on credit.

        1) Retail sales installment loans, retail charge agreements and revolving charge accounts.

        2) Other statutes restrict the amount of interest that can be charged in such transactions.

  3. If more than the statutory maximum rate is charged, the effect varies from state to state.

    a. Transaction is void as to excess interest only.

    b. Transaction is void as to interest but not as to principal.

    c. Entire transaction is tainted by usury and void as to principal and interest.

  4. In a few states the maximum rate of interest that may be charged is a floating rate because it is dependent upon the cost of capital in a specified market (e.g., certain Treasury notes).

  5. Distinguish lawful rate of interest (usury law) from legal and/or judgment rate of interest.

B. Gambling.

  1. Gambling or wagering involves creation of risk and distribution of property by chance among persons who have given consideration in order to participate.

  2. Distinguish.

    a. Contracts for property and life insurance which provide for shifting an existing risk.

    b. Futures contracts, contracts for future purchase or sale of commodities, purchase of stock on margin.

    c. Games of skill.

C. Sabbath (or Sunday) laws.

  1. The nature of statutes, restricting contracting on Sunday, varies as does their enforcement.

  2. If a statute prohibits formation or performance of a contract on a Sunday, contracts made or performable on Sunday are illegal, void and unenforceable.

  3. In some states, contracts may be entered into on Sunday but performance is prohibited except for labor of charity or necessity.

  4. Sunday laws have been held to be unconstitutional in a number of states.

D. Licensing statutes.

1. Statutes require that licenses be obtained in order to engage in certain trades, professions or businesses.

2. Enforceability of contracts made by unlicensed persons.

   a. Some statutes expressly provide that contracts which are made by unlicensed persons are void and unenforceable.

   b. If the object of a statute is regulatory (to protect the public from unauthorized practitioners), contracts are void and unenforceable.

   c. If the purpose of a statute is merely to raise revenue, contracts are enforceable.

E. Contracts to commit crimes.

   1. Agreements are void.

   2. If purpose or performance of the contract becomes illegal because of enactment of statute after the contract has been entered into, the parties are discharged from their obligations by operation of law. (See Chapter 14.)

II. Agreements that are contrary to public policy.

A. Agreements, which injure an established interest of or which have a negative impact on society, are void and will not be enforced.

B. Restraints of trade.

   1. Agreements containing covenants (promises) not to compete.

      a. An agreement, the sole purpose of which is not to compete, is contrary to public policy and not enforceable.

      b. An ancillary (subsidiary) promise or covenant not to compete will be enforced if it is reasonable (no more extensive than necessary, under the circumstances, to protect a property or other valuable interest of the promisee).
         1) Sale of business — Reasonableness determined by nature of business, period of duration and geographic area covered.
         2) Employment contracts.
            a) Enforceable if not excessive in scope or duration.
            b) Statutes in approximately 25% of the states prohibit restraint of trade clauses in employment contracts.

   2. Resale price maintenance — Today a promise by a dealer not to sell a manufactured product at a price below some established minimum will not be enforced.

C. Unconscionable agreements and clauses.

   1. Agreements that are unreasonably oppressive or excessive will not be enforced.

2. Exculpatory clauses — A promise to relieve another from potential liability based on tort, without regard to fault, will be strictly construed and often found to be violations of public policy.

3. Adhesion contracts — A contract may be unconscionable if a party, receiving an unusually greater benefit, has superior bargaining power ("take it or leave it" situation).

4. Courts may refuse to enforce unconscionable contracts or unconscionable clauses in contracts for sale of goods (U.C.C. Sec. 2-302).

D. Discriminatory contracts.

E. Agreements for the commission of crimes or torts — Courts will not aid parties who found their causes of action on criminally or civilly wrongful acts.

F. Agreements that result in obstruction of the administration of governmental function or injury to public service.

   1. Influencing governmental action improperly.

      a. Corrupting legislators or other public officials.

      b. Distinguish valid lobbying activities.

   2. Obstructing judicial process by concealing commission of a crime or promising not to prosecute.

   3. Surrendering right of access to justice.

      a. Forum selection clauses are usually upheld.

      b. Agreements to submit present disputes and future disputes (because of statutes) to arbitration are upheld.

III. Effect of illegality.

A. General rule — Illegal bargains are void and, therefore, unenforceable by either party.

B. Exceptions.

   1. Justifiable ignorance of the facts that cause the agreement to be illegal.

   2. Members of a class, intended to be protected by a statute prohibiting specific activities, may enforce contract.

   3. If the parties are not equally at fault, the innocent party may recover consideration paid to guilty party.

   4. Withdrawal from illegal bargain before full performance is rendered.

5. Severable, or divisible, contracts — Courts will enforce legal provisions if the illegal portions of a contract can be severed.

KEY WORDS AND PHRASES IN TEXT

Contracts that are contrary to statutes
Usury
Lawful rates of interest
Legal and judgment rates of interest
Retail installment loans
Retail revolving charge accounts
Gambling
Sabbath or Sunday laws
Licensing statutes
Agreements to commit crimes
Contracts that are contrary to public
    policy
Restraint of trade agreements
Antitrust statutes
Covenants not to compete

Resale price maintenance
Unconscionable clauses
Exculpatory clauses
Adhesion contracts
Discriminatory contracts
Contracts injuring public service
Agreements to obstruct legal process
Forum selection clauses
Arbitration clauses
Effect of illegality
Parties *in pari delicto*
Justifiable ignorance of facts
Members of a protected class
Blue Sky Laws
Severable or divisible contracts

FILL-IN QUESTIONS

1. Agreements, which violate _____ or _____ are illegal bargains and, therefore, void and unenforceable.

2. _____ statutes provide the maximum rate of interest that may lawfully be charged for a loan of money.

3. By statute a lender is prohibited from charging interest of more than 20 percent per year on a loan of money. If Larry lent Bob $100 and Bob agreed that he would repay the $100 in a year and give Larry an additional $40 at the time of repayment, Bob will have to pay Larry _____.

4. Contracts which provide for the creation of risk are _____ contracts and are illegal in most states. Contracts which provide for _____ risk, such as contracts of insurance, are legal.

5. A promise not to compete with another is termed a _____. The promise will be enforced if it is _____ and no more extensive than necessary to protect a property interest of the promisee.

6. A clause in a contract that provides that one party to the contract will be relieved of any liability to the other, without regard to fault or negligence, may be unenforceable because it is an unconscionable _____ clause.

MULTIPLE CHOICE QUESTIONS

1. An agreement to engage in an illegal act, such as robbing a bank, is an example of a:

    a. void contract.
    b. voidable contract.
    c. valid contract.
    d. quasi contract.

2. Contracts that are entered into by one who has not complied with a statute which requires a license for the practice of a business, trade or profession:
    a. may be enforced by the unlicensed party if the licensing statute is a revenue raising statute rather than a regulatory one.
    b. may be enforced by the unlicensed party if the licensing statute is a regulatory statute rather than a revenue raising one.
    c. may be enforced by the unlicensed party unless the statute states that such contracts are unenforceable.
    d. may be enforced by the unlicensed party as long as they are reasonable and not injurious to the other party to the contract.

3. An attorney, who has been admitted to practice law in North Dakota, but not in Missouri, performs legal services and conducts a trial for a client in Missouri.
    a. The client will be required to pay the attorney a fee for the legal services performed.
    b. The client will be required to pay the attorney a fee for the legal services performed and for conducting the trial.
    c. The attorney cannot collect a fee for performing the legal services but can collect a fee for conducting the trial.
    d. The attorney cannot collect a fee for any legal services performed in Missouri.

4. A transaction will be found to be usurious if the following has occurred:
    a. a lender makes a loan of money to a borrower.
    b. the borrower is required to repay the loan.
    c. a sum of money, in excess of the interest allowed by statute, is to be paid by the borrower to the lender.
    d. all of the above.

5. An insurance contract is not treated as an illegal gambling contract:
    a. because all states have statutes that so provide.
    b. because it provides for shifting an existing risk.
    c. unless the premium paid bears no reasonable relationship to the value of the property insured.
    d. unless it is for life insurance and the life insured is that of a child who is less than 18 years of age.

6. Smith purchased the Tiny Department Store from Timothy. All of the terms of the sale were contained in a writing, signed by Smith and Timothy. One of the terms provided that Timothy would not engage in the same business for ten years within a radius of five hundred miles of the Tiny Department Store. One year later Timothy opened the Hugh Department Store a half mile from the Tiny Department Store.
    a. Timothy has not breached the covenant because he did not use his own name or that of "Tiny" at his new store.
    b. The contract is unenforceable because the parties failed to comply with the Statute of Frauds.
    c. The covenant is contrary to public policy and is, therefore, illegal and void.
    d. The covenant is neither illegal nor void.

7. Johnson purchased the Warehard Hardware Store from Ware for $90,000. All of the terms of the sale were contained in a writing, signed by Johnson and Ware. One term provided that Ware would not engage in the same business for two years within one mile of the Warehard Store. Five months later Ware opened the Quick Hardware Store two blocks from the Warehard Store.
   a. Johnson can obtain an injunction because Ware has violated the terms of the contract.
   b. The contract is illegal because it provides for resale price maintenance by Johnson.
   c. This is an example of a restraint of trade which is unreasonable and, therefore, illegal and void.
   d. The contract violated the federal antitrust laws.

8. Seller Manufacturing Company produced widgets and contracted to sell 1,000 widgets to Buyer Retail Store. Buyer agreed that it would sell the widgets at a price of at least $7 each.
   a. Although the agreement is contrary to public policy, Buyer's promise is enforceable if the quantity being sold is insufficient to give Buyer a monopoly on such goods in its trading area.
   b. Although the agreement is contrary to public policy, Buyer's promise is enforceable because the federal antitrust laws so provide.
   c. The agreement will be treated as a restraint of trade today because it provides for resale price maintenance.
   d. The provision of the agreement is legal and Buyer may, therefore, be sued for breach of contract if it sells the widgets for $6 each.

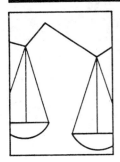

Chapter 12

Writing and Form

Although it is advantageous, contracts generally need not be reduced to writing in order to bind the parties. Some contracts, however, must be in writing and signed by the party against whom they are to be enforced because of the Statute of Frauds. Recall from Chapter 7 that one of the elements of a contract is that, if a contract is required by law to be in a particular form, an agreement must be in that form in order to be enforceable.

If a written instrument is regarded as an integration of the agreement of the parties to it, other evidence, which changes the effect of the writing, is not admissible because of the parol evidence rule. This rule and the rules of interpretation, upon which the courts rely when determining the meaning of unclear or ambiguous language in written agreements, are discussed in the final section of this chapter.

THINGS TO KEEP IN MIND

1. The Statute of Frauds does not require a formal document. All that is usually necessary is a signed memorandum indicating the essential terms.

2. If a contract does not comply with the Statute of Frauds, it is unenforceable, rather than void or voidable. This means that it cannot be proven in the manner required by law.

3. Usually the Statute of Frauds is raised as a defense. If the issue is not raised, an oral contract will be enforced.

OUTLINE

I. The Statute of Frauds.

A. In order to be enforceable, some contractual promises must be evidenced by a writing, which is signed by the parties against whom they are being enforced.

B. Contracts that must be in writing.

   1. Contracts for sales of interests in real property.

      a. Interests in land include:
         1) Contract for sale of land.
         2) Conveyances — Transfers of land for consideration. Usually a conveyance requires a contract for the sale of the land, the delivery of a deed and payment of the consideration.
         3) Life estates — Interests in land which last only for the lifetime of a named person.
         4) Mortgages — Conveyances given as security to lenders.
         5) Easements — Rights to use land.
         6) Leases — Rights to use and possess land for stated periods of time. Most states require that leases for more than one year be in writing.

      b. Contract may be taken out of the Statute of Frauds.
         1) Full performance of oral contract by one or both parties.
         2) Substantial part performance by a purchaser if his or her action is only explainable as being pursuant to an agreement.
            a) Part payment of consideration,
            b) Taking possession, and
            c) Making substantial improvements in reliance on oral contract.

   2. Contracts that cannot be performed within one year.

      a. If performance is possible, even if it is highly improbable, within one year, an oral contract is enforceable.

      b. The year begins from the date of the contract.
         1) Not the date performance is to begin.
         2) If time for performance is of uncertain duration, but depends upon some contingency, which may occur within a year, oral contract is enforceable.

      c. Full performance by one party within a year takes contract out of the Statute of Frauds.

      d. Some states have statutes requiring that contracts, not performable within the lifetime of the promisor, must be in writing.

   3. Collateral, or secondary, promises to answer for obligations of others.

      a. Promises to answer for the debts or to discharge duties of another. See the following diagram.

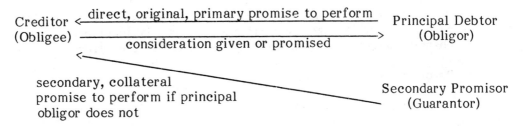

b. A promise is within the Statute of Frauds and must be in a signed writing if:
   1) The promise is made to the obligee (rather than the principal obligor) by one who is not presently liable for the debt or who does not have a present duty to perform.
   2) The liability of the guarantor is secondary or collateral to that of the principal obligor.

c. If the main purpose or leading object of the secondary promisor is to protect his or her own interest or to obtain a material benefit, an oral promise will be enforced.

d. Promises by executors or administrators to personally pay the debts of decedents' estates.

4. Unilateral promises made in consideration of marriage and prenuptial agreements.

5. Contracts for the sale of goods and other personal property (covered by U.C.C.).

   a. Contract for sale of goods for a price of $500 or more (U.C.C. Sec. 2-201). Exceptions:
      1) Partial performance — Buyer pays for or receives and accepts goods.
      2) Goods (not ordinarily suitable for resale) to be specially manufactured for buyer by seller, who has begun production of the goods.
      3) Sale between merchants, when either party, within a reasonable period of time, sends a written confirmation to which the other party fails to object within ten days.
      4) Admission, in pleadings or in court, that contract existed.

   b. Other Code provisions.
      1) Contracts for sale of securities (U.C.C. Sec. 8-319).
         a) Statute of Frauds is satisfied by payment or delivery and acceptance of securities.
         b) Statute of Frauds is satisfied by written confirmation.
      2) Security agreements (U.C.C. Sec. 9-203).
      3) Contracts for sale of miscellaneous personal property when price is more than $5,000 (U.C.C. Sec. 1-206).

C. Sufficiency of writing — Memorandum evidencing the contract need only contain basic, essential terms of the contract.

II. Parol evidence rule.

A. If a written instrument is regarded by the parties as their complete, integrated agreement, other oral or written evidence is inadmissible for purposes of changing, altering or contradicting the effect of the writing.

B. Parol evidence is admitted to show:

   1. A modification of the writing.

   2. The contract was void or voidable.

   3. The meaning of ambiguous or vague language.

   4. The writing was incomplete.

   5. A prior course of dealings or a trade usage (U.C.C. Sec. 2-203).

   6. Gross typographical or clerical errors.

   7. Another separate contract with a different subject matter.

III. Interpretation of contracts.

A. Over time, the courts have developed guidelines for determining the meaning of terms in a contract so as to give effect to the contract that the parties made. The objective of the rules of interpretation is to determine the intent of the parties from the language used in their agreement.

B. The plain meaning rule — When the words used in a writing are plain, clear, unequivocal and unambiguous, their meaning will be determined from the face of the written document alone.

C. If the words used in a writing are ambiguous or not clear:

   1. The interpretation which results in a reasonable, effective and legal contract is preferred over one which results in an unreasonable, ineffective or illegal agreement.

   2. A writing will be interpreted as a whole; all writings that are part of the same transaction will be interpreted together, and words will not be taken out of the context in which they are used.

   3. A word will be given its ordinary, commonly accepted meaning, and a technical term will be given its technical meaning.

   4. Specific terms will be given greater consideration than general language.

   5. Handwritten words prevail over typewritten words, and typewritten words prevail over preprinted words.

   6. When multiple meanings of language are possible, the language will be interpreted most strongly against the party who chose the words.

7. The court will admit evidence of usage in trade, prior dealings and course of performance.

KEY WORDS AND PHRASES IN TEXT

Statute of Frauds
Enforceability of contracts
Contracts involving interests in land
Real property
Fixtures
Life estate
Mortgage
Easement
Lease
Partial performance of an oral contract
Contracts whose terms cannot possibly be performed within one year from the date of formation
Collateral, secondary, ancillary promises made by third parties
Promise by an administrator or executor of an estate to personally pay a debt of the estate

Promise to answer for the debt, miscarriage, duty or obligation of another
Guaranty
Suretyship
Main purpose (or leading object) rule
Contracts for the sale of goods when price is $500 or more
Goods that are made specially to order
Written confirmation of an oral contract between merchants
Admissions
Sufficiency of signed writing
The parol evidence rule
Integrated contract
Rules of interpretation
Plain meaning rule
Trade usage
Prior dealings
Course of performance

FILL-IN QUESTIONS

1. Promises, required by the Statute of Frauds to be in writing and signed by the party against whom they are being enforced, include those _____
   _____
   _____
   _____.

2. Johnson said to the manager of a local store, "If Cooper does not pay for his purchases this month, I will pay for them." Johnson's promise is unenforceable because the Statute of Frauds requires that a promise _____
   _____ must be in
   writing and signed by the promisor. If Johnson told the manager of the store that he would pay for the purchases made by Clark, Johnson's employee, Johnson's promise would be enforceable because _____
   _____ and, therefore,
   is not within the Statute of Frauds.

3. A contract for the sale of goods when the price is $_____ or more is required to be in writing.

4. The Parol Evidence Rule provides that if a written instrument is regarded by the parties as a complete, integrated statement of their agreement, other oral or written statements, agreements or promises are _____ for the purposes of adding to, deleting from, changing, altering or contradicting the effect of the writing, which is the final expression of the rights and duties of the parties.

5. Parol evidence is admissible to show that a contract is _____ because of illegality, fraud in the execution, mistake as to the existence of the subject matter, or judicially determined incapacity, or _____ because of lack of capacity (minority, insanity, intoxication), fraud in the inducement, misrepresentation, mutual mistakes of fact, duress or undue influence.

6. With regard to a written contract, oral evidence is admissible to prove that the writing was not intended as the entire agreement of the parties or to prove _____
    _____
    _____
    _____.

7. If a written contract is clear and unambiguous, a court will not admit extrinsic evidence because of the parol evidence rule and the _____ rule of interpretation. If, however, the meaning of words in a written contract do not clearly express the _____ of the parties to the contract, a court will use rules of interpretation in order to clarify terms of the agreement. For example, if two interpretations of terms in a written contract are possible, one of which will result in the contract being void because of illegality and the other resulting in the contract being legal and valid, the interpretation which results in a _____ contract will be used by a court.

MULTIPLE CHOICE QUESTIONS

1. The Statute of Frauds requires that certain contracts be in writing and signed by the party against whom they are being enforced. If such a contract does not comply with the Statute:
    a. it is voidable.
    b. it is void.
    c. it is unenforceable.
    d. it is illegal.

2. The Statute of Frauds:
    a. is an old English statute that has no relevance today.
    b. applies to all contracts which, by their terms, require the payment of $500 or more.
    c. defines what constitutes fraudulent conduct by a party in inducing another to enter a contractual relationship.
    d. requires that a contract for the sale of an unimproved piece of real property for $100 be in writing.

3. Philo Stine owns ten acres of land on which there is a large house. Which of the following contracts that Philo contemplates entering into would not have to be evidenced by a signed writing in order to satisfy the statute of frauds?
    a. An agreement with Picasso to paint the house for $2,000.
    b. A two year lease of the house and one acre of land to Lolitta for $10,000.
    c. A four month easement over the land to Monet for $4.
    d. The right to remove stones from one acre of land for two months to Vladimir for $20.

4. A contract must be in writing and signed by the party to be charged if it provides for:

    a. a sale of goods when the price is more than $300.

    b. a lease of equipment for more than one month.

    c. a promise made to a third party to answer for the default of another.

    d. a promise made to a debtor to answer for his or her debt to another person.

5.   The section of the Statute of Frauds dealing with suretyship and guaranty refers to:

    a. promises to pay debts of others.

    b. contracts for the sale of securities.

    c. contracts for the sale of real property.

    d. mutual promises to marry.

6.   On November 1, 1988, Richards orally agreed to employ Everett for one year as a clerk at a salary of $600 per week. Everett began working a week later and performed satisfactorily, but on December 20, 1988, Richards terminated Everett's employment because of business reversals. Everett is suing Richards for damages for breach of contract.

    a. Everett will be successful if, on November 1, the parties had not fixed the date upon which Everett was to begin work.

    b. Everett will be successful if, on November 1, the parties had fixed November 8 as the date upon which Everett was to begin work.

    c. Whether or not the agreement stated the date upon which employment was to commence, it will not affect the outcome of the lawsuit.

    d. As the salary to be paid was more than $500 per week, Everett will not be successful because the agreement was not in writing.

7.   Marco Manufacturing Co. orally agreed to sell and the Reed Retail Store agreed to buy $2,000 worth of merchandise.

    a. If Marco fails to deliver the merchandise and Reed fails to pay the $2,000, Reed can enforce the contract against Marco.

    b. If Marco fails to deliver the merchandise and Reed fails to pay the $2,000, Marco can enforce the contract against Reed.

    c. If Marco delivers and Reed accepts the merchandise, the contract can be enforced by Marco against Reed.

    d. The Statute of Frauds does not apply to a sale of goods between merchants and the contract is therefore enforceable.

8.   The parol evidence rule:

    a. requires that certain contracts be in writing or evidenced by a writing in order to be enforceable.

    b. affects the evidence that may be offered if a prisoner wishes to be released from jail.

    c. prevents the introduction of oral testimony to alter the terms of a written agreement.

    d. applies to a contract for the sale of miscellaneous personal property when the price is more than $500.

9.   Gordon and Henry entered into a contract for the sale of goods. All of the terms were reduced to writing. Gordon is attempting to introduce another writing in evidence. In which of the following circumstances will Gordon *not* be able to introduce the evidence?

    a. The evidence relates to another agreement between the parties concerning a different subject matter.

b. The written contract indicates that it was intended as the "entire contract" between the parties and the point is covered in detail.

c. The evidence relates to statements made by Henry, to which Gordon assented, that the contract for the sale of the goods would become effective if the price of gasoline rose to $2 per gallon.

d. The written contract contains an obvious typographical error concerning the point in issue.

10. Karla and Victor entered into a contract for the delivery of goods, all of the terms of which were reduced to writing. Karla is attempting to introduce oral evidence. She will be prevented from doing so if the evidence relates to:

a. a mistake concerning the value of the goods.

b. the subject matter of the contract which was heroin.

c. another agreement concerning a loan of money.

d. a modification of the contract made a week after the writing of the contract.

11. Hughes and Ikes entered into a written contract for the sale of stapling equipment by Hughes to Ikes for $10,000 to be paid for by Ikes in six months. In the preprinted form supplied by Hughes, there was a statement to the effect that "interest at the rate of 18% will be charged." This statement was crossed out and followed by the following handwritten statement: "As interest, Ikes will pay Hughes $10,800 six months from the date of this contract."

a. A court will permit the introduction of extrinsic evidence showing that the current trade usage is to charge 22% interest.

b. A court will interpret the written contract and find that Ikes will have to pay $900 as interest.

c. A court will interpret the written contract and find that Ikes will have to pay $800 as interest.

d. A court will allow the introduction of evidence that Ikes and Hughes orally agreed that no interest would be payable.

Chapter 13

Third Party Rights

The relationship between the parties to a private contract, which creates reciprocal rights and duties, is referred to as privity of contract. Others, who are not parties to the agreement, usually lack privity and, therefore, have no contractual rights which a court will enforce.

A contract between two parties may involve a third party, who has rights or assumes obligations. The parties to a contract may expressly provide that a benefit be conferred upon a person, who is not a party to the contract (third party beneficiary contract). A party to an existing contract may transfer rights, which he or she has, to a stranger to the contract (assignment) or delegate performance of his or her duties to a third person (delegation).

THINGS TO KEEP IN MIND

1. In a third party beneficiary situation there is only one contract. When there is an assignment of rights or delegation of duties, usually there are two relevant contracts.

2. The one to whom performance is to be given under the terms of a contract has a "right," which may be assigned. The one who is required by a contract to render performance has a "duty," which may be delegated.

OUTLINE

I. Third party beneficiary contracts.

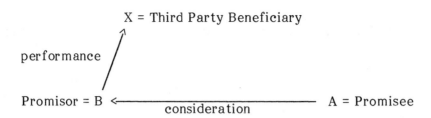

X = Third Party Beneficiary

performance

Promisor = B ⟵——————————— A = Promisee
                 consideration

A. The third party beneficiary is a stranger to the contractual relationship of the parties to the contract; he or she makes no promises and gives no consideration to the promisor, who is to render performance, but the intention of the parties is to confer a benefit upon him or her.

B. Creditor beneficiary — The promisee's intention is to discharge an obligation, owed to a third party, by having the promisor, with whom the promisee contracts, render performance to the third party.

C. Donee beneficiary — The promisee's intention is to confer a gift upon a third party by having the promisor, with whom the promisee contracts, render performance to the third party.

D. Rights of third party beneficiary.

  1. An intended donee or creditor beneficiary has a legal right to enforce the contract against the promisor. (Note that a creditor beneficiary also has rights against his debtor, the promisee.)

  2. Original contracting parties cannot modify, alter, or terminate contract if third party beneficiary:

     a. Learns of and assents to the contract, or

     b. Sues on the contract, or

     c. Materially changes his or her position in reliance on the contract.

  3. The beneficiary acquires rights, subject to the right of the promisor to raise any defenses that he or she might have against the promisee, against the beneficiary.

E. Incidental beneficiary — One, who is to receive an incidental benefit from the performance of a contract, may not enforce the contract if there was no intent to confer a benefit upon him or her.

II. Assignment of contract rights.

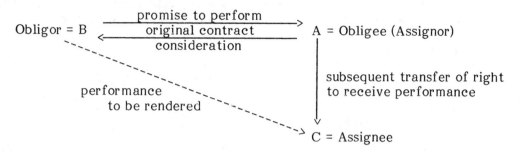

A. Assignment is an act whereby one party to an existing valid contract (the assignor) transfers the rights, which he or she has, to another person (the assignee), who is a stranger to the original contract, but who may enforce the contract.

B. No special formality is necessary in order to make an effective assignment.

   1. Compliance with Statute of Frauds.

   2. Consideration need not be given.

      a. Promise to make a future assignment must be supported by consideration in order that it be effective.

      b. If no consideration is given by assignee, assignment is revocable by assignor.

C. Rights that may be assigned without assent of obligor.

   1. Right to receive the payment of money.

   2. Right to delivery of a deed or goods.

D. Some rights may not be assigned because of express prohibitions.

   1. Statutory prohibitions.

   2. Reasonable contractual prohibitions in anti-assignment clauses.

   3. Claims for injuries due to torts may not be assigned prior to entry of judgment.

   4. Rights of an insured against an insurer may not be assigned prior to an actual insured casualty loss.

   5. At law, future or potential rights may not be assigned.

E. The right to receive personal or confidential services may not be assigned without the consent of the obligor.

F. An obligee, who is making an assignment, may not change the nature of the non-personal performance (which he has a right to receive) so as to increase the burden or risk to the obligor, without the assent of the obligor.

G. Effect of assignment.

    1. Assignee can enforce the contract against the obligor.

    2. Assignee takes claim subject to all defenses available against obligee/assignor even if consideration was given for the assignment.

    3. Clause, providing for waiver of right to assert defenses, in original contract is strictly construed.

H. Although it is not necessary to give notice of assignment to obligor, it is wise to do so.

I. Multiple assignments.

    1. Successive assignments of same rights by obligee to more than one assignee, who take in good faith and for value.

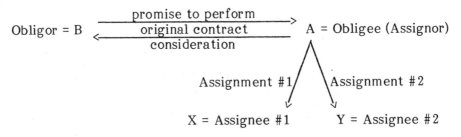

    a. Once an obligee makes an unrevoked assignment of all the rights that he or she possesses, a subsequent assignment of the same rights by the obligee to another assignee is wrongful.

    b. In some states, assignee, who first takes assignment, prevails even if he or she did not first give notice of assignment to obligor.

    c. In other states, assignee, who first notifies obligor of assignment, will prevail.

    2. Partial assignments will be effective.

    3. An assignee may reassign the contract rights to another person (sub-assignment).

III. Delegation of duties.

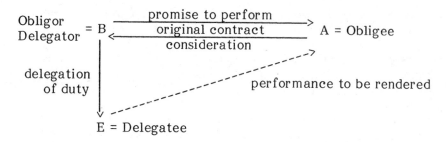

A. Performance of non-personal duties may be delegated by obligor.

B. Personal duties may not be delegated without assent of party to whom performance is to be rendered.

C. If a delegatee fails to perform, the obligee may sue:

1. The obligor, with whom the obligee had contracted, and

2. The delegatee. The obligee is treated as a third party creditor beneficiary of the contract formed by the obligor (delegator) and delegatee.

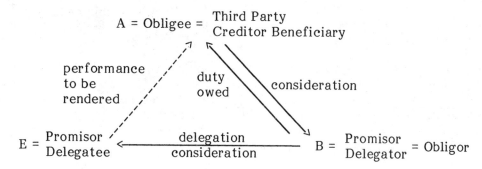

KEY WORDS AND PHRASES IN TEXT

Privity of contract
Third party beneficiary contracts
Intended beneficiary
Third party creditor beneficiary
Third party donee beneficiary
Incidental beneficiary cannot enforce contract
When rights of third party beneficiary vest so that he or she can enforce contract
Assignment of contract rights to third party
Effect of assignment of contract rights
A particular assignment may be covered by the Statute of Frauds

Legally sufficient consideration need not be given for assignments
Gratuitous assignments
Statutory prohibitions against certain assignments
Anti-assignment clauses in contracts
Performance of personal services or duties
Assignment cannot materially increase or alter the duties of the obligor
Assumption of mortgage
Due-on-sale provisions in mortgages
Notice of assignment to obligor
Delegation of contractual duties
Non-delegatable duties
Effect of delegation of duties

FILL-IN QUESTIONS

1. Usually a person who is not a party to a contract cannot enforce the contract because he or she lacks ___privity___ of contract.

2. If the parties to a contract expressly agree that one of them is to render his or her performance to a third party, the person to whom the performance is to be rendered may be a _3rd Party Donee_ or _3rd Party Creditor_ beneficiary.

3. Adams and Brady have made an agreement which provides that Adams will pay Brady $50 per week for twelve weeks, if Brady promises to cut the grass on Cotton's and Delmer's property. If Delmer is a friend of Adams, Delmer will be treated as a third party ___donee___ beneficiary if Adams intends to give him a gift of having his grass cut. If Adams owed Cotton $600, Cotton will be treated as a third party ___creditor___ beneficiary. Both Cotton and Delmer can enforce the contract but Nailer, a neighbor of Cotton's, although he will benefit from the performance of the contract, cannot enforce the contract because he is merely an ___incidental___ beneficiary.

4. If one transfers to another the rights he or she has because of a contract, he or she has made an _assignment_. The transferor is called the _assignor_ and the transferee is called the _assignee_.

5. The performance of non-personal duties may be _delegated_ by the party, who, under the terms of a contract, is required to render performance to the other contracting party.

6. In general, the parties to a contract may assign rights, which they have because of the contract, to strangers to the contract, unless (1) there is a _statutory prohibition_ against assignment, (2) there is an anti-assignment clause in the contract, (3) the contract requires the performance of personal services or duties, or (4) as a result of the assignment, the duties of the obligor will be _materially increased or altered._

MULTIPLE CHOICE QUESTIONS

1. Roberts took out a $10,000 life insurance policy on her own life with ABC Insurance Company and named Sanders as the beneficiary. Roberts paid all the premiums until her untimely death a year later. The insurance company has not paid Sanders, who is, therefore, suing it.
   a. Sanders is entitled to the payment of the $10,000 because he is a third party donee beneficiary.
   b. If Roberts made misrepresentations concerning material facts in the application for insurance, the ABC Insurance Company can successfully raise the defense that the contract was voidable because of fraud or misrepresentations against Sanders.
   c. Although Sanders gave no consideration and was not a party to the contract between Roberts and ABC Insurance Company, he is a proper party to enforce the insurance contract.
   d. All of the above.

2. A has agreed to pay B $3,000 if B promises to paint C's house.
    a. If C gave no consideration to A or B, C has no standing to sue B because there is no privity of contract between B and C.
    b. If C gave no consideration to A or B, C will be treated as a third party donee beneficiary and may enforce the contract against B.
    c. As C is a third party beneficiary, C may enforce the contract against B, who will be barred from raising any defenses against C that he could have raised against A.
    d. C is an assignee because A transferred his rights to have his (A's) house painted by B.

3. Hendon owed Borhan $200. On Monday, Hendon gave $200 to Katz, who promised to give the money to Borhan on the following Friday in order to discharge Hendon's debt. Katz did not deliver the money to Borhan. Borhan, a third party creditor beneficiary, will be successful if she sues Katz:
    a. because the parties to a contract, which provided for conferring a benefit upon a third person, cannot terminate their agreement if the third person learns of the original contract and detrimentally changes his or her position in reliance upon it.
    b. even though Hendon and Katz altered their agreement on Wednesday before Borhan learned of it and gave her consent.
    c. even though Hendon and Katz altered their contract on Tuesday before Borhan materially changed her position in detrimental reliance on the contract.
    d. because the parties to a contract, which provides for conferring a benefit upon a third person, lack the power to alter or terminate their contract, after they confer a benefit upon the third person.

4. The Acme Construction Co. contracted with Granite City to build a new court house. It was foreseen that blasting would be necessary, and Acme promised that it would pay for "any and all property damage caused by the blasting."
    a. MacDonald, a homeowner, can recover from Acme for damage to his home caused by the blasting, because he is an incidental beneficiary.
    b. Naughton, a homeowner, cannot recover from Acme for damage to her home caused by the blasting, because she is an incidental beneficiary.
    c. Oppenheimer, a tourist, can recover for damage to her car caused by the blasting, because she is a third party beneficiary.
    d. Only the city can recover from Acme for damage to its property, because it was a party to the contract.

5. The right to recover under a fire insurance policy may be assigned:
    a. by the insured at any time.
    b. by the insured after the policy has been in force for a reasonable period of time without incurring a loss.
    c. after a fire when the duty of the insurer to pay is fixed.
    d. never.

6. Simple Oil Distributing Co. contracted with Vital Service Station to supply its gasoline requirements for one year, estimated to be one million gallons, at a price of twenty cents above the price per gallon paid by Simple. All of the terms of the contract were reduced to writing. Simple was having difficulty obtaining gas supplies and, therefore, agreed with Best Oil Corp. that Best would "take over" Simple's contract with Vital by supplying Vital's requirements and receiving payment therefor from Vital.

    a. Simple was not obligated to deliver gasoline to Vital if it was unable to obtain supplies because the quantity of gasoline to be delivered and the price were uncertain.

    b. Simple cannot assign its right to be paid by Vital to Best without the assent of Vital.

    c. Simple has effectively assigned its rights and delegated its duties under the terms of its contract with Vital to Best.

    d. Simple is effectively released from any further obligation to perform under the terms of the contract with Vital.

7. Manson orally agreed to sell his truck to Jackson, who orally promised to pay Manson $510 within one week and $800 one year after delivery of the truck. Prior to delivering the truck, Manson orally assigned his right to be paid to Thompson.

    a. Thompson cannot enforce Jackson's agreement because the Statute of Frauds requires that the contract and the assignment be in writing.

    b. Thompson cannot enforce Jackson's agreement because he gave no consideration to Manson for the assignment.

    c. Thompson cannot enforce Jackson's agreement because Jackson did not assent to the assignment by Manson.

    d. Thompson can enforce Jackson's agreement.

8. On April 4, the Barnes Store sold $100 worth of merchandise on credit to Ames, who promised that she would pay the Barnes Store $100 on May 1. On April 6, the store assigned its right to be paid to the Careful Credit Corp. for $90.

    a. Careful Credit Corp. may not assign its rights to Doubtful Claims Inc.

    b. Careful Credit Corp. may not enforce Ames' promise to pay because Ames did not consent to the assignment.

    c. If Ames returns the merchandise to the Barnes Store, which accepts it, on April 8, Ames can raise a good defense if Careful Credit Corp. sues her for $100 after May 1.

    d. Since the Barnes Store is a merchant, it is prohibited from assigning its right to be paid by Ames until May 1 when the $100 is due and owing.

9. Rawson has a contract with Green, the owner of a professional basketball team, to play basketball for one year. In most states:

    a. Green may assign his contractual rights to the owner of another basketball team without Rawson's consent.

    b. Rawson may delegate his duty to play basketball and assign his right to be paid to Hubbard, without Green's consent, if Hubbard is a better basketball player than Rawson.

    c. Rawson may assign his right to be paid for playing basketball after he has rendered his performance without Green's consent.

    d. Rawson may not assign any rights or delegate any duties that he has because of his contract with Green to another person.

Chapter 14

Performance and Discharge

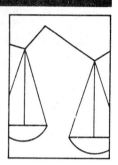

Most contracts are fully performed by the parties, resulting in their discharge. Contracting parties may be discharged by full performance, by breach of contract, by agreement and by operation of law.

THINGS TO KEEP IN MIND

1. If a contractual party fails to perform an absolute contractual promise, he or she is not discharged, but is liable to the other party for the breach of contract. The other party is discharged and, therefore, excused from performing.

2. If a contractual promise is conditional and the conditioning event occurs, the promisor's duty to perform does not arise or is terminated so that no liability attaches for failing to perform.

OUTLINE

I. Conditions — A condition is an operative event, the occurrence or nonoccurrence of which changes, limits, precludes, gives rise to or terminates a contractual obligation.

  A. Types of conditions.

    1. Condition precedent — Conditioning event must occur before performance by promisor is required. Until then the promisee has no right to receive performance.

    2. Condition subsequent — Occurrence of conditioning event extinguishes an existing contractual duty.

3. Concurrent condition — Performance of each party is conditioned on the performance of the other party.

B. How conditions arise.

1. Express — Condition clearly stated by parties.

2. Implied in fact — Condition that is understood or inferred.

3. Implied in law (constructive) — Imposed by court in order to achieve justice and fairness.

II. Discharge by performance.

A. Full, complete performance in manner prescribed by contract discharges performing party.

B. Tender of complete performance — An unconditional offer to perform by one ready, willing and able to do so, discharges party if his or her tender is not accepted.

C. Time for performance.

1. If time for performance is not stated, performance is to be rendered within a reasonable period of time.

2. If parties stipulate that time is of the essence (vital), the time requirement must be complied with.

3. If time for performance is stipulated, but not vital, performance prior to or within a few days of the stated time satisfies contract.

D. Part performance.

1. If partial performance is accepted, performing party can recover value of performance.

2. If performance is substantial (i.e., minor, trivial deviation from contractual obligation) and deviation is not the result of bad faith, the performing party is discharged, but is liable for his or her failure to render complete performance.

3. Partial performance, which is not substantial performance, is a breach of contract and results in the discharge of the party entitled to receive performance but not the discharge of the partially performing party.

E. Effect of contractual conditions on discharge by performance.

1. Strict compliance with express conditions is necessary.

2. Substantial performance of constructive conditions is necessary.

3. Express personal satisfaction condition — Promise of one party to pay may

be conditioned on that party's satisfaction with the other party's performance.

    a. If personal taste, preferences, aesthetics, fancy or comfort is involved, payment is excused if dissatisfaction is honest and in good faith, even though a reasonable person would have been satisfied.

    b. If satisfaction relates to operative fitness, merchantability or mechanical utility, payment is excused when dissatisfaction is honest and a reasonable person would have been dissatisfied.

III. Discharge by breach of contract.

  A. A breach of contract is the nonperformance of a contractual duty.

  B. A party, who totally fails to perform, is not discharged and is liable for damages for breach of contract. The other party is, however, discharged and need not hold himself or herself ready to perform.

  C. If a party performs in part, but his or her performance does not amount to substantial part performance, there is a material breach of contract.

    1. The partially performing party is not discharged and is liable for the material breach of contract.

    2. The other party is discharged and need not hold himself or herself ready to perform.

  D. If there is a minor, nonmaterial breach of contract, the breaching party is liable for damages if the breach is not cured. The nonbreaching party is not discharged and is required to perform.

  E. Anticipatory breach of contract.

    1. If a party repudiates a contract before he or she is required to perform, the other party may sue immediately and does not have to remain ready to perform.

    2. The doctrine of anticipatory breach does not apply to a promise to pay a stated sum of money, a unilateral contract or a bilateral contract that is executory on one side only.

IV. Discharge by agreement of the parties.

  A. Provision in original contract.

  B. New, subsequent, valid, enforceable contract.

    1. Elements of contract, including consideration, must be present.

    2. Mutual rescission — Parties agree to discharge and relieve each other of their obligations.

    a. If original bilateral contract was executory, consideration is present because each party gives up existing rights.

    b. If original contract was a unilateral or a bilateral one that was executed by one party, new consideration must be given to the party who performed in exchange for his or her promise to relieve the nonperforming party of his or her contractual duty to render the originally promised performance.

3. Release — Statement by one party relieving other party of contractual duty. A release often includes a promise not to sue for breach of contract.

4. Accord and satisfaction.

    a. Accord — Parties agree that a different (substitute) performance will be rendered by one party in satisfaction of his or her original obligation.

    b. Satisfaction — The substitute performance is actually rendered and accepted.

    c. Until substitute performance is rendered, the original contractual obligations are merely suspended.

5. Substituted agreement — Parties agree to enter a new agreement with different terms as a substitute for an original contract, which is expressly or impliedly discharged.

6. Novation — Parties agree with a third person that the contractual duties of one of the original parties will be assumed by the third person. The third person is substituted for one of the original parties with the consent of the party entitled to receive the performance.

V. Discharge by operation of law.

A. Material alteration of a written contract without consent.

B. Running of the statute of limitations, which operates to bar access to judicial remedies.

C. Discharge (decree) in bankruptcy.

D. Impossibility — Occurrence of a supervening, unforeseen event, making it impossible to perform.

1. Object of contract becomes illegal.

2. Death or serious illness or incapacitation of a party who was to perform personal services.

3. Destruction of specific subject matter of the contract.

4. Economic frustration — An unforeseen event occurs which frustrates the

purpose for which one of the parties entered the contract so that the value of the expected performance he or she is to receive is destroyed.

5. Commercial impracticability — An extreme change in conditions makes performance impracticable because it will be extremely difficult, burdensome or costly to render.

6. Temporary impossibility — When performance is temporarily suspended because of unexpected occurrences and subsequent circumstances make performance very difficult, parties may be discharged.

KEY WORDS AND PHRASES IN TEXT

Discharge of party to contract
Conditions
Condition precedent
Condition subsequent
Concurrent condition
Express condition
Implied in fact condition
Implied in law (or constructive) condition
Discharge by full complete performance
Reasonable expectations test
Substantial part performance
Material breach of contract
Performance to the personal satisfaction
   of another
Anticipatory breach (or repudiation)
   of contract
Time for performance
Discharge by agreement
Discharge because of mutual rescission
Discharge because of a novation

Discharge because of a substituted
   agreement
Settlement agreement
Discharge because of an accord and
   satisfaction
Discharge by operation of law
Material alteration of a written contract
Running of a statute of limitations
Discharge in bankruptcy
Discharge because of impossibility of
   performance
Objective impossibility
Death or incapacity of a party
Destruction of the subject matter of
   a contract
Change in law that renders performance
   illegal
Commercial impracticability
Temporary impossibility

FILL-IN QUESTIONS

1. If parties to a contract agree that one of them will not be required to perform upon the happening of some event, their contract contains a condition _precedent_ ; if, however, they agree that the occurrence of some event will terminate an existing contractual obligation, the contract contains a condition _subsequent_ .

2. Karen promised to pay Trina $2,000 in exchange for Trina's promise to paint Karen's house in a color to be selected by Karen. The contract between Karen and Trina contains an express condition _precedent_ . If Karen does not select a color of paint, Trina is _discharged_ from her obligation to paint the house.

3. National Sales Company is in the mail order business. A customer may order goods from the company and, if so, promises to pay the purchase price for the merchandise. National Sales Company agrees that when goods, which are ordered by a customer, do not meet with the customer's satisfaction, the customer can return the merchandise within 15 days and will not be required to pay the purchase

price. Contracts between National Sales Company and its customers thus contain express conditions _subsequent_ . If Beth orders three blouses from National Sales Company and returns one within 15 days, she is _discharged_ from her obligation to pay for the returned blouse. If Beth fails to pay for the two other blouses, she will be liable to the company for _breach_ of contract.

4. A party, who renders or tenders _full complete performance_ in the manner prescribed by a contract, is discharged.

5. A party to a contract is _discharged_ if he or she renders complete performance. If a party substantially performs, he or she is _discharged_ , but is liable for the minor, trivial breach of contract. If, however, there is a material breach of contract because a party only partially performs, he or she is not _discharged_ , but the other party, to whom the breaching party owed a contractual duty, is _discharged_ .

6. Sam agreed to sell 400 pens to Pam for $100. When Sam delivers the 400 pens, Sam is _discharged_ and Pam is obligated to pay $100 to him. If Sam delivers 396 pens, Sam is also _discharged_ . Pam will not, however, be _discharged_ until she pays $100 for the pens, less a deduction (probably of $1) because there has been a minor, trivial breach of contract by Sam. If Sam delivers only 40 pens, he is not _discharged_ because there has been a material breach of contract. Pam will not be required to pay for the pens because of Sam's material _breach_ of contract.

7. The parties to a contract may subsequently agree to discharge and terminate their existing agreement by making a new contract. The new agreement may be an accord and satisfaction, _mutual rescission, substituted agreement_ or _novation_ .

8. Parties to a contract are discharged by operation of law if there has been a material alteration of a written contract by one party without the assent of the other party or _the statute of limitations has run or a decree in bankruptcy has been issued_ .

9. A contract is discharged because of _impossibility_ if the subject matter has been destroyed or one of the parties, who was to perform personal services, has died.

MULTIPLE CHOICE QUESTIONS

1. Aunt Alice promised to give her niece, Betty, $5,000 if Betty spent her two month summer vacation in Europe. Betty is legally entitled to the $5,000 if she:
    a. spends three weeks in Europe and works at home for the remainder of her vacation.
    b. spends two months in Mexico and Brazil.
    c. spends seven weeks in Europe.
    d. all of the above.

2. On November 1, S and B entered into a written contract for the sale by S of a fully described tract of land for $20,000, delivery of the deed and payment by B to be due on December 1.

a. If B advises S on November 15 that he no longer wishes to purchase the land and is repudiating the contract, S can successfully sue B for breach of contract on November 17.

b. If S advises B on November 15 that he no longer wishes to sell the land and is repudiating the contract, B can successfully sue S for breach of contract on November 17.

c. If B advises S on November 15 that he no longer wishes to purchase the land and is repudiating the contract, S can successfully sue B for anticipatory breach of contract on November 17.

d. If S advises B on November 15 that he no longer wishes to sell the land and is repudiating the contract, B can successfully sue S for anticipatory breach of contract on November 17.

3. If a breach of contract is:
   a. material, the nonbreaching party may sue for damages but must perform his or her part of the contract.
   b. material, the nonbreaching party may not sue for damages if he or she has accepted the improper performance.
   c. minor, the nonbreaching party is excused from performing.
   d. minor, the nonbreaching party may sue for damages for the breach.

4. On July 10, Fred, the owner of a farm, contracted to sell 3,000 bushels of Grade A tomatoes on September 1 to the Prince Pizza Co. The tomatoes on Fred's farm were destroyed in a hail storm on August 8. If Fred fails to deliver 3,000 bushels of tomatoes on September 1:
   a. Fred may be sued for breach of contract successfully by Prince Pizza Co.
   b. Fred is discharged because of a condition subsequent.
   c. Fred is discharged by operation of law because of impossibility.
   d. Prince Pizza Co. may successfully sue Fred for anticipatory breach of contract.

5. On June 1, Frank, the owner of a farm, contracted to sell 2,000 bushels of Grade A corn from his farm on August 10 to Careful Corn Canners Inc. The corn on Frank's farm was destroyed by locusts on August 1. If Frank fails to deliver 2,000 bushels of corn on August 10:
   a. Frank may be sued for breach of contract successfully by Careful Corn Canners Inc.
   b. Frank is discharged because of a condition subsequent.
   c. Frank is discharged by operation of law because of impossibility.
   d. Careful Corn Canners Inc. may successfully sue Frank for anticipatory breach of contract.

6. Larry rented a room from Mike along Main Street on a Saturday for the purpose of watching a parade. Mike knew that this was the reason for renting the room. Unfortunately there was a bad snow storm and the parade was cancelled. Mike has sued Larry for the rent. In most states a court will determine that:
   a. the contract is discharged because of impossibility.
   b. the contract is discharged because of economic frustration.
   c. the contract is discharged because of the occurrence of a conditioning event.
   d. the contract is not discharged.

7. On March 1, Pick and Quick entered into a valid written contract that provided for the sale by Pick of 1,000 yo-yos to Quick for $1,000. All of the terms were clearly

and unambiguously contained in the writing. A week later Pick delivered 400 yo-yos but he has failed to deliver the remaining 600 yo-yos.

   a. Pick is not discharged and is liable to Quick for a material breach of the contract.

   b. Quick must remain ready, willing and able to pay Pick the $1,000.

   c. Even if Quick accepted the 400 yo-yos, he would not have to pay for them because there has been a material breach of contract.

   d. If Quick accepted the 400 yo-yos, Pick is discharged without liability and does not have to tender delivery of the remaining 600 yo-yos.

8.   Don promised to pay Cathy $100 if Cathy painted Don's portrait.

   a. If Cathy dies before completing the portrait, Cathy and Don are discharged.

   b. If Ellen, Cathy and Don agree that Ellen will paint the portrait and Don will pay Ellen rather than Cathy, the parties have entered a novation.

   c. If Cathy paints the portrait but Don fails to pay the $100, Cathy is discharged but Don is not discharged.

   d. All of the above.

Chapter 15

Breach of Contract and Remedies

A breach of contract occurs when a party fails to fully and correctly perform a contractual duty. The party to whom the duty is owed may bring an action against or sue the breaching party in order to enforce his or her rights or to obtain an appropriate remedy.

THINGS TO KEEP IN MIND

If there has been a breach of contract, when the nonbreaching party sues, the remedy that usually will be afforded will be compensatory damages, a sum of money which will be adequate in order to put him or her in the position that he or she would have been in had there not been a breach of contract.

OUTLINE

I. Remedies at law — Money damages.

    A. Compensatory damages — Awarded to a nonbreaching party in order to compensate him or her for the actual harm or loss caused by the breach.

    Measure of damages — Factual question.

        1. How much money will place the plaintiff in as good a position as he or she would have been in if the defendant had correctly performed?

        2. Usually this amounts to the loss of normal, expected profit plus any sums previously paid or incidental expenses incurred by the nonbreaching party.

            a. Sales of goods — Difference between the contract price and market price.

   b. Sale of land — Usually the difference between the contract price and
       market price.

   c. Construction contracts — Damages vary depending upon which party has
       failed to perform and at what stage construction is at time of breach.

   d. Employment contracts.
       1) Breach by employer — Salary for unexpired term less earnings of
           employee from job of similar nature or, if such job is available,
           compensation which the employee would have received if he or she
           had accepted the position.
       2) Breach by employee — Cost of procuring replacement employee less
           contracted salary or wages.

B. Consequential or special damages — Speculative, unforeseeable, remote,
    indirect or unexpected damages, which do not ordinarily flow from a breach of
    contract, are not recoverable unless contemplated by nonperforming party
    because he or she was given notice thereof.

C. Punitive or exemplary damages — Unusual award by court to punish for willful,
    wanton, malicious (tortious) harm caused to a nonbreaching party.

D. Nominal damages — Inconsequential sum, which establishes that plaintiff had a
    cause of action but suffered no measurable pecuniary loss.

E. Mitigation of damages — A party, who suffers damages, must reduce actual
    damages, if he or she is able to do so.

F. Liquidated damages — The parties may provide in their contract that a stated
    sum of money or property will be paid or, if previously deposited, forfeited, if
    one of the parties fails to perform in accordance with the contract. Such
    provisions will be enforced unless they are unreasonable and, therefore, are
    penalties.

II. Equitable remedies.

   A. Not available if:

       1. Remedy at law (usually money damages) is adequate, determinable and
           available.

       2. Aggrieved party has shown bad faith, fraud, etc.

       3. Aggrieved party has unnecessarily delayed in bringing an action (laches).

       4. Court will have to supervise execution of remedy.

   B. Rescission and restitution.

       1. Rescission means cancellation or abrogation of a contract. It may be
           mutually agreed to by parties to a contract or awarded as a remedy by a
           court.

   2. Usually restitution is also given by a court so that previously rendered consideration, or its value, is returned.

C. Specific performance — An order by a court to render a contractually promised performance.

   1. Specific performance will be granted when:

      a. Contract involves unique personal property or real property, which is always considered to be unique.

      b. Performance that is to be rendered is clear and unambiguous.

   2. Specific performance will not be granted when performance to be rendered involves personal services.

D. Injunction — An order enjoining or restraining a person from doing some act.

E. Reformation — A court may correct an agreement so that it will conform to the intentions of the parties.

F. Quasi contract — A court may require that one who has received a benefit pay for the benefit conferred in order to prevent unjust enrichment.

III. Election of remedies.

A. In the past a plaintiff was required to elect either a legal remedy (compensatory money damages) or equitable relief.

B. Today, generally, both legal and equitable relief will be available if they are not inconsistent.

IV. Limitations on liability for breach of contract.

A. Waiver of breach — A party may relinquish, repudiate or surrender the right which he or she has to seek a remedy for breach of contract by accepting defective performance.

B. Contractual limitations on liability (limitation of liability clauses) will be enforced unless they are unconscionable or the result of unequal bargaining power.

   1. Mutual assent to limitation on liability clause, based upon notice thereof, is necessary.

   2. Parties may agree to limit liability for certain types of breaches of contract or conduct but may not exclude liability for gross negligence or intentional torts.

   3. Parties may agree to fix a maximum sum that can be recovered if there is a breach of contract.

   4. Parties may agree to limited remedies.

C. UCC provisions.

KEY WORDS AND PHRASES IN TEXT

Breach of contract
Remedies
Damages
Compensatory damages
Measure of damages
Quantum meruit
Consequential (special) damages
Punitive (exemplary) damages
Nominal damages
Mitigation of damages
Liquidated damages
Penalties
Equitable remedies

Rescission
Restitution
Specific performance
Involuntary servitude
Reformation
Quasi contract
Unjust enrichment
Election of remedies
Waiver of breach
Pattern of conduct
Limitation of liability clauses
Requirement that there be mutual
    assent to limitation on liability

FILL-IN QUESTIONS

1. A plaintiff, who is suing a party with whom he has contracted, may recover _Compensatory money_ damages to compensate him or her for the foreseeable injury sustained because of a breach of contract.

2. In an action based on a breach of a contract for the sale of property, the measure of damages will usually be the difference between _Contract price_ and _Market price_.

3. Sam agreed to sell his house to Baker for $70,000. Baker was unable to obtain a mortgage and, therefore, did not complete the purchase. The fair market value of the house was $64,000. If Smith sues Baker for breach of contract, Smith can recover _compensatory_ damages in the amount of $ _6000_ because the appropriate measure of damages is the loss of profit, or the difference between the contract price and the _market price_.

4. Consequential, or _special_, damages are those that indirectly flow from a _breach of contract_ and are awarded only when they were, or should have been, reasonably foreseeable to the parties at the time that the contract was formed.

5. If a provision in a contract states that a certain sum of money will be forfeited by a party who fails to perform a contractual duty, the provision is referred to as a _liquidated damages_ clause and will be enforced as long as the amount _____.

6. _Rescission + restitution_ will be granted by a court if a minor or a party, whose assent was not real, wishes to disaffirm a voidable contract to which he or she was a party.

7. Equitable relief, such as _rescission + restitution_, _Specific Performance_ and _injunction_, will be granted if a legal remedy, such as compensatory damages, is _inadequate_ or unavailable.

8. Mark was 17 years of age when he entered into a written contract to purchase a car. Because Mark was a minor, the contract for the purchase of the car is _Voidable_ by Mark. Two months later, Mark decided that he wished to return the car to the seller and get back the purchase price, which he had paid to the seller. Mark will seek the equitable remedies of _rescission_ and _restitution_.

MULTIPLE CHOICE QUESTIONS

1. In an action based upon a refusal of a buyer to accept and pay for $100 worth of pencils instituted by the seller, a court will probably:
   a. award nominal damages only.
   b. award compensatory damages only.
   c. grant a decree of specific performance.
   d. grant a decree of specific performance and compensatory damages.

2. In an action based upon a breach of an employment contract by an employee, a court will probably:
   a. award nominal damages.
   b. award punitive damages.
   c. award compensatory damages.
   d. grant a decree of specific performance.

3. Nominal damages refer to:
   a. a small sum awarded to a plaintiff whose rights have been infringed upon as a result of a defendant's breach of contract if the plaintiff incurred no actual loss.
   b. a specific sum of money that one party agrees to pay to another in the event that he fails to perform in accordance with a major provision in a contract.
   c. an award by a court when it is determined that a liquidated damages clause in a contract was excessive because it did not bear a reasonable relationship to the actual damage incurred.
   d. the difference between the contract price and the market price of goods that were the subject matter of a contract that has not been performed by either the buyer or seller of the goods.

4. When a contract provision requires that a party, who fails to perform as agreed in a contract, pay a specified sum to the other party, the amount is referred to as:
   a. specific performance.
   b. nominal damages.
   c. liquidated damages.
   d. punitive damages.

5. Specific performance is:
   a. the remedy used when the subject matter of a contract is unique.
   b. the first remedy a court will grant if there is a breach of contract.
   c. used when a party has failed to mitigate damages.
   d. infrequently used in cases of breach of contracts for the sale of real property.

6. In an action based upon a breach of a contract:
   a. whenever possible a court will require specific performance.

b. if a party can be adequately compensated by money damages, he will not be granted an injunction.

c. the party to whom damage is done because of the breach will be awarded money damages only if the contract is rescinded.

d. the party to whom damage is done because of the breach will usually be awarded money damages as well as rescission or an injunction.

7. Cassie and Dave entered into a written agreement stipulating that Dave would deliver 100 tons of sand to Cassie within three days. There was a mistake in the written document because it had been their intention to provide that delivery would be within thirty days. If Cassie insists upon delivery within three days, Dave would seek the remedy of:

a. reformation.
b. rescission.
c. specific performance.
d. special damages.
e. punitive damages.

8. One who suffers damage, because the party with whom he has contracted has failed to perform, has a duty to reduce his actual damages if possible. This is referred to as:

a. making an election of remedies.
b. limiting liability.
c. liquidating damages.
d. mitigating damages.

9. David contracted to sell a set of dueling pistols to John for $50,000. Both David and John believed that the pistols had been owned by Aaron Burr. It is learned that they made a mutual mistake of fact and John wishes to avoid the contract. The most appropriate remedy is:

a. nominal damages.
b. compensatory damages.
c. rescission.
d. reformation.

10. Reynolds promised to sell 500 shares of stock to Ingram for $10,000 but has failed to deliver the stock certificates to Ingram. A court will issue a decree for specific performance if it is established that:

a. Ingram used false representations of fact in order to induce Reynolds' assent to the contract.

b. the shares of stock are those of a corporation, whose shares are publicly traded on a national stock exchange.

c. a provision of the contract stipulated that if Reynolds did not deliver the stock certificates she would pay Ingram $100, which was the foreseeable amount of damages that would be incurred.

d. the shares of stock are those of a small corporation which are not readily available for purchase.

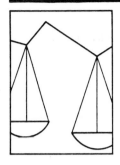

COMMERCIAL TRANSACTIONS AND THE UNIFORM COMMERCIAL CODE

The objective of this unit is to familiarize you with some of the more frequently occurring types of business transactions. Much of the law relating to such transactions has been codified in the Uniform Commercial Code, an internally consistent, comprehensive statement of applicable basic principles of law.

The Code applies to most aspects of a commercial transaction, involving personal property, but does not relate to those involving real property or the performance of services. Included are rules relating to agreements for the sale of goods by original manufacturers, by wholesalers and other distributors and, ultimately, by retailers, who sell them to the final consumers; the transportation and storage of goods; methods available for financing the purchase of goods and for securing payment of the purchase price. Note that, if the parties wish that a rule, different than that provided for by the Code, apply to their dealings, they may so agree.

References are given in the material in the subsequent chapters to sections found in the Uniform Commercial Code, the provisions of which are reproduced in the text. (See Appendix B.)

Chapter 16

Introduction to Sales Contracts and Their Formation

The law of sales deals with the rights and duties of the buyers and sellers of goods in the entire chain of purchases-and-sales, from their original production to their ultimate purchase for consumption or other use. Transactions involving sales of goods for consideration are covered by Article 2 of the Uniform Commercial Code. The Code provides for flexibility and establishes standards of good faith and reasonableness for parties engaging in sales transactions. Provisions of the Code, that change some of the rules of law with which you became familiar when you studied the law of contracts, are highlighted.

THINGS TO KEEP IN MIND

1. An agreement for the sale of goods is a contract. All of the elements of a contract, therefore, must be present for it to be valid and enforceable. Some of the rules of contract law, however, are relaxed under the U.C.C.

2. Often special rules are applicable if one or, in some cases, both parties are merchants.

OUTLINE

I. Nature of sales transactions.

A. The most common commercial transaction is the sale and purchase of goods (tangible personal property).

B. Modern sales law is derived from the Law Merchant. Today many of the principles of the law of sales are codified in Article 2 of the U.C.C.

C. A sale is a present transfer of ownership rights (title) to existing, identified goods for consideration, known as the price, by a seller to a buyer.

1. The price may be money, goods, real property, personal property or services.

2. Goods — Items that are tangible and moveable.

   a. Goods associated with realty (real property) (Sec. 2-107):
      1) Mineral or similar natural resources, found beneath the surface, to be severed by the seller.
      2) Growing crops and similar things attached to land to be severed by the buyer or seller.
      3) Things attached to realty to be severed by the buyer or seller, without material harm to the land.

   b. It is sometimes difficult to distinguish goods from service, to which the Code is not applicable.

   c. Special classifications (Sec. 2-105):
      1) Unborn young of animals.
      2) Rare coins and money treated as a commodity.
      3) Items specially manufactured.

3. Merchants, to whom special rules apply (Sec. 2-104) are those who:

   a. Deal in goods of the kind involved in the transaction, or

   b. Hold themselves out, because of their occupations, as having knowledge and skills peculiar to the business or goods involved in the transaction, or

   c. Employ merchants to act on their behalf.

II. Formation of sales contract.

A. Contract law principles apply to sales agreement, unless modified by the Code. (See Exhibit 16-2 in text for summary.) The Code applies standards of good faith and reasonableness in many instances.

B. Offer.

1. Moment at which contract became effective may be undetermined (Sec. 2-204).

2. If intention to form a contract is found, contract will not fail for indefiniteness because some terms are left open.

   a. Quantity — Requirements and output contracts (Sec. 2-306).

   b. Price (Sec. 2-305).
      1) If parties intended to form contract, but did not set price or provide method by which it was to be determined, the price will be the reasonable price at the time of delivery.
      2) If buyer or seller is to set price, he or she must do so in good faith.

           3) If price is not fixed through fault of one party, other party may treat contract as cancelled or fix a reasonable price.

    c. Place of delivery (Sec. 2-308) — If not specified:
        1) Seller's place of business or, if he or she has none, his or her residence.
        2) If goods are at a location other than seller's place of business, and both parties know it, at that location.

    d. Time of delivery (Sec. 2-309) — If not specified, within a reasonable time.

    e. A party, terminating an ongoing contract for delivery of goods, when no period is specified for its duration, must give reasonable notice (Sec. 2-309).

    f. If the terms for payment are not specified, payment is due at the time and place at which the buyer is to receive the goods (Sec. 2-310).

    g. Merchant's firm offer will be irrevocable without consideration, if it is in writing and signed by the merchant (Sec. 2-205).

C. Acceptance.

  1. Method of acceptance — If none is specified, any commercially reasonable means of communication may be used (Sec. 2-206).

  2. Offer to buy for prompt shipment is accepted when seller promises to ship or promptly ships conforming goods. If seller ships nonconforming goods as an accommodation, it is not an acceptance. (Sec. 2-206.)

  3. Offeree communicates that he or she intends to accept an offer, but adds different or new terms (Sec. 2-207).

    a. If either or both of the parties are not merchants, it is an effective acceptance of terms agreed upon and proposal for new or different terms.

    b. If the parties are merchants, the new or different terms become part of the contract unless:
        1) Offer expressly limits acceptance to only its terms, or
        2) The terms materially alter the offer (such that they result in hardship or surprise), or
        3) The offeror notifies the offeree of his or her objections to the terms within a reasonable period of time.

  4. If an offeree to a unilateral contract does not notify the offeror within a reasonable period of time that he is beginning his or her performance, the offer lapses (Sec. 2-206).

D. Consideration.

  1. Consideration is not necessary for contract modifications if made in good faith (Sec. 2-209).

2. A writing is, however, necessary if:

   a. Agreement of the parties so provides, or

   b. The contract, as revised, is required to be in writing in order to be enforceable under the Statute of Frauds.

3. See also Chapter 9 — Consideration for contracts.

E. Statute of Frauds (Sec. 2-201).

   1. If price for the sale of goods is $500 or more, a writing or memorandum (indicating the parties, nature of goods, price and quantity, unless covered by open term provisions), signed by the party against whom it is being enforced, is required.

   2. Sales between merchants — If one party sends a written confirmation of oral agreement within a reasonable time, and the other party does not object within ten days, both parties are bound.

   3. Writing not required in following cases:

      a. Contract for goods to be specially manufactured for a particular buyer when:
         1) Goods are not suitable for resale in the ordinary course of business, and
         2) Seller has begun production.

      b. Party admits in court or pleadings that contract had been formed.

      c. Receipt and acceptance of goods.

      d. Payment for goods.

F. Parol evidence rule — Even if writing is a complete statement of the agreement of the parties, parol evidence is admissible to explain or supplement the writing by showing trade usage, a course of dealings or a course of performance, which is not inconsistent with the terms of the writing (Sec. 2-205 and 2-208).

   1. Trade usage — Any regular or customary practice or method of dealing in the particular place, trade or vocation, which one is justified in expecting will be observed with regard to the transaction.

   2. Course of dealings — Prior conduct of the parties, while engaged in similar transactions.

   3. Course of performance — Subsequent conduct of the parties, which is indicative of their intentions.

G. Unconscionability — Contracts or severable contract provisions, that are grossly unfair or one-sided, will not be enforced (Sec. 2-302).

III. Leases of goods.

A. Article 2A of the U.C.C., which repeats many of the provisions of Article 2, applies to transactions in which goods are leased rather than sold and to which neither Article 2 (Sales of Goods) nor Article 9 (Secured Transactions) apply.

B. Lease agreement — The understanding of the parties as to the transfer of the right to possession and use of the goods.

C. Parties.

1. Lessor — Person who sells the right to possession and use of goods under a lease.

2. Lessee — Person who acquires the right to possession and use of goods under a lease.

KEY WORDS AND PHRASES IN TEXT

The Uniform Commercial Code (U.C.C.) — Article 2
The sale of goods
Goods associated with real property
Goods associated with services
Merchants
Formation of a contract for the sale of goods (offer and acceptance)
Indefinite (or open) terms
Open price terms
Open payment terms
Open delivery terms
Duration of an ongoing contract
Options, cooperation, good faith and commercial reasonableness regarding performance
Merchant's firm offer
Methods of acceptance
Distinction between conforming and nonconforming goods
Goods shipped as an accommodation
Statute of Frauds provision in U.C.C.

Acceptance containing additional or different terms (when one or more of the parties is not a merchant and when all of the parties are merchants)
Modification that materially alters terms of contract (consideration not required but signed writing may be necessary)
Written confirmation when parties to contract are merchants
Specially manufactured goods
Admissions in pleadings or in court
Partial performance
Parol evidence rule
Prior course of dealings
Usage of trade
Course of performance
Unconscionability
Standard form contracts
Leases of goods
Lease agreement
Lessor
Lessee

FILL-IN QUESTIONS

1. A sale is a contract which provides for a ___transfer___ of title or ownership rights to existing, identified _goods or property_ for consideration known as the ___price___.

2. Article 2 of the Uniform Commercial Code contains special rules if the parties to a contract are ___merchants___, because they _deal in goods of the kind involved in the sales transaction_ or hold themselves out, because of their occupations, as having the special knowledge

and skills peculiar to the business or goods involved in the transaction, or employ others with such knowledge and skills.

3. In order for an offer to be effective at common law, all of the material terms must be clear, definite and certain. This rule is relaxed by the Uniform Commercial Code. For example, the _price_, and in output and requirements contracts the _quantity_ of goods, which are the subject matter of a contract of sale, may be left open.

4. A buyer and seller, in good faith, may modify a contract for the sale of goods in order to change the date upon which the goods are to be delivered without any _new consideration_. The modification would have to be in writing, signed by the seller, in order to be enforceable by the buyer, if _the contract as modified for a price of $500 or more_ or the agreement of the parties so provides.

5. If a merchant makes a written signed offer to buy or sell goods and gives an assurance that the offer will remain open, the offer is _irrevocable_ for the specified period of time if a period is stated or, if no time is specified, for a _reasonable_ period of time.

6. In general, an acceptance, which includes one or more terms that are different than or in addition to the terms contained in an offer for the sale of goods, will be treated as an effective acceptance. If one or more of the parties is not a _merchant_, the additional or changed terms will be construed as proposals for additions to or changes in the contract. Between _merchants_, the additional or changed terms become part of the contract unless (1) the offer limits acceptance to the terms contained in the offer, or (2) _additional or changed terms alter the offer_, or (3) notification of objection to the additions or changes has been or is given within a reasonable time after notice of the addition or change is received.

7. With regard to contracts for the sale of goods, the general rule is that, if the price of the goods is _$500 or more_, the contract is not enforceable unless there is a writing, which evidences the contract between the parties and which is signed by the party against whom enforcement is sought.

MULTIPLE CHOICE QUESTIONS

1. A contract providing for the transfer of title to four automobile tires is not covered by Article 2 of the Uniform Commercial Code if:
    a. the bargained for consideration is services to be performed by the recipient.
    b. there is no bargained for consideration given by the recipient.
    c. the tires are to be specially manufactured for an antique fire engine.
    d. the price for the tires is less than $500.

2. Article 2 of the Code applies to the sale of tangible, moveable personal property, including:
    a. minerals, if removed from realty by the buyer.
    b. things attached to realty, which are to be severed by the seller, without regard to the harm to the realty.
    c. things not yet in existence.
    d. unborn animals.

3. Polk owns 100 acres of woodland. He agrees to sell a specified amount of the timber growing on it to the Lewiston Lumber Co. and the right to extract coal from the land to the Comet Coal Co. for one year.
    a. The transaction with Lewiston Lumber Co. involves a sale of goods if the timber is to be cut by Lewiston.
    b. The transaction with Comet Coal Co. does not involve a sale of goods.
    c. The transaction with Lewiston Lumber Co. involves a sale of goods if the timber is to be cut by Polk.
    d. All of the above.

4. Ware orally contracts to specially manufacture two pairs of glasses with prescription lenses for Ohl for $600.
    a. The transaction is not covered by Article 2 of the Code because it provides for the sale of goods to be specially manufactured.
    b. The transaction is not covered by Article 2 of the Code because it is a contract for the performance of services.
    c. Although the agreed upon price is more than $500, the contract will be enforceable against Ohl because Ware sent a written confirmation of the agreement immediately and Ohl failed to object within ten days.
    d. Although the agreed upon price is more than $500, the contract will be enforceable against Ohl, if Ware has begun grinding the lenses, because the glasses are not suitable for resale in the ordinary course of business.

5. If it is established that a buyer and seller had contractual intent, their contract will be enforced even though:
    a. the buyer had not communicated his assent to the seller's offer.
    b. it provides for the sale of an illegal substance.
    c. it calls for the sale of all the carpeting manufactured at the seller's plant for one year, although the quantity of goods to be sold is indefinite.
    d. it calls for the sale of all the carpeting that the buyer may wish to buy for one year, because the quantity of goods to be sold is indefinite.

6. Lee is the owner of a clothing store. On January 2, she called the Demarre Dress Manufacturing Co. and placed an order for 100 dresses, at a price of $20 per dress, to be delivered on January 20. Lee refused to accept the dresses, which conformed to the contract, on January 20.
    a. Lee is liable to Demarre, if Demarre sent a writing on January 3, confirming the agreement, which was received by Lee, who did not respond.
    b. Lee is liable to Demarre, if Demarre sent a writing on January 3, stating that the price would be $25 per dress, which was received by Lee, who did not respond.
    c. Lee is liable to Demarre because the Statute of Frauds provision of the Code is not applicable when the buyer and seller of goods are both merchants.
    d. Lee is not liable to Demarre because the dresses were not delivered to her place of business.

7. A merchant's offer to sell goods states that it will remain open and not be revoked by the seller. The offer is revocable:
    a. unless consideration is given by the buyer if the offer is oral.
    b. unless the period of time, during which it is to be held open, is stated in the offer.
    c. unless the offer is evidenced by a writing, signed by the buyer.
    d. if the period of time, during which it is held open, is reasonable.

8. Wright Box Corp. offered to sell 1,000 #4 cardboard boxes at a price of $100 to the Pomfert Packing Co. and stated that it would not withdraw the offer for one month.
    a. The offer is a firm offer and irrevocable, without consideration, for three months, if it is in writing.
    b. The offer is a firm offer and irrevocable, without consideration, for the period stated, if it is in writing.
    c. The offer is a firm offer and irrevocable, without consideration, for a reasonable period of time, if it is oral.
    d. Pomfert Packing Co. is bound by the agreement, if it does not object within ten days.

9. Kabot agrees to sell and Long agrees to buy 100 pounds of flour at a price to be determined by Kabot, the seller.
    a. The flour is to be delivered at Long's place of business, because the parties did not expressly state where it was to be delivered.
    b. There is no contract, because the parties did not agree to the place of delivery.
    c. There is no contract, because Lond did not agree to a price.
    d. Long will be required to pay the price set in good faith by Kabot.

Chapter 17

SALES
Title, Risk, and
Insurable Interest

Although for some purposes, such as taxation, inheritance and creditors' rights, it is necessary to determine which party has title (rights of ownership) to the goods that are the subject matter of a contract for sale, under the Uniform Commercial Code, the concept of title does not have major importance in determining the rights and responsibilities of the parties to a sales transaction. To a great extent, it has been replaced by concepts of identification of the goods to the contract, risk of loss and insurable interest, which are explained in this chapter. These concepts affect the liabilities of the parties, if the goods are damaged, destroyed or lost, their rights to obtain insurance, as well as the rights of their creditors.

THINGS TO KEEP IN MIND

1. The rules discussed in the chapter apply only if the parties have not specified in their contract when identification of the goods or transfer of the risk will occur.

2. Goods that are in existence are usually identified when the contract is made, at which time the buyer has an insurable interest although he may neither have possession nor title nor bear the risk of loss.

3. If a buyer has a contract right to receive goods that are not in existence (future goods), the earliest point at which he or she has an insurable interest, bears the risk of loss or obtains title, is when the goods come into existence and are identified to the contract.

OUTLINE

I. Identification of the goods — Designation of goods that are the subject matter of a sales contract (Sec. 2-501).

A. Identification determines when the buyer has a right to obtain insurance on the goods, recover from a third person, who damages the goods and, in some cases, obtain the goods from the seller.

B. The parties may specify in their agreement when identification will occur.

C. If parties do not so specify, identification occurs:

1. At the time the contract is made, if goods are existing and identified.

2. In general, at the time future goods come into existence and are marked, shipped or identified by the seller.

D. Fungible goods.

1. Every unit is exactly like every other unit.

2. Fungible goods may be identified as a specified portion, weight or quantity of an identified bulk or larger mass.

II. Terms that are used when goods are being shipped, or transported, by a carrier.

A. The effect is to indicate whether or not certain charges are included in the price of the goods to be paid by the buyer and, therefore, whether the seller or buyer is to pay the charges.

B. The terms also are considered to be delivery terms (Sec. 2-319).

C. F.O.B. — Free on board at a stated place, which may be point of delivery or destination (Sec. 2-319).

D. F.A.S. —Free alongside a vessel at a port, which may be point of delivery or destination (Sec. 2-319).

E. C.I.F. — Price includes cost of goods and insurance and freight charges (Sec. 2-320).

F. C. & F. — Price includes cost of goods and freight charges (Sec. 2-320).

G. Delivery ex-ship — Seller's obligations do not end until the goods are delivered and unloaded from the carrying vessel at the specified port of destination (Sec. 2-322).

III. Passage of title (Sec. 2-401).

A. Title does not pass until goods are in existence and identified.

B. Parties may agree on manner of and conditions under which title passes.

C. Applicable rules, if parties have not otherwise agreed.

1. Existing goods, identified at the time of contracting.

    a. If contract does not provide for issuance of a document of title or delivery to a bailee, other than for movement or shipment — Title passes at time of contracting.

    b. If contract provides for delivery of document of title by the seller — Title passes at time and place document of title is delivered.

    c. If contract provides for goods to be held by a bailee without issuance of document of title — Title passes at time and place of contracting.

2. Future goods — Title passes when seller completes duty of physically delivering goods.

    a. Contract provides for shipment to buyer (F.O.B. point of shipment) — Title passes at time and place goods are delivered to carrier.

    b. Contract provides for delivery at destination (F.O.B. point of destination) — Title passes at time and place goods are tendered at specified destination.

D. Sale of goods on trial basis — Buyer has privilege of returning conforming goods to seller (Sec. 2-326).

1. Sale on approval — Goods are delivered primarily for use.

    a. Title passes to buyer upon approval (acceptance by buyer).

    b. Until that time, buyer's creditors have no rights with respect to the goods.

2. Sale or return — Goods are delivered primarily for resale.

    a. Title passes to buyer in accordance with III.B and III.C, *supra*, unless seller reserves title.

    b. Goods are subject to buyer's creditors' claims while they are in buyer's possession.

3. Consignment — Owner of goods (consignor) delivers goods to a consignee for sale by the consignee.

    a. If consignee sells goods, he or she pays consignor for the goods; if the goods are not sold, consignee returns them to consignor.

    b. While goods are in consignee's possession, consignee has title to them and consignment is treated as a sale or return transaction, unless consignor:
      1) Complies with applicable law providing for consignor's interest or the like to be evidenced by a sign; or
      2) Establishes that the consignee is generally known by his or her creditors to be in the business of selling the goods of others; or
      3) Complies with filing provisions relating to secured transactions.

IV. Transfer of risk of loss to buyer (Secs. 2-509 and 2-510).

A. Risk of loss does not shift to buyer until goods are in existence and identified.

B. Parties may agree as to how and when risk of loss will shift to buyer.

C. Applicable rules, if parties have not otherwise agreed.

   1. Existing goods identified at time of contracting.

      a. If contract does not provide for issuance of document of title or delivery to a bailee, other than for shipment or movement, risk is transferred to buyer:
        1) When buyer received goods from merchant seller.
        2) When nonmerchant seller tenders the goods.

      b. If the contract provides for delivery of negotiable document of title by the seller, risk is transferred to the buyer at time and place of buyer's receipt of document of title.

      c. If the contract provides for delivery of a nonnegotiable document of title by the seller, risk is transferred to the buyer after the buyer has received the document and has had a reasonable time to present it to the bailee and demand the goods.

      d. If the contract provides for goods to be held by bailee, without issuance of document of title, risk is transferred to buyer at time and place bailee acknowledges buyer's right to possession.

   2. Future goods — Seller completes duty of physically delivering goods.

      a. Shipment contract — Risk shifts to buyer at time and place goods are delivered to carrier.

      b. Destination contract — Risk shifts to buyer at time and place goods are tendered at specified destination.

D. Sale of goods on trial basis.

   1. Sale on approval — Goods are delivered for use.

      a. Risk of loss remains with seller until goods are accepted.

      b. Buyer must exercise right of returning goods within specified time or, if none is specified, a reasonable time, in which case seller bears expense of returning goods.

   2. Sale or return — Goods are delivered for resale.

      a. Risk of loss is on buyer.

      b. Buyer bears expense and risk of return.

E. Effect of breach of sales contract on risk of loss.

   1. Breach by seller.

      a. Defect in goods discovered immediately — Risk does not pass until defect cured or buyer knowingly accepts defective goods.

      b. Defect in goods discovered after goods accepted — Buyer can revoke acceptance. To the extent buyer is not covered by insurance, seller bears the loss.

   2. Breach by buyer.

      a. Loss shifts to buyer for a reasonable period of time after seller learns of breach by buyer, if goods are identified.

      b. To the extent seller is not covered by insurance, buyer bears the loss.

V. Insurable interest (Sec. 2-501).

  A. Insurance is discussed in Chapter 54.

  B. A buyer has an insurable interest:

   1. In existing goods that have been identified as soon as a sales contract is made.

   2. In future goods when the goods come into existence and are identified.

  C. A seller has an insurable interest as long as he or she retains title and, after title has passed, if he or she retains a security interest in the goods. (Security interests are discussed in Chapters 29 and 30.)

VI. Bulk transfers — A transfer (usually a sale) in bulk of a major portion of assets, such as inventory, materials, furniture, fixtures, etc., that is not in the ordinary course of the transferor's business.

  A. Effect is to jeopardize creditors' ability to collect debts owed by seller.

  B. Article 6 of the Code provides for giving notice to seller's creditors.

   1. As between seller and buyer, sale is valid, without compliance with Article 6.

   2. Buyer notifies seller's creditors at least ten days before sale so that they can protect their own interests.

      a. Seller furnishes list of creditors.

      b. Seller and buyer provide schedules of property.

   3. If Article 6 is not complied with, property in hands of buyer is subject to claims of seller's creditors within a specified period of time.

VII. Sales by nonowners (Sec. 2-403).

  A. One, who sells goods, can only transfer to another that interest which he or she has.

B. Imperfect title — Seller lacks good title because he or she does not possess full ownership rights.

    1. Void title — Purchaser, in good faith for value, from a seller, whose title was void, does not acquire title.

    2. Voidable title.

        a. A seller may avoid or disaffirm a contract for the sale of goods if he or she is a minor or if the buyer used fraud in order to induce the contract, etc., while the buyer has possession of the goods.

        b. If the buyer has resold the goods to one who is a good faith purchaser for value, the subsequent purchaser acquires valid title. The seller's only remedy is damages.

        c. If the buyer has resold the goods to one who is not a good faith purchaser for value, the actual owner (the original seller) can reclaim the goods from the subsequent purchaser.

C. Entrusting goods to nonowner — If an owner of goods entrusts possession of them to a merchant, who deals in that kind of goods, the merchant has power to transfer the entruster/owner's title to a purchaser in the ordinary course of business.

D. Seller's retention of sold goods — Retention is evidence of seller's intent to defraud creditors, unless seller is a merchant who retains possession for a "commercially reasonable time" for some legitimate purpose.

KEY WORDS AND PHRASES IN TEXT

Contract to sell goods
Passage of title
Goods that are in existence
Goods that are identified to the contract
Future goods
Fungible goods
Title passes when goods exist and are
    identified
Title may pass in accordance with terms
    of agreement
In absence of agreement, title passes
    when seller physically delivers goods
Shipment contracts
Destination contracts
Document of title (bill of lading or
    warehouse receipt)
Transfer of risk of loss
F.O.B., F.A.S., C.I.F., C. & F. and
    delivery ex-ship
Tender of delivery

Delivery of goods without movement
    or shipment
Delivery of goods to bailee
Sale on approval
Sale or return
Consignment
Risk of loss when there is a breach of
    contract for the sale of goods
Commercially reasonable time
Bulk transfer not made in the ordinary
    course of transferor's business
    (U.C.C. Article 6)
Sale by nonowners
Good title
Imperfect title (void or voidable title)
Good faith purchaser
Entrusting possession of goods
Seller's retention of sold goods
Insurable interest of buyer
Insurable interest of seller

FILL-IN QUESTIONS

1. A contract for the sale of goods may provide for a sale of goods presently in existence or <u>a K to sell goods in the future</u>

2. Identification of existing goods occurs at the time <u>K is formed</u>; identification of goods not yet in existence does not take place until the goods come into existence and are properly <u>marked, shipped</u> or identified by the seller.

3. If a buyer, who purchased goods for his or her own use, has a right to return conforming goods to the seller, the sale is a sale <u>on approval</u>; if he or she purchased the goods for resale, the transaction is a sale <u>or return</u>.

4. If the parties to a contract for the sale of goods do not indicate the place of delivery or the manner in which the goods are to be delivered, the place of delivery is the merchant <u>seller's place of business</u>, and the price of the goods does not include charges for shipment, storage or insurance.

5. If parties have not otherwise agreed in their contract for the sale of existing goods to be delivered by a merchant seller to the buyer, title passes and the buyer has an insurable interest at the time <u>of contracting</u> but the risk of loss is not transferred to the buyer until <u>buyer receives goods from merchant</u>.

6. A contract for the sale of future goods, that are to be shipped from the seller to the buyer, may indicate which of the parties is to pay certain transportation and other charges. F.O.B. means <u>free on board</u> at a stated place, and F.A.S. means <u>free along side</u> a vessel at a port. If the stated place is in the city, or port, in which the buyer is located, the <u>seller</u> must pay the shipping charges. These terms also are treated as delivery terms and determine when title and <u>risk of loss</u> shifts from the seller to the buyer.

7. C.I.F. indicates that the price of the goods includes their cost and <u>insurance & freight costs</u>. C. & F. indicates that the price of the goods includes their cost and <u>freight charges</u>.

8. If parties have agreed in their contract for the sale of future goods that the goods are to be shipped F.O.B. to a carrier in the city in which the seller maintains its business, it is a <u>shipment</u> contract. Title and risk of loss to the buyer will pass when the goods are <u>delivered to carrier</u>, although the buyer has <u>an insurable interest</u> when the goods come into existence and are identified.

MULTIPLE CHOICE QUESTIONS

1. Under a contract for sale of goods, a buyer may return goods after they have been delivered but before they are accepted.
   a. If the goods are the kind that are used by the buyer, the buyer's creditors can make a claim with regard to the goods.
   b. If the goods are the kind that are used by the buyer, and they are stolen, the risk of loss falls on the buyer.
   c. If the goods have been purchased for ultimate resale by the buyer, the buyer's creditors can make a claim with regard to the goods.

d. If the goods have been purchased for ultimate resale by the buyer, the seller bears the expense of returning the goods, if the buyer exercises his right of returning the goods.

2. In general, the buyer is deemed to have waived his right of inspection when an agreement for sale is:
a. a shipment contract.
b. a destination contract.
c. an identification.
d. a documentary sale.

3. Frank lent his bicycle to his friend, Pat. Pat then sold the bicycle to Bob for a fair price. Bob did not know how Pat had acquired the bicycle. When Frank learned what Pat had done, he demanded that Bob return the bicycle to him.
a. Frank can enforce his demand.
b. Frank cannot enforce his demand, because he was not a minor.
c. Frank can enforce his demand only if Pat was the owner of a bicycle store and Bob was a customer.
d. Frank can enforce his demand only if Pat was insolvent at the time of the sale.

4. On Monday, Frankel purchased a bicycle for $150 from The Cycle Shop but left it with the seller so that some adjustments could be made. On Tuesday, Brady purchased the bicycle for $155, without knowing that it was Frankel's property. The sale to Brady was:
a. effective because the Cycle Shop's title was voidable, because Frankel was a minor.
b. effective because Frankel had entrusted the bicycle to the Cycle Shop, which dealt in bicycles.
c. not effective because the Cycle Shop did not have title to the bicycle.
d. not effective because the Cycle Shop's title was void.

5. Theeve stole two personal computers from the Own P C Store. He sold one to Abby for $1,000 and gave one to Bob as a gift.
a. Own P C Store does not have a right to recover either the computer sold to Abby or the one given by Theeve to Bob.
b. Own P C Store has a right to recover both the computer sold to Abby and the one given by Theeve to Bob.
c. Own P C Store has a right to recover the computer that Theeve gave to Bob because he was not a purchaser for value but cannot recover the computer purchased by Abby.
d. Own P C Store has the right to recover the computer that Theeve gave to Bob if Bob subsequently sold it to Carla for $1,010.

6. Krupp sold all of his business property to Stone. Caruso, a creditor of Krupp, will be able to reach some of this property because the bulk transfer was ineffective because:
a. a schedule of the property to be transferred was not filed with a court thirty days prior to the bulk transfer by Krupp or Stone.
b. the list of creditors and schedule of property which was transferred was not retained for two years after the bulk transfer.
c. although Stone did not know it, Krupp did not prepare a complete, accurate list of her creditors.

    d. Stone did not request that Krupp supply him with a complete, accurate list of her creditors.

7. The provisions relating to bulk sales and transfers in Article 6 of the UCC:
    a. protects the creditors of the seller. As a general rule, if the Code is complied with, such creditors must look to the proceeds of the sale only.
    b. protects the creditors of the buyer. As a general rule, if the Code is not complied with, such creditors must look to the proceeds of the sale only.
    c. requires that a list of creditors and a schedule of property be filed with a designated official of the State or Country.
    d. must be complied with in order that the contract of sale be enforceable by a seller against a buyer.

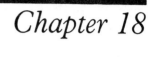*Chapter 18*

SALES
Performance
and Obligation

As is true of any contract, the parties to a contract for the sale of goods assume certain express duties to perform in accordance with their agreement—the seller to transfer and deliver and the buyer to accept and pay for goods that conform to the contract. In addition, the Uniform Commercial Code imposes obligations on each of the parties to exercise good faith in performing and to do nothing to impair the expectations of the other party that the contract will be duly performed.

THINGS TO KEEP IN MIND

1. Many of the seemingly intricate rules explained in this chapter are effective if the parties have used certain commercial terms, with which you should become familiar. Often, if you give some thought to it, you will realize that the consequences of using a particular term is implicit from the wording of the term itself.

2. In the law of sales, the word "delivery" does not necessarily mean a physical delivery of the goods. A seller is required to make the goods available to the buyer, which may be accomplished by a tender of delivery of a document of title, rather than the goods themselves.

OUTLINE

I. Duty of good faith and commercial reasonableness — Standards of good faith and commercial reasonableness are read into every contract for the sale of goods.

   A. If a party is to fill in particulars of performance, he or she must do so "in good faith and within limits set by commercial reasonableness" (Sec. 2-311).

B. In the case of a merchant, this means honesty and "observance of reasonable commercial standards of fair dealing" (Sec. 2-103(1)(b)).

C. Parties are expected to be cooperative and not take advantage of each other.

II. Performance of a sales contract — The seller has an obligation to transfer and deliver goods that conform to the contract and the buyer has an obligation to accept and pay for them (Sec. 2-301).

A. If the parties have not otherwise agreed, the obligations of the seller and buyer to perform are concurrent conditions.

B. A party must either perform as required by the contract or, under certain circumstances, tender correct performance or be excused from tendering his or her performance.

III. The seller's obligations.

A. Tender of delivery (Sec. 2-503).

1. Tender of delivery by the seller must occur at a reasonable time and in a reasonable manner.

2. A seller, holding conforming goods, must give reasonable notice to the buyer to enable him or her to take delivery.

3. Place of delivery. (Also see Chapter 17.)

a. In situations in which the place of delivery is not specified and transportation by carrier is not required, the place of delivery is:
1) Seller's place of business; if he or she has none, seller's residence.
2) When the parties know that goods are at a location, other than the seller's place of business, at that location.
3) When the goods are held by a bailee, seller tenders delivery of document, which will enable the buyer to obtain goods (Sec. 2-308).

b. Carrier cases (Secs. 2-319 through 2-322).
1) Shipment contract — Seller must:
a) Put goods in carrier's possession, and
b) Make reasonable contract for transportation of the goods,
c) Deliver or tender to the buyer any documents necessary to enable the buyer to obtain possession of goods from carrier, and
d) Notify buyer promptly of shipment.
2) Destination contract — Seller must tender conforming goods at specified destination.
3) Delivery F.O.B. (free on board) at a named place — Seller's duty, risk and expense ends when goods are at the designated place.
4) Delivery F.A.S. (free alongside) to a named vessel — Shipment contract — Seller's duty, risk and expense ends when goods are delivered to dock and seller obtains receipt (usually the bill of lading), which is tendered to the buyer.

    5) Delivery ex-ship (from the carrying vessel) — Destination contract — Seller bears duty, risk and expense until the goods are unloaded.

    6) C.I.F. (purchase price includes cost of the goods, insurance during transit and freight charges) — Shipment contract.
      a) Seller is obligated to load goods, pay freight, obtain proper insurance, receipt and other necessary documents, prepare invoice and tender all documents to buyer.
      b) Risk of loss is borne by buyer.
      c) C. & F. — Price includes cost of goods and freight charges.

B. Perfect tender rule — In order to be entitled to payment, the seller is required to tender conforming goods in a manner that accords completely to the terms of the contract.

  1. If the goods and/or tender do not conform to the contract, the buyer may:

    a. Reject all the goods, or

    b. Accept all the goods, or

    c. Accept some and reject the rest of the goods (Sec. 2-601).

  2. Exceptions.

    a. Parties may agree otherwise.

    b. Cure — Seller may repair, replace or, in some cases, make a price adjustment for nonconforming goods.
      1) Buyer is required to disclose nature of defect.
      2) If time for delivery has not expired, seller is merely required to give notice of intention to give proper delivery and make such delivery within contracted time.
      3) If seller delivered nonconforming goods reasonably believing that the buyer would accept tender of nonconforming goods, but buyer rejects the goods, seller has a reasonable time within which to make proper delivery (cure) after giving notice to buyer, even though contracted time for delivery has expired (Sec. 2-508).

    c. If there is no material delay or loss, the buyer may not reject the goods because of inappropriate shipping arrangements (Sec. 2-504).

    d. Seller may substitute a different means of delivery, if the agreed manner of delivery becomes impracticable or impossible to use, without fault of the seller (Sec. 2-614).

    e. Installment contract — Delivery of goods in installments may be contemplated in the contract or because of circumstances necessitating delivery in lots (Secs. 2-307 and 2-612).
      1) Buyer may reject a nonconforming installment, which cannot be cured and which substantially impairs the value of the installment.
      2) There is a breach of the entire contract if one or more nonconforming installments substantially impair the value of the entire contract.

      f. Commercial impracticability — If performance of a contract is commercially impracticable because of an unforeseen supervening occurrence, not contemplated by the parties at the time of contracting, nondelivery or a delay in delivery does not constitute a breach (Sec. 2-615).

      g. Destruction of identified goods without fault of either party before risk of loss passes to buyer (Sec. 2-613).
        1) Seller is excused from performing, if the goods are totally destroyed.
        2) If the goods are partially destroyed, the buyer may:
          a) Treat the contract as avoided, or
          b) Accept the goods with a deduction from the contract price.

IV. The buyer's obligations.

A. The buyer is obligated to accept the goods and to pay for them in accordance with the terms of the contract for sale (Secs. 2-301 and 2-607).

B. Payment — If no provision is made in the contract:

  1. Unless sale is made on credit, payment is to be made at the time and place that the goods are received by the buyer (Sec. 2-511).

  2. Payment can be in cash or another commercially acceptable medium (Sec. 2-511).

  3. If sale is made on credit, the credit period begins on the date of shipment (Sec. 2-310).

C. Right to inspection of goods (Sec. 2-513).

  1. Buyer has a right to inspect goods before making payment unless buyer has agreed to:

    a. C.O.D. (collect on delivery) shipment, or

    b. Payment upon presentation of document of title. (This is so when a bill of lading is tendered with a C.I.F. or C. & F. contract.) (Sec. 2-513.)

  2. Place, time and manner of inspection must be reasonable.

D. Acceptance (Sec. 2-606).

  1. Manifested expressly or by conduct if buyer:

    a. After opportunity to inspect, indicates that the goods are conforming or that they are acceptable despite nonconformity.

    b. After opportunity to inspect, fails to reject the goods.

    c. Performs an act that is inconsistent with the seller's ownership.

  2. Acceptance may be revoked by notifying seller of a breach within a reasonable period after buyer discovers or should have discovered the breach (Sec. 2-607).

V. Right to adequate assurance of performance (Sec. 2-609) and to cooperation (Sec. 2-311).

   A. If either the seller or buyer has reasonable grounds to believe that the other party will not perform, he or she may make a written demand for reasonable "adequate assurance of due performance."

   B. Until such assurance is received, the party who has reasonable grounds for insecurity may suspend performance for which he or she did not receive consideration.

   C. When one party's performance depends on the other's cooperation, and cooperation is not forthcoming, the other party can suspend performance.

VI. Anticipatory repudiation — If, prior to the time for performance, either party communicates his or her intention not to perform to the other party, the aggrieved party may:

   A. Wait for the other party to perform correctly or retract the repudiation.

   B. Resort to an appropriate remedy.

   C. Suspend his or her own performance (Sec. 2-610).

KEY WORDS AND PHRASES IN TEXT

Both buyer and seller owe duties of
   exercising good faith and cooperation
Commercial reasonableness
Performance of contract for sale of goods
Seller's duty to transfer and deliver
   conforming goods
Buyer's duty to accept and pay for
   conforming goods
Seller's obligation to deliver goods and
   buyer's obligation to pay in
   accordance with the contract are
   concurrent conditions of performance
Seller's obligation to tender delivery of
   conforming goods
Place of delivery
Shipment contracts
Destination contracts
The perfect tender rule
Cure

Substitution of carriers
Contracts providing for delivery of goods
   in installments
Substantial impairment of value of
   contract
Commercial impracticability
Destruction of identified goods
Buyer's obligations
Credit period
Buyer's right to inspect
C.O.D. (collect on delivery) shipments
Payment due upon receipt of document
   of title
Acceptance of delivered goods by buyer
Revocation of acceptance
Notice of revocation
Partial acceptance
Assurance of due performance
Anticipatory repudiation

FILL-IN QUESTIONS

1. In order to perform, a seller is obligated to transfer and deliver goods _that conform to the K_____ to the buyer, who has an obligation to accept and _pay for_____ the goods. If the parties have not otherwise specified, the seller's

and buyer's obligations are to be rendered at the same time because they are _Concurrent_ conditions.

2. If a seller is to deliver goods to a carrier under a shipment contract, the seller is required to (1) _put goods in possession of carrier_, (2) make a commercially reasonable contract for transportation, and (3) promptly notify the buyer.

3. Delivery F.A.S. and ex-ship are terms used when goods are to be transported by ship. If delivery is F.A.S. a named vessel, the seller's duty ends when the goods are _delivered to dock "alongside" of ship_ and the seller obtains a receipt, which is duly tendered to the buyer. If the goods are to be delivered ex-ship, the seller's duty, risk and expense continue until the goods are _unloaded_.

4. The distinction between a C.I.F. and a C. & F. contract is that, with a C.I.F. contract, the purchase price includes the cost of the goods, _insurance during transit_ and _transportation or freight charges_, whereas with a C. & F. contract, only the _cost of goods + transp. + fr. charges_ are included. With both C.I.F. and C. & F. contracts, the risk of loss during shipment is borne by the _buyer_.

5. If a seller tenders goods that do not conform to the contract, the buyer has a number of options. He or she may (1) _accept all goods_, (2) _reject all goods_, or (3) _accept some + not others that don't conform_.

6. When the parties have not indicated any terms of payment but goods have been properly tendered for delivery by a seller, a buyer has an obligation to pay at the time and place the goods are _received by buyer_ by using cash or _any other acceptable method_ for payment.

7. If, before the date when his or her performance is due, one party to a contract for the sale of goods indicates that he or she clearly does not intend to perform in accordance with the contract, an _anticipatory breach_ has occurred.

MULTIPLE CHOICE QUESTIONS

1. Upon the delivery of nonconforming goods, a buyer may:
    a. reject all the goods.
    b. accept all the goods.
    c. accept those units which conform but reject the rest.
    d. all of the above.

2. Beyer, in Kansas City, Missouri, ordered 1,000 fully described pots and pans from Deelar, a wholesaler, in Pittsburgh, Pennsylvania. The pots and pans were in existence and to be shipped by truck. If the pots and pans were to be shipped:
    a. F.O.B. Kansas City, and the goods were lost in transit, the risk of loss is borne by Beyer.
    b. F.O.B. Kansas City, and the goods were lost in transit, the risk of loss is borne by Deelar.
    c. C.I.F. and the goods were lost in transit, the risk of loss is borne by Deelar.
    d. C. & F. and the goods were lost in transit, the risk of loss is borne by Deelar.

3. The New England Candy Co. of Boston, Massachusetts, contracted for the purchase of a stated quantity of sugar from Sweet Sugar Inc. of Louisiana. Assume that the contract provided that the sugar was to be shipped:
   a. F.O.B. Boston. The expense of loading is borne by New England Candy Co.
   b. F.A.S. Coastal Queen (a freighter), New Orleans. The expense of loading is borne by Sweet Sugar Inc.
   c. Ex-ship Boston. The expense of loading is borne by Sweet Sugar Inc.
   d. C. & F. The expense of loading is borne by New England Candy Co.

4. The New England Candy Co. of Boston, Massachusetts, contracted for the purchase of a stated quantity of sugar from Sweet Sugar Inc. of Louisiana. Assume that the contract provided that the sugar was to be shipped by sea, to arrive November 1.
   a. Assume that Sweet Sugar learns that shipment by truck will be less expensive and ships by truck, rather than by sea in accordance with the contract. New England Candy Co. may reject the goods, which arrived on October 30 in Boston because of the seller's failure to make a perfect tender.
   b. Assume that there is a hurricane off the coast of New Orleans and that Sweet Sugar, therefore, ships the sugar by truck, rather than by sea. New England Candy Co. may not reject the goods, which arrived on October 30 in Boston, because of Sweet Sugar's failure to perform in accordance with the contract.
   c. Assume that the goods arrived by ship in Boston on October 30 but were stolen from the vessel on October 31. New England Candy Co. bears the risk of the loss, even though Sweet Sugar failed to notify it that the goods were being shipped.
   d. Assume that the goods arrived by ship in Boston on October 30 but were stolen from the vessel on October 31. Sweet Sugar bears the risk of loss, even though it sent and New England Candy received the bill of lading through normal banking channels.

5. Shuman Auto Parts Inc. entered into a contract for the sale of 3,000 spark plugs to Wright Auto Supplies Distribution Co. The 3,000 spark plugs were marked, packaged and held by Shuman at its plant. Wright was notified that the spark plugs were available. A week later, a fire occurred at Shuman's plant and the spark plugs were destroyed.
   a. If no delivery terms were specified in the contract for the sale of the spark plugs, Shuman made a tender of delivery and has fully performed its contractual obligations.
   b. Shuman is excused from performing because identified goods were destroyed before the risk of loss was transferred to Wright.
   c. Both Shuman and Wright are excused from performing because of commercial impracticability.
   d. Wright may treat the contract as avoided because the goods have been destroyed.

6. The Bertown Bridge Club placed an order for 100 decks of playing cards with McDonald. No date was specified for delivery. A week later, McDonald tendered 100 decks of cards to the Bridge Club. The Bridge Club discovered that 50 of the decks were missing the ace of diamonds and immediately notified McDonald that the goods were nonconforming and unacceptable.
   a. McDonald's action may be treated as an anticipatory repudiation. The Bertown Bridge Club can, therefore, suspend its performance.
   b. The Bertown Bridge Club's action may be treated as an anticipatory repudiation. McDonald may, therefore, sue the Bridge Club for damages.

    c. McDonald will cure the defect by supplying the missing aces of diamonds within a reasonable period of time.

    d. McDonald will cure the defect by reducing the price of the 50 decks by three percent.

7. Selk and Buckingham had a contract for the sale of three electric typewriters, which were delivered by the seller, Selk, in the manner prescribed by the contract. Buckingham has a right to inspect the typewriters before paying for them:

    a. unless Selk notified Buckingham that the typewriters did not conform to the contract because they were green instead of blue and were being shipped as an accommodation.

    b. unless the contract specified that the typewriters were to be shipped C.O.D.

    c. only if the contract so provided.

    d. only if Buckingham accepts delivery at Selk's place of business.

8. Schain had delivered ten window screens to Barton in the manner prescribed by the contract of sale, and Barton paid for the screens.

    a. If Barton resells the screens to a third person, Barton will be treated as having accepted them.

    b. If Barton discovered that the screens were defective three months later, while she was putting them up, and notified Schain of the defect, Barton will not be treated as having accepted them.

    c. If Barton discovered that the screens were defective three months later, while putting them up, but did not notify Schain of the defect for six months, Barton will not be treated as having accepted them.

    d. If Barton inspected the screens when they were delivered, without noticing the defects, which became apparent when she put the screens up, Barton may not revoke her acceptance.

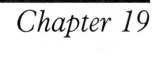

Chapter 19

SALES
Remedies of
Buyer and
Seller for Breach

If one of the parties to a contract for the sale of goods repudiates the contract or fails to properly perform or becomes insolvent, a number of different remedies are available to the aggrieved party under the Uniform Commercial Code. The reason for the variety of remedies is to ensure that appropriate relief will be afforded to an aggrieved party in order to put him or her in as good a position as he or she would have been had the other party correctly performed (Sec. 1-106). Parties to a sales contract may, if they wish, create or provide their own remedies as well.

THINGS TO KEEP IN MIND

Some of the Code remedies revolve around acceptance by a buyer of identified, conforming goods. Acceptance usually is signified by (1) receipt and retention of goods by a buyer, after inspection reveals that the goods conform to the contract, or (2) an indication by a buyer that he or she will take nonconforming goods, or (3) the failure of a buyer to reject.

OUTLINE

I. Rights and remedies of the seller.

    A. Seller's lien (Sec. 2-703) — Seller has a right to retain possession of goods until receipt of payment of the price, unless right is waived or lost by:

        1. Express agreement of the parties.

        2. Acts inconsistent with its existence. If transaction is a sale on credit, seller has no right to lien until credit period expires or buyer becomes insolvent.

3. Payment or tender of payment by buyer. If buyer gives a promissory note, lien is not discharged until note is paid.

4. Unconditional and voluntary delivery of the goods to the buyer or a bailee or agent of the buyer.

B. Withhold delivery of goods — Seller may retain goods if:

1. There is a breach of contract by the buyer or buyer repudiates part of contract by wrongfully rejecting, revoking acceptance or failing to make proper payment (Sec. 2-703).

2. Buyer becomes insolvent (Sec. 2-702(1)).

C. Stop delivery of goods (Sec. 2-705).

1. Seller may stop the goods in hands of carrier or other bailee.

a. If there has been a breach of the contract by the buyer, seller may stop carload or other large shipment.

b. If buyer is insolvent, size of shipment is immaterial.

2. Seller must give timely notice to bailee and pay any charges resulting from the stoppage. Bailee need not obey, if negotiable document of title, which had been issued, is not surrendered.

3. Right to stop in transit ends when:

a. Buyer receives goods.
    1) Physical possession, or
    2) Bailee, other than carrier, acknowledges to buyer that goods are held for the buyer.

b. Carrier acknowledges to buyer that goods are held by reshipment or as a warehouse.

c. Negotiable document of title has been negotiated to buyer.

D. Reclaim goods in possession of an insolvent buyer (Sec. 2-702).

1. Within ten days after buyer's receipt of the goods.

2. Anytime, if buyer misrepresented his solvency, in writing, within three months prior to delivery of the goods.

3. Right to reclaim is lost, if buyer resold goods to good faith purchaser.

E. Identify goods to contract notwithstanding fact that there has been a breach of contract by the buyer (Sec. 2-704).

1. When goods are identified to the contract, seller may hold buyer liable to pay purchase price or resell the goods.

2. Seller may identify:

    a. Goods that are finished and conform to the contract.

    b. Unfinished goods. Seller must exercise reasonable commercial judgment in order to mitigate loss and either:
      1) Cease manufacturing and resell for scrap or salvage value, or
      2) Complete manufacturing and identify goods.

F. Resell the goods (Sec. 2-706).

  1. Buyer wrongfully rejected goods or revoked acceptance, failed to pay or repudiated contract.

  2. Seller has possession of goods, because of proper withholding, stoppage in transit or reclamation.

  3. Resale must be made in good faith in a commercially reasonable manner; it may be public or private.

  4. Seller must give buyer reasonable notice of resale, unless goods are perishable.

  5. Seller may recover:

    a. Difference between resale price and contract price, and

    b. Incidental damages.

  6. Seller is not liable to buyer for any profits made at resale.

  7. Purchaser at sale takes free of any claims of buyer to the goods.

G. Recover purchase price plus incidental damages (Secs. 2-709 and 2-710).

  1. Buyer accepted goods and has not revoked acceptance.

  2. Conforming goods were lost or damaged after risk of loss passed to buyer.

  3. Breach of contract by buyer occurred after goods were identified, but seller is unable to resell them at a reasonable price.

H. Sue for damages (Sec. 2-708) — Usually the measure of damages is the difference between the contract price and the market price at the time and place of tender of goods.

I. Cancel contract.

  1. Buyer wrongfully rejects goods, revokes acceptance of conforming goods, fails to pay for the goods or repudiates (Sec. 2-703).

  2. All unperformed duties of buyer and seller are terminated, but seller may sue for breach of contract (Sec. 2-106(4)).

J. No right to repossession of goods — Unless provided for in contract.

II. Rights and remedies of buyer.

A. Reject nonconforming or improperly delivered goods (Sec. 2-601) — Buyer may:

1. Reject all the goods,

2. Accept all the goods, or

3. Accept one or more commercial unit or units and reject remainder.

B. Revoke acceptance (Sec. 2-608).

1. Buyer accepted goods without knowing that they were nonconforming.

a. Defect difficult to discover.

b. Buyer assumed nonconformity would be cured, but it was not.

2. Buyer notified seller within a reasonable time after defect was discovered or should have been discovered, and before any substantial change in condition of goods, not caused by defect, occurred.

3. Defect substantially impaired the value of the goods to the buyer.

C. Cover (Sec. 2-712).

1. Buyer contracts with another seller for purchase of goods in substitution for those due from seller if:

a. Buyer rightfully rejected or revoked acceptance of goods.

b. Seller repudiated contract or failed to deliver goods.

2. Measure of damages is the difference between cost of cover (= market price) and contract price plus consequential and incidental damages.

3. Buyer is not required to cover and may seek alternative remedy.

D. Recover damages.

1. For nondelivery or repudiation of contract (Sec. 2-713) — Measure of damages is difference between market price when buyer learned of breach and contract price, plus any incidental and consequential damages, less expenses saved because of seller's breach.

2. For breach, although nonconforming goods were accepted by the buyer and notice given to seller.

a. Damages resulting from seller's breach of contract.

b. Damages resulting from seller's breach of warranty.

       1) Measure — Difference, at time and place of acceptance, between value of goods as accepted and value that they would have had if they had been as warranted.

       2) If goods were resold by the buyer and he or she is sued by his or her customer, buyer may:

          a) Notify original seller of pending litigation. Notice may provide that seller may come in and defend and, if seller does not do so, he or she is bound by determination.

          b) Defend against customer's suit and later bring action against seller.

E. Recover identified goods upon seller's insolvency (Sec. 2-502).

   1. Seller becomes insolvent within ten days after receiving first payment.

   2. Buyer tenders unpaid balance of purchase price.

F. Obtain specific performance (Sec. 2-716(1)) — When goods are unique or buyer's remedy at law is inadequate.

G. Bring action to replevin the goods (Sec. 2-716(3)) — Recover identified goods in possession of a seller, who is wrongfully withholding them, when buyer is unable to effect cover.

H. Retain and enforce security interest in the goods (Sec. 2-711(3)) — After breach by seller, buyer may enforce a security interest for any payments of price made and reasonable expenses incurred.

I. Cancel the contract (Sec. 2-711(1)).

   1. Seller wrongfully fails to make proper delivery or repudiates contract or buyer rightfully rejects or revokes acceptance of the goods.

   2. Right to cancel may be lost, if buyer delays in exercising right.

   3. All unperformed duties of buyer and seller are terminated, but buyer may sue for breach of contract occurring before cancellation.

J. Sue seller for fraud under applicable state law.

III. Statute of limitations.

A. Actions for breach of sales contract, brought under Uniform Commercial Code, must be commenced within four years after the cause of action arose (Sec. 2-725).

   1. Cause of action for breach of warranty accrues when seller makes tender of delivery, even though buyer did not know of defect.

   2. A breach of future performance warranties does not occur until time for performance begins.

B. Causes of action, based upon non-Code claims, are subject to applicable state statutes of limitations.

IV. Contractual provisions affecting remedies.

    A. Liquidation of damages (Sec. 2-718) — Must be reasonable and approximately equal to anticipated or actual loss caused by the breach.

    B. Limitation of remedies (Sec. 2-719).

        1. Buyer and seller may expressly provide for additional remedies, substitute remedies, a different measure of damages or that a particular remedy be an exclusive or sole remedy.

        2. If circumstances cause the purpose of an exclusive remedy to fail, the aggrieved party may pursue remedies provided by the Uniform Commercial Code.

        3. A limitation or exclusion of consequential damages will be enforced, unless it is unconscionable.

    C. Waiver of defenses — The buyer may agree, in the contract for sale, that he or she will not assert defenses, which he or she has against the seller, against an assignee or holders to whom commercial paper is transferred.

V. Lemon laws.

    A. When an automobile, which is under warranty, has a defect that significantly affects its value or use and the defect has not been remedied by the seller within a specified number of opportunities, the buyer has a right to a new car, replacement of defective parts or return of all consideration paid.

    B. Usually, disputes are heard by arbitration panels such as appeal juries.

KEY WORDS AND PHRASES IN TEXT

Seller's right to withhold delivery of goods

Seller's right to stop delivery of goods while they are in transit

Seller's right to reclaim goods that are in the possession of an insolvent buyer

Seller's right to identify and/or resell goods after learning of buyer's breach of contract

Seller's right to resell the goods

Seller's right to recover the purchase price plus incidental and consequential damages

Seller's right to damages for buyer's wrongful repudiation or nonacceptance of the goods

Seller's right to cancel the contract

Seller's lien

Buyer's right to reject nonconforming or improperly delivered goods

Rejection must be timely and reasons given for rejection

Merchant buyer's duties when goods are rejected

Buyer's right to recover identified goods from an insolvent seller

Buyer's right to obtain specific performance

Buyer's right to bring action for replevin of the goods

Buyer, who has rightfully rejected goods or revoked acceptance, has right to retain goods in order to enforce a security interest in the goods

Buyer's right to cancel the contract

Buyer's right of cover

Buyer's right to recover damages for nondelivery or repudiation by seller

Buyer's right to recover damages for breach when goods are nonconforming or defective

Measure of damages for breach of warranty

Buyer's rights with respect to the seller when a purchaser from the buyer sues the buyer for breach of warranty

Statute of limitations

Liquidated damages

Limitations of remedies

Limiting consequential damages

Waiver of defenses

Lemon laws

FILL-IN QUESTIONS

1. If there is a breach of contract by a buyer who wrongfully rejects goods, revokes a prior acceptance, fails to make a proper payment or repudiates part of a sales contract, or becomes insolvent, a seller may _withhold delivery of goods_ or _stop delivery in possession of bailee_ .

2. If there is a wrongful breach or repudiation of a sales contract, a seller may:
    (1) exercise his or her seller's lien;
    (2) _recover purchase price_ ;
    (3) _sue for damages_ ;
    (4) _identify goods to the K_ ;
    (5) _resell goods that he has in possession_ ; or
    (6) _cancel K_ .

3. If a buyer becomes insolvent, the seller may, under certain circumstances, _reclaim goods from buyer_ .

4. If there is a breach of a sales contract by a seller, prior to acceptance by the buyer, the buyer may:
    (1) reject nonconforming or improperly delivered goods;
    (2) _recover identified goods if seller is insolvent (within 10 days of payment)_ ;
    (3) _effect cover by contracting for substitute goods_ ;
    (4) _replevin the goods_ ;
    (5) _obtain order for specific performance_ ;
    (6) _sue for damages_ ;
    (7) _cancel K_ ; or
    (8) _resell properly rejected goods if there is a security interest_ .

5. A seller can recover the contract price as compensatory damages if the buyer has not paid for goods, which have been _accepted_ , or if the buyer has _rejected_ the goods and the goods cannot be reasonably resold.

6. When a seller has failed to deliver goods, in most cases, the measure of the damages that the buyer can recover is the difference between _K price_ and the cost of cover in addition to any _incidental_ or consequential damages.

7. A stipulated damages clause is enforceable as a liquidated damages clause provided

the amount or formula is __reasonable__ and approximately equal to the anticipated or actual harm caused by the breach of contract.

MULTIPLE CHOICE QUESTIONS

1. Salisbury sold a refrigerator to Benton, who paid for it with a check. Benton stopped payment on the check before Salisbury cashed it.
   a. Salisbury has a right to take and retain the refrigerator.
   b. Salisbury does not have the right to exercise a seller's lien.
   c. Salisbury has the right to take and retain the refrigerator, if it is in the possession of a good faith purchaser in the ordinary course of Benton's business.
   d. Salisbury has the right to revoke the buyer's acceptance.

2. If there is a breach of a contract of sale by the buyer, the seller may stop the delivery of goods in the possession of a carrier when:
   a. the size of the shipment is a carload or less.
   b. the carrier acknowledged to the buyer that it was holding the goods for the buyer as a warehouseman.
   c. the seller gives timely notice to the carrier and surrenders a negotiable document of title to the carrier.
   d. a negotiable document of title has been negotiated to the buyer.

3. Edson purchased a radio from the Radio Store for cash. Later Ogden, a competitor of the Radio Store, demanded that Edson turn over the radio to him, because he (Ogden) could prove that it had been stolen from his store. Edson relinquished the radio to Ogden and demanded his money back from the Radio Store.
   a. Edson will not be able to get his money back, because the doctrine of *caveat emptor* is applicable.
   b. Edson will not be able to get his money back, because the contract of sale provided that the seller make no express warranties.
   c. Edson will be able to get his money back, because of the breach of warranty of merchantability by the Radio Store.
   d. Edson will be able to get his money back, because of the breach of warranty of good title by the Radio Store.

Questions 4 and 5 are based on the following fact situation: Fleur Sweater Co. purchased yarn from Scott Yarns Inc., a manufacturer of yarn. The yarn was delivered, accepted and paid for by the buyer. The yarn was used to manufacture 5,000 sweaters, which were subsequently sold throughout the United States. Months after the sweaters had been sold to consumers, Fleur Sweater Co. began to receive complaints that, due to defects in the yarn, the sweaters were disintegrating. Fleur Sweater Co. notified Scott Yarns Inc. that, unless it came into the litigation, it would be bound by any and all judicial determinations. Scott Yarns Inc. has not responded.

4. Fleur Sweater Co. can successfully:
   a. sue Scott Yarns Inc. for money damages, including the amounts consumers have recovered from it.
   b. revoke its acceptance of the yarn.
   c. exercise its remedy of cover.
   d. all of the above.

5. Assume that the contract for the sale of the yarn had been made in January 1986; the yarn was delivered and accepted by Fleur Sweater Co. in March 1986; the sweaters were manufactured in April 1986; the sweaters were sold to consumers in 1987 and 1988; and complaints were first received from consumers in February 1988.
   a. Scott Yarns Inc. can cancel its contract with Fleur Sweater Co.
   b. Fleur Sweater Co. will not be able to obtain money damages for breach of warranty.
   c. Fleur Sweater Co. will be able to exercise its remedy of replevin.
   d. The measure of damages recoverable by Fleur Sweater Co. is the difference between the market price, when it learned of the breach by Scott Yarns Inc., and the contract price.

6. Sassafrass Distributors entered into a contract for the sale of goods to Blake. Blake refused to pay for the goods. Sassafrass Distributors will *not* be able to recover the price for the goods if:
   a. Blake accepted the goods but wishes to return them.
   b. the goods were destroyed after the risk of loss passed to Blake.
   c. Blake refused to accept delivery of the goods and the goods were resold by Sassafrass Distributors in the ordinary course of business.
   d. the goods were identified to the contract and Sassafrass Distributors made a reasonable effort to resell them at a reasonable price but was unable to do so.

7. In accordance with a contract for sale, Dainty Dish Manufacturers shipped 100 sets of dishes to M Mart Store. The shipment arrived on Monday, earlier than it was expected. The receiving department made a perfunctory examination of the dishes and put them in a storeroom. When ten sets of the dishes were taken from the storeroom on Wednesday morning, it was discovered that the quality of the dishes was inferior to that specified in the contract. Which of the following statements is correct?
   a. M Mart Store must retain the dishes because it accepted them and had an opportunity to inspect them upon delivery.
   b. M Mart Store's only remedy is to bring an action for rescission.
   c. M Mart Store has no rights against Dainty Dish Manufacturers if the dishes are of merchantable quality.
   d. M Mart Store can reject the dishes upon its subsequent discovery that they are not in accordance with the contract specifications.

Chapter 20

SALES
Introduction to Sales Warranties

A manufactured item, that had been the subject matter of a contract of sale, may prove to be defective or not fit for the normal or a particular use for which it was purchased, causing personal injury or property damage to the buyer; or the seller may not have had the right to sell the item, so that, after it was in the hands of the buyer, a third person asserted claims to it. Often a buyer, seeking redress, may rely on a contractual theory of warranty.

A seller has certain obligations to the buyer, because he or she makes warranties, or assurances, concerning the goods he or she sells. The seller is responsible for transferring good title and for furnishing goods that function in the expected manner and are suitable for the buyer's need.

THINGS TO KEEP IN MIND

All sellers of goods are treated as making certain implied warranties, unless they have made effective disclaimers. Warranties may also be expressly made by sellers, who make factual assertions, affirmations, representations, etc.

OUTLINE

I.   Warranties of title (Sec. 2-312).

    A. In most contracts for the sale of goods, the seller makes warranties concerning his or her right to sell the goods free of claims to them by other persons.

        1. Good title — Seller warrants that he or she has valid title to the goods and that the transfer of title to the buyer is rightful.

2. No liens — Seller warrants that there are no liens, security interests or other encumbrances, of which the buyer has no knowledge.

3. No infringements — If seller is a merchant, he or she warrants that the goods are free from any adverse copyright, patent, trademark or similar claims. This warranty against infringement does not apply if the goods were made to the buyer's specifications.

B. Warranties of title may be expressly excluded, disclaimed or modified in the contract.

C. Warranties of title are excluded if sale occurs under circumstances which clearly indicate that no such assurances are being made by the seller.

II. Warranties of quality.

A. Express warranties — A factual assertion, representation, affirmation or promise, relating to the goods, or description, model or sample of the goods, which becomes "part of the basis of the bargain" (Sec. 2-313).

1. Assurances and representation made by a seller before, at the time of and after contracting.

2. No particular words need be used to create a warranty.

3. Statements of opinion and value do not create warranties as to quality, unless made by experts.

4. In some cases, a seller may not make any warranties or may effectively disclaim those which he or she has made, by unambiguous language to that effect in the contract.

B. Implied warranties — Arise, unless expressly excluded.

1. Merchantability (Sec. 2-314).

   a. Made by merchant, who deals in the kind of goods sold.

   b. Goods are merchantable if:
      1) Of the average or usual quality existing in the market.
      2) Reasonably fit for the normal, ordinary purposes for which they are used.
      3) Properly "contained, packaged and labeled."

   c. Merchant seller is absolutely liable for breach of warranty of merchantability.

   d. Warranty of merchantability is made in a sale of food or drink for consumption on the premises or elsewhere.

   e. Warranty of merchantability may be disclaimed or modified by:
      1) Using expressions such as "as is" or "with all faults."

   2) Using conspicuous language, which must include the word "merchant-ability."

   3) An inspection conducted by the buyer, or a refusal by the buyer to examine the goods or a sample. (There is no warranty as to defects, which a reasonable examination would reveal.)

   4) Trade usage, course of dealing or course of performance (Sec. 2-316).

  2. Fitness for a particular purpose (Sec. 2-315).

   a. Seller warrants that the goods are fit for the particular purpose intended by the buyer.

   b. The warranty is made by a seller, who need not be a merchant, having reason to know the particular purpose for which the buyer purchases the goods.

   c. The buyer relies on the skill and judgment of the seller in selecting the goods.

   d. Warranty of fitness for particular purpose may be disclaimed or modified by:
    1) Using expressions such as "as is" or "with all faults."
    2) The disclaimer must be in writing and conspicuous, but need not have a reference to fitness for particular purpose.
    3) An inspection conducted by the buyer, or a refusal by the buyer to examine the goods or a sample. (There is no warranty as to defects, which a reasonable examination would reveal.)
    4) Trade usage, course of dealing or course of performance (Sec. 2-316).

III. Overlapping warranties — More than one warranty may be made by a seller in a sales transaction (Sec. 2-317).

 A. If the warranties are consistent with each other, a buyer can base an action against the seller on all of them.

 B. If multiple warranties are inconsistent, the intention of the parties will determine which will prevail. The following rules are used as guides in order to determine their intentions.

  1. Technical specifications prevail over inconsistent models, samples or general descriptions.

  2. A "sample from an existing bulk" prevails over inconsistent general descriptions.

  3. Implied warranty of fitness for particular purpose takes precedence over express warranties.

  4. Express warranties take precedence over implied warranties of merchant-ability and title.

IV. Common law doctrine of privity of contract. (See Chapter 13.)

A. One, who has not consented to a contractual relationship, neither acquires rights nor assumes obligations.

B. There are obligations and, therefore, liability for failure to carry out obligations only if there is privity of contract.

C. If there is a breach of an express or implied warranty by a seller:

    1. The buyer can sue his seller for the breach, but

    2. An injured user or other remote, noncontracting party, who was not in privity with the seller, cannot sue a seller for the breach. (Remember, this is the common law rule, which is subject to change.)

D. Prior to the adoption of the Uniform Commercial Code, the limitations on liability, based on the concept of privity, had been eroded in many states, in which courts recognized that, with modern marketing techniques, consumers purchased products because of the name of the manufacturer and its advertising campaigns, and held that:

    1. Warranties, made by a seller, extended to those persons who could reasonably be foreseen by a manufacturer as potential users of the manufactured item.

    2. Warranties, relating to food and drink, and, in some cases, other items, which, if deleterious, were dangerous to human life, extended to remote users.

E. Modification of the doctrine of privity in the Uniform Commercial Code (Sec. 2-318) — With regard to potential liability arising from breach of warranty, the requirement of contractual privity has been considerably obviated by the Code.

    1. The effect is to make certain persons, such as lessees, family members, donees and bystanders, third party beneficiaries of express and implied warranties that are made by sellers of the goods. Note that three alternative provisions have been proposed by the drafters of the U.C.C.

    2. Warranties extend to any person who is reasonably expected to use, consume or be affected by the goods and who is injured (third party beneficiaries of warranties).

        a. Persons who are covered by Sec. 2-318.
            1) Alternatives A and B extend only to natural persons.
            2) Alternative A is limited to natural persons who are members of the family or household or guests in the home of the purchaser.
            3) Alternative C extends to natural and other persons, such as corporations.

        b. Types of injuries covered by Sec. 2-318.
            1) Alternatives A and B cover only those who incur personal injuries and, therefore, exclude property damage.
            2) Alternative C does not restrict coverage to only personal injuries and, therefore, extends coverage to property damage.

V. Disclaimers, exclusion and modifications of warranties.

    A. Express and implied warranties may be excluded, or disclaimed or modified, as discussed herein at I.B, II.A.4, II.B.1.e and II.B.2.d.

    B. The Magnuson-Moss Warranty Act (The Federal Trade Commission Improvement Act).

        1. Provides for conspicuous disclosure of information, concerning written warranties, extended to buyers of goods, purchased for consumption, when the price is more than $10.

        2. Modifies Uniform Commercial Code warranty provisions.

KEY WORDS AND PHRASES IN TEXT

Caveat emptor
Warranty
Implied warranty of good title
Implied warranty that there are no liens, security interests or encumbrances against the goods
Implied warranty that there are no infringements upon the rights of others
Disclaimer of warranty of title
Express warranty
Statements of opinion, value and puffing do not create express warranties (general rule)
Implied warranty of merchantability

Implied warranty of fitness for a particular purpose
Effect of overlapping warranties
Privity of contract
Third party beneficiaries of express and implied warranties
U.C.C. Sec. 2-318 alternative provisions
Disclaimers of warranties
Implied warranties may arise or be excluded or modified because of course of dealing, course of performance or usage of trade
Unconscionable disclaimers of warranties
Magnuson-Moss Warranty Act
Federal Trade Commission

FILL-IN QUESTIONS

1. A seller, whether or not he or she is a merchant of goods, impliedly warrants that he or she is transferring good title to the buyer, that he or she has the right to do so and that the goods are _free from liens, security interests or encumberances_.
A seller, who is a merchant, also warrants against infringements, which means that the goods are _free from claims based upon patents, trade marks, etc._.

2. A seller, who makes a statement or representation concerning the quality of the goods that he sells, has made an _express_ warranty if the assertion, statement or representation deals with a _factual_ characteristic of the goods, as distinguished from a statement of opinion or value.

3. Even though a seller of goods makes no express warranties concerning the quality of the goods that he or she is selling, it is implied that the goods are _marketable_ and _fit for the particular purpose they are intended_.

4.   A merchant, who deals in the kinds of goods that are the subject matter of a sale to a consumer, makes an implied warranty of merchantability. He or she warrants that the goods are (1) _fit for particular use as intended_, (2) _average or usual quality_ and (3) contained, packaged and labeled as provided in the contract, unless he or she has effectively disclaimed or modified the implied warranty. He or she may do so by using conspicuous language, which includes the word _merchantability_.

5.   If the intentions of the parties are not clear as to whether or not an express warranty made by the seller was to take precedence over an inconsistent implied warranty, the implied warranty of _____ will prevail over an inconsistent _____ warranty. If, however, an express warranty is inconsistent with an implied warranty of merchantability or title, the _____ warranty will prevail over the inconsistent _____ _____.

6.   Today, under the U.C.C., one who was not a purchaser, but was injured by a defective manufactured product, may recover from the seller, based on a breach of an express or implied warranty, because he or she is treated as a _____ _____ of the sales contract. In all states, however, he or she will have to show that he or she was a person who was reasonably expected to _____ by the goods.

MULTIPLE CHOICE QUESTIONS

1.   In a contract for the sale of goods, express warranties are created by the seller, if he or she:
     a. represents that the goods will increase in value by at least 20 percent in two months.
     b. states that in his or her opinion, the goods will prove satisfactory for the buyer's purpose.
     c. assures the buyer that the goods will be the same as a sample which he exhibits.
     d. says that his or her goods are better than those of his competitors.

2.   Obedin owned and operated a small precision machine manufacturing business. Kendall contracted with Obedin for the manufacture of a metal cutting machine, for which Kendall supplied specifications. Obedin produced and delivered the machine, which conformed to the specifications, and Kendall paid the contract price. The machine performed satisfactorily. Six months after delivery of the machine to Kendall, Cutter Machine Tools brought action against Obedin and Kendall for infringement of its patent rights. Kendall, in turn, brought an action against Obedin, based upon breach of warranty. Kendall will *not* be successful, if his action is based upon breach of:
     a. an express warranty, because an implied warranty against infringement takes precedence over a conflicting express warranty.
     b. an implied warranty against infringement, because the machine was made in accordance with specifications furnished by the buyer.
     c. an implied warranty of good title, because an implied warranty of good title is displaced by an implied warranty against infringement when the seller is a merchant.
     d. an implied warranty that the machine was free of liens or other encumbrances because such a warranty is not made when goods are specially manufactured.

3. Langer, who was not a merchant, sold a computer to Vannan for use in an educational project. Langer made no express warranties. Vannan claims and is able to show that the computer does not perform the operations needed for her project. She, therefore, sues Langer for breach of warranty. Vannan will probably be successful because Langer breached the implied warranty:
   a. of merchantability.
   b. of fitness for a particular purpose.
   c. that the item sold was fit for the ordinary purpose for which computers are normally used.
   d. that there were no security interests or other encumbrances which would interfere with Vannan's use of the computer.

Questions 4, 5 and 6 are based upon the following fact situation: Charlotte went to Katherine's store in order to purchase a new ladder so that she could paint the trim on her 15-foot ceilings. Charlotte asked to see a ladder manufactured by X, which Katherine showed her. Katherine also showed Charlotte a ladder manufactured by Y and one by Z, stating that she believed that the Y ladder was the "best buy" of the three and that the X ladder would not prove satisfactory for Charlotte's purposes. You are to assume that the entire transaction was conducted orally.

4. Charlotte purchased the X ladder. She was injured when the ladder collapsed while she was painting the trim on her ceiling. With regard to a breach of warranty of fitness for a particular purpose, which of the following statements is true?
   a. There has been a breach of warranty of fitness, because Katherine knew the purpose for which Charlotte was making the purchase.
   b. There has been no breach of warranty of fitness, because Charlotte did not rely on Katherine's skill and judgment in making her selection.
   c. There has been no breach of the warranty of fitness, because Katherine used conspicuous language to effectively exclude the warranty of fitness.
   d. There has been a breach of warranty of fitness, because the ladder was not fit for the normal purpose for which ladders are used.

5. Charlotte purchased the Y ladder. She was injured when the ladder collapsed while she was painting the trim on her ceiling. With regard to a breach of warranty of merchantability, which of the following statements is true?
   a. There was a breach of the warranty of merchantability because the ladder was not reasonably fit for the purpose for which one usually uses a ladder.
   b. A warranty of merchantability takes precedence over express warranties.
   c. Katherine effectively disclaimed the warranty of merchantability.
   d. Katherine's express statements created an express warranty of merchantability.

6. Charlotte purchased the Z ladder. She was injured when the ladder collapsed while she was painting the trim on her ceiling.
   a. Katherine is not liable for breach of any warranties because she made no assertions or representations of facts concerning the Z ladder.
   b. An implied warranty of merchantability can be expressly excluded by contract if the seller is a nonmerchant, but not by Katherine because she was a merchant.
   c. An implied warranty of merchantability would have been effectively excluded if the defect had been revealed by Charlotte's inspection.
   d. A disclaimer of the warranty of merchantability by Katherine would not be effective unless it was conspicuous and in a writing, which included the word "merchantability."

7. Cautious T.V. and Radio Store wishes to exclude implied warranties as to quality from its future sale of television and radio sets. It can effectively do so by:
    a. selling only brand name merchandise.
    b. using a written contract form which states conspicuously that, "All warranty protection by Cautious T.V. and Radio Store is expressly excluded by the seller."
    c. using a written contract form which states conspicuously that, "There are no warranties which extend beyond the description contained in this contract of sale."
    d. using a written contract form which states conspicuously that, "The merchandise is sold as is and with all faults."

8. Freyberg became violently ill after eating a hamburger purchased at Speedy Burger Palace, and it has been determined that his illness was caused by poisonous substances in the hamburger, causing it to be unfit for human consumption. Freyberg sues the Speedy Burger Palace, basing his cause of action on a breach of implied warranty of merchantability and warranty of fitness for a particular purpose.
    a. Freyberg may base his cause of action upon either or both of the warranties.
    b. Freyberg may base his cause of action upon one of the warranties but not both of them.
    c. The implied warranty of merchantability does not apply, because Freyberg did not consume the hamburger at the Speedy Burger Palace, but ate it while seated in his own car.
    d. The implied warranty of fitness for a particular purpose does not apply, because Speedy Burger Palace was not informed by Freyberg of the particular purpose for which he was purchasing the hamburger.

9. Huber purchased a case of beer from Beere's Beverages. He drank one can of the beer without any harmful effects and used the remainder of it to wash his car. As a result, the paint on the car was permanently damaged.
    a. Beere's Beverages is liable to Huber for breach of the warranty of merchantability.
    b. Beere's Beverages is liable to Huber for breach of the warranty of fitness for a particular purpose.
    c. Beere's Beverages is not liable for breach of any implied warranties as to quality, because Beere's Beverages did not know the purpose for which Huber was purchasing the beer and Huber used the beer for an unusual purpose.
    d. Beere's Beverages is not liable for breach of any implied warranties as to quality, because such warranties do not apply to food or drink.

10. Mink sold Beaver twenty fur coats in accordance with a written signed contract. The contract contained no specific provisions regarding warranties of title, but stated that the coats were sold to Beaver "with all faults and defects." Two of the coats that were sold to Beaver had been stolen and were reclaimed by the rightful owner. Which of the following is a correct statement?
    a. The implied warranty of title is eliminated by the parol evidence rule.
    b. The disclaimer "with all faults and defects" effectively negates any and all implied warranties.
    c. Beaver assumed the risk of Mink's title being void because there was no express warranty of good title.
    d. The contract automatically contained a warranty that good title was conveyed, which could only be excluded by specific language.
    (This question has been adapted from AICPA Examination, November 1983.)

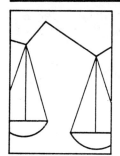

Chapter 21

SALES
Product Liability

If a manufactured product is defective, it may be the cause of personal or property injuries to the purchaser or third persons, such as other users or bystanders. The product may have been the subject matter in a chain of numerous sales transactions and, as a result, many sellers may have potential liability to those injured by the defective item. Who bears the burden of liability is determined by the theory of law upon which the injured person bases his or her cause of action. Liability for defective products may be imposed because of tort, contract and/or statutory law.

The diagram below illustrates the numerous potential parties. Some may be parties because they have been injured and are plaintiffs; others may be parties because they were in the "chain" of purchases and sales. Note that often it is the remote user or bystander, rather than the ultimate buyer, who will seek to impose liability on one of the sellers in the vertical chain of sales.

Producer of component part
↓
Manufacturer of item that caused damage because of defect
↓
Wholesaler or other distributor
↓
Retailer
↓
Buyer ————————> Second hand purchaser (remote party)

————> Donee or guest (remote party)

————> Lessee or other user (remote party)

————> Injured bystander (remote party)

THINGS TO KEEP IN MIND

1. In the diagram, those in the vertical chain are potential defendants. The buyer and remote parties in the horizontal chain represent potential plaintiffs. The ultimate buyer may be a defendant as well as a plaintiff.

2. Many of the concepts of contract and tort law were formulated before modern methods of production and distribution for mass consumption existed.

OUTLINE

I.   Contract liability — Based.on the theory that a seller is regarded as making certain warranties relating to the products that he or she sells. (See Chapter 20.)

II. Tort liability. (Also see Chapter 4.)

  A. In an action based upon tort, an injured party need not show that privity of contract existed between the injured party and the defendant.

  B. Misrepresentation.

    1. Fraudulent misrepresentation — A buyer who is injured because he or she reasonably relied upon a representation of a material fact that was false and made in order to induce a contract, may recover for the tort of fraud.

    2. Nonfraudulent misrepresentation — In many jurisdictions, if a misrepresentation is innocently made by a seller, without the intention of deceiving a buyer, the buyer may also recover in tort for the injuries which he or she incurred because of the misrepresentation.

  C. Negligence — Failure to exercise reasonable care.

    1. Manufacturer (as well as other sellers) must exercise reasonable care to make products that are safe for the purpose for which they are intended to be used.

    2. A manufacturer is liable to one who is injured because of a defective product if:

      a. It was foreseeable that the defect would cause the product to be dangerous to life, and

      b. The manufacturer failed to correct the defect or make a reasonable inspection, which would disclose the defect.

    3. Defenses.

      a. Defendant exercised reasonable care.

      b. Lack of showing of proximate cause between defendant's failure to exercise reasonable care and the plaintiff's injury.

    c. Comparative or contributory negligence.

    d. Assumption of the risk.

D. Statutory liability — Federal and state statutes, in addition to the Uniform Commercial Code, impose duties on manufacturers of goods purchased for consumption with regard to labeling, advertising, selling, etc.

    1. If a manufacturer has violated such a statute, it may be treated as negligence *per se.*

    2. Some relevant federal legislation.

        a. The Consumer Product Safety Act provides for regulation of all potentially hazardous consumer products.

        b. Federal Food, Drug, and Cosmetic Act, Federal Hazardous Substances Labeling Act, Federal Flammable Fabrics Act.

E. Strict tort liability — Theory used in some cases and suggested in Restatement (Second) of Torts, Section 402A.

    1. Manufacturer or other seller is liable, regardless of fault, if:

        a. The product was in a defective condition when sold by the defendant manufacturer or other seller;

        b. The defect resulted in the product being unreasonably dangerous to a user or consumer or his or her property when used for its ordinary purpose;
            1) Product was dangerous beyond the expectation of the ordinary consumer, or
            2) A less dangerous alternative was economically feasible for the manufacturer but the manufacturer failed to produce it.

        c. Plaintiff incurred a physical injury;

        d. The defect was the proximate cause of the injury;

        e. The product reached the plaintiff without any substantive change in its condition after its sale by the defendant; and

        f. The defendant is normally engaged in selling such products.

    2. The injured party need not establish privity of contract or that the manufacturer, or other seller, was negligent or that its conduct was intentional.

    3. Liability sharing — In some jurisdictions, when a plaintiff is unable to prove which of many sellers of a harmful product supplied the particular product that caused plaintiff's injury, industry-wide liability may be imposed and allocated based upon the respective market shares of multiple sellers of the product.

4. Limitations on recovery and defenses — In *some*, but not all, of those states in which the strict liability theory is applied, the following defenses may be effective:

    a. Property damage, rather than personal injuries, was incurred.

    b. The product was misused.

    c. The defect occurred after the product left the defendant's control and possession.

    d. The plaintiff's existence was not foreseeable — he or she is too remote a party.

    e. With regard to automobiles, "ordinary use" of an automobile does not include involvement in a collision. (Some courts, however, have adopted the "crashworthiness doctrine.")

    f. Plaintiff, while knowing of and appreciating the risk, which was created by the defect, unreasonably and voluntarily engaged in the risk although he or she realized the potential danger. (Assumption of the risk.)

    g. Plaintiff's negligence or intentional conduct contributed to his or her own injuries (minority rule).

    h. The injury occurred after the period of time specified in statute of limitations or statute of repose.

KEY WORDS AND PHRASES IN TEXT

Products liability
Contract liability based upon warranty theory (see Chapter 20)
Tort liability (also see Chapter 4)
In actions based upon tort liability, it is not necessary to establish privity of contract
Tort of negligence
Exercise of reasonable/due care
Defenses to negligence
Violation of statutory duty
Negligence per se
Fraudulent and innocent (nonfraudulent) misrepresentation
Doctrine of strict tort liability
Restatement (Second) of Torts, Section 402A

Unreasonably dangerous defective product
Liability imposed as a matter of public policy
Requirements for imposition of doctrine of strict liability for defective products
Limitations on recovery based upon strict liability
Statutes of repose
Assumption of the risk defense
Misuse of the product defense
Application of defense of comparative negligence in strict liability cases
Liability to bystanders
Crashworthiness doctrine
Strict liability of suppliers of component parts and lessors

FILL-IN QUESTIONS

1. _____ generally refers to the liability of sellers, manufacturers and distributors of goods to buyers of the goods and other people who have incurred injuries caused by the products.

2. A buyer of goods that prove to be defective may bring an action against the seller, with whom he or she contracted, based on contract, if he or she can show that there was a breach of an express or implied _____. If the buyer bases his cause of action on tort, he or she will have to establish that the seller was either _____ or strictly liable.

3. If a seller of goods made representations concerning the goods which were false, but induced the buyer to purchase the goods, the buyer may recover in contract from the seller, based on a theory of breach of _____ and, in tort, based on fraud in the inducement, if the buyer _____ and was _____.

4. Prior to the adoption of Sec. 2-318 of the Uniform Commercial Code, in many states, one, who was not a purchaser, but was injured by a manufactured product, could not recover from the seller of the product in an action based on breach of warranty because of lack of _____. For this reason, he or she would base his or her cause of action on the tort of _____, but would have to show that the seller _____.

5. Based on the tort doctrine of strict liability, any person who is injured by a manufactured product, including the buyer, a bystander or remote user, may successfully recover from the manufacturer or other seller of the item by establishing that he or she was injured by the product, which was defective, and that _____ _____ _____.

MULTIPLE CHOICE QUESTIONS

Unless otherwise indicated in a question below, assume that the fact situations, given in the following questions, arise in a state which has adopted the Uniform Commercial Code and which is following the recent trends in the United States so that the courts are imposing strict liability on all the sellers of defective products.

Questions 1, 2 and 3 are based on the following fact situation: Thirsty purchased a 75¢ bottle of soda, manufactured by the Soke Company, at a neighborhood grocery store. Thirsty took the bottle home, where he drank some and shared the rest with Parched. Thirsty and Parched became violently ill because they swallowed slivers of glass that were in the bottle of soda. The grocery store and Soke Company exercised extraordinary care to prevent such an occurrence.

1. At common law, the grocery store would be liable to:
   a. Thirsty for breach of warranty of merchantability, because there was privity of contract between it and Thirsty.
   b. Parched for breach of warranty of merchantability, because there was privity of contract between it and Parched.

c. Thirsty for the tort of negligence.

d. Parched for the tort of negligence.

2. With regard to the liability of Soke Company, which of the following statements is *incorrect?*

a. It is liable to Thirsty and Parched for breach of warranties.

b. It is liable to Thirsty and Parched in tort, even though it exercised a high degree of care.

c. It is not liable to Thirsty and Parched for the tort of negligence, because it used due care in the manufacture of its product in order to insure that it was safe, if used for the purpose for which it was intended.

d. It is not liable to Thirsty and Parched in tort because a reasonable person would have inspected the bottle and its contents before consuming the soda.

3. Which of the following statements is correct?

a. Soke Company could have effectively disclaimed all liability to buyers and other consumers of its product by putting a carefully worded disclaimer on the label.

b. Federal and state consumer product safety protection statutes would not apply to Soke Company, because soda is not normally a hazardous product.

c. The Magnuson-Moss Warranty Act does not have any applicability to Soke Company's liability to Parched or Thirsty.

d. The Magnuson-Moss Warranty Act insures that the implied warranty of merchantability is extended to Parched as well as Thirsty.

Questions 4 and 5 are based on the following fact situation: Tillie purchased a new typewriter, manufactured by the BMI Corp., from a seller of business equipment, for $350. When she brought the typewriter home, she tested it by typing her name. As she touched the "L" key, all of the keys flew out of the machine, severely injuring Tillie. On her written contract of sale there was a conspicuous statement to the effect that the sale was covered only by the manufacturer's warranties and that the seller did not warrant that the typewriter was fit for the particular purpose intended by the buyer nor make any warranties as to its merchantability. There was a conspicuous written twelve month warranty attached to the typewriter, promising that BMI Corp. would replace the typewriter if it proved to be defective.

4. With regard to the seller from whom Tillie purchased the typewriter:

a. it is liable to Tillie for breach of the warranty of merchantability.

b. it is liable to Tillie for breach of warranty of fitness for a particular purpose.

c. it is not liable to Tillie for negligence, if it can show that it exercised reasonable care.

d. it is not liable to Tillie in tort for personal injuries but is liable for property damage.

5. The warranty statement attached to the typewriter:

a. was binding on BMI Corp. and the seller with whom Tillie dealt.

b. was binding on BMI Corp. only.

c. does not have to comply with the Magnuson-Moss Warranty Act, because the typewriter was purchased for Tillie's personal use.

d. limits BMI Corp.'s liability to Tillie for personal injuries.

6. Acro purchased a set of Goodmonth tires from Tyre, a dealer in tires, who made no express warranties. The tires were put on Acro's delivery truck. After the truck had been driven 100 miles on the new tires, one of them blew out, causing the truck

to go out of control. As a result, the truck was completely wrecked and Ernest, the driver employed by Acro, was injured, as was Innocent, the driver of the automobile into which Acro's truck collided. Neither Ernest nor Innocent was negligent.

a. Tyre is the only party liable to Acro for breach of warranty.

b. Goodmonth is liable for personal injuries, incurred by Ernest, in tort and in contract for breach of warranty.

c. Goodmonth is not liable for personal injuries, incurred by Innocent, in tort or in contract for breach of warranty.

d. Tyre is relieved of any liability because he did not manufacture the defective tire.

7. Conny Sumer purchased a television set from Rea Taylor, who had purchased the set (and nine others, which she had sold to other buyers in her appliance store) from the Manu Facturing Co. When Conny's son turned the television set on, the screen shattered, severely cutting his face. Conny Sumer and her son are, therefore, suing Rea Taylor and Manu Facturing Co., basing the actions on torts and contract.

a. Conny Sumer's son can recover for his personal injuries from either Rea Taylor or Manu Facturing Co. in contract and tort.

b. Conny Sumer can recover for property damage from either Rea Taylor or Manu Facturing Co. in contract.

c. In some states, Conny Sumer cannot recover for property damage from Rea Taylor or Manu Facturing Co. in tort unless she can show that they were negligent.

d. All of the above.

8. Evans incurred an injury due to a malfunction of a power tool which he had purchased at a local hardware store. The tool was manufactured by Cautious Tool Company. Evans has commenced an action against the hardware store and Cautious Tool Company based upon strict tort liability. Which of the following statements is correct?

a. Privity of contract will not be a valid defense against Evans in his lawsuit.

b. Evans' suit against the hardware store will be dismissed because the hardware store was not at fault.

c. Cautious Tool Company will not be liable to Evans if it manufactured the tool in a nonnegligent manner.

d. Evan's lawsuit will be dismissed because strict liability has not been applied in product liability cases in most jurisdictions.

(This question has been adapted from AICPA Examination, November 1983.)

9. Dieffenbacher is suing the manufacturer, the wholesaler, and the retailer for bodily personal injuries suffered by her as a result of using a lawnmower that she had purchased. Under the theory of strict tort liability:

a. Privity of contract will be an absolute bar insofar as the wholesaler is concerned if the wholesaler did not have a reasonable opportunity to inspect the lawnmower.

b. Contributory negligence on the part of Dieffenbacher will always be a bar to recovery.

c. The manufacturer will avoid liability if it can show that it followed the custom of the industry.

d. Dieffenbacher may recover despite the fact that she cannot show that any negligence was involved.

(This question has been adapted from AICPA Examination, November 1983.)

10. Kaye leased a new automobile from R&R Rent A Car in August. In October, while operating the car in a correct, safe and lawful manner, Kaye was injured when the auto crashed into a highway divider. The crash occurred because the brakes on the auto failed to properly operate. Kay has brought a tort action based upon strict liability against the manufacturer and R&R Rent A Car. Based upon recent trends in the law:

   a. Kaye may be able to recover from either the manufacturer or R&R Rent A Car even though he had leased, rather than purchased, the automobile.

   b. Kaye may be able to recover from R&R Rent A Car even though he had leased, rather than purchased, the automobile but may not recover from the manufacturer with whom he did not have privity of contract.

   c. Kaye will have to establish that the automobile was extraordinarily dangerous.

   d. Kaye may be able to recover from the manufacturer even though R&R Rent A Car had made modifications on the automobile at Kaye's request.

Chapter 22

Basic Concepts of Commercial Paper

You are familiar with many types of writings that are used to facilitate commerce and trade. For example, money in the form of currency is used daily by most of us. Recall, from the material in Unit Two, that many contractual agreements are reduced to writing and often the rights of the parties are assignable. In addition, in order to facilitate the delivery of goods, documents of title are issued, and investment securities, such as stocks and bonds, are issued by business organizations and frequently bought and sold by investors. These writings are all forms of intangible personal property, for one who is in possession of them has rights associated with ownership. Such instruments are used in business because there is relative ease in transferring them.

Special kinds of paper, the subject of this and the following five chapters, are referred to as "commercial paper" when they contain written promises or orders to pay money. They are forms of personal property, representing contract rights, which are easily transferable and used to facilitate trade. You are familiar with checks, for you have probably received and/or used them to pay for goods and services. Checks are one type of commercial paper. In addition, there are also promissory notes, drafts and certificates of deposit. These kinds of instruments have been used in the business community for hundreds of years.

THINGS TO KEEP IN MIND

It is important to become familiar with the terminology presented in this short chapter. Be sure you understand the meanings of the terms discussed.

OUTLINE

I.   Functions and purposes of commercial paper.

    A. Substitute for money — For convenience and safety.

B. Credit device — One wishing to extend the time for payment for goods, services or the use of money (a loan) may give a creditor a written instrument. The creditor, in turn, if he or she wishes to have cash immediately, may sell the instrument received from the debtor, but will have to "pay for" the immediate cash by paying interest in advance (discounting).

C. Historical origins of the law relating to commercial paper.

   1. Used by traders and merchants.

   2. The Law Merchant.

   3. Court recognition of the legal rights of traders.

   4. Uniform Negotiable Instruments Act.

   5. Article 3 of the Uniform Commercial Code.

II. Types of commercial paper.

   A. Promissory note — Written promise, signed by the promisor (the maker) to pay a sum of money to another person, at a definite time, or on demand.

      1. Used to borrow money, buy goods, obtain services, or as evidence of indebtedness.

      2. Types of promissory notes.

         a. Mortgage note — Promise to repay a loan of money, secured by real property.

         b. Collateral note — Promise to repay a loan of money, secured by personal property.

         c. Installment note — Promise to pay indebtedness in specified periodic installments.

         d. Certificate of deposit — Acknowledgement by a bank of a receipt of money with a promise to repay.

         e. Judgment note — In some states the maker of a note authorizes the immediate confession and entry of a judgment against him or her by a court of record, if he or she fails to pay in accordance with the terms of the note.

   B. Draft — Written order, direction or command by one person, the drawer, to another person, the drawee, to pay a sum of money to a third person, the payee.

      1. Parties to draft.

         a. Drawer — Issues paper, giving direction that a sum of money be paid.

      b. Drawee — Person, to whom draft is directed, who is to pay and who is already or may become obligated to the drawer.

      c. Payee — Person to whom money is to be paid.

      d. One person may be more than one party to a draft. E.g., drawer may be drawee or payee.

  2. Used to:

      a. Collect an account.

      b. Finance purchase of goods or the furnishing of services.

      c. Transfer funds.

  3. Draft may be accepted — Drawee engages or promises that he, she or it will pay.

  4. Draft may be payable on demand, or at sight (upon presentment to drawee), or at a future stated time or at a stated period of time after date or after sight (after it has been presented to the drawee).

  5. Types of drafts.

      a. Trade acceptance — Draft drawn by and payable to the seller of goods.
        1) Seller is drawer and payee.
        2) Buyer is drawee, who accepts draft by placing his or her signature on the face of the paper.
        3) Usually draft is payable in the future.

      b. Check — Demand draft, drawn on a bank by a drawer, who has money on account at the drawee bank, payable to another person.

III. Other types of commercial paper.

  A. Other forms of checks used in the banking system. See Chapter 27 herein.

  B. Traveler's check — Check drawn by financial institution, which requires the signature of the payee in order to become payable.

  C. Letter of credit — Agreement that issuer will pay drafts drawn by a specified person.

IV. Other ways of classifying commercial paper — Commercial paper may be classified as to:

  A. When it is payable — Demand or time paper.

    1. Demand or sight paper — Payable whenever it is presented for payment by the person in possession of it.

2. Time paper — Payable at a time in the future.

B. To whom it is payable — Commercial paper may be payable to:

1. A named person, the payee, or his or her order, or

2. Bearer, who is anyone in possession of the paper, which is payable to bearer, or cash, or other designation indicating that it is not payable to a named person.

C. Whether it is negotiable or nonnegotiable.

1. Negotiable — The paper contains all the requisites specified in Sec. 3-104.

2. Nonnegotiable — One or more of the requisites prescribed by Sec. 3-104 is missing.

V. Parties to commercial paper.

A. Original parties.

1. To a promissory note:

a. Maker — Issuer who signs and is promising to pay.

b. Payee — Party to whom promise is made; a note may be issued to bearer.

2. To a draft:

a. Drawer — Issuer who signs and is ordering the drawee to pay.

b. Drawee — Party to whom direction or order to pay is directed.

c. Payee — Party to whom payment is to be made; may be issued to bearer.

B. Other parties who may come in contact with commercial paper.

1. Indorser — Transferor who signs his or her name on the back of the commercial paper.

2. Indorsee — Transferee to whom or to whose order paper is payable.

3. Holder — Person in possession of a negotiable instrument that was issued or indorsed to him (or her) or his (or her) order or to bearer.

4. Holder in due course — A good faith holder to whom a negotiable instrument is transferred for value, who has a special status because certain defenses cannot be raised by the person, required to ultimately pay the instrument, against a holder in due course.

5. Holder through a holder in due course — A holder who is not himself or herself a holder in due course, but acquires his rights from or through another person who is a holder in due course.

6. Acceptor — Drawee of draft or check who, by placing his or her signature on the paper, agrees to pay when it is due.

7. Accommodation party — One who signs an instrument in order to lend his or her name and/or credit to it. Accommodation party is liable in the capacity in which he or she signs to all parties except the accommodated party.

KEY WORDS AND PHRASES IN TEXT

Commercial paper
Article 3 of the Uniform
    Commercial Code
Functions of commercial paper
    (substitute for money and
    credit device)
Discounting
Draft (bill of exchange)
Time draft
Sight draft
Trade acceptance
Check
Promissory note
Certificate of deposit (CD)
Letter of credit
Demand instrument
Time instrument
Order to pay (draft or check)

Promise to pay (promissory note or
    certificate of deposit)
Negotiable instrument
Nonnegotiable instrument
Parties to commercial paper
Maker of promissory note or
    certificate of deposit
Drawer of draft or check
Drawee of draft or check
Payee
Indorser
Indorsee
Bearer
Holder
Holder in due course
Holder through a holder in due course
Acceptor
Accommodation party

FILL-IN QUESTIONS

1. Written promises or orders to pay sums of money are referred to as _____.

2. A draft is commercial paper that contains a written _____ to pay money. A check is a special form of draft, which is payable on _____ and is drawn on a drawee that is a _____.

3. Trade acceptances are frequently used in order to finance the purchase of goods. A trade acceptance is a draft that is accepted by the buyer, who is the _____ of the draft and who, after the draft has been accepted, is referred to as the _____. The seller of the goods is often both the _____ and the _____ of a trade acceptance.

4. A promissory note is a written _____ to pay a sum of money. The person who issues the promissory note is the _____. The one to whom a promissory note is payable is referred to as the _____.

5. Promissory notes and drafts may be payable _____ or at a future time. If they are payable in the future they are referred to as _____.

6.

> January 4, 1989
>
> At sight, I promise to pay John
> Jones the sum of $20.
>
> *Mary Smith*

The instrument is a promissory _____. The _____ is Mary Smith and the payee is _____. It is a _____ instrument because it is not payable at a future time.

7.

> January 6, 1989
>
> Pay to the order of bearer the sum of $100 on January 6, 1990.
>
> To: Ben Beier
>
> *David Duke*

The instrument is a _____. _____ is the drawer and _____ is the drawee. Since it is not payable to a named person, it is _____ paper. It is _____ paper because it is payable on a fixed date in the future.

MULTIPLE CHOICE QUESTIONS

1. A draft is:
    a. a collateral note.
    b. a time instrument.
    c. payable to bearer.
    d. a three party instrument.

2. On a check, the drawee is:
    a. the one who wrote the check.
    b. the person cashing the check.
    c. a bank.
    d. a bank or other person.

3. An essential difference between a draft and a promissory note is:
    a. a promissory note is payable on a specific date.
    b. a draft is payable to a specific person.
    c. the drawer and drawee of a draft have a debtor-creditor relationship.
    d. two or more persons are required to sign a promissory note.

4. Little owes Adams money. Instead of Adams being paid the money, the money is to be paid to Brown. The draft will be signed by:
    a. Adams.
    b. Little.

c. Brown.

d. Little and Adams.

5. Smith made a contract to purchase a washing machine on credit from the Acme Appliance Co. He signed a paper in which he stated that he promised to pay $350, the purchase price, in six months from the date of the writing. It also stated that the paper was secured by the washing machine. Acme Appliance Co. transferred the paper to Easy Finance Corp., which paid Acme eighty percent of the face value. Smith was notified that Easy Finance Corp. was now in possession of the paper.

a. The instrument was discounted by Easy Finance Corp.

b. The instrument was a mortgage draft.

c. The drawer of the instrument was Acme Appliance Co.

d. The drawee of the instrument was Easy Finance Corp.

Questions 6 and 7 are based on the following fact situation: Betty Barnes has ordered merchandise for her art supply store located in Baltimore from Sam's Best Paints Inc. in New York City. The merchandise is to be shipped. Sam's Best Paints Inc.'s bank has sent a bill of lading covering the shipment and the following document to Betty Barnes' bank.

February 2, 1989

To: Betty Barnes
      Betty's Art Shop
      Baltimore, Maryland

On April 2, 1989, pay to the order of Sam's Best Paints Inc.
Five Thousand and 00/100 Dollars ($5,000).

Accepted at Baltimore, Maryland
on February _____, 1989   Sam's Best Paints Inc.

                                                 by___*Sam Evans*___

by_____   Sam Evans, President
Payable at Second National Bank of Baltimore

Betty Barnes' bank has notified her of its receipt of the document and asked her to come to its main office in order to sign the document.

6. The document is:

a. a sight draft.

b. a trade acceptance.

c. a time check.

d. an accommodation bill of exchange.

7. Sam's Best Paints Inc. is:

a. the drawer and drawee. Betty Barnes is the payee and will be the accepter when she signs the instrument.

b. the drawer and payee. Betty Barnes will not sign the document because she correctly knows that one person cannot be the drawer and payee of a draft.

c. the drawer and payee. Betty Barnes' bank is the drawee, and when Betty Barnes signs the draft she will be the acceptor.

d. the drawer and payee. Betty Barnes is the drawee, and when she signs the draft she will be the acceptor.

8. While visiting a friend, Fred, in Fresno, California, Bill's wallet was stolen. Bill was in need of funds and wished to cash a personal check drawn on the Mellon Bank in Pittsburgh, Pennsylvania. A bank in Fresno was willing to cash the check if Fred signed the check on the back, which Fred did. With regard to the check:
    a. Bill is the drawee, the Mellon Bank is the drawer and Fred is an indorser.
    b. Bill is the drawer, the Mellon Bank is the drawee and Fred is an accommodation maker.
    c. Bill is the drawer, the Mellon Bank is the drawee and Fred is an accommodation drawer.
    d. Bill is the drawer, the Mellon Bank is the drawee and Fred is an accommodation indorser.

Chapter 23

COMMERCIAL PAPER
The Negotiable Instrument

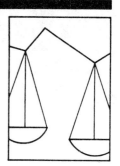

Commercial paper may be negotiable or nonnegotiable. If it is negotiable, unique, special rules, found in Article 3 of the Uniform Commercial Code, govern the rights and obligations of the parties to it, as well as others to whom it may be transferred. If it is nonnegotiable, the law of contracts applies. Recall, from the chapter dealing with the rights of third parties (Chapter 13), that an obligor can raise a defense, which he or she can assert against the obligee (who assigns his or her rights to a third person), against an assignee. As a result, negotiable promissory notes, certificates of deposit, drafts and checks are more freely transferable and more readily acceptable as substitutes for money and credit and are, therefore, more desirable than nonnegotiable instruments.

THINGS TO KEEP IN MIND

In order to be treated as a negotiable instrument, commercial paper must conform to certain formal requisites, all of which must be found within the four corners of the face of the writing. It must be in writing, signed by the maker or drawer, contain a single, unconditional promise or order to pay a sum certain in money, on demand or at a definite time in the future, and it must be payable to the order of a named payee or to bearer (Sec. 3-104).

OUTLINE

I.   Contract law versus Article 3 of the U.C.C.

    A. The transfer of a nonnegotiable instrument to a third party is an assignment of contractual rights. (See Chapter 13.)

       1. The transferor is an assignor and the transferee is an assignee.

2. When the nonnegotiable instrument becomes due and payable, the obligor (i.e., the maker of a promissory note or the drawee of a draft) may raise any defenses, which he or she could have asserted against the original obligee/assignor (usually the payee), against the assignee.

B. In addition to being an assignment, the proper transfer of a negotiable instrument by a holder to a third party is referred to as a negotiation.

1. The transferee, who takes the instrument for value, in good faith and without notice that is overdue or has been dishonored or that there are claims to or defenses against it, qualifies as a holder in due course (HDC).

2. When the negotiable instrument becomes due and payable, the obligor (i.e., the maker of a promissory note or the drawee of a draft) may not raise some of the defenses, which he or she could have asserted against the original obligee (usually the payee), against the HDC.

3. If a negotiable instrument is not properly negotiated, its transfer is merely an assignment of rights, and any defenses, which could have been asserted against the original obligor (i.e., the maker of a promissory note or the drawee of a draft), may be raised against the transferee/holder.

II. The forms of negotiable instruments (Sec. 3-104).

A. Promises to pay — Promissory notes and certificates of deposit.

B. Orders to pay — Drafts and checks.

III. Requirements for negotiability (Sec. 3-104).

A. A writing which is relatively permanent, preservable, portable, moveable and tangible.

B. Signed by the maker of a note or certificate of deposit, or the drawer of a draft or check.

1. A symbol or mark intended by the user to authenticate the writing.

2. Need not appear at bottom right hand corner of the writing (a subscription).

3. A signature may be provided by an authorized representative (Sec. 3-403).

C. Contains a single, express, absolute, unequivocable, unconditional promise or order to pay (Sec. 3-105).

1. Promise — An express affirmative undertaking, if instrument is a promissory note.

a. Not merely an acknowledgment of indebtedness, without the inclusion of words such as, "due on demand."

b. In a certificate of deposit, the acknowledgement of a receipt of money and an engagement to repay it indicates a promise to pay.

2. Order — An express, precise, mandatory direction or command to the drawee, who is identified, if instrument is a draft or check.

3. Unconditional nature of promise or order — The holder does not have to look outside of the paper in order to determine his or her right to payment.

    a. Nonnegotiable, if promise or order is subject to or governed or burdened by another agreement, but *negotiable* if:
      1) Subject to implied or constructive conditions, such as good faith.
      2) States the consideration or transaction which gave rise to the instrument, by using notations such as, "as per contract" or "arising out of the sale of goods."
      3) Refers to another separate collateral agreement by using words such as, "secured by a mortgage" or "secured by a security interest in certain property." (These words make the paper "better.")

    b. Nonnegotiable, if paper states that it is payable out of a particular fund or source, because payment would depend upon the existence and sufficiency of the source of funds.
      1) Use of words such as, "payable only from account number 3," "pay out of proceeds of sale," etc.
      2) *Negotiable* if:
        a) Indicates particular fund out of which reimbursement is to be made or an account to be debited.
        b) Payable out of a particular fund, when paper is issued by a governmental body or agency to be paid out of specified revenue funds, or issued by a partnership, estate or trust payable only out of its assets.

D. Sum certain in money — At the time that the holder receives the instrument, the holder must be able to know the present value of the instrument, in terms of the existing medium of exchange, without referring to a source outside the paper.

1. Sum certain (Sec. 3-106).

    a. At the time that the holder receives the instrument, he or she must be able to ascertain, from the face, the exact minimum amount that he or she will receive when it is paid, and

    b. At the time or maturity, the holder must be able to determine the definite sum that he or she will be paid. The exact sum to be paid must be stated or capable of being made certain by computation from the face of the instrument.

    c. *Negotiable* if it provides that instrument is to be paid:
      1) With stated interest or in stated installments.
        a) Negotiable if it states:
          (1) Payable with interest at the contract (lawful) rate or at the judgment (legal) rate, if the statutory rate is not a fluctuating rate.
          (2) Payable with interest, which is interpreted as the statutory judgment rate of interest (Sec. 3-118(d)).

> b) Nonnegotiable if it states that interest is to be payable at "prevailing" or "current bank rate."
>
> 2) With different stated interest rates before and after default or on a specified date, or
>
> 3) With reasonable court costs and attorney fees upon default, in those states which permit such clauses, or
>
> 4) With a stated discount or additional sum if payment is made before or after the date fixed for payment.

2. Payable in money only.

   a. Money is the "medium of exchange authorized or adopted by a domestic or foreign government as a part of its currency" (Sec. 1-201(24)).

   b. If instrument is payable in foreign currency, it may still be negotiable, but it is deemed payable in equivalent United States dollars.

   c. If instrument provides for payment in a commodity (other than money), instead of or in addition to money, it is not negotiable.

E. Payable on demand or at a definite time.

   1. Payable on demand — Payment is required whenever instrument is tendered, at sight or on presentment (Sec. 3-108).

      a. "At sight" or "on presentment."

      b. If no date is stipulated in an instrument for payment, it is payable on demand.

   2. Payable at a definite time (Sec. 3-109) — The holder must be able to determine the latest possible date on which the instrument will be paid.

      a. An instrument is negotiable if it is payable:
         1) On or before a stated date.
         2) At a fixed period after a stated date or after issue or sight.
         3) At a definite stated time but subject to acceleration. (The time for payment will be accelerated upon the happening of some event, such as the failure of the obligor, who is usually the maker of a note, to make a payment of interest or an installment that is due.)
         4) At a definite, stated time but subject to an extension:
            a) To another stated date, so that the outer limit in time for payment is known. (Think of it as being payable at the date to which it may be extended, but subject to acceleration to the earlier stated date.)
            b) At the option of the holder, with no outer limit stated. (Think of it as being demand paper.)

      b. An instrument is not negotiable:
         1) If it is payable upon the happening of an event, the date of which is not certain (such as the arrival of a ship, death of a named person).
         2) At a definite stated time, subject to an extension at the option of the obligor.

F. Payable to order or to bearer — The words of negotiability.

    1. Order instrument (Sec. 3-110).

        a. Pay to the order of a named payee (who may be the maker, drawee or drawer as well).

        b. Pay to a named payee or his, her or its order.

        c. Pay to the order of multiple payees, together (jointly) or in the alternative.

        d. Pay to the order of the representative of an estate, trust, etc., or a partnership or unincorporated association.

    2. Bearer instrument (Sec. 3-111).

        a. Pay to bearer.

        b. Pay to order of bearer.

        c. Pay to the order of a named person or bearer (or his or her assigns).

        d. Pay to cash or payroll or similar designation.

G. If an instrument is a draft or check, the drawee must be identified.

IV. Terms and omissions that do not affect negotiability (Sec. 3-112) — An instrument is negotiable although it:

A. Omits a statement of consideration or the place where drawn or payable.

B. Contains a statement that collateral is given.

C. Contains a provision that the payee, by indorsing or cashing the instrument, acknowledges that it is accepted as full satisfaction of an obligation.

D. Does not state the date of issue, unless such date is necessary in order to determine the date upon which payment is due.

E. Is postdated or antedated.

V. Rules of interpretation.

A. If there is a conflict between typewritten and preprinted words, the typewritten words control. If there is a conflict between handwritten words and those that are typed or preprinted, the handwritten words control.

B. If there is a conflict between words and symbols, such as numbers, that represent the words, the words control.

KEY WORDS AND PHRASES IN TEXT

Assignment of rights
Requirements for a negotiable instrument
   (U.C.C. Section 3-104)
Writing that has permanence and
   portability
Signature of the maker or drawer
Signature by authorized representative
Unconditional promise or order to pay
Implied or constructive conditions
Statement of consideration (is not
   necessary in order for instrument to
   be negotiable)
Reference to other agreements or writings

Statement that instrument is secured
Indication of a particular fund or account
   out of which instrument is to be paid
Sum certain in money
Payable on demand (or at sight or upon
   presentation)
Payable at a definite time
Acceleration clause
Extension clause
Payable to order
Payable to bearer
Bearer instrument

FILL-IN QUESTIONS

1. Section 3-104(1) provides that in order for an instrument to be negotiable, it must
    be in writing, signed by the _____ (if it is a promissory note or
    certificate of deposit) or the _____ (if it is a draft or a check), contain
    an unconditional promise (if it is a promissory note) or _____ (if it is a
    draft or check) to pay a sum certain in _____ on demand or at a
    _____, and be payable to order of a named payee or to
    _____.   A draft and a check must indicate the name of the
    _____, to whom the order to pay is directed.

2.

   | To: Tenth State Bank |
   | Pay to John Jonry the sum of fifty-four dollars ($54.00). |

   The instrument satisfies the following requirements for negotiability _____
   _____
   but it is not negotiable because _____
   _____.

3. You are given the following instrument:

   May 1, 1989

   On June 3, 1991, I promise to pay to the order of
   N. Barnes one hundred dollars ($100.00), this note being
   payable out of the proceeds of the sale of my 1928
   antique Ford automobile.

   Roger Colen

The instrument satisfies the following requirements for negotiability _____

_____

_____

but it is not negotiable because it does not contain _____

_____

_____.

4. You are given the following instrument:

> May 1, 1989
>
> Fifty years from date I, ___*Cynthia Smart*___,
> promise to pay to the order of Lucy Loring the sum of
> ($1,000.00) one thousand dollars, but should my aunt,
> Priscilla Smart, die before the maturity date hereof, this
> note shall become payable two weeks after her death.

The instrument satisfies the following requirements for negotiability _____

_____

_____

but it is not negotiable because _____

_____.

MULTIPLE CHOICE QUESTIONS

1. The signature of the maker of a negotiable promissory note must appear:
    a. on the instrument.
    b. in ink.
    c. as a subscription.
    d. in the lower right hand corner.

2. The following writing is given to you:

> 8/19/88
>
> Pay to Jack Johnson fifty dollars ($50.00).
> To: The First State Bank
>
> *John Jackson*

    a. It is an example of a negotiable demand draft.
    b. It is an example of an order bill of exchange.
    c. It is an example of a nonnegotiable promissory note.
    d. It is an example of a nonnegotiable sight draft.

3. When no time of payment is specified in a promissory note, the note is payable:
    a. on demand.
    b. within a reasonable period of time.

    c. within one year.
    d. thirty days after issue.

4. The following paper is given to you:

> Pay to the order of Peter Squires or bearer $33.00.
>
> To: R. Carey
>   5487 Main St.   *Thomas Poole*

    a. It is an example of a negotiable check.
    b. It is an example of a nonnegotiable check.
    c. It is an example of a time draft.
    d. It is an example of a negotiable sight draft.

5. A promise to pay out of a particular fund does not destroy negotiability of an instrument, provided the promise is made by:
    a. a banker.
    b. a business corporation.
    c. a municipal corporation.
    d. none of the above.

6. The negotiability of an instrument is destroyed if it contains the terms:
    a. this note is secured by a chattel mortgage, dated June 4, 1988.
    b. this note is subject to the terms of a mortgage dated September 22, 1988.
    c. this check is given in payment of rent for June.
    d. this instrument is given as per agreement entered on the date of issue.

7. A so-called "I.O.U." is:
    a. a draft.
    b. a promissory note.
    c. order paper.
    d. an acknowledgment of an obligation.

8. The following words in a promissory note would destroy negotiability:
    a. subject to our agreement of March 2, 1988.
    b. payment for five crates of oranges.
    c. payable in three monthly installments.
    d. together with interest at the legal rate.

9. A check, payable "to the order of U.S. Treasurer," is:
    a. not negotiable because it is not payable to a named person's order or to bearer.
    b. a negotiable order check.
    c. a negotiable bearer check.
    d. treated as time paper.

10. The negotiability of an otherwise negotiable promissory note is affected by:
    a. post-dating the note.
    b. a clause authorizing payment in silver.
    c. a clause authorizing payment in Mexican pesos.
    d. a clause providing for acceleration of payment.

Chapter 24

COMMERCIAL PAPER
Transferability
and Negotiation

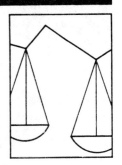

The manner in which commercial paper is transferred depends first of all upon whether it is negotiable or nonnegotiable. If it is negotiable, it is transferred by negotiation; if it is nonnegotiable, transfer is by assignment. Negotiation of order paper is by delivery and indorsement, but bearer paper may be negotiated by delivery alone.

An indorsement will have certain characteristics, which are not mutually exclusive. An indorsement indicates (1) how subsequent negotiation is to be effected (blank or special), (2) limitations on the liability of the indorser (qualified or unqualified), and (3) the type of interest being transferred (restrictive or nonrestrictive).

THINGS TO KEEP IN MIND

1. One, who signs his or her name on a negotiable instrument, acquires liability to subsequent holders.

2. One, whose signature is not on a negotiable instrument, is not liable on the instrument, except if he or she had been a holder of a bearer instrument, he or she will be liable to his or her immediate transferee.

3. No indorsement can change the negotiable character of paper. If commercial paper is negotiable on its face, it remains negotiable.

OUTLINE

I. Methods by which commercial paper is transferred.

   A. Nonnegotiable paper — Transfer is by assignment and, therefore, delivery of the instrument by the maker or drawer, who issues the instrument (Sec. 3-102(1)(a)).

Thereafter, an assignee may make a subassignment, in order to transfer his or her rights.

B. Negotiable instrument — Transfer is by "negotiation" — A transfer that results in the transferee being a holder, one in possession of a negotiable instrument, drawn, issued or indorsed to him or her or his or her order or bearer (Sec. 1-201(20)). The manner in which negotiation is effected depends on whether the instrument is order or bearer paper.

    1. Transfer of paper from original maker or drawer to the person to whom he or she intended to be the recipient — Contract law applies.

    2. Bearer paper is negotiated by physical delivery alone.

    3. Order paper is negotiated by a physical delivery and a necessary indorsement by the transferor (the payee or an indorsee).

II. Indorsement.

A. Signature of a transferor, usually on the back of the instrument.

B. If instrument is payable to the order of a named payee, the payee must indorse it in order to transfer his or her rights to a holder.

C. If instrument is payable to bearer, the transferee may request that his or her transferor indorse it.

D. If there is no space for an indorsement on the back of an instrument, indorsement is effective if written on an *allonge,* a separate paper that is firmly affixed to the original instrument.

E. One can change the manner required in order to transfer commercial paper by the type of indorsement used, but cannot change the negotiable character of the paper by indorsement.

F. One, who indorses, becomes secondarily liable to subsequent holders.

III. Types of indorsement.

A. Manner of indorsement determines how paper is transferred or negotiated in the future, what rights are transferred and the liability of parties.

    1. Indorser is liable to pay subsequent holder if primarily liable party does not pay.

    2. One, who indorses without indicating that he or she is indorsing in a representative capacity, is liable in his or her individual capacity.

B. Future manner of negotiating instrument is determined by blank or special indorsement (Sec. 3-204).

    1. Blank indorsement.

a. Holder or one in possession signs name.

b. Results in paper being considered bearer paper. Negotiation is by delivery alone.

2. Special indorsement.

a. Holder or one in possession indicates a specific person, to whom he or she intends to make the instrument payable, by writing, "Pay to the order of," or, "Pay to," the specified person and signs name.

b. Results in paper being considered order paper. Negotiation thereafter is by delivery and indorsement of indorsee.

3. Order paper can be changed to bearer paper and *vice versa* by using a blank indorsement and special indorsement.

C. Liability of indorser is described by qualified or unqualified indorsement (Sec. 3-414).

1. Qualified — Indorser signs name and writes, "without recourse," so that he or she has limited liability to subsequent holders.

2. Unqualified — Indorser signs, in blank or specially, without qualification and is secondarily liable to subsequent holders.

D. Type of interest being transferred is described by restrictive or nonrestrictive indorsement (Secs. 3-205 and 3-206).

1. Restrictive — Restricts or conditions rights of indorsee, but does not change obligations of party who created the paper.

a. An instrument is not negotiable if the issuer imposes such restrictions. A restriction or condition in an indorsement, however, does not destroy the negotiability of the paper.

b. Transferee from an indorsee, whose rights were restricted by a restrictive indorsement, must comply with direction in indorsement.

c. Kinds of restrictive indorsements.
   1) Conditional — Rights of indorsee are subject to the happening of some event. (Pay X only if he delivers the merchandise.)
   2) Prohibition against further transfer — Interpreted as a special indorsement. (Pay to X only.)
   3) Indorsement for deposit or collection — Results in the indorsee (usually a bank) being an agent for purposes of obtaining payment for indorser.
   4) Trust indorsement — Payment to indorsee must be consistent with the restriction.

2. Nonrestrictive — No conditions or restrictions are imposed upon the indorsee.

IV. Miscellaneous.

   A. Indorsement on negotiable instrument, using words of assignment, is a negotiation (Sec. 3-202).

   B. If name of indorsee is misspelled, indorsee may negotiate by indorsing in misspelled name, correct name, or both (Sec. 3-203).

   C. Depositary bank is agent of customer for purposes of supplying a missing indorsement of customer unless there is a specific prohibition on the instrument (Sec. 4-205).

   D. Multiple payees (Sec. 3-116) — If payable:

      1. In the alternative — Either may indorse (e.g., "Payable to A or B").

      2. Jointly — All must indorse (e.g., "Payable to A and B").

   E. Unindorsed order paper (Sec. 3-201) — Transferee is treated as an assignee but may obtain transferor's indorsement, if transfer was made for value.

   F. Instrument drawn or indorsed payable to an estate, partnership, unincorporated association, etc., may be indorsed by an authorized representative of the organization (Sec. 3-110).

V. Forged or unauthorized indorsements and imposters.

   A. Forgeries and signatures of unauthorized persons (Sec. 3-404) — Loss falls on one who took from forger.

      1. Forger or unauthorized indorser is personally liable.

      2. Not considered to be the signature of the person, by whom it appears to have been written, unless he or she ratifies it.

      3. If signature was necessary for negotiation, transferee is not a holder.

      4. Payor is liable to rightful owner.

   B. Imposters (Sec. 3-405) — Loss falls on maker or drawer if:

      1. Imposter, representing that he or she was another person, convinces maker or drawer to issue instrument in name of person that he or she is representing.

      2. Employee or agent issues instrument to a named payee, who may be ficticious, intending that the payee have no interest in the instrument.

      3. Employee or agent supplies the name of a payee, or ficticious person, to employer or principal, who issues instrument.

VI. Warranties — See Chapter 26.

KEY WORDS AND PHRASES IN TEXT

Negotiable instrument is issued by maker
    or drawer
Transfer by assignment (transferee is an
    assignee)
Transfer by negotiation (transferee is a
    holder)
Negotiable order paper is negotiated by
    delivery of instrument with an
    indorsement
Special indorsement
Negotiable bearer paper is negotiated by
    delivery
Converting order paper to bearer paper
    and bearer paper to order paper
Indorsements
Allonge
Blank indorsement
Special indorsement
Qualified indorsement
Unqualified indorsement

Restrictive indorsement
Conditional indorsement
Indorsement prohibiting further
    indorsement
Indorsement for deposit or collection
Trust indorsement
Nonrestrictive indorsement
Unauthorized or forged signature
Imposter
Ficticious payee
Correction of misspelled name
Indorsement by bank as agent for its
    customer
Multiple payees
Instrument payable in the alternative
Instrument payable jointly
Unindorsed order paper is transferred by
    assignment
An authorized representative, agent or
    officer can indorse an instrument
    that is payable to a legal entity

FILL-IN QUESTIONS

1.   A negotiable instrument is transferred by _____. An instrument that is payable on its face to a named payee is order paper and is negotiated by the payee by delivery of the instrument with an _____. In order to indorse the instrument, the payee must place his, her or its _____ on the instrument.

2.   A _____ is one who is in possession of a negotiable instrument that has been issued to him, her or it or to bearer, or specially indorsed to his, her or its order, or to him, her or it, or to bearer or in blank.

3.   A blank indorsement consists of merely the _____ of the payee or indorser. In order to negotiate the instrument to another person, all that is necessary is a _____ of the instrument.

4.   A _____ indorsement indicates the person to whom the indorser intends to make a negotiable instrument payable. In order for the indorsee to further negotiate the instrument, he, she or it must place his, her or its _____ on the instrument. If the indorser merely signs the instrument, the paper is then considered to be bearer paper and may be negotiated by _____ alone; if the indorser specifies to whom the instrument is to be paid, the paper is then considered to be order paper and may be negotiated by _____.

5.   You are given the following instrument:

```
                                          30 March 1989

    Pay to the order of Lucy Low----------------------$25.00
    Twenty-five and 00/100----------------------------dollars

    Tenth State Bank
                                    Howard How
```

Write the appropriate indorsement in order to transfer the instrument to Tom Trustee for the benefit of Benny Fishiary: _____
_____.

Write the appropriate indorsement in order to transfer the instrument from Tom Trustee to Henry Hunt so that it becomes bearer paper: _____
_____.

Write the appropriate indorsement so that Henry Hunt can deposit or cash the check at his bank: _____.

MULTIPLE CHOICE QUESTIONS

1. An order instrument:
   a. is merely an assignment.
   b. may be changed to bearer paper by indorsement.
   c. may be negotiated without an indorsement.
   d. is payable to bearer.

2. An instrument that is bearer on its face:
   a. is always bearer paper.
   b. is a draft.
   c. cannot be a check.
   d. may be changed to order paper.

3. An indorsement that specifies the person to whom the instrument is payable:
   a. changes order paper to bearer paper.
   b. is a restrictive indorsement.
   c. is a special indorsement.
   d. cannot be transferred subsequently to another person.

4. Delivery and indorsement are the two elements of a valid negotiation for:
   a. negotiable instruments.
   b. commercial paper.
   c. order paper.
   d. bearer paper.

5. A qualified indorsement is best epitomized by the words:
   a. For deposit only.
   b. Without recourse.
   c. Pay to the order of X only.
   d. Any of the above.

6. The payee of a check signed his name on the back and wrote, "Pay to Richard Roe." This is:
   a. a qualified, nonrestrictive, blank indorsement.
   b. an unqualified, nonrestrictive, special indorsement.
   c. an unqualified, restrictive, special indorsement.
   d. an unqualified, nonrestrictive, blank indorsement.

7. The last indorsement on the back of a check reads, "Arthur's Annex, for collection only." It is:
   a. a qualified, nonrestrictive, blank indorsement.
   b. a qualified, restrictive, blank indorsement.
   c. an unqualified, restrictive, special indorsement.
   d. an unqualified, restrictive, blank indorsement.

8. "John Doe, without recourse" is written on the back of a promissory note. It is:
   a. a qualified, nonrestrictive, blank indorsement.
   b. a qualified, restrictive, blank indorsement.
   c. an unqualified, restrictive, blank indorsement.
   d. an indorsement that will prevent the further negotiation of the note.

9. The "imposter rule" may be described as:
   a. an exception to the usual rule that a payor is liable to one whose signature is forged.
   b. a restatement of the general rule that a payor is not liable to one whose signature has been forged.
   c. a restatement of the general rule that a payor is liable to a true payee if the payor pays a forger rather than the payee.
   d. none of the above.

10. Zack wrote a check, payable to the order of Vera, who claimed that she was collecting money for the United Fund. Vera was not really collecting for the United Fund, but she cashed the check at Zack's bank.
    a. Zack must incur the loss.
    b. Vera had good title to the check.
    c. The bank must incur the loss because it paid out on a forged signature.
    d. The bank must incur the loss even though there was no forgery.

Chapter 25

COMMERCIAL PAPER
Holder in Due Course

As will become clearer in Chapter 26, a holder in due course possesses greater rights than a person who is simply a holder. It is important that you be able to recognize whether or not a particular holder of an instrument is a holder in due course. A holder in due course (HDC) is a holder, who takes a negotiable instrument for value, in good faith, without notice that the instrument is defective or overdue or has been dishonored or that there are defenses or claims that may be asserted against it.

THINGS TO KEEP IN MIND

One who is not a holder, in possession of a negotiable instrument, drawn or issued to his or her order or to bearer or indorsed to him or her specially or in blank, cannot be a holder in due course.

OUTLINE

I. Contract law versus law of commercial paper.

    A. Contract law of assignment.

        1. Contract law applies when contract rights are assigned to a third person, the assignee.

            a. Nonnegotiable commercial paper transferred to a third person.

            b. Negotiable instrument transferred, without a proper negotiation, to a third person.

        2. Assignor transfers only those rights which he or she has. Original obligor

can, therefore, raise defenses, existing between contracting parties, against the assignee, who was not a party to the original contract.

B. Special rules of Article 3 of the Uniform Commercial Code apply to transferee of a negotiable instrument that has been properly negotiated to him or her. The transferee may be deemed to be a holder or a holder in due course.

II. Holder — A person in possession of an instrument drawn, issued or indorsed to him or her or to his or her order or to bearer or indorsed in blank (Sec. 1-201(20)) so that he or she is entitled to receive payment (Sec. 3-301).

A. An original party to the issuance of an instrument, such as the payee, may be a holder.

B. A holder has the right to:

1. Transfer or negotiate the instrument.

2. Demand payment.

3. Assert any rights, which his or her transferor might have asserted. This is so because a holder has the status of an assignee.

III. Holder in due course (HDC) — A holder of a negotiable instrument who takes the instrument for value, in good faith, without notice that it is overdue or that it has been dishonored or that any person has a defense against it or a claim to it (Sec. 3-302).

A. HDC takes instrument for value (Sec. 3-303).

1. Value must have been actually given rather than promised, unlike consideration for a contract.

2. A donee of a gift does not give value.

3. Holder takes instrument for value to the extent that the agreed consideration has been performed. Consideration may be services performed, property sold or money (not necessarily the face amount of the instrument).

4. Adequacy of consideration is immaterial. (The question of adequacy may, however, go to the issue of good faith.)

5. Value is given if an instrument is given as security.

6. Value is given if an instrument is given in payment of an antecedent (pre-existing) debt or claim.

7. Value is given if an instrument is exchanged for a negotiable instrument or if an irrevocable commitment is made to a third person.

8. Sufficient value is *not* given if a holder acquired instrument:

a. At a judicial sale or under legal process.

    b. In taking over an estate.

    c. As part of a bulk transfer that was not in the ordinary course of business (Sec. 3-302).

B. HDC takes instrument in good faith (Sec. 1-201(19)).

    1. Holder acts honestly and subjectively believes that the instrument is regular, even if a more prudent person would have been suspicious or put on notice that something was wrong at the time he or she acquires the instrument.

    2. If the consideration given by a holder is inadequate, relative to the purported value of an instrument, the holder does not take it in good faith.

C. HDC takes instrument without notice of certain defects (Sec. 3-304).

    1. Notice.

        a. At the time instrument is acquired.

        b. Actual knowledge, receiving notification or having knowledge of available facts or circumstances, such that he or she should have known certain things. (Knowledge is, therefore, imputed.)

    2. Without notice that the instrument was overdue.

        a. Time instrument.
          1) Considered overdue on the day after specified maturity date.
          2) Presence of an acceleration clause in installment paper is not notice that instrument may be overdue.

        b. Demand instrument.
          1) Knowledge that a demand had been already made.
          2) Acquire instrument after it has been outstanding an unreasonable period of time.
            a) Check — 30 days (Sec. 3-304(3)(c)).
            b) Draft — Less than 60 days (business usage).
            c) Note — 60 days (business usage).

    3. Without notice that instrument was dishonored — Presented for payment or acceptance, which was refused.

    4. Without notice that there are defenses against the instrument or claims to it.

        a. Defects that are apparent from the examination of the instrument because it is incomplete or irregular — Erasures, alterations, incomplete or incorrect indorsements, material omissions or blanks, when author of paper did not authorize completion (Sec. 3-304).

        b. Defects that are extraneous to the instrument but apparent from facts surrounding the transaction.

       1) Knowledge that transferor's title is defective because of theft, illegality, fraud, etc.

       2) Knowledge that obligation of a party is void or voidable or that all parties were discharged.

       3) Knowledge will not be imputed if:

          a) Instrument is antedated or postdated.

          b) Public notice by filing, etc., has been given.

   5. Payee, who was not an actual party to issuance of instrument, may be a holder in due course.

IV. Holder through a holder in due course.

   A. A holder, who derives his or her interest or title from a holder in due course, may acquire the rights of a holder in due course because he or she is an assignee, who acquires the rights that his or her assignor possessed, unless he or she was a party to an irregularity, such as fraud or illegality (Sec. 3-201).

   B. Limitations on this shelter principle.

     1. A holder, who reacquires an instrument, is entitled to the status he or she previously had.

     2. A holder cannot improve his or her status by reacquiring an instrument from a holder in due course.

KEY WORDS AND PHRASES IN TEXT

Holder in due course (HDC)

Holder in due course takes negotiable instrument free of most defenses and claims of other parties

Assignee takes commercial paper subject to claims and defenses that existed between prior parties

Requirements for holder in due course status

Holder in due course must be a holder

Holder in due course must have taken negotiable instrument for value

Value

Performance of agreed upon consideration

Instrument taken as security for an obligation

Instrument taken in payment for antecedent (preexisting) debt

Instrument taken in exchange for another negotiable instrument

Holder in due course must take negotiable instrument in good faith

Holder in due course must take negotiable instrument without notice that instrument is overdue or has been dishonored or that there is a defense against or claim to it

Notice

Overdue time instruments

Overdue demand instruments

Dishonored instrument

Claims to or defenses against instrument

Incomplete and irregular instruments

Voidable obligations

When payee may be a holder in due course

Holder through a holder in due course (the shelter principle)

Limitations on the shelter principle

Instances in which holder takes instrument for value but is not accorded holder in due course status

FILL-IN QUESTIONS

1. One is considered to be a holder if he or she is in possession of an instrument that is drawn, issued or indorsed to him or her or to his or her order or to _____ or indorsed _____ .

2. A holder in due course of a negotiable instrument is one who took the instrument, _____ and without notice that it was _____ or that it had been _____ or without notice of _____ or claims to it on the part of any person.

3. Giving value, as a requisite for being a holder in due course, differs from consideration necessary to support a contract because value must be _____ _____ , whereas consideration may be something promised. One is not considered as having given value if nothing is given or if something, such as _____ , is promised but not given, or if an instrument is acquired at a judicial sale or _____ _____ in taking over an estate or as part of a bulk transfer _____ _____ .

4. If you are in possession of a note, payable to the order of John Doe, and indorsed by John Doe, you are a _____ . If you paid $10 to your transferor in exchange for the note, in good faith and without notice that _____ _____ , you are also a holder in due course.

MULTIPLE CHOICE QUESTIONS

1. Henry Hunt needed $100 in a hurry. He asked Frank Franklin, an acquaintance, if Frank would give him $100 for a piece of paper that looked like this on its face:

> To: Earl Earl
>
> Pay to the order of Paula Paul the sum of $120.00.
>
> *Roberto Roberts*
> Roberto Roberts

The only writing on the back of the paper was Paula Paul's signature.
a. Earl Earl was a holder but not a holder in due course.
b. Paula Paul could not have been a holder because she was the payee.
c. Henry Hunt will have to indorse the instrument in order for Frank Franklin to have the status of a holder in due course.
d. Frank Franklin will be a holder in due course if he has no notice of any defects in the paper or defenses available against it.

2. Mary Munroe, the assistant to the treasurer of the XYZ Corporation, prepared the monthly payroll and the checks for the corporation. Ms. Munroe added the name of Jane Joker, a ficticious person, to the payroll and prepared a check to Jane Joker's order. The treasurer, who did not know the true facts, signed the check in good faith. Mary Monroe then indorsed the check with the name of Jane Joker,

negotiated the check to Kevin Kansas, obtained the money and disappeared. Kevin Kansas cashed the check at the corporation's bank.
a. XYZ Corporation can recover the amount of the check from the bank.
b. Kevin Kansas was a holder in due course.
c. Jane Joker was a holder in due course.
d. Mary Munroe was a holder in due course.

3. Peter Pill, in exchange for $800, offers you a piece of paper. One side looks like this:

> I promised to pay to the order of Barney Beaker the
> sum of One Thousand and   dollars
> on November 30, 1994.
>
>   *Arthur Aspirin*
>   Arthur Aspirin

The back looks like this:

> *Barney Beaker*
> *Pay to Z. Zink*
> *Z. Zink*

You will not be a holder in due course because:
a. there is a blank on the face of the instrument.
b. the date upon which the instrument was issued has been omitted.
c. the consideration you give will not be adequate value.
d. the name of Peter Pill, who will be your transferor, does not appear on the back.

4. Quoit paid Ridge for services performed by Ridge with a check payable to Ridge's order. Ridge indorsed it in blank and gave the check to Strata as a gift.
a. Strata is neither a holder nor a holder in due course.
b. Strata is a holder but not a holder in due course.
c. Strata is a holder and a holder in due course.
d. If Strata transfers the check for value to Tracer, Tracer will be a holder through a holder in due course.

5. Viper induced Walsh to write a check payable to Viper's order by making a misrepresentation of a material fact, upon which Walsh reasonably relied. The next day Viper gave the check to Houlder, who took it in good faith, for value, without notice of any defects in the paper or defenses against it or claims to it. Two days later, Houlder indorsed the check, payable to Ingram's order. Ingram, who knew of the original transaction between Viper and Walsh, gave value to Houlder and is the present holder of the check.
a. Houlder was a holder in due course.
b. Houlder was not a holder in due course but had the rights of a holder through a holder in due course.
c. Ingram is a holder in due course.

d. Ingram is not a holder in due course but had the rights of a holder through a holder in due course. ·

6. On June 1 Macon sold Norris defective goods, for which Norris paid with a check. On June 3 Norris discovered that the goods were defective and stopped payment of the check. On June 8 Macon learned of the stop payment order. On July 4 Macon specially indorsed the check to Loring for value. Loring knew neither of the defective goods nor the stoppage of payment.
   a. Macon was a holder in due course.
   b. Loring was a holder in due course.
   c. Loring was not a holder in due course because the instrument was overdue when he acquired it.
   d. Loring was not a holder in due course because he acquired the instrument on a national holiday.

7. Henderson sold an $800 negotiable promissory note, which was payable in one month to her order, to Dumas for $790. When she delivered the note to Dumas, Henderson neglected to sign her name on the back. Dumas:
   a. qualifies as a holder in due course.
   b. qualifies as a holder.
   c. has a specifically enforceable right to obtain Henderson's unqualified indorsement.
   d. has a better right to receive payment of the note than Henderson had.
   (This question has been adapted from AICPA Examination of May 1982.)

8. In order to be a holder of a bearer negotiable promissory note, the transferee must:
   a. give value for the note.
   b. take the note in good faith.
   c. acquire the note before receiving notice that another person has a claim to the instrument.
   d. have physical possession of the instrument.
   (This question has been adapted from the AICPA Examination of May 1984.)

9. Which of the following will not constitute giving value in determining whether or not a person is a holder in due course?
   a. The exchange of a negotiable instrument for consideration to be performed in one month.
   b. The taking of a negotiable instrument as security for a six month loan of money.
   c. The giving of one's own negotiable note in connection with the purchase of another negotiable instrument.
   d. The performance of services rendered to the payee of a negotiable draft accompanied by indorsement by the payee.
   (This question has been adapted from the AICPA Examination of May 1984.)

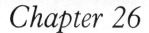

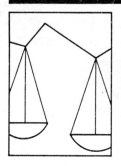

COMMERCIAL PAPER
Defenses, Liability,
and Discharge

A party to commercial paper, who is obligated to pay, may have one or more defenses, which can be raised against a holder seeking payment of an instrument. Certain defenses, termed personal defenses, are not available against a holder in due course; other defenses, referred to as real defenses, are available against all holders, including holders in due course.

Parties, who issue or transfer commercial paper, acquire liability to subsequent holders of such instruments. Recall that commercial paper is a special form of contract. For this reason, any party, whose signature appears on the instrument, is liable in contract. A party, who makes an unconditional promise to pay, such as a maker of a note or an acceptor of a draft, is absolutely and primarily liable in contract to pay. The contract liability of other parties to instruments, such as drawers of drafts, unqualified indorsers and accommodation parties, is secondary and conditioned upon (1) the proper and timely presentment of the instrument to one, who is required to pay or required, in the case of a draft, to accept, (2) dishonor, a refusal to pay or accept, and (3) notification of the dishonor.

Parties, who transfer or present commercial paper, are also treated as having made certain implied warranties, the effects of which are to cut off defenses that ordinarily might be raised. As a result, additional unconditional liability may be imposed upon such parties.

The liability of one or more parties to pay the face amount of an instrument may be terminated or discharged. Normally commercial paper is discharged by payment or other satisfaction but some or all parties may be discharged by cancellation or renunciation; a correct tender of payment; impairment of a right of recourse (to obtain reimbursement) against a party or collateral security; reacquisition; a fraudulent, material alteration; certification of a check; a draft varying acceptance; an unexcused delay in presentment and/or notice of dishonor; or any act which would discharge a simple contract for the payment of money. No discharge, however, will be effective against a holder in due course, who lacked notice of the discharge when the instrument was negotiated to him or her.

THINGS TO KEEP IN MIND

In addition to the liability discussed in the chapter, remember that some underlying transaction gives rise to the issuance of commercial paper so that the parties to the underlying transaction have contractual rights and obligations, which are merely suspended by the issuance of an instrument. The same is true when commercial paper is transferred. For example, if R draws a check, payable to P, on his bank, in order to pay for goods purchased from P, R remains contractually obligated to pay P for the goods should the drawee bank refuse to honor the check. Similarly, had P negotiated the check to H, in exchange for the performance of some services, P's liability to pay H for the services is merely suspended until H receives payment of the instrument.

OUTLINE

I.   Defenses — May be raised by a party, who is liable to pay on an instrument.

   A. Real or universal defenses — Can be raised against all holders, including holders in due course and holders through holders in due course. Usually a void transaction is involved.

      1. Forgery or unauthorized signatures (Sec. 3-401 and 3-404).

      2. Fraud in the execution (Sec. 3-305(2)(c)).

      3. Material alteration of a completed instrument, if carelessness is not present, to the extent of the alteration (Sec. 3-407).

      4. Discharge in insolvency or bankruptcy proceedings (Sec. 3-305(2)(d)).

      5. Illegality when state statute provides that transaction is void (Sec. 305(2)(b)).

      6. Incapacity.

         a. Infancy to the extent it is a defense to a simple contract.

         b. Mental incompetency, if state law provides that contracts are void.

      7. Extreme duress.

      8. Statute of limitations.

   B. Personal or limited defenses — Can be raised against a holder but not a holder in due course or a holder through a holder in due course (Sec. 3-306).

      1. Breach of contract.

      2. Lack or failure of consideration.

3. Lack of real assent because of fraud in the inducement, misrepresentation, mistake, undue influence or ordinary duress.

4. Illegality and incapacity, which renders a contract voidable, rather than void.

5. Discharge by payment or other satisfaction or cancellation of an instrument which is permitted to circulate (Secs. 3-601(1)(a) and 3-602).

6. Unauthorized completion of an incomplete instrument (Secs. 3-304(4)(d) and 3-407).

7. Conditional delivery or nondelivery (Sec. 3-306(c)).

II. Limitations on holder in due course rule when commercial paper is issued in conjunction with a consumer credit transaction.

A. State legislation including Uniform Consumer Credit Code.

B. Federal Trade Commission rule protects consumers who obtain goods or services or loans in order to finance the purchases of goods or services.

1. Installment sales contracts and sales contracts that include promissory notes, issued in order to finance consumer credit transactions, must contain a notice preserving the right of the debtor to assert any defenses, which he or she could have asserted against the creditor with whom the debtor dealt, against a subsequent transferee or holder.

2. A holder of such a contract or note, therefore, does not possess all of the benefits that he or she normally would have as a holder in due course.

III. Liability of parties.

A. Liability based on signatures.

1. No one is liable on a negotiable instrument unless his or her signature appears thereon (Sec. 3-401(1)).

a. A signature may be handwritten, typed, printed or some mark, such as a thumb print.

b. A signature indicates a "present intention to authenticate a writing" (Sec. 1-201(39)).

c. One, whose signature has been used without authorization, may ratify its use on a negotiable instrument (Sec. 3-404(2)).

d. One, who signs another's name without authority or forges another's signature, is liable on a negotiable instrument (Sec. 3-404(1)).

e. One, whose name is signed by another without authorization, is not liable on a negotiable instrument (Sec. 3-404(1)).

2. A signature may be provided by an authorized representative, such as an agent (Sec. 3-403).

    a. Usually an agent gives the appropriate signature of his or her principal and signs his or her name, indicating that he or she is signing in a representative capacity, in which case only the principal is liable.

    b. An agent, who signs in his or her own name only, is personally liable on the instrument (Sec. 3-403(2)).

    c. If an agent signs for a principal and provides his or her own signature, without indicating that he or she is acting in a representative capacity, both the principal and agent are liable on the instrument (Sec. 3-403(2)). Parol evidence is admissible between the original parties in order to establish the agency relationship.

    d. If an agent signs his or her own name and indicates that he or she is signing in a representative capacity but fails to indicate the name of the principal, parol evidence is admissible between the original parties in order to establish the agency relationship.

B. Contractual liability — One, whose signature appears on a negotiable instrument, by his or her own hand or that of another authorized person, acquires either primary liability or secondary liability based on contract.

1. Primarily liable parties.

    a. The maker of a promissory note.
       1) Maker promises to pay according to original tenor of note or according to terms as completed, if it was incomplete when issued (Sec. 3-413(1)).
       2) Maker admits the existence of the payee and his or her capacity to indorse (Sec. 3-413(3)).
       3) The underlying obligation, for which the note is given, is suspended until payment of the note. Upon dishonor, the maker can be sued either on the note or the underlying obligation (Sec. 3-802(1)).

    b. Acceptor of a draft (Sec. 3-410).
       1) No one is primarily liable on a draft when it is issued.
          a) If a draft is presented for acceptance to a drawee by a holder, the drawee becomes an acceptor upon acceptance of the draft.
          b) A drawee, who is not an acceptor, is not liable to a presenter if he, she or it fails to pay or accept a draft. A drawee's contractual liability is only to the drawer.
       2) Certification of a check is treated as an acceptance (Sec. 3-411).
       3) Acceptor:
          a) Promises to pay according to the tenor of the instrument at the time of acceptance.
          b) Admits the existence of the drawer, the genuineness of the drawer's signature and the drawer's capacity.
          c) Admits the existence of the payee and the payee's capacity to indorse (Sec. 3-413).
       4) Draft must be presented when:

   a) Instrument requires presentation, as in the case of trade accep-
      tance.
   b) Draft is payable at a place other than the address of the drawer.
   c) Payment date of draft is dependent upon presentment.

2. Secondarily liable parties.

   a. Liability of drawer, unqualified indorser and accommodation party (other
      than an accommodation maker) is conditioned upon:
      1) Correct, timely presentment for payment or acceptance (Sec. 3-501).
      2) Dishonor — Refusal of payment or acceptance (Sec. 3-507(1)).
      3) Timely notice of dishonor to party, who is secondarily liable (Sec. 3-
         508) or notice of protest if instrument is drawn or payable outside the
         U.S. or its territory (Sec. 3-509).

   b. Rights against a secondarily liable party are preserved by complying with
      conditions of presentment and notice of dishonor or protest.

   c. Presentment and notice of dishonor or protest or a delay thereof may be
      excused, or waived (Sec. 3-511).

   d. Parties who are secondarily liable.
      1) Drawer engages that he or she will pay if a draft is dishonored and
         notice of dishonor given (Sec. 3-413(2)).
      2) Indorsers (Sec. 3-414).
         a) Unqualified indorser engages that he or she will pay according to
            the tenor of the instrument at the time of indorsement, if it is
            dishonored and notice of dishonor is given.
         b) A qualified indorser is relieved of contractual liability on an
            instrument.
      3) Accommodation party (Sec. 3-415).
         a) Signs for purposes of lending his or her name and credit to a party
            to an instrument.
         b) Obligation depends on capacity in which he or she signs.
         c) Accommodation party is not liable to the party accommodated
            and may obtain reimbursement for amounts paid on instrument
            from accommodated party.

C. Implied, unconditional warranty liability of parties.

   1. Warranties, which are made upon transfer, by one, who negotiates an instru-
      ment and receives consideration (Sec. 3-417).

      a. If transfer has been by indorsement and delivery, warranties apply to:
         1) Immediate transferee, and
         2) Subsequent holders, who take instrument in good faith.

      b. If transfer was by delivery alone, warranties run only to immediate
         transferee.

      c. Warranties of transferor.
         1) Transferor has good title or is authorized to obtain payment or accep-
            tance on behalf of a person, who has good title.

2) All signatures are genuine or authorized.

3) The instrument has not been materially altered.

4) No defense of any party is available against the transferor. A qualified indorser merely warrants that he or she has no knowledge of any such defenses.

5) The transferor has no knowledge of insolvency proceedings instituted against the maker, acceptor or drawer of an unaccepted draft.

2. Warranties made upon presentment by a person presenting instrument for acceptance or payment to a maker, acceptor or drawee (Sec. 3-417(1)).

   a. Good title.

   b. No knowledge that signature of maker or drawer is unauthorized.

   c. Instrument has not been materially altered.

IV. Discharge of parties to paper — A discharge is not effective against a holder in due course, who lacks notice of the discharge, when the instrument is negotiated to him or her (Sec. 3-602).

A. Discharge by payment or other satisfaction given to holder (Secs. 3-601(1)(a) and 3-603).

   1. A party is not discharged if payment was made in bad faith or in a manner inconsistent with a restrictive indorsement.

   2. Payment by an indorser discharges that indorser and subsequent indorsers.

   3. Tender of payment does not discharge obligation to pay face amount, but discharges liability for interest, costs and attorney fees (Sec. 3-604).

B. Discharge by cancellation or renunciation (Sec. 3-605).

   1. Cancellation — Intentional destruction, mutilation, etc., of instrument discharges all parties. Crossing out an indorsement discharges liability of that indorser and subsequent indorsers.

   2. Renunciation — Surrender of instrument or present, absolute surrender of rights in a signed writing.

C. Discharge because of material, fraudulent alteration (Secs. 3-407 and 3-601(f)).

   1. An alteration is material if it changes the obligations of a party.

   2. Parties are discharged to the extent of the alteration.

D. Discharge by impairment of the right of recourse, which is a source of reimbursement, against a party or collateral security (Secs. 3-601 and 3-606).

   1. Holder releases or agrees not to sue a party from whom an indorser can obtain reimbursement.

2. Holder agrees to suspend the right to enforce an instrument against a party.

3. Holder discharges prior indorsers by cancellation.

4. Holder, without justification, impairs collateral that had been given as security that the instrument would be paid.

E. Discharge by reacquisition — When a prior holder reacquires an instrument, intervening parties are discharged (Sec. 3-601(3)(a)).

F. Discharge by an unexcused failure or delay in presentment or notice of dishonor (Secs. 3-502 and 3-601(1)(i)).

G. Discharge by any act or agreement that would discharge a simple contract for the payment of money, such as a release, accord and satisfaction, etc. (Sec. 3-601(2)).

KEY WORDS AND PHRASES IN TEXT

Real defenses
Forged or unauthorized signature
Fraud in the execution (*in factum* or from the inception)
Material alteration of a completed instrument
Discharge in bankruptcy
Minority (to the extent that it is recognized as a real defense under state law)
Illegality
Mental incapacity or incompetency
Extreme duress
Personal defenses
Breach of contract
Fraud in the inducement
Illegality (if not treated as real defense)
Ordinary duress
Undue influence
Federal Trade Commission rule limiting rights of holder in due course in consumer transactions
Liability based upon contract
Contract liability based upon signature
Effect of unauthorized signature
Agent's signature
Agent's personal liability
Primary liability (based upon contract) of maker, acceptor and certifying bank
Secondary liability (based upon contract) of drawer and unqualified indorsers

Secondary liability is conditioned upon the instrument having been properly and timely presented
Secondary liability is conditioned upon the instrument having been dishonored
Secondary liability is conditioned upon timely notice of dishonor being given to secondarily liable party
Accommodation parties are liable in the capacity in which they sign instrument
Warranty liability of parties
Transfer warranties
Transferor has good title
Transferor warrants that all signatures are genuine or authorized
Transferor warrants that instrument has not been materially altered
Transferor warrants that no defense of any party is good against transferor (qualified indorser warrants that he or she has no knowledge of any defenses)
Transferor has no knowledge of institution of insolvency proceeding against maker, acceptor or drawer of unaccepted draft or check
Transfer warranties extend to all subsequent holders (who took in good faith) if transferor transferred order paper by indorsement and delivery

Transfer warranties extend only to immediate transferee if transferor transferred bearer paper by delivery without indorsement

Presentment warranties

Presenter has good title or is authorized to obtain payment or acceptance on behalf of a person who has good title

Presenter has no knowledge that signature of maker or drawer is not authorized

Presenter warrants that instrument has not been materially altered

Discharge by payment or other satisfaction

Unauthorized completion of an incomplete instrument

Nondelivery

Discharge by cancellation

Discharge by reacquisition

Discharge by impairment of right of recourse against a party or collateral

FILL-IN QUESTIONS

1. A party to a negotiable instrument may be liable if the instrument is not paid when it is due if his or her _____ appears on the instrument. He or she may be liable based upon the underlying obligation, _____ _____ or an implied warranty.

2. Parties, who are primarily liable based on contract, include _____ _____. Parties, who are secondarily liable, include _____ _____.

3. One of the purposes of giving a _____ to indorsers, following a proper presentment and dishonor, is to inform them, as secondarily liable parties, that the maker of a promissory note has failed to meet his or her obligations.

4. If a draft is presented by a holder for acceptance, the presenter warrants to the drawee/acceptor that he or she has (1) _____, (2) _____, and (3) _____.

5. A personal defense, such as _____, is one that cannot be raised against a holder in due course; a real defense is one that can be raised against _____.

MULTIPLE CHOICE QUESTIONS

1. For breach of any of the warranties of transferors, imposed by the Uniform Commercial Code upon both qualified and unqualified indorsers, the transferor is:
   a. liable to his or her transferee and subsequent holders.
   b. never liable for unintentional acts.
   c. liable only to his or her transferee.
   d. liable only to subsequent holders.

2. Signing a note, when it is believed that only an autograph is requested, gives rise to:
   a. no defense.
   b. the defense of illegality.
   c. a personal defense.
   d. a real defense.

3. With regard to a negotiable instrument, the following is usually considered to be a personal (limited) defense:
   a. The statute of limitations.
   b. Breach of contract.
   c. Fraud in the execution.
   d. Discharge in bankruptcy.

4. With regard to a negotiable instrument, the following is usually considered to be a real (universal) defense:
   a. Fraud in the execution.
   b. Fraudulent concealment.
   c. Failure of consideration.
   d. All of the above.

5. A party, who indorses a negotiable instrument with the words, "without recourse," avoids:
   a. all liability if the instrument is not paid when due.
   b. liability, based on warranty, if the instrument is not paid when due.
   c. liability, based on the contract, which is implied in the instrument, but not liability based on an underlying contract, which gave rise to the instrument.
   d. liability, based on the contract, which is implied in the instrument, as well as liability based on an underlying contract, which gave rise to the instrument.

6. A principal is liable on a negotiable instrument, signed by his or her agent in the name of the agent:
   a. if the agent has authority to issue negotiable instruments on behalf of his or her principal.
   b. if the agent has signed only his or her own name.
   c. and in the name of the principal.
   d. only if the agent indicates that he or she is signing in his or her representative capacity.

7. Carson executed a promissory note in the amount of $4000 payable to Donaldson. On the due date, Donaldson went to Carson's place of business and told Carson, "Your note is due today but I wish to renounce all my rights in connection with it." The note is:
   a. effectively discharged by renunciation and cancellation.
   b. effectively discharged by payment or other satisfaction.
   c. not effectively discharged because Carson has not given value to Donaldson.
   d. not effectively discharged unless the note is surrendered or Donaldson's statement is contained in a signed writing.

8. Ink, in order to borrow $2000 from his local bank, asked Pencil to sign a note as an accommodation maker. Pencil agreed and both he and Ink thereupon executed the note as makers by signing the face of the instrument.
   a. Pencil is liable as an accommodation indorser.
   b. Pencil is not liable to pay if Ink tendered the $2000, plus the interest that was due to the bank when the note became due.
   c. Ink may recover from Pencil if Ink tendered the $2000, plus the interest that was due to the bank when the note became due.
   d. Ink and Pencil are completely discharged if Ink tendered the $2000, plus the interest that was due to the bank when the note became due, if the bank refused to accept the payment.

9. Martin made a contract to purchase a television set on credit from TV City Inc. She signed a negotiable promissory note for the purchase price. TV City Inc. transferred the paper to the Careful Credit Co., which paid TV City Inc. ninety percent of the face value of the note. Martin, who was notified that Careful Credit Co. was now in possession of the note, has failed to pay Careful Credit Co. although the note is now due. Careful Credit Co. is, therefore, suing Martin, who claims (1) she has been discharged in a state insolvency proceeding and (2) the television set had not been delivered by TV City Inc. Careful Credit Co. had no notice of the existence of these defenses when it purchased the instrument.
    a. Both defenses can be successfully raised against Careful Credit Co.
    b. Martin can successfully raise the defense of discharge in an insolvency proceeding against Careful Credit Co. but not the defense of breach of contract.
    c. Martin can successfully raise the defense of failure of consideration against Careful Credit Co. but not the defense of discharge in an insolvency proceeding.
    d. Martin cannot successfully raise either defense against Careful Credit Co.

Chapter 27

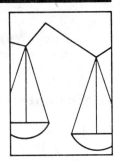

COMMERCIAL PAPER
Checks and the Banking System

The most frequently used form of commercial paper is the check, a demand draft which is drawn on a financial institution. The provisions of Article 3 of the Uniform Commercial Code, many of which have been discussed in the preceding chapters, apply to checks. In addition, Article 4 of the Code contains rules, pertaining to the bank deposit and collection system and the relationship between a bank customer and his or her bank, as well as other banks that may be involved in the collection process for checks and other types of commercial paper. These rules are meant to expedite the smooth flow of money, credit and business transactions.

The Expedited Funds Availability Act of 1987 (EFAA) and Regulation CC adopted by the Board of Governors of the Federal Reserve System in 1988 to implement this federal statute provide for limitations on the amount of time during which banks can restrict withdrawal of deposited funds by depositors and improvements in the check collection and return process. In some instances, EFAA preempts provisions in the U.C.C.

THINGS TO KEEP IN MIND

1. Checks are orders, issued by depositors, directing their banks to pay out funds, which the depositors have previously placed with the banks (demand deposits).

2. Often a holder of a check, who wishes to obtain cash for it or deposit it in his or her own bank account, does not use the bank upon which the check is drawn. It is, therefore, necessary that the check be forwarded through a network of intermediary banks by the holder's bank for collection and payment purposes.

OUTLINE

I. Checks.

A. A check is a draft, drawn on a bank, ordering it to pay a stated sum certain in money on demand (Sec. 3-104(2)(b)).

B. Usually a check is negotiable because it is signed by the drawer, contains a single, unconditional order to pay a sum certain in money on demand to the order of bearer or a named payee (Sec. 3-104(1)).

C. A postdated check is treated as a negotiable time draft.

D. A check is not an assignment of funds (Sec. 3-409). Until final payment is made, there is no effect on the depositor's account and the underlying obligation, for which the check is given, is not discharged.

E. Special kinds of checks.

   1. Cashier's check — A check drawn by a bank upon itself so that it is the drawer and drawee. A cashier's check is treated as being accepted in advance.

   2. Traveler's check — Check drawn by a financial institution, which requires the signature of the payee in order to be transferred.

   3. Certified check — Personal check, drawn by a depositor on his or her bank, which is accepted by the drawee bank (Sec. 3-411).

      a. The bank, which certifies, unconditionally promises that the check will be paid when presented.

      b. The bank immediately charges the depositor's (drawer's) account.

      c. If certification is obtained by the drawer, the drawer remains secondarily liable. Prior indorsers are discharged.

      d. If certification is obtained by a holder, the drawer and prior indorsers are discharged.

   4. Teller's check — Check provided to a customer drawn by the customer's bank on another bank or payable through or at another bank.

F. Relationship between bank and its customer.

   1. A customer is a person, having an account with a bank or for whom a bank has agreed to collect items (instruments for the payment of money) (Sec. 4-104(e) and (g)).

   2. Depositor is a creditor of his or her bank and a principal. The bank is a debtor and agent of its depositor.

   3. Duties of bank.

      a. Honor and pay checks of customer, who has sufficient funds in his or her account.

1) Bank is obligated to honor checks even if there are insufficient funds in the customer's account if it has agreed to honor overdrafts.
2) Bank is not required (but may) pay stale checks — Uncertified checks presented more than six months after the date of the check (Sec. 4-404).
3) Bank may honor checks of deceased or legally incompetent depositor until it knows of death or incompetency of a depositor. Even if it receives knowledge of the death of a depositor, it may pay or certify checks that were issued by a deceased depositor for ten days after the date of death (Sec. 4-405).

b. Follow order from a depositor to stop payment (Sec. 4-403).
1) Only customer may give stop payment order.
2) Bank must receive stop payment order at such time and in such a manner so that it has a reasonable opportunity to comply.
3) Duration — 14 days if oral; six months if written. Stop payment order may be renewed.
4) If bank fails to comply with order, it is liable to customer for the amount of actual loss incurred.

c. Liability of bank for payment on forged signatures.
1) Bank maintains signature cards of depositors and is required to check signatures of drawers.
2) Bank is liable if it pays an item, on which the signature of its customer, the drawer, is forged (Sec. 3-419). Exceptions:
   a) Drawer's negligence contributed to the forgery (Sec. 3-406).
   b) Imposter situation (Sec. 3-405).
   c) Customer fails to promptly notify bank of forgery after receipt of statement and cancelled checks (Sec. 4-406).
3) If bank pays on a forged indorsement, it cannot rightfully charge the drawer's account, but may recover from the person, who presented item for payment, because of warranties made upon presentment.

d. Liability of bank for payment on an altered check, if drawer was not negligent.
1) Bank may charge drawer's account for the amount of the check as originally issued.
2) Bank bears loss to the extent of the raised amount, if it pays out on a check with a raised amount.
3) Bank may recover from the person, who presented the check for payment, based on warranty liability.

II. Accepting deposits and the check clearing process.

A. Definitions (Sec. 4-105).

1. Depositary bank — First bank to receive a check or other item for purposes of collection.

2. Payor bank.

a. The drawee bank, upon which a check is drawn, that is required to pay an item.

   b. In Federal Reserve System regulations, the payor bank is referred to as the "paying bank."

3. Collecting bank — Any bank, other than a payor bank, handling an item during the collection process.

4. Intermediary bank — Any bank, other than the depositary bank or the payor bank, handling an item.

B. Check collection process when holder and drawer are customers of the same bank.

   1. The check is referred to as an "on-us" item.

   2. Bank charges (credits) drawer's account and debits depositor's account.

   3. Considered paid on the opening of the second banking day after check was deposited (Sec. 4-213(4)(b)).

C. Check collection between customers of different banks.

   1. Depositary bank arranges for presentment of check to drawee bank directly or through intermediary banks in the Federal Reserve system or a clearing house.

   2. Each intermediary bank must pass the check on before midnight of the next day following its receipt (Sec. 4-202).

   3. Depositor remains the owner of item until it clears. Intermediary banks are subagents of the depositor.

D. The Expedited Funds Availability Act of 1987 (EFAA) and supplemental Federal Reserve System Regulation CC.

   1. Limitations are imposed upon banks' "hold" periods—the periods between the time bank customers deposit funds and the time the funds are to be made available for withdrawal by customers.

      a. When funds are to be made available at the start of a business day, the funds can be withdrawn at the later of 9:00 a.m. or the time that the depositary bank's teller facilities, including automated teller machines (ATMs), are available for customer withdrawal.

      b. Next day availability for certain deposits.
         1) Cash deposits and electronic payments.
         2) U.S. Treasury check when deposited in account of payee.
         3) Certain other checks when deposited in account of payee and deposited in person to a bank employee.
            a) U.S. Postal Service money order.
            b) Federal Reserve Bank or Federal Home Loan Bank check.
            c) State or local government check when depositary bank is in same state.

        d) Cashier's, certified or teller's check.

        e) An on-us check.

    4) The first $100 deposited by check or checks.

  c. Distinction between "local" and "nonlocal" checks.
    1) Local check — Check drawn on a bank that is located in the same check processing region as the branch or proprietary ATM of the depository bank at which the check was deposited.
    2) Nonlocal check — Check drawn on a bank that is in a different check processing region.

  d. Temporary availability schedule in effect September 1, 1988—September 1, 1990.
    1) Local checks — Funds are to be made available on the third business day following the banking day on which the deposit was made.
    2) Nonlocal checks — Funds are to be made available on the seventh business day following the banking day on which the deposit was made.

  e. Permanent availability schedule in effect September 1, 1990.
    1) Local checks — Funds are to be made available on the second business day following the banking day on which the deposit was made.
    2) Nonlocal checks — Funds are to be made available on the fifth business day following the banking day on which the deposit was made.

  f. There are a number of exceptions.

2. Certain disclosures must be made by banks to their customers.

3. Provisions of EFAA affect payment of interest by banks on accounts.

4. There also are provisions for standardized bank indorsements and improvements in the check collection and return process.

KEY WORDS AND PHRASES IN TEXT

Checks
Cashier's checks
Traveler's checks
Certified checks
Drawer's request for certification
Holder's request for certification
Alteration of a certified check
Uniform Commercial Code Article 4
Relationship between banks and their customers (creditor-debtor and principal-agent)
Duty of bank to honor checks
Stale checks
Bank may supply missing indorsement of customer

Effect of death or incompetency of a customer
Duty of bank to honor stop-payment order
Effect of payment by bank on forged signature of the drawer
Overdrafts
Customer's duties to exercise care and examine cancelled checks
Bank's liability if it pays on a forged indorsement
Bank's liability for payment on an altered check
Commercial banks accept deposits
Check collection system
Depositary bank

Payor bank   Midnight deadline
Collecting bank (intermediary bank)   Provisional credit
Bank's liability for paying when there is   The Federal Reserve System
    a restrictive indorsement   Expedited Funds Availability Act
"On-us" item   "Hold" on a deposited check

FILL-IN QUESTIONS

1. A check is a demand draft, drawn on a bank or other financial institution. The bank
    is the drawee. The drawer of a check is termed the bank's _____. When
    the bank pays out on the check, it is referred to as the _____ bank.

2. Often, particularly when a person is making a large purchase, a seller is concerned
    that the buyer's personal check will be dishonored. In order to ensure against a
    dishonor, the buyer will use a cashier's check or a certified check. A
    _____ is a check drawn by a bank upon itself. A _____ is a
    personal check, drawn by the buyer on his or her own bank, which is accepted by
    the drawee bank.

3. If certification of a check is obtained by _____, the drawer remains
    secondarily liable; if certification is obtained by _____, the drawer is
    relieved of secondary liability. In either case _____ are discharged by
    certification.

4. There is a contractual relationship between a depositor and his or her bank. The
    bank, therefore is required to honor checks drawn on the depositor's account, unless
    (1) there are insufficient funds in the account and the bank has not agreed to honor
    overdrafts; (2) _____
    (3) _____
    (4) _____
    (5) _____.

MULTIPLE CHOICE QUESTIONS

1. The status of a bank is such that:
    a. it is an agent of its depositor.
    b. its status varies so that sometimes it is classified as an agent and other times as
       a holder of instruments in its own right.
    c. it acquires its status based on the classification given it by its depositor.
    d. it is a holder.

2. In theory, a bank is liable for making a payment in all but one of the following
    situations. That situation is:
    a. It pays on an altered instrument, such alteration being the result of the drawer's
       negligence.
    b. It pays on a check on which the drawer's signature is missing.
    c. It pays after receipt of a valid stop payment order given by its depositor.
    d. It pays a check on which the signature of the drawer is forged in such a way
       that the forgery cannot be detected.

3. A written stop payment order is effective for:
   a. 14 days.
   b. one month.
   c. six months.
   d. one year.

4. A drawee bank is not generally obligated to pay a check, which is presented for payment more than:
   a. three months after the date of the check.
   b. six months after the date of the check.
   c. a reasonable period after the issue of the check.
   d. one year after the issue of the check.

5. Under the U.C.C., if a check is presented to a drawee bank for payment, the drawee bank is under a duty to pay or dishonor such check:
   a. before the opening of business on the second banking day following the day of presentment.
   b. before the close of banking business on the day upon which the check is presented to it.
   c. within three business days.
   d. immediately upon presentment and agreement to pay.

6. April paid a debt that she owed to May with a check that was drawn upon her account with the Farmers' Bank. May took the check to the Farmers' Bank and requested and obtained certification of the check. May then indorsed the check to June, in order to pay a debt owed to June. Before June cashed the check, the Farmers' Bank became insolvent.
   a. June may receive the face amount from either April or May because, if a bank that has certified a check becomes insolvent, the drawer and indorsers remain secondarily liable.
   b. June may not recover from either April or May because the effect of certifications was to discharge their secondary liability.
   c. June may recover the face amount of the check from April because, even though the check was certified by the drawee bank, the drawer remains secondarily liable.
   d. June may recover the face amount of the check from May because the certification did not discharge the liability of an indorser who indorsed after certification.

7. On Monday, September 12, 1988, McColgin deposited a $6,000 check in his account at a bank in Dallas, Texas. The check was drawn on another bank in Dallas. If McColgin wished to withdraw the funds, he could have withdrawn:
   a. the entire $6,000 on Tuesday, September 13, 1988.
   b. $1,000 on Tuesday, September 13, 1988 and the remaining $5,000 on Wednesday, September 14, 1988.
   c. $1,000 on Tuesday, September 13, 1988 and the remaining $5,000 on Thursday, September 15, 1988.
   d. $100 on Tuesday, September 13, 1988 and the remaining $5,900 on Thursday, September 15, 1988.

8. Assume that on Monday, September 10, 1990, McDevitt deposits a $4,000 check in her account at a bank in Newark, New Jersey. The check is drawn on a bank

located in Seattle, Washington. If McDevitt wishes to withdraw the funds by check, she may withdraw:

a. the entire $4,000 on Tuesday, September 11, 1990.

b. $100 on Tuesday, September 11, 1990 and the remaining $3,900 on Wednesday, September 12, 1990.

c. $100 on Tuesday, September 11, 1990 and the remaining $3,900 on Monday, September 17, 1990.

d. $1,000 on Tuesday, September 11, 1990 and the remaining $3,000 on Wednesday, September 19, 1990.

Chapter 28

Electronic Fund Transfers

An electronic fund transfer (EFT) is a transmission of money that is accomplished through the facilities of an electronic fund transfer system (EFTS) using a computer, terminal, telephone or magnetic tape. When funds are so transferred, the transaction is completed instantaneously and there is no physical movement of cash or other paper documentation in the form of a deposit slip and/or a negotiable instrument, such as a check. Thus, electronic banking dispenses with the use of checks and eliminates "float" time, the period between the time that a check is issued and the time that it is charged to the drawer's account by his or her bank. At the present time, electronic fund transfers are governed by common law and, in the case of consumer transactions, the federal Electronic Fund Transfer Act (EFTA).

THINGS TO KEEP IN MIND

1. The Expedited Funds Availability Act and Regulation CC (discussed in Chapter 27) include provisions for next day availability of electronic payments when an automated clearinghouse credit transfer (such as a direct deposit of wages by an employer) or a commercial, nonconsumer wire transfer is effected. Certain consumer EFTs that are governed by the EFTA, however, are excluded from EFAA coverage. The funds availability provision of EFAA applies to transfers conducted at automated teller machines (ATMs) at which natural persons may perform account transactions but not to point-of-sale terminals or machines that only dispense cash.

2. It is expected that changes will be made in the future in the Uniform Commercial Code, in order to incorporate provisions relating to new systems for payments.

OUTLINE

I. Types of electronic transfers.

A. Access to an EFTS requires entering personal identification number (PIN) and, in some cases, use of an access card containing encoded data.

B. Automated teller machine (ATM).

    1. May be referred to as a customer-bank communication terminal or remote service unit because terminal is connected to bank's or other financial institution's computer.

    2. An electronic device at which a natural person may make deposits and payments to an account and perform other account transactions, such as withdrawing and transferring funds, and obtain credit card advances after inserting access card and entering PIN.

C. Point-of-sale electronic system.

    1. On-line terminal at checkout counter in store connects to computer at customer's bank or other financial institution which has issued an access card to customer.

    2. After insertion of customer's access card, computer verifies customer's balance and debits account for amount of purchase.

D. Automated clearinghouse (ACH).

    1. Facility that processes debit and credit transfers of funds.

    2. Entries are made by electronic signals without checks.

    3. Distinguish from check clearinghouse association—arrangement by which participant banks exchange deposited checks on a local basis.

    4. ACH credit transfer.

        a. Originator orders that originator's account be debited and another account be credited (an electronic payment).

        b. Includes direct deposits of social security benefits and employer payroll and pension payments at recipient's bank.

    5. ACH debit transfer.

        a. Originator, with prior approval, orders that another account be debited and the originator's account be credited.

        b. Customer may authorize bank or other financial institution to make automatic payments from account (in which customer has made deposits) at regular, recurrent intervals to a third party.

        c. Examples — Insurance premiums, utility bills and home mortgage and automobile or other installment loan payments.

E. Pay-by-telephone system.

1. Customer may access financial institution's computer system by telephone using PIN.

2. Customer may then direct transfer of funds from one account to another or from his or her account to another person, such as a utility company.

II. The Electronic Fund Transfer Act of 1978 (EFTA).

A. EFTA is a disclosure statute, the objective of which is to benefit consumers.

B. EFTA is administered by the Federal Reserve System which has adopted Regulation E in order to protect EFTS users.

C. EFTA does not apply to commercial (nonconsumer) electronic fund transfers between businesses or between businesses and financial institutions.

D. EFTA establishes the rights, liabilities and responsibilities of participants in consumer electronic fund transfers.

   1. Applies to financial institutions (including banks, savings and loan institutions, credit unions and other entities that directly or indirectly hold accounts) which offer electronic fund transfer services to consumer account holders.

   2. Covers electronic fund transfers to and from demand, savings and other asset accounts established for personal, family or household purposes pursuant to a prearranged plan under which periodic or recurring transfers are contemplated.

      a. A preauthorized transfer is one that the institution is empowered to make at least once in each successive sixty day period at substantially regular intervals.

      b. If preauthorized transfers are contemplated, the authorization must be in writing, a copy of which must be supplied to the customer.

E. Disclosure must be made by financial institution concerning:

   1. Charges for using the EFTS.

   2. What systems are available and any limits on frequency and dollar amounts.

   3. The customer's right to receive evidence of transactions in writing from financial institution.

      a. Receipt must be given at the time of the transfer for each transfer made from an electronic terminal.
         1) Not required for telephone transfers.
         2) Contents of receipt — Date, type and amount of transfer, identity of customer's account, identity of any third party involved in the transaction and location of terminal used.

      b. Periodic statements must be furnished.

1) Contents of statement — Dates, types and amounts of transfers, identity of any third parties involved in the transactions, fees charged and locations of terminals used for each account through which an EFTS provides access.
2) Monthly statement for every month in which there is an electronic transfer and quarterly statement if there are no electronic transactions.

c. If an automatic deposit is not made as scheduled, customer must be notified.

4. How errors can be corrected.

a. Customer must notify institution of any errors in periodic statement.
   1) Oral or written notification must be given within sixty days after institution has sent periodic statement.
   2) Contents of notice:
      a) Customer's name and account number.
      b) A sentence explaining that an error has been made, including the alleged amount involved.
      c) The reasons the customer believes that an error has been made.

b. Institution must make a good faith investigation and given written report to customer.
   1) Results must be reported within ten business days.
   2) If more time is needed for investigation and resolution of problem, institution must recredit customer's account after ten days and has forty-five days within which to continue investigation.
   3) If institution finds that an error occurred, it must adjust customer's account within one business day.
   4) If institution finds that no mistake was made, it must give customer a full written report with conclusions.
   5) Institution may be liable for treble damages if it fails to make a good faith investigation.

5. The customer's right to stop payments.

a. Once an EFT transaction has been made, customer cannot reverse or "stop payment."

b. If customer does not wish a preauthorized transfer to be made, he or she must notify the institution at least three days before scheduled date of EFT; institution may require written confirmation within fourteen days if notification was orally given.

6. The customer's liability for unauthorized transfers resulting from the loss or theft of the access card, code or other access device. (See below for EFTA provisions.)

7. Whom and what telephone number to call in order to report a loss or theft.

8. The financial institution's liability to the customer. (See below for EFTA provisions.)

9. Rules concerning disclosure of account information to third parties.

F. Customer's liability for unauthorized electronic fund transfers.

1. Liability may be imposed on customer when EFT resulted from the use of an accepted means of access and customer was provided with a means of identifying himself or herself to that means of access (an access card and/or PIN).

2. Liability when access card or other device is lost, stolen or misplaced.

   a. If customer notifies institution within two business days of learning of the loss or theft, customer's liability for any unauthorized transfers is limited to $50.

   b. If customer notifies institution more than two business days after learning of the loss or theft, customer's liability for any unauthorized transfers is limited to $500.

   c. If customer fails to notify institution of the loss or theft within sixty days after receipt of periodic statement reflecting an unauthorized transfer, customer has unlimited liability when the institution proves that:
      1) Customer and institution had an agreement under which customer assented to unlimited liability;
      2) Customer knew that access device had been lost, stolen or misplaced; and
      3) In the event of an unauthorized EFT appearing on the periodic statement, the loss of funds due to the unauthorized transfer would not have occurred but for the customer's failure to notify the institution within the sixty day period.

   d. If there are extenuating circumstances which prevented the customer from notifying the institution within the sixty day period, he or she must do so "within a reasonable time, under the circumstances."

3. Criminal liability may be imposed if customer knowingly or willfully commits certain acts, such as giving false information or using a forged access card.

G. Liability of the financial institution.

1. Institution is civilly liable for all damage proximately caused by its failure to make an EFT in accordance with the terms and conditions of its agreement with its customer (the account holder) in the correct amount and in a timely manner when the customer properly instructs it to do so.

   a. Exceptions:
      1) Customer's account had insufficient funds through no fault of the institution.
      2) Funds in the account were subject to legal process.
      3) Transfer would exceed an established credit limit.
      4) An ATM had insufficient cash.
      5) Circumstances beyond the control of the institution prevented the transfer.

b. Customer may recover actual damages and, if bad faith is shown, punitive damages of not less than $100 nor more than $1,000.

c. In specific situations, class actions can be brought, in which case punitive damages are limited to the lesser of $500,000 or one percent of the institution's net worth.

2. Criminal liability.

a. Certain violations of EFTA are federal misdemeanors, for which the penalty may be a fine of up to $5,000 and/or imprisonment for up to one year.

b. Other more serious violations involving interstate commerce are felonies, in which case the sanctions may be a fine of up to $10,000 and imprisonment for as long as ten years.

III. Commercial electronic fund transfers.

A. Commercial EFTs are governed by private agreements, case law and, in some cases, regulations of the Federal Reserve System.

B. Commercial EFTs include automated clearinghouse and wife transfer services.

1. Automated clearinghouse (ACH) — Facility that processes debit and credit transfers, such as the Federal Reserve System and the New York Automated Clearinghouse Association.

a. Originally, ACHs were designed to handle consumer "high-volume low-dollar" transfers.

b. Today, ACHs handle commercial transfers as well.

c. The National Automated Clearinghouse Association (NACHA) has adopted rules for consumer and commercial payments and endorses General Electric Information Services Company (GEISCO) as a private system for processing payments as an alternative to the Federal Reserve System.

2. Wire transfer — Unconditional order to an institution to pay money to a beneficiary that is transmitted by electronic or other means over networks used primarily to transfer funds between commercial accounts.

a. Examples — Society for Worldwide Interbank Financial Telecommunications network (SWIFT); Clearing House Interbank Payments System (CHIPS) operated by the New York Clearing House; Federal Reserve Fedwire.

b. Includes transfers made over public communications networks, such as ITT's telex services.

C. Applicable law.

1. Issues arise concerning allocation of the risk of error, fraud and loss among

the EFTS's users, failure to effect a transfer as ordered, awarding of consequential damages and the effect of insolvency of a party.

2. Some disputes are settled by the parties based upon their agreement or
customary course of dealing.

3. Courts have taken into consideration contract and tort principles, analogous
rules in the U.C.C., Federal Reserve System Regulation J and operating
circulars, and the facts in the particular case.

IV. Future developments.

A. In 1974, the Permanent Editorial Board of the Uniform Commercial Code and
the American Law Institute began work on a project for drafting a New Payments Code, a uniform set of rules governing payment systems other than cash.

B. Since 1987, a new project, "Commercial Code—Current Payment Methods," has
been undertaken in order to draft revisions of articles 3 and 4 of the U.C.C. and
a new article 4A—Wire Transfers, encompassing commercial electronic fund
transfers.

C. It is anticipated that in the future legislation will be enacted which will provide
guidance in defining the rights, obligations and liabilities of parties utilizing
EFT systems.

KEY WORDS AND PHRASES IN TEXT

Electronic fund transfer
Electronic fund transfer system
Float time
"Checkless" society
Electronic Fund Transfer Act
Access card
Personal identification number (PIN)
Automated teller machine (ATM)
Point-of-sale system
Automated clearinghouse
Direct deposit
Automatic payment
Pay-by-telephone system
Federal Reserve System Regulation E
Disclosure of terms and conditions by
    financial institutions

Financial institutions
Consumer accounts established for
    personal, family or household purposes
EFT transaction receipt
Preauthorized transfer
Reversibility (stop payment order) for
    preauthorized transfer
Corrections of mistakes
Unauthorized transfers
Consumer liability for unauthorized
    transfers
Liability of financial institutions under
    EFTA
Commercial electronic fund transfer
Commercial electronic fund transfer
    system

FILL-IN QUESTIONS

1. The United States has been referred to as a _____ society because of
the widespread use of checks. Today, in many instances, not even checks are used
because of the availability of _____ systems.

2. _____ refers to the period of time between the issuance of a check and its final payment, during which the drawer retains the use of funds, which is eliminated when an electronic fund _____ is used.

3. At an _____ (ATM), a customer of a bank or other financial institution who is provided with access to an electronic fund transfer system initiates an electronic transfer by inserting his or her _____ and typing in his or her _____ (PIN).

4. The Electronic Fund Transfer Act of 1978 applies to consumer electronic transfers and, therefore, demand, savings and other asset accounts that are established for _____ purposes; but not to _____ electronic transfers which are electronic transactions between businesses or between businesses and financial institutions.

5. The Electronic Fund Transfer Act is a disclosure statute and requires that the terms and conditions of electronic fund transfers be disclosed to customers of a bank or other financial institution. Among the terms that must be disclosed are the following: the charges for using the electronic fund transfer system; the system which is available and any limits on frequency of use or dollar amounts; _____ _____; the financial institution's liability to the customer; and rules concerning disclosure to third parties.

6. In addition to disclosing information to customers at the time of an agreement, with regard to each electronic fund transfer, a bank or financial institution must provide a customer with a _____ indicating the amount, date and type of transfer, the customer's account number, the identity of any third party involved and the _____ of the terminal which was used. The financial institution must also provide a _____ statement for every month in which there is an electronic transfer of funds.

7. The Electronic Fund Transfer Act provides that a bank customer's liability for unauthorized electronic transfers when his or her access card is lost or stolen will be limited to $50 if the loss or theft is reported within _____ business days after he or she learns of the loss or theft. If such notification is given to the bank later, the liability of the customer is limited to $_____ as long as the notification is given within _____ days after the customer has received a bank statement reflecting unauthorized transfers.

MULTIPLE CHOICE QUESTIONS

1. Lori has a checking account at the Sun City Bank. She also has borrowed $5,000 from the bank and has agreed that the monthly loan payments of $225 will be automatically withdrawn from her checking account and transferred to the bank on the fifteenth day of each month. Which of the following statements is correct?
   a. Lori has agreed to a preauthorized transfer for which the Sun City Bank need not furnish a receipt.
   b. The Sun City Bank must provide Lori with a monthly statement of her checking account transactions.

c. Lori will be unable to stop the transfer of next month's loan installment payment to Sun City Bank.

d. If Sun City Bank makes a mistake by transferring $450 from Lori's account on the fifteenth day of this month, Lori is entitled to an immediate credit of $225.

2. Elmco Inc. has an account at the Bank of Elm County, as do its twenty employees. Rather than issue paychecks, Elmco has agreed to make weekly payroll payments directly to the accounts of its employees at the bank.

a. If Elmco does not notify its employees that the weekly payroll deposits are being made, the Bank of Elm County is required to so notify the employees who are also its customers.

b. Because Elmco's account at the Bank of Elm County is not established for personal, family or household use, the transactions covering the direct payroll deposits are not within the purview of the Electronic Fund Transfer Act.

c. If the Bank of Elm County fails to make payroll transfers this week because there are insufficient funds in Elmco's account, the bank will be liable to Elmco for all damages proximately caused by its failure to make the electronic fund transfers.

d. If the Bank of Elm County fails to make payroll transfers this week because severe storms have resulted in four days discontinuance of electric service to the bank, the bank will be liable to Elmco employees for all damages proximately caused by its failure to make the electronic fund transfers.

3. Jo's bank maintains an automated teller machine (ATM) for the use of its customers. The bank has complied with the Electronic Fund Transfer Act. At has, therefore, made disclosures to its customers, including a disclosure that the maximum amount that can be withdrawn from an ATM on any one day is $300. On May 2, Jo deposited checks totaling $872 at the ATM. She also withdrew $300 in cash on May 5 at the ATM. She received a bank statement on June 1 which listed the May 2 deposit as being for $800 and the May 5 withdrawal as being for $3,000. On Monday, June 2, Joe notified the bank of the errors.

a. The bank need not do anything for ten business days, at which point it must begin a good faith investigation.

b. After 45 days, during which the bank must conduct a good faith investigation, the bank must credit $2,772 to Jo's account if it cannot find the cause of the error.

c. The bank must conduct a good faith investigation and report the results thereof to Jo before June 13 and, if it is unable to find the error, credit $2,772 to Jo's account.

d. After ten business days, the bank must credit Jo's account for $72. Thereafter, it must conduct a good faith investigation and report the results to Jo before June 13 and, if it is unable to find the error, credit $2,700 to Jo's account.

Questions 4, 5, 6, 7 and 8 are based upon the following fact situation: The Second Massachusetts Bank had properly notified its customers of its policy of permitting a maximum of $300 per day from one of its ATMs. Harold, who is a customer of the Second Massachusetts Bank, lost his access card on July 5. Unbeknown to Harold and the bank, the card was found by Lucky, who used the card in order to make five successive withdrawals of $300 on July 6, 7, 8, 9 and 10.

4. Assume that on July 6, Harold notified the bank that his access card was lost. Harold will be liable for:

    a. no more than $50.
    b. no more than $500.
    c. the entire $1,500.
    d. nothing.

5.   Assume that Harold notified the Second Massachusetts Bank of the loss of his access card on July 8. Harold will be liable for:
    a. no more than $50.
    b. no more than $500.
    c. the entire $1,500.
    d. nothing.

6.   Assume that Harold had difficulty remembering his personal identification number (PIN) and, therefore, wrote his PIN on his access card. If Harold notified the bank on July 6 that his access card was lost, he will be liable for:
    a. no more than $50.
    b. no more than $500.
    c. the entire $1,500.
    d. nothing.

7.   Assume that Harold notified the Second Massachusetts Bank of the loss of his access card in September after receiving two bank statements on which the withdrawals by Lucky were included. Harold will be liable for:
    a. no more than $50.
    b. no more than $500.
    c. the entire $1,500.
    d. nothing.

8.   Assume that on July 5, Harold was injured in an automobile accident. As a result of his injuries, he was unable to notify the Second Massachusetts Bank of the loss of his access card until August 9 after receiving a bank statement on which the withdrawals by Lucky were included.
    a. Harold will be liable for a reasonable amount.
    b. Harold will be liable for the entire $1,500.
    c. Harold will be liable for nothing.
    d. A court will take into consideration the extenuating circumstances in determining the extent of Harold's liability.

Unit Four

CREDITORS' RIGHTS AND BANKRUPTCY

The material in this unit deals with the rights of debtors and creditors. Some of the methods available to creditors for ensuring that legally owing obligations will be paid and the protection afforded to borrowers and purchasers before and after they enter credit transactions are discussed in Chapters 29 and 30. The subject matter of Chapter 31 is the federal bankruptcy law, the purpose of which is to provide orderly procedures for discharging, rehabilitating or reorganizing debtors, who are unable to pay their debts, while providing for the equitable distribution of their assets among their creditors.

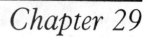

Chapter 29

Secured
Transactions

Secured transactions, which are covered by Article 9 of the Uniform Commercial Code, are credit transactions that are coupled with security interests in personal property. In a secured transaction, the buyer or borrower, who is referred to as the debtor, gives security rights in personal property to a seller or lender, who is called the secured party, in addition to an assurance that an obligation will be paid or otherwise performed. If the debtor defaults by failing to carry out the underlying obligation (which is usually for the payment of money), the secured party can look to the security as a substitute for the debtor's performance. Such devices are used to finance purchases made by manufacturers, retailers, other businesses and consumers.

Attention is given to the concept of a "floating lien," which is created by a security agreement which provides that a security interest attaches to (1) the proceeds of a sale or other disposition of covered collateral by a debtor, (2) after-acquired property of a debtor, and/or (3) future advances to be made by a creditor, the secured party.

The material in the latter part of the chapter deals with the priorities that secured parties have if they have perfected their security interests in collateral and the rights and duties of secured parties before and after a default by a debtor.

THINGS TO KEEP IN MIND

1. In order for a secured transaction to be effective between the parties to it, the debtor and the secured party, the security interest must "attach" to the collateral; in order that the secured transaction be effective against third parties it must be "perfected."

2. The objective of secured transaction devices is to protect creditors, who have extended credit, by giving them security interests in personal property which is typically in the possession of their debtors. Under the Code, lesser protection is

afforded to debtors and others who may also have extended credit or otherwise dealt with the same debtors.

3. Federal statutes and case law as well as Federal Trade Commission rules also govern some secured transactions.

OUTLINE

I. Definitions used in secured transactions covered by Article 9.

   A. Security interest — An interest in personal property or fixtures which secures payment or performance of an obligation (Sec. 1-201(37)).

   B. Secured party — A lender or seller who obtains a security interest in personal property (Sec. 9-105(1)(m)).

   C. Debtor — The party owing the obligation to pay money or otherwise perform (Sec. 9-105(1)(d)).

   D. Security agreement — An agreement which creates or provides for a security interest in personal property (Sec. 9-105(1)(l)).

   E. Collateral — Personal property that is subject to a security interest (Sec. 9-105(1)(c)). Classifications:

     1. Goods — Things that are moveable at the time that the security interest attaches or fixtures (Sec. 9-105(1)(h)).

       a. Includes standing timber, which is to be cut and removed, growing crops and unborn young of animals.

       b. Does not include moveables that are included in other classifications of collateral.

       c. Goods are classified in accordance with their primary use (Sec. 9-109). They may be:
         1) Consumer goods — Used or bought primarily for personal, family or household use.
         2) Equipment — Used or bought primarily for business use.
         3) Farm products — Crops, livestock or supplies used or produced in farming operations or products of crops or livestock in their manufactured state and in the possession of the debtor, who engages in farming or ranching.
         4) Inventory — Goods held for sale or lease, materials used or consumed in business and work in progress.

     2. Writings evidencing rights:

       a. Instruments — Commercial paper (negotiable and nonnegotiable), certificated investment securities (such as stocks and bonds) and writings evidencing rights to receive money that are not themselves security agreements or leases (Sec. 9-105(1)(i)).

    b. Documents of title — Bills of lading, dock warrants or receipts, warehouse receipts or other documents which, in the regular course of business or financing, are treated as evidencing that the person in possession is entitled to receive, hold and dispose of the document and the goods covered by the document (Secs. 1-201(15), 7-201 and 9-105(1)(f)).

    c. Chattel paper — A writing or a group of writings, evidencing a monetary obligation and a security interest in or lease of specific goods (Sec. 9-105(1)(b)).

  3. Accounts and general intangibles (Sec. 9-106).

    a. Account — Right to payment for goods sold or leased or services performed which is not evidenced by an instrument or chattel paper.

    b. General intangible — Personal property other than goods, accounts, chattel paper, documents, instruments and money.

F. Financing statement — Document which is filed with a government office to give notice that a security interest exists in particular collateral (Sec. 9-402).

II. Creating a security interest.

A. Transaction is one that is covered by Article 9 of the Code.

B. Attachment — A security interest is enforceable between the debtor and the secured party so that the secured party is assured that certain predesignated property will be available to satisfy a debt should the debtor default, only if attachment has occurred (Sec. 9-203). Requisites for attachment:

  1. Written agreement — Providing for security interest.

    a. Signed by debtor.

    b. Contains description of collateral.

    c. A writing is not necessary if the secured party is given possession of the collateral (a pledge).

  2. Value is given by the secured party. A secured party gives value if he or she acquires a security interest (Sec. 1-201(44)):

    a. In return for any consideration sufficient to support a simple contract, or

    b. In satisfaction of or as security for a preexisting obligation, or

    c. In return for a commitment to extend credit.

      3. Debtor has rights in the collateral.

III. Purchase money security interest — A security interest in specific collateral is taken by a seller of the collateral or a creditor, who advances funds or incurs an obligation, enabling the debtor to acquire the collateral (Sec. 9-107).

IV. Perfecting a security interest — Process whereby a secured party obtains priority over other third parties having claims against the debtor. The method used for perfection is determined by the classification of the collateral that is the subject of the security interest.

    A. By possession (Sec. 9-305).

        1. Common law pledge.

        2. Required method of perfection for instruments, other than instruments which constitute part of chattel paper (Sec. 9-304).

        3. The secured party or a bailee may be given possession.

    B. By attachment if a purchase money security interest is created in consumer goods, other than motor vehicles and fixtures (Sec. 9-302(1)(d)).

    C. By filing a financing statement.

        1. Contents of financing statement.

            a. Signature of debtor.

            b. Addresses of debtor and secured party.

            c. Description of collateral.

        2. Required method of perfecting unless the secured party is given possession or the secured transaction involves a consumer purchase money security interest.

        3. Where to file. The code gives three alternatives. (Sec. 9-401.)

            a. Central filing with state official, such as the secretary of state.

            b. Local filing with official of county.

            c. Combination of local filing for consumer and/or farm goods and central filing for other collateral.

    D. Perfected security interest covers collateral that is subsequently moved to another state for the remaining perfection period or four months (whichever is shorter) (Sec. 9-103).

V. The scope of a security interest and the floating lien concept (Sec. 9-204).

A. Financing statement is effective for five years. Provision is made for renewal.

B. Floating lien (Sec. 9-306).

    1. A security agreement may cover proceeds of the sale of collateral that was the subject matter of the agreement.

        a. Proceeds include whatever is received by the debtor when the collateral is sold, exchanged, collected or otherwise disposed of.

        b. Automatic perfection for ten days.

        c. May be provided for in the security agreement.

    2. A security agreement may cover advances to be made by a secured party in the future.

    3. A security agreement may cover after-acquired property, personal property, such as inventory, purchased or otherwise acquired by the debtor after the execution of the security agreement.

VI. Parties prevailing over a secured party who has failed to perfect his or her security interest (Sec. 9-301).

A. Persons who have prior perfected security interests in the same collateral.

B. Persons who have become lien creditors, including trustees in bankruptcy.

C. Buyers in the ordinary course of business.

D. Buyers or other transferees in bulk, not in the ordinary course of business, to the extent that they give value and receive delivery of the collateral without knowledge of the security interest. (Bulk Transfers are covered in Article 6 of the UCC.)

E. Transferees of accounts and general intangibles, to the extent that they give value and lack knowledge of the security interest.

VII. Priorities (Sec. 9-312).

A. One, whose security interest in the collateral has attached and been perfected, prevails over those who have not perfected their security interests.

B. If two or more parties have perfected security interests in the same collateral, the first to perfect has priority.

C. If two or more parties have unperfected security interests in the same collateral, the party whose security interest attached first prevails.

D. Exceptions.

    1. Buyers of goods in the ordinary course of business take free of security interests in sellers' inventory (Sec. 9-307).

    2. Secondhand purchaser of consumer goods, who gives value, purchases the goods for personal or household use and lacks knowledge of the existence of a security interest in the goods, takes free of a security interest of a seller whose purchase money security interest was automatically perfected without filing (Sec. 9-307).

    3. A subsequent purchaser of chattel paper or an instrument, in the ordinary course of business, who gives value and takes possession, has priority over a secured party with a prior security interest that had been perfected by filing (Sec. 9-308).

VIII. Rights and duties of parties before default or termination of a security interest when the parties have not otherwise agreed.

A. A secured party may release or assign all or part of collateral covered by a security interest (Secs. 9-405 and 9-406).

B. The financing statement can be amended (Sec. 9-402).

C. A secured party in possession of collateral must use reasonable care in order to preserve it; the debtor bears the expense and the risk of loss or damage (Sec. 9-207).

IX. Rights and duties of parties upon default.

A. What constitutes default is usually stated in the security agreement.

B. A secured party may obtain a judgment based upon the underlying obligation or enforce the security interest (Sec. 9-501).

    1. A secured party with a security interest in collateral in the form of accounts, chattel paper and instruments may collect such obligations directly (Sec. 9-306).

    2. A secured party may take possession of collateral covered by a security agreement (Sec. 9-503).

        a. The secured party must do so without breach of the peace.

        b. The secured party must use reasonable care in the custody and preservation of collateral (Sec. 9-207).

        c. The secured party may have the debtor assemble the collateral and have it available at a mutually convenient location.

        d. If the collateral is difficult to remove, the secured party may have it rendered unusable by the debtor and dispose of it on the debtor's premises.

3. A secured party may accept the collateral in satisfaction of the obligation and retain it (Sec. 9-505).

   a. Written notice must be given to the debtor and other secured parties, who have given written notice of claims, so that they may exercise their rights of redemption (Sec. 9-506).

   b. A secured party may not retain consumer goods if more than 60% of the price has been paid.

4. A secured party may dispose of collateral and apply proceeds to the obligation (Sec. 9-504).

   a. Private or public sale, lease or any commercially reasonable means to produce the maximum benefit to both parties.

   b. Notice must be given to the debtor and other secured parties, who have given notice of claims, so that they may exercise their rights of redemption, unless the goods are perishables (Sec. 9-506).

   c. Effect of disposition of collateral — A purchaser or other transferee takes free of claims of the debtor and the secured party (Sec. 9-504(4)).

   d. Order of distribution of proceeds (Sec. 9-504).
      1) Expenses of sale, possessing, holding and preparing for sale, including attorney fees.
      2) Satisfaction of debt.
      3) Subordinate security interest holders who gave written notification.
      4) Usually a debtor is entitled to any surplus. (Usually a debtor is responsible for a deficiency.)

X. Termination — When the debt is paid or other obligation satisfied, the secured party files a termination statement with the official with whom the original financing statement was filed (Sec. 9-404).

KEY WORDS AND PHRASES IN TEXT

Secured transaction
Article 9 of the Uniform Commercial Code
Security interest in personal property or fixtures
Attachment
Perfection
Security interest in personal property
Secured party (creditor)
Debtor
Security agreement
Collateral
Tangible goods (consumer goods, equipment, farm products, inventory and fixtures)

Indispensable paper (chattel paper, documents of title and instruments)
Intangible collateral (accounts and rights to payment that are not evidenced by instrument or chattel paper and general intangibles)
Requisites for creating a security interest (attachment of security interest to collateral)
Agreement between secured party and debtor (in writing, signed by debtor, unless secured party is given possession of the collateral)
Security party must give value

Debtor must have rights in the collateral

Purchase money security interest

The floating lien concept

Security agreement may cover proceeds of sale of collateral, after-acquired property and/or future advances

Line of credit

Perfection of security interest

Secured party perfects by taking possession of the collateral (pledge)

Secured party perfects when purchase money security interest in consumer goods attaches or when a person assigns a small portion of accounts receivable

Perfection by filing a financial statement

Location of filing office (depends upon classification of collateral)

Secured party's protection when collateral is moved to another jurisdiction

Lien creditor

Effective time of perfection

Priorities when there are conflicting security interests in the same collateral (the first in time to perfect has priority)

Exceptions to perfection priority rules

In general, a secured party with a perfected purchase money security interest prevails over a secured party with a nonpurchase money security interest in after-acquired collateral

Buyer in the ordinary course of business takes the goods free from any security interest in the merchant seller's inventory

Secondhand goods sold by a consumer to a consumer

Buyers of chattel paper and instruments

Rights and duties of debtors and secured parties before default

Secured party may make an assignment of a security interest

Secured party may release debtor

Financing statement may be amended

Party, who is in possession of the collateral, must use reasonable care in order to preserve it

Cumulative rights, duties and remedies following default by debtor

Secured party's right to take possession of collateral and duty to use care in order to preserve it

Assembling the collateral

Retention of collateral by secured party after default

Disposition of collateral in commercially reasonable manner

Application of proceeds from disposition of collateral

Deficiency judgment

Redemption rights

Termination of security interest

FILL-IN QUESTIONS

1. A secured transaction is one in which a debtor, who has an obligation (usually to pay a sum of money), gives a _____ in personal property or fixtures to a lender or seller, known as the _____.

2. The personal property, which is subject to a security interest, is called _____.

3. Goods, which may be the subject matter of a secured transaction, are classified in accordance with the primary purpose for which they are purchased and used. If they are used primarily by the debtor for personal, family or household use, such goods are termed _____. If they are used or consumed by a business in the manufacturing process, they are part of _____.

4. A security interest is enforceable by a secured party against a debtor, who has defaulted, if the security interest has _____ to the collateral. The secured party, however, will only have priority over other creditors if he or she has _____ his or her security interest.

5. A security interest attaches when (1) a debtor has _____,
    (2) the secured party has _____, and (3) the parties have entered into an
    agreement, which is required to be in writing if the secured party does not have
    possession of the collateral.

6. A security agreement is referred to as a floating lien if it provides that a security
    interest will attach to the proceeds of the sale or other disposition of specified
    collateral, _____ or _____.

7. A secured party, whose security interest has attached to collateral belonging to a
    debtor, but has failed to perfect his interest, will not prevail over _____
    _____
    _____.

8. Even if a secured party has perfected his or her security interest, he or she will not
    prevail over one who has a possessory lien for services and/or material furnished in
    repairing, storing, etc., collateral in his or her possession, or one who has purchased
    goods, which were part of inventory covered by a security agreement, if the
    purchase was made _____.

9. If two secured parties have security interests in the same collateral and neither of
    them has perfected, the one _____
    will have priority over the other.

10. Upon default by a debtor, a secured party may take possession of the collateral, to
    which his or her security interest attached, and retain the collateral or _____
    _____
    _____.

MULTIPLE CHOICE QUESTIONS

1. Article 9 of the Uniform Commercial Code, dealing with secured transactions, does
    not apply to the creation of a security interest in:
    a. personal property which has a value of $500 or less.
    b. personal property in which the debtor has no rights.
    c. personal property which is in the possession of a debtor.
    d. personal property which is in the possession of a secured party.

2. An automobile, purchased by Landau and secured by a purchase money security
    interest, will be classified as inventory if:
    a. Landau is in the business of selling automobiles and the automobile in question
       was purchased for resale.
    b. Landau is a salesman and uses the automobile in order to call on customers.
    c. Landau purchased the automobile for his mother.
    d. Two of the above.

3. Boyne borrowed $500 from Rater and signed a writing. The writing provided that
    Boyne promised to repay the $500 to Rater on March 1 and gave Rater the right to
    take possession of and sell her fully described television set if she failed to repay
    the money.
    a. It is not a security agreement because the words, "security interest," are not
       included in the writing.

    b. A security interest has been created in the television set only if the money borrowed was used to purchase the television set.

    c. Rater is the secured party and has a security interest in the television set.

    d. A security interest did not attach to the television set because Rater did not sign the writing.

4. A security interest will attach to specified collateral, in which the debtor has an interest, if a written security agreement containing a description of the collateral is:

    a. signed by the debtor and the secured party gives value by making a commitment to extend credit.

    b. filed with the designated state or local official.

    c. signed by a secured party who lends money to a debtor.

    d. signed by a debtor and states the addresses of the debtor and the secured party.

5. A negotiable draft usually:

    a. may not be used as collateral for a secured transaction.

    b. is considered to be goods if used for a secured transaction.

    c. may be used as collateral for a secured transaction which is perfected by possession.

    d. may be used as collateral for a secured transaction which is perfected by filing.

6. Public notice of a security interest in personal property is provided by filing a:

    a. security agreement.

    b. chattel mortgage.

    c. bill of sale.

    d. financing statement.

7. Brennan, a manufacturer of clothing, and Carver, a producer of fabric, signed an agreement whereby Carver agreed to sell Brennan $10,000 worth of fabric, to be paid for in six months. The agreement provided that the transaction would be secured by a security interest in Brennan's present and future inventory and that Carver agreed to provide Brennan with a continuing line of credit for a period of 18 months.

    a. In order for the agreement to be binding on both Brennan and Carver, a financing statement must be filed with an appropriate government official.

    b. The agreement is ineffective to give Carver a security interest in additions to Brennan's inventory, after the expiration of the six-month period.

    c. The agreement provides for a valid floating lien and it is binding on Brennan and Carver.

    d. If Carver advances $30,000 to Brennan 11 months later, Carver is an unsecured creditor to the extent of the $30,000.

8. TV Town Inc., a seller of television sets, maintains a large inventory of television sets which it obtains from manufacturers on credit. The manufacturers/creditors have all taken security interests in the appliances and the proceeds therefrom and have made the necessary filings in order to perfect their security interests. TV Town Inc. sells to many consumers; some pay cash and others buy on credit. TV Town Inc. takes a security interest when it makes a credit sale but it does not file a financing statement.

    a. The television sets in TV Town Inc.'s hands are consumer goods.

    b. Since TV Town Inc. takes purchase money security interests in the goods which it sells to customers, its security interests are perfected upon attachment.

c. The manufacturers can enforce their security interests against the television sets in the hands of the purchasers who paid cash for them.

d. A subsequent sale by one of TV Town Inc.'s customers to a purchaser for value will be subject to TV Town Inc.'s security interest.

9. C was an appliance dealer. She financed her inventory with her local bank and signed a security agreement using the inventory as security. B purchased a freezer from C. C defaulted on her payments to the bank.

a. A security agreement of this kind is illegal.

b. The bank may reclaim the freezer from B because its security interest never attached to the freezer.

c. The bank may reclaim the freezer from B because its security interest has been perfected.

d. B takes the freezer free of any security interests of C or the bank.

10. Nestler owned a candy store and was the holder of a warehouse receipt, which provided that the goods stored were to be delivered to the order of Nestler. Nestler borrowed money from Hirshy and gave Hirshy the warehouse receipt as security.

a. This is not a secured transaction because a warehouse receipt cannot be collateral in which a creditor may have a security interest.

b. Hirshy has not perfected his security interest unless a financing statement was properly filed.

c. Goodbard, who lent Nestler money before the transaction between Nestler and Hirshy, has priority over Hirshy with regard to the warehouse receipt.

d. Hirshy has perfected his security interest and has priority over other creditors of Nestler with regard to the warehouse receipt.

11. Epsilon sold Delta a CB radio for $180. Delta paid $50 immediately and agreed to pay $10 a month for thirteen months. Their agreement was reduced to writing and signed by both Epsilon and Delta. It included a provision under which Epsilon has the right to repossess the radio if Delta defaulted in her payments. Nothing else was signed, recorded or filed. The next week Epsilon and Delta had an argument. Since that time Delta has continued to use the CB but has not made any of the agreed payments.

a. Epsilon, the debtor, and Delta, the secured party, have entered into an effective secured transaction.

b. The security interest has attached to the CB radio and Epsilon has the right to repossess the CB and either retain the CB in satisfaction of the unpaid purchase price or sell it and apply the proceeds of the sale to the unpaid balance.

c. If Delta's car is wrecked in an accident, in which the CB is totally destroyed, Epsilon has priority over other unsecured creditors of Delta with regard to Delta's remaining personal property.

d. The security interest has attached to the CB radio and Epsilon has the right to repossess the CB, but will be required to sell it and apply the proceeds of the sale to the unpaid balance.

12. At a properly conducted public sale of property that was collateral for a secured transaction:

a. the debtor is liable for any deficiency, if the sale does not produce enough to satisfy all of the incurred charges and the debt.

b. the debtor may not purchase the collateral being sold.
c. the secured party may not purchase the collateral being sold.
d. junior secured parties may not participate in any excess proceeds.

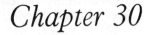

Chapter 30

Rights of Debtors and Creditors

The law dealing with the rights of creditors to be paid obligations, which are legally owed to them, has undergone considerable change, particularly in recent years because of the expansion of consumer oriented legislation. In this chapter the authors review some of the means available to creditors to ensure payment of debts owed to them as well as recent debtor protection statutes.

THINGS TO KEEP IN MIND

A creditor, who has lent money or extended credit to others, has a contractual right to be paid when the obligation is due. You are already familiar with some methods available to a creditor to ensure payment, such as the use of commercial paper, which was discussed in Unit Three, and secured transactions, the subject matter of Chapter 29. In order to have security that an obligation will be performed, a creditor may require that the debtor obtain a surety or guarantor. A creditor may obtain a lien on property, owned by a debtor, which can be sold in order to satisfy the obligation.

OUTLINE

I. Laws assisting creditors.

    A. A lien is a claim or charge on a debtor's property that must be satisfied before the property (or proceeds of its sale or other disposition) is available in order to satisfy claims of other creditors.

        1. A consensual lien is based upon an agreement of the parties.

        2. A lien creditor has priority only to the extent of the value of his or her collateral.

B. Some liens, which enabled creditors to reach their debtors' property, were recognized at common law; today, many liens are provided for by statute.

   1. Mechanic's (or materialman's) lien on real property — If a debt arises because an owner of real property fails to pay for labor, services or materials furnished for purposes of making improvements on real property, the party, to whom the obligation is owed, may obtain a lien on the improved property, which may be enforced ultimately by sale of the property.

   2. Artisan's lien on personal property — Possessory lien, enforceable by a bailee, who has improved or stored another's property and not been paid for services and/or value added.

   3. Innkeepers or hotelkeepers lien — A hotel, or other facility offering similar accommodations to the public, that has possession of a guest's property, may have a possessory lien for the value of unpaid hotel charges.

   4. A warehouse may have a possessory lien for unpaid storage charges.

   5. Statutes provide for recording, giving notice to the debtor, foreclosure and sale of property subject to such liens.

C. Judicial procedure which is generally used when a creditor is not paid and which results in creation of judicial liens.

   1. A lawsuit, instituted by a creditor, results in a judgment against a debtor for the amount of the debt plus interest and costs.

   2. If the judgment is not paid, the creditor can obtain a writ of execution, a court order directed to the sheriff to seize specified property of the debtor, sell it and give the proceeds to the judgment creditor.

   3. In some states by complying with statutes, a creditor may get an order for attachment of specified property of a debtor, before obtaining a judgment.

   4. By complying with statutes, a judgment creditor can reach property of a debtor in the hands of a third party, such as wages due to an employee (the debtor), in a garnishment proceeding.

      a. Federal and state statutes ensure that a specified minimum amount of wages cannot be reached by garnishment.

      b. Employer cannot discharge employee because his or her wages are subject to garnishment unless (in some states) wages are subject to multiple garnishments.

D. Bulk sales law — Article 6 of the UCC — See Chapter 17.

E. Secured transactions — Article 9 of the UCC — See Chapter 29.

F. Mortgage foreclosure on real property.

1. A creditor, who lends money, secured by real property, enters into a mortgage agreement with the debtor. The creditor is the mortgagee and the debtor is the mortgagor.

2. If the mortgagor defaults, foreclosure procedures may be instituted by the mortgagee. Methods of foreclosure:

   a. Strict foreclosure — Only permitted in a few states.

   b. Entry or writ of entry — Only permitted in a few states.

   c. Power of sale in accordance with mortgage agreement — Permitted in most states.

   d. Judicial sale — Usual method of foreclosure.
      1) Proceeds are used to satisfy the cost of foreclosure and the debt.
      2) Any surplus is paid to the debtor. If there is a deficiency, a deficiency judgment can be thereafter obtained by the creditor.

G. An unpaid creditor can apply to a court in order to have a fraudulent conveyance, which was made by a debtor to a third party, set aside.

II. Other creditors' remedies based upon common law principles.

   A. Debtor and two or more creditors may enter into an agreement providing that each creditor:

      1. Will accept a sum less than the amount owed by the debtor (a composition), or

      2. Will extend the period of time within which the debtor will pay the full amount owed (an extension), or

      3. Will accept a partial cash payment and a scaling down of the amount owed, payable over a stated period of time (a composition and extension).

   B. Assignment for the benefit of creditors — Debtor transfers his or her assets to an assignee or trustee, who liquidates the assets and distributes the proceeds pro rata among the creditors of the debtor.

III. Common law creditor protection based on contract — Guaranty and suretyship.

   A. Suretyship.

      1. A surety is a third party, who promises a creditor that he or she will be liable for an obligation along with the primary debtor. A surety is a joint obligor.

      2. A surety is primarily liable to a creditor. His, her or its promise need not be in writing, unless required by statute to be written.

      3. If the principal debtor defaults, the creditor may make an immediate demand upon the surety for payment.

B. Guaranty.

    1. A guarantor makes a separate, collateral, secondary promise to the creditor that, if the debtor does not pay, he, she or it will pay the obligation.

    2. The guarantor is promising to answer for the debt, default or miscarriage of another (the principal debtor). The guarantor's liability is, therefore, secondary and the promise to pay must be in writing in order to comply with the statute of frauds.

    3. If the debtor defaults, the creditor must first make a demand on the debtor before making a demand for payment on the guarantor.

C. Defenses that may be raised by a surety or guarantor against the creditor.

    1. Material modification of the obligation owed by the principal debtor without the assent of the surety or guarantor.

    2. Discharge of the primary obligor.

    3. Tender of proper payment by the primary obligor.

    4. Surety or guarantor may raise any defense that may be asserted by the principal debtor, except minority and discharge in bankruptcy.

IV. Protection of the debtor.

A. State statutory exemptions.

    1. Real property — Homestead exemption. If the family home is sold in order to satisfy a judgment, a specific amount of the sale price must be reserved for the debtor so that he or she can provide shelter for his or her family.

    2. Personal property — Usually a specified dollar amount of household furnishings, clothing, personal possessions, pensions received from the government based upon military service and a proportion of disposable income are exempt from satisfaction for debts.

B. Federal Consumer Credit Protection Act (The Truth-in-Lending Act).

    1. A lender or seller, who is extending credit, must disclose the loan or credit terms, including finance charges.

    2. C.C.P.A. applies to creditors, who, in the ordinary course of business, lend money, extend credit or arrange for the extension of credit to natural persons for purchases for personal, family, household or agricultural use, if the price is less than $25,000.

    3. The Fair Credit Billing Act, which amends the CCPA, relates to credit reports and collection procedures.

C. Uniform Consumer Credit Code.

1. Adopted in a few states.

2. Similar to the federal Truth-in-Lending Act.

3. Alters the holder in due course rule.

D. Debt collection — Federal and state statutes have been enacted to prevent the use of abusive practices.

E. Real estate transactions — Federal legislation includes the Interstate Sales Full Disclosure Act, designed to prevent fraudulent land sales, and the Real Estate Settlement Procedures Act.

F. A Federal Trade Commission rule limits the rights of holders in due course of negotiable instruments. See Chapter 26.

KEY WORDS AND PHRASES IN TEXT

Lien
Consensual lien
Common law and statutory liens
Mechanic's (materialman's) lien on real
   property
Possessory lien
Artisan's lien on personal property
Innkeeper's (hotelkeeper's) lien on personal
   property
Writ of execution
Attachment
Prejudgment remedy
Writ of attachment
Garnishment
Garnishee
Creditors' composition agreements
Mortgage foreclosure on real property
Mortgagor
Mortgagee
Deed of trust
Foreclosure sale
Deficiency judgment
Equity of redemption
Statutory period of redemption
Assignment for the benefit of creditors

Bulk sale or transfer
Fraudulent conveyances
Suretyship
Surety enters into express contract with
   creditor and is primarily liable
Guaranty
Guarantor makes promise to answer for
   debt, default or miscarriage of
   another and is secondarily liable
Defenses of surety and guarantor
Rights of surety and guarantor (subroga-
   tion, reimbursement, contribution)
Defenses of surety and guarantor
Rights of surety and guarantor (subroga-
   tion, reimbursement, contribution)
Protection of the debtor
Exempt property
Homestead exemption (real property)
Exempt personal property (furniture,
   clothing, vehicle, animals)
Consumer protection statutes
Federal Consumer Credit Protection
   Act (Truth-in-Lending Act)
Uniform Consumer Credit Code
Federal Trade Commission holder in
   due course rule

FILL-IN QUESTIONS

1. A _____ is one who is primarily liable because he or she joins an obligor in promising to pay a debt to a creditor; a _____ is secondarily liable because his or her promise to pay an obligation is conditioned on the failure of the primary obligor to pay a debt to a creditor.

2. If a debt is incurred, but not paid, by the owner of real property for services rendered or materials furnished in order to improve the property, the creditor, who furnished the services or supplied the materials may obtain a _____ lien, which will be enforceable by the sale of the real property.

3. A bailee in possession of personal property, which he or she has stored, cared for and repaired, has an _____ lien, if the charges for storage and improvements are not paid.

4. If a judgment creditor has not been paid the amount of the judgment, he or she may apply for a writ of execution, which is a court order _____ _____.

5. _____ is a procedure whereby a court order is obtained, directing the sheriff to reach specified property of a debtor in the hands of a third person so that it can be applied to reduce the amount of a judgment.

6. Following the foreclosure of a real property mortgage, if the proceeds of the judicial sale are inadequate to satisfy the cost of foreclosure and the debt, the _____ is liable for any deficiency.

7. Statutes provide that certain property of a debtor cannot be reached in order to satisfy his or her debts. Usually such property includes a specific amount of the sale price realized on the sale of _____ as well as clothing and personal possessions. Certain income is also exempt because a creditor cannot reach _____ _____.

MULTIPLE CHOICE QUESTIONS

1. Certain creditors may have common law and/or statutory liens on the real property owned by their debtors. Such liens are referred to as:
    a. mechanics' liens.
    b. artisans' liens.
    c. prejudgment writs of execution.
    d. homestead exemptions.

2. Pine supplied lumber to Holmes for the construction of a barn on Holmes' land. Carpenter was employed by Holmes to build the barn. Neither Pine nor Carpenter have been paid by Holmes. By complying with state statutes, requiring recording and notice to a debtor, Pine and Carpenter may obtain and enforce:
    a. mechanic's liens on Holmes' real property.
    b. mechanic's liens on Holmes' personal property.
    c. artisan's liens on Holmes' real property.
    d. artisan's liens on Holmes' personal property.

3. Wage garnishment statutes enable a creditor of a debtor who is employed to obtain a portion of the wages due to the employed debtor from his or her employer. There are, however, statutory provisions that protect the debtor when the remedy of garnishment is used. For example:
    a. Some minimum amount of wages cannot be used in order to satisfy a garnishment.

b. Usually, the creditor must first obtain a judgment against the debtor.

c. The employer is prohibited from discharging the employee because the employee's wages are subject to a garnishment.

d. All of the above.

Questions 4 and 5 are based on the following fact situation: Dunstone owns no real property but she owns an automobile worth $4,000, a television set worth $300 and miscellaneous personal property worth $5,000. She is employed at a salary of $400 per week. Dunstone owes a local bank $2,000 for a loan that is past due.

4. The bank can obtain:

   a. a writ of execution for the immediate seizure of Dunstone's automobile.

   b. an order for garnishment immediately of a proportion of Dunstone's salary.

   c. a lien on Dunstone's television set and/or her automobile by recording its lien and notifying Dunstone.

   d. a writ of execution for the seizure of Dunstone's television set, after obtaining a judgment against Dunstone.

5. If the bank obtains a judgment against Dunstone and an appropriate court order:

   a. a proportion of Dunstone's salary cannot be reached through garnishment.

   b. for the seizure and sale of Dunstone's property, a specific amount of the sale price must be set aside so that Dunstone can provide shelter for her family.

   c. the bank will have liens on Dunstone's property, which may then be foreclosed.

   d. the bank will not be able to recover from any of Dunstone's assets because of statutory exemptions.

6. An agreement which provides that a creditor/lender will have a security interest in real property which is owned by a debtor/borrower, who retains title to the real property, is called a mortgage.

   a. The debtor/borrower is the mortgagee and the creditor/lender is the mortgagor. If the mortgagor defaults in making payments on the loan, the mortgagor may bring an action for foreclosure.

   b. The debtor/borrower is the mortgagor and the creditor/lender is the mortgagee. If the mortgagor defaults in making payments on the loan, the mortgagee may bring an action for foreclosure.

   c. The debtor/borrower is the mortgagor and the creditor/lender is the mortgagee. If the mortgagor defaults in making payments on the loan, the mortgagee may obtain a deed of trust in a court procedure.

   d. The debtor/borrower is the mortgagee and the creditor/lender is the mortgagor. If the mortgagor defaults in making payments on the loan, the mortgagor may bring an action for foreclosure subject to the mortgagee's right of redemption.

7. David owed Goliath a $1,000 debt, due November 1. On October 15, for consideration, Rocke promised in writing that he would pay Goliath the $1,000 if David failed to pay it. On November 1, David failed to pay Goliath.

   a. Rocke is a surety and is, therefore, primarily liable to Goliath.

   b. Rocke is a guarantor and is, therefore, primarily liable to Goliath.

   c. Rocke is a surety and is, therefore, secondarily liable to Goliath.

   d. Rocke is a guarantor and is, therefore, secondarily liable to Goliath.

8. Beta owed Kappa a $400 debt due December 1. On November 15, Xi for consideration promised Kappa orally that he would pay the $400 if Beta did not pay. On

December 1, Beta failed to pay Kappa. Kappa demanded that Xi pay the $400 but Xi refused, saying that his promise was not legally enforceable.
a. Xi's promise to act as surety is unenforceable because it is not in writing.
b. Xi's promise to act as a guarantor is unenforceable because it is not in writing.
c. Xi is a surety and, therefore, Kappa must proceed against Beta before demanding payment from Xi.
d. Xi is a guarantor and, therefore, Kappa need not proceed against Beta before demanding payment from Xi.

9. Deb loaned Mollie $10,000 for one year. Mollie obtained a bond from the Sue-Us Bonding Company, which guarantied payment of the $10,000 to Deb. Mollie did not pay Deb, and Deb is suing the bonding company for payment.
a. The guaranty made by Sue-Us Bonding Company did not have to be in writing in order to be enforceable.
b. If Mollie was a minor, spent the money and disaffirmed her promise to repay the loan, Deb may not recover from the bonding company.
c. If Mollie had given Deb a promissory note for $20,000 in exchange for the $10,000 loan, the defense of usury can be successfully raised by the Sue-Us Bonding Company.
d. Sue-Us Bonding Company can successfully raise the defense of bankruptcy, if Mollie has been discharged in bankruptcy.

10. The Truth-in-Lending Act:
a. applies to any lender or seller who, in the ordinary course of business, lends money or extends credit to others, if the amount lent or the amount of credit given is less than $25,000.
b. applies to any lender or seller who, in the ordinary course of business, lends money or extends credit to natural persons for purchases, not exceeding $25,000, for personal, household or business use.
c. establishes a maximum percentage amount that can be charged for extending credit.
d. is a disclosure statute, requiring lenders and sellers to disclose the cost of credit.

Chapter 31

Bankruptcy and Reorganization

Article I, Section 8 of the United States Constitution empowers Congress to enact uniform bankruptcy laws. In accordance with this authorization, Congress first passed a bankruptcy act in 1898. The most current federal bankruptcy statute is the Bankruptcy Reform Act of 1978, as amended (codified in Title 11 of the United States Code), which substantially changed and modernized the law relating to bankruptcy.

The goals of bankruptcy law are to provide relief for an honest debtor from the oppressive burden of indebtedness and for the fair, ratable distribution of a debtor's assets among creditors. As with the prior bankruptcy law, provision is made (but simplified in the present law) for alternative debtor rehabilitation solutions in the form of reorganization and adjustments of debts of individuals and family farmers.

THINGS TO KEEP IN MIND

1. In addition to the federal bankruptcy law, other methods are available for insuring a fair distribution of the assets of an insolvent debtor among his, her or its creditors, so that the debtor has an opportunity to financially rehabilitate himself, herself or itself. State insolvency statutes, which do not conflict with the U.S. Constitution (by impairing the obligations of contracts) or the federal bankruptcy statutes, and affect only property within the state, may be utilized. Other solutions, based upon principles of contracts, trusts and/or equity, such as compositions and/or extensions, assignments for the benefit of creditors and equitable receivership, may also be used.

2. Definitions of insolvency.

    Balance sheet insolvency — Liabilities exceed assets.

    Equitable involvency — Current liabilities exceed current assets so that debtor cannot pay debts as they mature or become due.

OUTLINE

I.   The Bankruptcy Reform Act of 1978, as amended (U.S.C., Title 11).

    A. Establishes Bankruptcy Courts with jurisdiction over all controversies affecting the debtor or his, her or its estate.

    B. Provides procedures for:

        1. Voluntary and involuntary liquidation (bankruptcy) of "bankruptcy estates" of natural persons, firms, partnerships, corporations, unincorporated companies and associations (Chapter 7).

        2. Reorganization of persons, firms and corporations (Chapter 11).

        3. Adjustment of debts of individuals with regular income (Chapter 13).

        4. Adjustment of debts of family farmers (Chapter 12).

II. Liquidation — Ordinary or straight bankruptcy.

    A. Voluntary liquidation.

        1. Commenced by any natural person, firm, association or corporation, except railroad, banking, insurance or municipal corporation or savings or building and loan association (to which other chapters of the Act apply).

        2. Petitioning debtor need not be insolvent, unless it is a partnership.

        3. Debtor will be granted an order for relief if petition is proper and debtor had not been discharged in bankruptcy within the past six years.

    B. Involuntary liquidation.

        1. Commenced against any debtor, except railroad, banking, insurance or municipal corporation, building or savings and loan association, credit union, nonprofit organization, rancher or farmer.

        2. Creditors, who have noncontingent, unsecured claims amounting to $5,000 or more, file a petition with the Bankruptcy Court.

            a. If there are 12 or more creditors, three of them must join in the petition.

            b. If there are less than 12 creditors, one or more may sign the petition.

            c. If a party so requests, a temporary trustee may be appointed to take possession of the debtor's property in order to prevent loss.

        3. The court will grant an order for relief if the debtor fails to file an answer or, if debtor files an answer, creditors prove that:

            a. The debtor is not paying debts as they become due, or

    b. A general receiver, assignee or other custodian was appointed or took possession of the debtor's property within 120 days preceding the filing of the petition.

C. Automatic stay.

    1. The filing of a voluntary or involuntary petition stays or suspends most litigation or other action that might be taken by creditors against the debtor or the debtor's property, such as commencing or continuing actions in order to enforce or perfect liens or security interests.

    2. Secured creditors may, however, apply for relief from an automatic stay if they are not adequately protected and the Bankruptcy Court may require that the debtor make periodic payments or provide additional collateral.

D. Debtor must file completed official forms with Bankruptcy Court — Contents:

    1. A list of secured and unsecured creditors with their addresses and the amounts owed.

    2. A schedule of assets.

    3. A statement of financial affairs.

    4. A list of current income and expenses.

    5. A schedule of exempt property, if debtor wishes to claim exemptions. Debtor has option of taking exemptions provided by either the law of the state in which he, she or it is domiciled or the Federal Bankruptcy Act, which provides for the following exemptions:

        a. Equity in home and burial plot, not exceeding $7,500.

        b. Interest in one motor vehicle, up to $1,200.

        c. Interest in personal household goods, clothing, books, animals, etc., up to $200 for any single item, but not exceeding a total of $4,000.

        d. Interest in jewelry, up to $500.

        e. Other property, worth up to $400, plus up to $3,750 of the unused part of the $7,500 exemption for equity in a home and/or burial plot.

        f. Items used in a trade or business, up to $750.

        g. Interests in life insurance policies.

        h. Professionally prescribed health aids.

        i. Federal and state benefits, such as social security, veterans' disability, and unemployment benefits.

    j. Alimony and child support, pensions and annuities.

    k. Rights to receive certain personal injury and other awards.

E. Order for relief is entered and interim or provisional trustee is appointed.

F. Bankruptcy estate.

    1. All tangible and intangible property, wherever located, in which the debtor had legal and/or equitable interests at the time that the petition was filed.

    2. The estate includes:

        a. Property that may be exempt.

        b. Community property; property that the debtor transferred but which trustee can reach because transfer is voidable; causes of action; and proceeds, rents and profits generated by property in the estate.

        c. Property that was received by debtor as a gift and/or inheritance and property acquired in a settlement with a spouse or as a beneficiary of life insurance within 180 days after filing of the petition.

G. First meeting of creditors — Within ten to thirty days after the order for relief is entered, the court calls the meeting of creditors, which is attended by the debtor and at which a trustee is elected, or interim (provisional) trustee becomes permanent trustee.

H. Claims of creditors.

    1. Filed within six months of the first meeting of creditors.

    2. Claims, which arose before the filing of the petition, are allowed, unless objected to or unenforceable or excluded:

        a. Claims for interest accruing after petition was filed.

        b. Claims of landlords or employees, based upon breach of lease or contract, for no more than one year's rent or wages.

I. The trustee.

    1. The trustee takes title to property that is included in the debtor's bankruptcy estate.

    2. Duties and powers of trustee — Trustee administers the estate of the debtor, by collecting assets, reducing them to cash and approving claims.

        a. Trustee may assume or reject executory contracts.

        b. Trustee may bring actions to avoid transfers of the debtor's assets, which the debtor or a judgment, lien or unsecured creditor would have had a right to avoid under state law or the Bankruptcy Act.

    c. Trustee is empowered to avoid transfers of property interests that were not perfected when the petition was filed.

    d. Trustee may avoid preferential transfers — Transfers of property or payments that favor one creditor over other creditors. With some exceptions, a preferential transfer includes those made:
      1) When the debtor was insolvent.
      2) To or for the benefit of a creditor for or on account of an antecedent debt.
      3) During the 90 days before the petition was filed.
      4) Resulting in the receipt by the creditor of a greater percentage of payment than would be made under the provisions of the bankruptcy law.

    e. Fraudulent transfers are voidable by the trustee.
      1) Transfer made in order to hinder, delay or defraud creditors or for less than reasonable consideration when the debtor was insolvent or, as a result of the transfer, becomes insolvent.
      2) Trustee has the power to avoid conveyances made within one year before the filing of the petition or the state statutory period, which is usually two to five years.

J. Priority of payment of claims upon distribution.

  1. Secured creditors, having valid liens or security interests in property, are entitled to exercise their security interests.

    a. A secured creditor can accept the collateral in full satisfaction of the debt.

    b. A secured creditor has the option of foreclosing on the collateral and using proceeds in order to pay off the debt.
      1) If proceeds exceed debt:
        a) Excess may be used to cover reasonable costs incurred by secured creditor because of debtor's default.
        b) Trustee gets any remaining balance.
      2) If there is a deficiency, secured creditor becomes an unsecured creditor as to balance.

  2. Priorities of payment of claims of unsecured creditors — Each class of debts must be fully paid before next class is entitled to share in remaining proceeds; if there are insufficient proceeds to fully pay a particular class of creditors, proceeds are distributed pro rata and remaining classes receive nothing.

    a. Costs and expenses of preserving and administering the debtor's estate.

    b. In an involuntary proceeding, claims arising in the ordinary course of business, after the commencement of the action but before the election of the trustee.

    c. Claims of wage earners, not exceeding $2,000 per claim, for wages earned within 90 days before the filing of the petition.

    d. Claims, not exceeding $2,000 per employee, for employee benefit plan contributions, arising within 180 days before filing of the petition.

    e. Claims (not exceeding $2,000) of farm producers and fishermen against debtors who own or operate grain storage facilities or fish produce storage or processing facilities.

    f. Claims for deposits made for consumer purchases, up to $900 per claim.

    g. Taxes and penalties legally due and owing within three years before filing of the petition.

    h. Claims of general creditors (including any unpaid balances owed to creditors who had limited priorities) on a pro rata basis.

    i. Any balance is returned to the debtor.

K. Discharge of debtor from debts.

  1. Claims that are not discharged.

    a. Back taxes (three years) which are not paid in full.

    b. Those based upon fraud, embezzlement, misappropriation or defalcation against the debtor, acting in a fiduciary capacity.

    c. Alimony and support.

    d. Intentional tort claims.

    e. Property or money obtained by debtor under false pretenses or fraudulent representations.

    f. Student loans obtained within five years.

    g. Unscheduled claims.

    h. Claims from prior bankruptcy action in which the debtor was denied a discharge for a reason other than the six year limitation.

    i. Consumer debts of more than $500 for luxury goods or services owed to a single creditor within 40 days of the order for relief.

    j. Cash advances aggregating more than $1,000 as extensions of open-end consumer credit obtained by the debtor within 20 days of the order for relief.

    k. Judgments or consent decrees awarded against the debtor for liability incurred as a result of the debtor's operation of a motor vehicle while intoxicated.

  2. Denial of discharge of a debtor.

    a. Assets are distributed, but debtor remains liable for unpaid portion of the claims.

    b. Discharge will not be granted if the debtor:
       1) Waives the right to discharge.
       2) Failed to appear at the first meeting of creditors or to participate in proceedings, involving objections raised to the application for discharge.
       3) Committed a bankruptcy crime.
       4) Unjustifiably failed to keep records from which his, her or its financial and business conditions could be ascertained.
       5) Refused to obey an order or answer material questions of the court.
       6) Concealed, transferred, etc., property.

J. Reaffirmation of a debt, which has been discharged, is effective if:

  1. Reaffirmation is made before a bankruptcy court grants a discharge.

  2. Agreement is filed with the court.

  3. Court approval is given, when debtor is not represented by an attorney, and court finds that there is no undue hardship and agreement is in the best interest of the debtor.

  4. Debtor may rescind within 60 days of filing of the agreement. (Rescission period must be clearly and conspicuously stated in the agreement.)

III. Reorganization.

A. Any individual, business firm or corporate debtors who are eligible for Chapter 7 liquidations (except stockbrokers and commodities brokers) and railroads are eligible for Chapter 11 reorganization.

B. A voluntary or involuntary petition may be filed, and automatic stay and entry or order for relief provisions apply.

C. Debtor remains in possession and may continue to operate his, her or its business.

D. Fair and equitable plans for settling claims and/or extending time for payment in order to avoid liquidation are approved by the court.

E. Debtor may file a plan within 120 days after the order for relief. If debtor does not do so or if the plan is not approved, the trustee, creditors or shareholders committee, appointed by the court, or any party in interest, may file a plan within 180 days after the order for relief.

F. Plan must be approved by a majority in number and two-thirds in amount of each class of creditors and shareholders, whose claims and interests will be impaired.

G. Although not accepted by a class of creditors or shareholders, if the court finds that the plan is fair and confirms it, the plan is binding on all parties.

H. Provision is made for the conversion of a reorganization into a liquidation proceeding.

I. Creditors may prefer private negotiated adjustments of creditor-debtor relations (out-of-court workouts).

J. A debtor can reject an existing collective bargaining agreement if the debtor has proposed modifications and the union has rejected the modifications without good cause.

IV. Adjustment of debts of an individual with regular income (Chapter 13).

A. An individual debtor, who is a wage earner or engaged in business, may voluntarily file a petition for adjustment of his or her debts.

1. Debtor's noncontingent, liquidated, unsecured debts amount to less than $100,000 and secured debts to less than $350,000.

2. Debtor remains in possession.

3. Automatic stay provisions apply.

4. Debtor submits a plan that may provide for a reduction in the amount of his or her obligations and/or for additional time within which to pay his or her debts. (Plan is comparable to a composition and/or extension.)

B. A reasonable plan, which provides for timely payments and is made in good faith, will be confirmed by the court. In most instances, the plan will have to be approved by all the secured creditors. Approval by unsecured creditors is not necessary.

C. Most plans call for payments of all or a portion of future income or earnings to be made to a trustee for a three year period, which may be extended for up to five years; most debts are discharged after the three year period.

D. A Chapter 13 proceeding may be converted into a Chapter 7 liquidation or Chapter 11 reorganization.

V. Family Farmer Bankruptcy Act (Chapter 12).

A. Provisions of Chapter 12 are similar to Chapter 13.

B. Petition may be filed by a family farmer, who is an individual, partnership or closely held corporation, whose gross income is at least 50 percent dependent upon farming and whose debts are at least 80 percent farm-related and less than $1,500,000.

C. Automatic stay provisions apply; farmer-debtor remains in possession.

D. Farmer-debtor files plan (providing for payment of debts) within 90 days after order for relief; court confirmation is necessary.

E. Debtor is discharged after completion of payments called for in plan during a three year period (or longer if extended by the court).

F. A Chapter 12 proceeding may be converted into a Chapter 7 liquidation or Chapter 11 reorganization.

VI. The 1984 amendments provided for special business functions, including grain storage facilities, long term shopping center leases, repurchase agreements and time shares in homes and condominiums.

KEY WORDS AND PHRASES IN TEXT

U.S. Constitution, Article I, Section 8
Bankruptcy Reform Act of 1978 as amended
Bankruptcy Court
Goals of bankruptcy
Core proceedings
Debtor
Consumer debtor
Chapter 7 liquidation (straight or ordinary bankruptcy)
Filing the petition in bankruptcy
Voluntary bankruptcy
Involuntary bankruptcy
Contents of petition (schedules)
Order for relief
Automatic stay
Adequate protection doctrine
Interim or provisional trustee
Permanent trustee
Creditors' meeting
Filing of proof of claims by creditors
Bankruptcy estate
Property of the debtor
Exempt property
Trustee's powers
Powers of avoidance
Voidable contract
Preferential transfer or payment
Statutory liens
Fraudulent transfers
Distribution of property
Secured creditor

Unsecured creditor
Order of priority for classes of debts owed to unsecured creditors
Discharge in bankruptcy
Exceptions to discharge
Objections to discharge
Effect of discharge
Revocation of discharge
Reaffirmation of debt that has been discharged
Chapter 11 reorganization
Out-of-court workout (negotiated adjustment of creditor-debtor relations)
Debtor in possession
Creditors' committee
Chapter 11 plan of rehabilitation (contents, filing, acceptance and confirmation)
Cram down provision of Bankruptcy Code
Rejection of collective bargaining agreement
Chapter 13 adjustment of debts of an individual with regular income
Chapter 13 proceeding can be initiated only by the filing of a voluntary petition by the debtor
Chapter 13 plan (contents, filing, confirmation, modification of and objections to plan)
Chapter 13 discharge
Chapter 12 Family Farmer Bankruptcy Act
Chapter 12 plan (contents, filing, acceptance and confirmation)

FILL-IN QUESTIONS

1. There is a uniform bankruptcy law in the United States because Article I, Section 8 of the _____ provides that _____ is empowered to enact "uniform Laws on the subject of Bankruptcies throughout the United States."

2. The goals of the bankruptcy law are to provide relief and protection to debtors and to provide a fair method of distributing a debtor's assets among the _____.

3. When voluntary or involuntary petitions are filed for liquidations or _____ or voluntary petitions are filed for adjustments of debts of individuals with regular income or family farmers, most litigation against a debtor is suspended. This is called an _____, which bars creditors from commencing or continuing actions against a debtor.

4. A debtor, who is a natural person, _____, other than a railroad, banking, insurance or municipal corporation or building or savings and loan association, may voluntarily petition for liquidation under Chapter 7 of the federal bankruptcy statute. If such a debtor owes more than $_____, his, her or its creditors may file a petition for _____, provided that the debtor is not a rancher, farmer or nonprofit organization.

5. In a liquidation proceeding instituted under the federal bankruptcy law, usually the creditors elect the trustee for the debtor's estate at the first meeting of the creditors, which is called by _____. Creditors have _____ from the date of the meeting within which to file their claims.

6. The trustee in bankruptcy may avoid transfers of the debtor's property if _____ or a judgment, lien or unsecured creditor would have had the right to avoid the transfer under state law or the federal bankruptcy act.

7. A preferential transfer by a debtor is one in which the debtor transferred money or property to one creditor which resulted in _____ and may be avoided by _____.

8. Either debtors or their creditors may commence liquidation proceedings (under Chapter 7) or _____ proceedings (under Chapter 11) but only a debtor may apply for _____ (under Chapter 13).

MULTIPLE CHOICE QUESTIONS

1. A debtor, who is in financial difficulty and transfers all of his property to another, in trust, for distribution among his creditors, has:
    a. entered into a composition.
    b. agreed to an extension.
    c. made an assignment for the benefit of creditors.
    d. made a voidable fraudulent conveyance.

2. An insolvent debtor owes many creditors and has filed a petition for voluntary liquidation. If he had transferred title to his $5,000 automobile to one creditor a month before filing the petition, he has made a voidable:
    a. fraudulent conveyance.
    b. assignment for the benefit of creditor.
    c. admission of debt.
    d. preferential transfer.

3. Although Johns has assets valued at $500,000, he has many unpaid current debts, totaling $300,000. Johns has not been paying his debts as they become due and

appears to have been in financial difficulty for some time. A month ago, he transferred title to his $8,000 automobile to Charles and two weeks later, he transferred all of his remaining property to Thomas, in trust for purposes of distributing the proceeds of their sale among his creditors. Yesterday, a group of almost all of his creditors filed a petition with the Bankruptcy Court for involuntary liquidation of Johns' property. Which of the following statements is correct?

a. The transfers of the automobile to Charles and all of Johns' property to Thomas were fraudulent conveyances which may be voided by the trustee in bankruptcy.

b. The transfer of the automobile to Charles was a voidable transfer because Charles received a preference but a trustee in bankruptcy will be unable to avoid the transfer.

c. The petition will be dismissed and no order for relief granted because Johns is not insolvent.

d. An order for relief may be granted because Johns transferred all of his property to Thomas, who was a custodian or general receiver of Johns' assets.

4. Organizations that may be subjected to involuntary liquidation under the federal bankruptcy statute include:

a. manufacturing corporations.

b. banking corporations.

c. insurance corporations.

d. charitable associations.

5. Spendthrift is in financial difficulty. She is insolvent in the bankruptcy sense but has not filed a petition for voluntary liquidation. A few of her creditors are threatening to force her into liquidation.

a. If she makes an assignment of her property to a third person, as custodian, for the benefit of her creditors, the bankruptcy court will grant an order for relief following the filing of a petition for involuntary liquidation.

b. If she has ten creditors, whose claims are not contingent as to liability and amount to more than $5,000, a petition for involuntary liquidation must be signed by at least three of them.

c. As long as she is able to meet current obligations, there is no basis for creditors to file a petition for involuntary liquidation.

d. She cannot file a voluntary petition for liquidation without the approval of her creditors.

6. Environmental Heat Inc. is a medium sized corporation that has been having some difficulty paying current bills. For example, checks issued by it have not been honored by its bank because of insufficient funds. The principal creditors have held a meeting in order to consider possible alternative courses of action. At the meeting they have learned that Environmental Heat Inc. has sufficient assets to meet liabilities in the event of liquidation and that potentially the corporation will be profitable in the next five years.

a. The best action that the creditors can take is to file a petition for involuntary liquidation.

b. The bankruptcy court will not grant an order for relief if the creditors file a petition for involuntary liquidation because Environmental Heat Inc. is not insolvent in the bankruptcy sense.

c. If the creditors file a petition for involuntary reorganization, Environmental Heat Inc. will have to submit a plan for reorganization and all creditors will have an opportunity to vote on the plan.

d. If the creditors file a petition for involuntary reorganization, the bankruptcy court may confirm a plan for reorganization, submitted by the shareholders, even if the plan was not accepted by two-thirds of one class of creditors.

Questions 7, 8, 9 and 10, which have been adapted from AICPA Examination, May 1987, are based on the following fact situation: On March 10 last year, the creditors of Stowe, a sole proprietor engaging in the business of selling hardware, filed an involuntary petition in the Bankruptcy Court for liquidation of Stowe's property in accordance with Chapter 7 of the Bankruptcy Code. Stowe's nonexempt property has been converted to cash which is available to satisfy the following expenses and unsecured claims as may be appropriate:

Expenses

Administration costs necessary to preserve the property of Stowe's bankruptcy estate	$20,000
Salary to Stowe for services rendered in operating the hardware business after the commencement of the bankruptcy action	30,000

Unsecured Claims

Claims by two of Stowe's employees for wages earned within 90 days of the filing of the bankruptcy petition in the amount of $4,000 and $3,000, respectively	$ 7,000
Claim by Hammond Hammer Co. for delivery of merchandise to Stowe on February 20, which was prior to the filing of the petition	9,000

7. What amount will be distributed as salary to Stowe if the cash available for distribution is $15,000?
   a. $0.
   b. $5,000.
   c. $7,500.
   d. $15,000.

8. What amount will be distributed as salary to Stowe if the cash available for distribution is $55,000?
   a. $0.
   b. $2,000.
   c. $22,000.
   d. $30,000.

9. What amount will be distributed to the two employees if the cash available for distribution is $25,000?
   a. $0.
   b. $4,000.
   c. $5,000.
   d. $7,000.

10. What amount will be distributed to the two employees if the cash available for distribution is $62,000?
    a. $4,000.
    b. $3,000.
    c. $6,000.
    d. $7,000.

Unit Five

AGENCY AND EMPLOYMENT

The efficient operation of a business, whether it is a sole proprietorship, partnership or a large corporation, depends upon employing other people, some of whom are considered to be agents. How agency relationships are created and terminated is discussed in Chapter 32. If an agency relationship exists, the agent and the person employing him or her, the principal, owe certain duties to each other (a subject matter of Chapter 32), and acts committed by an authorized agent will be treated as being the acts of the principal. As a result, a principal will be liable in contract to third parties, with whom the agent has dealt, and in tort to those who have been injured by an agent, acting within the scope of his or her authority. The extent of contractual and tort liability is explored in Chapter 33. Chapter 33 concludes with a discussion of employment relationships.

Chapter 32

AGENCY RELATIONSHIPS

An agency is a representative relationship which arises when one person, the agent, represents or acts for and in the place of another person, the principal. It is a consensual relationship. In most cases, consent of the parties to the creation (and the termination) of an agency relationship is, in fact, given. In other instances, the parties may be treated as having consented because of their conduct.

If an agency relationship exists, the principal and agent owe each other those duties which are specified in their agreement and other duties, which are implicit because of the agency relationship. Some of these duties are based on the fact that an agency relationship is a fiduciary one founded upon trust and confidence. As a result, agents and principals are required to act with good faith, honesty and loyalty toward each other.

In this chapter, the authors first discuss the nature of the agency relationship and the ways in which it is created. Next, there is a section devoted to the duties which are owed by the principal and agent to each other. The manner in which principal-agent relationships may be terminated is the subject matter of the final portion of the chapter.

THINGS TO KEEP IN MIND

1. It is sometimes necessary to distinguish agency relationships from those of employment or independent contractors. Although there are no hard and fast rules for doing so, usually the issue is resolved by examining the relative amount of independent discretion given and the amount of control exercised by the principal/employer.

2. Duties, owed by principals and agents, may arise out of the fact that the agency relationship is usually a contractually created one. Generally, actions based upon a

failure of either party to perform or an agent to account or a principal to compensate an agent are founded on contract. Actions based upon a breach of the fiduciary duty (competing with one's principal, acting for a third person's benefit, failing to reveal material information or making a secret profit) are founded on tort and do not require a showing of fraud or actual, measurable damages.

OUTLINE

I.   The nature of agency.

   A. By using a representative or agent, one person may conduct multiple business operations.

   B. A corporation can function only by using agents.

II. Agency distinguished from other relationships.

   A. Principal—agent relationship.

      1. An agent acts on behalf of and instead of a principal in engaging in business transactions.

      2. An agent may bind his or her principal in contract with a third person.

      3. An agent has a degree of independent discretion.

   B. Employer (master)—employee (servant) relationship.

      1. In order to determine if a relationship is one of employment, a court will examine surrounding circumstances.

         a. Employer controls or has right to control the employee in the performance of physical tasks.

         b. Employees have little or no independent discretion.

         c. Employees are paid for time rather than results.

      2. The rights and duties of an employee differ from those of an agent. Today the distinction is important for purposes of applicability of legislation, such as tax, social security, unemployment, workplace safety and workers' compensation statutes. (See Chapter 49.)

   C. Independent contractor.

      1. An independent contractor engages to bring about some specified end result and is normally paid at the completion of performance.

      2. The person employing an independent contractor does not exercise control over the details of the performance.

3. An independent contractor cannot bind the person employing him or her in a contract with a third party.

4. An independent contractor usually uses his or her own materials, equipment and employees.

III. Formation of agency relationship.

  A. In general.

    1. An agency may be formed for any legal purpose.

    2. An agency is a consensual relationship but not necessarily a contractual one. Consideration need not be given by a principal.

    3. Generally, no special formalities are required in order to create an agency.

      a. Unless required by the statute of frauds or other statute, a writing is not necessary.

      b. If the appointment of an agent is in a writing, the writing is called a "power of attorney."

    4. Capacity.

      a. A principal must have legal (contractual) capacity because contracts, entered into by his or her agent, are treated as contracts of the principal. If a principal lacks capacity, such contracts are voidable by the principal but not the third party.

      b. An agent need not have legal (contractual) capacity in order to act as agent, but the contract of agency may be avoided by the agent, who lacks capacity (but not the principal).

  B. Agency created by agreement.

    1. The agent and principal affirmatively indicate that they consent to the formation of the agency.

    2. The agreement may be an express one or implied from the conduct of the parties.

  C. Agency created by ratification.

    1. The principal's consent to the agency is given after the purported agent acted on behalf of the principal.

    2. Ratification may be express or implied.

    3. Ratification relates back to the time that the agent acted without authorization.

D. Agency created by estoppel. A person may be estopped to deny the existence of an agency if he or she caused a third party to reasonably believe that a person was his or her agent because there is an appearance that an agency relationship exists.

E. Agency created by operation of law.

    1. A court may find that an agency exists in order to carry out a social policy. (Purchases of necessaries by family members.)

    2. Statutes provide that a state official will be treated as having been appointed as an agent to receive service of process under certain circumstances.

IV. Types of agencies.

A. Gratuitous agencies or agencies for hire.

B. Agency coupled with an interest.

    1. Agency may be created for the benefit of the agent or a third person.

    2. Agent has a beneficial interest in the subject matter of the agency.

C. Subagent — One appointed by an agent to assist agent in conducting affairs of the principal.

V. Agent's duties to principal.

A. Some of the duties of an agent are specified in the agency agreement, others are implied from the agency relationship.

B. Duty to perform — An agent is required to follow instructions, use reasonable skill and diligence in carrying out agency obligations, and use special skills, which he or she possesses, if they are applicable.

C. Duty to notify principal of material information that relates to the subject matter of the agency.

D. Duty of loyalty.

    1. An agent may neither compete with his or her principal nor act for another principal, unless full disclosure is made to the principal and the principal consents.

    2. After termination of an agency, the agent may not disclose trade secrets, confidential information, customer lists, etc., acquired in the course of his or her employment.

    3. Conflicts of interest — Any secret profits or benefits, received by an agent, acting adversely to his or her principal, belong to the principal, who may recover them from the agent. (A court may impose a constructive trust.)

E. Duty to account — An agent must account to his or her principal for any moneys or property, rightfully belonging to the principal, which have come into the agent's hands. An agent should not commingle such property with his or her own property or that of others.

F. Remedies available to principal for breach of duties by agent.

    1. Principal's right to indemnification — If a principal is required to pay damages to an injured party for an agent's tortious conduct or, as a result of an agent's violation of the principal's instructions, incurs a loss, the principal may recover the amount of resulting damages from the agent.

    2. A principal may seek remedies based upon breach of contractual duties or in tort, based upon a breach of the fiduciary duty.

    3. Transactions engaged in by an agent, which violate the fiduciary duty, are voidable by the principal.

    4. A court will impose a constructive trust on property received by an agent, who has used his or her agency position in conflict with those of his or her principal, so that the property (or the proceeds of its sale) is treated as held for the benefit of the principal.

VI. Principal's duties to agent.

A. Some of the duties of a principal are specified in the agency agreement; others are implied from the agency relationship.

B. A principal has an obligation to perform in accordance with his or her contract with an agent.

C. Duty to compensate, indemnify and reimburse agent.

    1. A principal is required to pay any agreed compensation to his or her agent.

    2. If no compensation is specified, a principal is required to pay expenses, losses and reasonable compensation for services rendered by the agent, unless the agency is a gratuitous one or there are circumstances, such as a family relationship, indicating that compensation had not been intended.

    3. There is no duty to pay compensation to an agent who has failed to perform his or her duties.

D. Duty of cooperation — A principal is required to assist an agent in performing his or her duties and to do nothing to prevent such performance.

E. Duty to provide safe working conditions.

F. Remedies available to agent for breach of duties by principal.

    1. Indemnification — A principal may be required to indemnify an agent for payments or liabilities, incurred in executing his or her obligations, and for losses, caused by the failure of the principal to perform his or her duties.

2. An agent may obtain a lien against his or her principal's property.

3. An agent may sue for breach of contract or counterclaim if sued by his or her principal.

4. An agent may bring an action for an accounting.

5. An agent may withhold further performance.

VII. Termination of agency relationship.

A. Termination by act of the parties.

1. Lapse of time.

a. Agency expires at the end of a specified time if one is stated.

b. Agency terminates after the expiration of a reasonable period of time if no term has been specified.

2. Purpose accomplished. Agency is terminated when the objective for which it was created has been achieved.

3. Occurrence of specific event. An agency ends upon the happening of a particular event if its formation had been so conditioned.

4. Mutual agreement. The parties may consent to the termination of an agency.

5. Termination by one party.

a. A principal may revoke the authority of an agent or an agent may renounce his or her appointment as an agent.

b. Either party may have the power but not necessarily the right to terminate an agency.
    1) If an agency is an agency at will (not for a stated term or for a particular purpose), either party has the power and right to terminate the agency.
    2) If an agency is not an agency at will, a party may have the power but not the right to terminate the agency and is, therefore, liable to the other party for the wrongful termination, which is a breach of contract.

c. An agency may be terminated for cause.

d. A principal has neither the power nor the right to terminate an agency coupled with an interest (which is also referred to as a power coupled with an interest or a power given as security).
    1) The agency is said to be irrevocable.
    2) Distinguish situations in which an agent merely derives proceeds or profits from transactions.

B. Termination by operation of law.

    1. Death or insanity terminates an agency.

        a. Knowledge of the death or insanity is not required.

        b. An agency coupled with an interest is not automatically terminated.

        c. Statutory exceptions exist.

    2. Bankruptcy of the principal terminates the agency.

        a. Insolvency does not terminate the relationship.

        b. Bankruptcy of the agent does not necessarily terminate the agency relationship.

    3. Impossibility.

        a. Destruction of the subject matter of the agency.

        b. Outbreak of war.

        c. Change in law making further conduct of the agency illegal.

    4. Unforeseen change in circumstances.

C. Notice required for termination.

    1. If termination is by act of a party, the agency continues between the principal and agent until notice is given by principal, who is revoking, or agent, who is renouncing authority.

    2. Notice must be given to third persons.

        a. Actual notice must be given to third persons who dealt with the agent.

        b. Constructive notice must be given to those who knew of the agency by publication in a newspaper, posting of a sign, etc.

    3. The party terminating the agency or another person may give the notice.

    4. Notice generally is not required if the agency is terminated by operation of law. (See Chapter 27 herein regarding Uniform Commercial Code, Sec. 4-405.)

KEY WORDS AND PHRASES IN TEXT

Agency relationship exists between principal and agent

Derivative authority

Distinctions between relationships in which employees, agents or independent contractors perform services in accordance with agreements with those who employ them

State and federal employment laws apply to employer-employee (master-servant) relationships

Factors used in order to distinguish one relationship from another

Extent of control and supervision that may be exercised by one in superior position

Extent of independent discretion that may be exercised by person who is employed

Which person furnishes tools and place of work?

Length of employment

Method of payment (is compensation given for time or completion of a job?)

Degree of skill required by the person employed

Commingling of the relationships

Formation of the agency relationship

Power of attorney

Equal dignity rule

Agency formed by express or implied agreement of principal and agent

Agency resulting from express or implied ratification

Agency created by estoppel

Agency created by operation of law

Agent's duties to principal

Agent's duty to use diligence and skill in performing work

Agent's duty to notify principal of matters that come to his or her attention concerning subject matter of agency

Agent's fiduciary duty of loyalty

Agent's duty of obedience

Agent's duty to account for principal's property (including funds)

Duties owed by subagents

Unauthorized subagents

Principal's duties to agent

Principal's duty to compensate, reimburse and indemnify agent

Principal's duty of cooperation

Principal's duty to provide safe working conditions

Agent's rights and remedies against principal

Principal's rights and remedies against agent (constructive trust, avoidance and indemnification)

Termination of agency by act of parties

Termination because of lapse of time, achievement of purpose, occurrence of specified event or mutual agreement

Termination because of act of one party (agent's renunciation or principal's revocation)

Agency coupled with an interest (irrevocable agency)

Agency terminated by operation of law (death or insanity, unforeseen circumstances such as impossibility, changed circumstances, bankruptcy, outbreak of war)

Notice required for termination

FILL-IN QUESTIONS

1. A person who agrees to work for another, subject to his or her control and directions, for an agreed hourly rate, would most likely be considered an _____ rather than an _____.

2. A person who agrees to construct a house for another, furnishes the materials, supplies and employees and is to be paid a lump sum upon completion of the house would most likely be considered to be an _____.

3. An agency may be created by agreement of the parties, _____ _____ or _____.

4. Most agencies are created for the benefit of the principal. An agency _____ _____, however, is created for the benefit of the agent or a third person.

5. An agent is contractually obligated to his or her principal to perform in accordance with their agency agreement. This means that an agent is required to _____ _____ _____.

6. An agent is a fiduciary. As a result, an agent must act _____ _____. He or she must reveal information, relating to the subject matter of the agency to his or her principal, and will have to account to his or her principal for any secret profit or benefit obtained, while acting for the principal. If an agent violates the fiduciary duties, the contract of agency is _____ by the principal.

7. A principal is obligated to pay his or her agent _____ unless the agency agreement or other circumstances clearly indicate that such services were to be rendered gratuitously.

8. A principal has a right to _____ if, as a result of the failure of his or her agent to carry out instructions, he or she incurs a loss. An agent has a similar right of _____ for payments made or liabilities incurred in executing his or her agency duties.

9. A principal may terminate an agency by _____ the authority of his or her agent, without liability to the agent, if _____ _____.

10. An agency is terminated by operation of law upon the death or insanity of either the principal or agent, _____ or _____.

MULTIPLE CHOICE QUESTIONS

1. Creation of an agency relationship does not require:
   a. consent of the agent.
   b. contractual capacity on the part of the principal.
   c. consideration.
   d. any of the above.

2. An agency relationship:
   a. must be evidenced by a writing.
   b. creates a power of attorney.
   c. may be terminated only by the principal.
   d. may be created by estoppel.

3. Parmer sends Anders a letter requesting that Anders act as his agent to sell an acre of land which Parmer owns. Anders accepts by signing a carbon copy of the letter and returning it to Parmer. This is an example of:
   a. an agency created by express agreement of the parties.

  b. an agency created by implied agreement of the parties.
  c. a formal contract of ratification.
  d. an illegal power of attorney.

4. As to third parties, an agency by estoppel:
  a. is the same thing as an agency created by operation of law.
  b. is the same thing as an agency created by ratification.
  c. can be imposed upon the principal even though there is, in fact, no agency relationship created by agreement.
  d. will be found to exist if a third party sold goods to a minor or did not pay for them even though they were necessaries.

5. Pearson, a minor, entered into a contract of agency with Argyle, an adult. Argyle made a contract with Yeager, while acting as agent for Pearson. The contract:
  a. of agency is voidable by Argyle.
  b. of agency is voidable by Pearson.
  c. with Yeager is voidable by Argyle.
  d. with Yeager is voidable by Yeager.

6. Prince, an adult, enters into a contract of agency with Queen, a minor. Queen made a contract with Zephir, while acting as agent for Prince.
  a. The contract of agency is not binding on Prince.
  b. The contract of agency is not binding on Queen.
  c. The contract with Zephir is not binding on Prince.
  d. The contract with Zephir is not binding on Zephir.

7. As security, a lender is given authority to collect rents due to a borrower and to apply these rents to the payment of a debt owed to the lender.
  a. This does not create an agency.
  b. The agency is created by operation of law.
  c. This is an agency coupled with an interest.
  d. The agency is terminated by the death of the borrower.

8. An agent owes a duty of loyalty to his or her principal:
  a. because the agent occupies a fiduciary relation with the principal.
  b. which is violated if the agent acts in a negligent manner.
  c. and if this duty is violated, the agent is liable only for actual losses incurred by the principal as a result of the breach.
  d. but this duty prohibits an agent from making a secret profit while representing the principal only if the interests of the principal are adversely affected.

9. An agent, employed by both the buyer and seller of certain personal property, will be considered as violating his fiduciary duty:
  a. although both the buyer and seller know of his dual position and consent thereto.
  b. although no actual monetary damage can be shown.
  c. but is entitled to retain compensation paid for his services by the seller.
  d. but neither the buyer nor the seller can rescind an executory contract made on his behalf by the agent.

10. J. P. Metty hired Leopard as his agent for purposes of finding a building contractor and supervising the construction of a new mansion for Metty. It was anticipated that the cost would be at least $500,000. For his services Leopard would receive a

fee of $30,000. Leopard contacted Castle Construction Co., which agreed to construct the stately manor house for Metty for $500,000 and an addition to Leopard's house at no charge. The Metty mansion and the addition to Leopard's house have been completed and Metty has paid the $500,000 to Castle Construction Co. Leopard is liable to Metty because:

a. he failed to inform Metty that the mansion could be constructed for less than $500,000.

b. he acted disloyally by failing to obtain the most favorable terms for Metty.

c. he failed to account for a benefit he received as a result of the agency.

d. all of the above.

11. Paul appointed Fred as his agent to purchase 500 shares of ETT Co. stock for $18 per share. Unknown to Paul, Fred owned 500 shares of ETT Co. stock. Fred sold his own shares to Paul at $18 per share.

a. Paul must carry out his duty of compensating Fred for the services performed.

b. A court will impose a constructive trust on the 500 shares of ETT Co. stock now held by Paul.

c. The contract of sale is voidable by Paul so that he can return the 500 shares of stock to Fred and recover the $9,000 paid therefor.

d. If the value of the stock increases to $24 per share, Paul has no basis for suing Fred.

12. A principal engages an agent for three months as its exclusive agent to sell its product in a three state area.

a. The contract creating the agency must be in writing.

b. If the principal sells its product in the three state area through another agent, it will be liable for damages to the first agent.

c. The principal does not have the power to terminate the agency because it is an agency coupled with an interest.

d. The principal can disaffirm contracts made by the agent when it is discovered that the agent is a minor.

13. M's agent, Q, had access to a secret formula which M developed and used for the manufacture of a substance that absorbs snow causing it to disappear. Q sold the trade secret to S.

a. M cannot discharge Q without liability.

b. M can recover the consideration paid by S to Q although the sale of the trade secret occurred after Q left M's employ.

c. M can recover the consideration paid by S to Q or recover in tort for the breach of Q's fiduciary duty, but not both.

d. There is no basis for a suit by M against S.

14. April was an agent of Primmer. April died last month. The agency is, therefore, terminated by:

a. mutual assent.

b. revocation of authority.

c. implied agreement of the parties.

d. operation of law.

15. Marple has been authorized to act as Christie's agent until December 31, 1989. The agency will be terminated without liability to either Marple or Christie:

a. on December 31, 1989, only.

b. upon the insolvency of Christie, before December 31, 1989.
c. upon the death of Marple, before December 31, 1989.
d. upon the dismissal, without cause, of Marple by Christie.

16. In order to terminate the authority of an agent to bind his or her principal, actual notice to creditors who dealt with the agent or extended credit to the principal through the agent, must be given:
a. if the principal is bankrupt.
b. to the attorney general of the state in which the principal resides.
c. if a change in law makes the further continuation of the agency illegal.
d. if the principal revokes the authority of the agent.

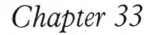

Chapter 33

Liability to Third Parties and Employer-Employee Relationships

A named principal is liable as a party to an act or transaction engaged in or conducted by his or her agent. As a result, a principal may be liable in contract or tort to a third party. The third party in such case will have to establish that there was an agency relationship and that the agent was acting within the scope of his or her actual or apparent authority or that the act of the agent was later ratified by the principal. In this chapter the authors discuss the nature of the liability of employers as well as the rights and liabilities of principals and agents with regard to third parties.

THINGS TO KEEP IN MIND

An agent's authority to do a particular thing may have been expressly or impliedly conferred by his or her principal, in which case the agent has actual authority. An agent may lack the actual power to perform a particular act but may possess apparent authority if, because of his or her principal's words or conduct, a third party reasonably and justifiably believed that the agent had the necessary authority.

OUTLINE

I. Liability of principals to third parties based on contract.

    A. A principal is liable as a party to a lawful contract made for and on his or her behalf by his or her agent, while acting within the scope of his or her actual or apparent authority, or subsequently ratified by the principal.

    B. Third party must show that:

        1. The agency relationship existed, and

    2. The agent acted within the scope of his or her authority.

C. Authority of agent.

    1. Actual — Conferred by principal upon the agent in order to accomplish the purpose of the agency.

        a. Express actual authority.
            1) May be given orally or in a writing.
            2) "Equal dignity" statutes may provide that, if a contract being executed by an agent is required to be in writing, the agent's authorization must also be in writing.

        b. Implied actual authority.
            1) Inferred because of conduct of principal.
            2) Conferred because of custom.
            3) Reasonably necessary to carry out express authority.
            4) Arising because of an emergency which necessitates action by the agent to protect or preserve the property or rights of the principal.
            5) An agent has limited power to delegate performance of his or her duties to subagents.

    2. Apparent authority and estoppel.

        a. The principal manifests to a third person that his or her agent has authority and the third person reasonably relies upon the principal's statement or conduct, deals with the agent and is injured.

        b. Apparent authority cannot be based upon declarations or conduct of the agent.

        c. Apparent authority may arise if a principal gives possession and evidence of ownership of his or her property to a purported agent.

        d. The principal is estopped from asserting that the agent lacked authority.

D. Ratification — The affirmation by a principal of a previously unauthorized contract or act.

    1. The principal must have knowledge of all material facts surrounding the transaction.

        a. If the principal lacks complete knowledge, he or she may repudiate the ratification, unless the third person has changed his or her position in reliance on the ratification.

        b. It does not matter that the lack of knowledge results from the agent's wrongful conduct or a mistake.

    2. The effect of ratification is to bind the principal as if the act or contract had been originally authorized.

    3. The entire transaction must be ratified.

4. The agent must have held himself or herself out as acting for the person who subsequently ratifies.

5. The principal must have had capacity at the time the act was performed and at the time it was ratified.

6. Ratification may be express.

7. Ratification may be implied.

   a. Acceptance of benefits.

   b. Failure to repudiate.

8. Death, insanity or withdrawal of third party before ratification prevents principal from effectively ratifying.

II. Contract liability of agent to third party.

A. If a contract is made in the principal's name and authorized by the principal, the agent is not a party to the contract and, therefore, does not incur contract liability. (The parties to the contract are the principal and the third party.)

B. If a contract is made in the name of a principal by an agent who lacks authority, and the contract has not been ratified by the principal, the agent is not liable as a party, but is liable to the third party based upon breach of implied warranty of authority.

C. An agent is liable to a third party if he or she expressly obligates himself or herself or guarantees performance by his or her principal.

III. Liability when principal is undisclosed.

A. An undisclosed principal is one whose existence and identity are not disclosed to a third party with whom an agent deals.

B. The agent is a party to the contract and is liable as such.

C. If the agent had authority:

   1. The agent is entitled to indemnification from the principal.

   2. The third party can recover from the principal, unless:

      a. The third party elected to look only to the agent.

      b. Liability is based upon a negotiable instrument, because the principal's signature does not appear thereon.

   3. The third party can recover from either the principal or the agent but not both.

D. The principal can enforce the contract against the third party, if it was entered on his or her behalf by an authorized agent, unless:

1. Liability is based upon a negotiable instrument and the principal did not acquire rights thereto.

2. The third party was being defrauded by the principal.

3. The contract was for the performance of personal services by the agent.

E. The principal bears the loss if his or her agent acted dishonestly.

F. Partially disclosed principal.

1. Third party knows of principal's existence but not identity.

2. The principal and the agent may both be treated as parties to the contract.

IV. Liability to third party for torts.

A. An agent is personally liable for his or her torts, even if they were authorized.

B. The doctrine of *respondeat superior* — A superior, such as an employer or principal, is vicariously liable for torts committed by a subordinate, such as an employee or an agent, if the subordinate was acting within the scope of his or her employment or agency, in furtherance of the superior's business.

1. The principal/employer normally cannot disclaim vicarious liability for subordinate's torts.

2. The principal is liable for tortious acts of employees and subagents hired by an agent, who had authority to hire.

3. An employer, who has the right to control employees who are "borrowed," is liable to third parties.

4. One employing an independent contractor is not liable for torts of the independent contractor or those of his or her employees.

C. A superior is not liable if a subordinate substantially deviates from his or her required duties and goes on a "frolic of his or her own."

D. A principal is liable for the intentional tort of fraud or misrepresentation, if his or her agent had the authority to make representations concerning the subject matter with which he or she dealt on behalf of the principal.

E. The one in a superior position, having the right to control the activities of his or her subordinate, is liable for the subordinate's negligence and intentional torts and has a duty to restrain subordinates from engaging in reckless acts.

F. Notice of material facts, relating to a principal's or employer's business, received by an agent or employee, will be imputed to the principal or employer.

V. Liability for crimes.

    A. An agent or employee is liable for his or her own crimes, even if he or she was acting within the scope of authority or employment.

    B. A principal or employer is not liable for the criminal actions of an agent or employee, even if the agent or employee was acting within the scope of authority or employment, unless:

        1. The principal or employer participated in the crime or expressly directed or authorized its commission.

        2. A specific statute imposes liability on the principal or employer.

VI. Employer-employee relationships.

    A. For applicable statutory regulations of employment, see Chapter 49.

    B. Employment relationships are generally created by contracts to which contract rules of law apply.

        1. Contract provisions may be embodied in a collective bargaining agreement between an employer and a union, acting as a representative of employees.

        2. A contract may contain any terms as long as they are not contrary to statute or public policy.

        3. A reasonable covenant not to compete with an employer after termination of employment, which is a subordinate part of an employment contract, is usually enforceable by injunction.

        4. A contract provides for payment of compensation to the employee.

        5. The shop right doctrine — Employer has a nonexclusive right to use an invention developed by an employee whose duties do not include research and making inventions.

            a. Employer does not have to pay royalties to the employee.

            b. Employee may obtain a patent in his or her own name, retains ownership rights and may sell rights to others or license others to use.

            c. The employer's shop right is irrevocable, even after employment relationship is terminated.

        6. Termination of employment.

            a. If contract is for employment at will, either employer or employee can end employer-employee relationship without liability to the other party.

            b. Today, in some jurisdictions, an employer will be liable for wrongful discharge if discharge violated a statute or an established public policy or is based upon bad faith.

        1) Civil rights laws.
        2) Whistle blowing — Reporting, testifying against or aiding in an investigation of an employer who is violating the law.
        3) Discharge for refusing to violate the law, serving on a jury or exercising established rights, such as filing a worker's compensation claim or participating in union activities.
        4) Lack of good faith and fair dealing.
        5) Implied promise of continued employment which may be established by policy statements made by employer, a course of dealing or personnel manual.

    c. An employment contract for a specified duration can be terminated without liability for good and sufficient cause.
        1) If employer wrongfully terminates employment, employer is liable for damages, the measure of which is usually the compensation due under the contract for the remainder of the term of employment.
        2) If employee wrongfully terminates employment, employee is liable for damages, the measure of which is usually the difference between the amount that the employer will have to pay a new employee and the compensation that the employer had been paying to the terminating employee.

C. Employment torts.

  1. Liability of employer for injuries incurred by an employee while working within the scope of employment.

    a. Common law — Employer is liable for negligence but can assert defenses, such as contributory negligence and the fellow servant rule.

    b. Workers' compensation statutes — A fixed amount of compensation, including lost wages, medical and death benefits, is paid by the employer or the employer's insurer to an employee for an injury that occurs as a result of an accident arising in the course of employment without regard to fault.

  2. Employer's liability for intentional torts and negligence — See material above at IV.

KEY WORDS AND PHRASES IN TEXT

Scope of authority
Express and implied actual authority
Power of attorney
Equal dignity rule
Apparent authority based upon estoppel
Emergency powers of agents
Express and implied ratification
Requirements for ratification
Principal's and agent's liability for contracts

Disclosed, partially disclosed and undisclosed principals
Warranties made by agent
Warranty of authority
Principal's liability for tortious conduct
Principal's authorization of tortious conduct
Principal's and agent's liability for torts of an agent
Misrepresentations made by agent

Negligence of agent
Doctrine of *respondeat superior*
Scope of employment
Liability for independent contractor's acts
Liability for agent's crimes
Liability of principal for torts committed
    by subagent
Liability of employer for tort committed
    by borrowed employee
Employer-employee relationships based
    upon contracts
Covenant not to compete

Employee's right to compensation
Shop right doctrine
Termination of contract of employment
Employment at will
Employment contract for specified
    duration (term)
Employers' liability for their own acts
Workers' compensation statutes
Employers' liability to third parties for
    torts of employees (negligence and
    intentional torts)
Notice of dangerous conditions

FILL-IN QUESTIONS

1. The extent of an agent's power to engage in transactions on behalf of his or her principal is referred to as the agent's _____.

2. Actual authority may be _____, if a principal uses words to confer authority upon an agent, or implied, because such authority is incidental to and clearly necessary or logically inferred from the express powers granted or based upon _____.

3. When a third party deals with an agent (who in fact lacks express or implied actual authority) reasonably believing that the agent has authority to act on behalf of his or her principal and the third party changes his or her position in reliance on the principal's words or conduct, the principal may be _____ from denying that his or her agent lacked actual authority. In such a case, the agent is said to be acting within the scope of his or her _____ authority.

4. A principal is liable on a contract made in his or her name by an agent, acting within the scope of his or her authority or subsequently _____ by the principal. In such case, the agent is _____ liable to the other contracting party as a party to the contract. If the agent lacked authority, he or she is liable to the other contracting party based upon the _____.

5. A disclosed principal is one whose existence and identity are known by a third party at the time that he or she is dealing with the principal's agent. A partially disclosed principal is a principal whose existence is known but whose _____ is not known by a third party at the time that he or she is dealing with the principal's agent. An _____ _____ is a principal whose existence and identity are not known by a third party at the time that he or she is dealing with the principal's agent.

6. The doctrine of *respondeat superior* results in one in a superior position being vicariously liable without actual fault for _____ committed by his or her subordinates, while acting within _____
_____.

MULTIPLE CHOICE QUESTIONS

1. An agent is liable for performance of a contract to the third party, with whom he or she deals, on a contract that he or she has entered into on behalf of his or her principal:
    a. whenever the agent exceeds his or her authority.
    b. whenever the agent acts in behalf of a nonexistent principal.
    c. whenever the agent acts in behalf of a principal, who did not have contractual capacity at the time of the transaction.
    d. only if the agent expressly assumes liability and thus becomes a party to the contract.

2. An agent is thought of as possessing the same authority as is possessed by other agents in similar positions. Such authority is normally:
    a. express actual authority.
    b. express apparent authority.
    c. implied actual authority.
    d. implied express authority.

3. If a principal leads a third party to believe that he or she has conferred authority on his or her agent, although he or she has not conferred such authority on the agent in fact, the agent will be considered as having:
    a. express actual authority.
    b. implied actual authority.
    c. apparent authority.
    d. no authority.

4. Arnold is the manager of a snow clearing service. Although not expressly authorized to do so, Arnold would have:
    a. implied authority to discharge an employee who has refused to lift a shovel and has thrown snowballs at customers.
    b. implied authority to borrow money to purchase twenty snowblowers.
    c. apparent authority to borrow money to purchase twenty snowblowers.
    d. actual authority to cancel an order for snow plows, placed by the purchasing agent of the snow clearing service.

5. Cramer, chief clerk for Morris, is asked by Morris to assume management of his store, while Morris is on special undercover assignment for the CIB. If Morris cannot be reached for advice, Cramer is justified in:
    a. discharging an incompetent employee.
    b. borrowing money in Morris's name for purposes of enlarging the store.
    c. lending Egger, an employee in the store, $9,000.
    d. all of the above.

6. If a principal accepts the benefits of a contract, entered into by his agent, acting without the scope of his authority, the principal will be considered to have ratified the contract:
    a. in its entirety.
    b. although he lacked actual knowledge of some of the material terms of the agreement.
    c. although the other party to the contract has withdrawn.
    d. retroactive to the date upon which it was entered, although at that time the principal was incompetent.

7. Paul has authorized Arthur to purchase a television set from Exeter on his (Paul's) behalf. Instead of purchasing a television set, Arthur, fully disclosing the agency relationship, purchased a CB radio. Paul used the CB radio for one month but neither he nor Arthur paid Exeter for it.
    a. Only Arthur is liable for the purchase price of the CB radio.
    b. Paul is liable for the purchase price of the radio because he ratified the transaction by accepting the benefits.
    c. Paul is liable for the purchase price of the radio because Arthur had actual authority to purchase it.
    d. Paul is not liable for the purchase price of the radio because he made no implied warranty as to his capacity.

8. Auten is an agent for a disclosed principal, Pine. On May 1, Auten entered into an agreement with Taupte Corp. on behalf of Pine, although she lacked authority to do so. On May 5, Taupte Corp. learned of Auten's lack of authority and immediately notified Auten and Pine that it was withdrawing from the May 1 contract. On May 7, with full knowledge of all the material facts, Pine ratified the May 1 contract in its entirety. If Taupte Corp. refuses to honor the agreement and Pine brings an action for breach of contract, Pine will:
    a. prevail because the May 1 contract was ratified by Pine in its entirety.
    b. prevail because Pine's capacity to act as a principal was known to Auten.
    c. lose because the May 1 contract was void due to Auten's lack of authority.
    d. lose because Taupte Corp. notified Auten and Pine of its withdrawal before Pine's ratification.
    (This question has been adapted from AICPA Examination, May 1987.)

9. Bauten is an agent for a disclosed principal, Plane. On May 1, Bauten entered into an agreement with Teme Corp. on behalf of Plane, although she lacked authority to do so. On May 5, with full knowledge of all the material facts, Plane ratified the May 1 contract in its entirety. On May 7, Teme Corp. learned of Bauten's lack of authority and immediately notified Bauten and Plane that it was withdrawing from the May 1 contract. If Teme Corp. refuses to honor the agreement and Plane brings an action for breach of contract, Plane will:
    a. prevail because the May 1 contract was ratified by Plane in its entirety.
    b. prevail because Plane's capacity to act as a principal was known to Bauten.
    c. lose because the May 1 contract was void due to Bauten's lack of authority.
    d. lose because Teme Corp. notified Bauten and Plane of its withdrawal within a reasonable time.

10. An agent, who has been appointed by a principal to move lumber that is obstructing a road which the principal is required to keep clear:
    a. is liable to a third person, who is injured while trying to climb over the lumber, which the agent failed to remove.
    b. is not liable to a third person, who is injured by a falling two by four, because the agent has moved the lumber but stacked it in a negligent manner.
    c. is liable to a third person, with whom she gets into a dispute while in the process of moving the wood and hits him with a two by four.
    d. is not liable to a third person if her principal, under the doctrine of *respondeat superior*, is liable for the tort committed by the agent.

11. If an employee has, while acting within the scope of employment, committed both negligent and intentional acts that resulted in injuries to third parties, the employer:

    a. may be liable to the third parties, even if the employee's acts were unauthorized.

    b. may effectively limit its liability to the injured third parties if the agent has signed a disclaimer absolving the employer from liability.

    c. will be liable under the doctrine of *respondeat superior* only for the intentional acts.

    d. will never be criminally liable unless it actively participated in the acts with its employee.

(This question has been adapted from AICPA Examination, May 1987.)

12. Watson was an employee of the H and M Contracting Corp. Watson was specially trained in procedures to be used in blasting operations with particular emphasis on safety precautions. H and M Contracting Corp. had contracted to construct a factory. In order to put in the foundation, it was necessary to do some blasting and Watson's services were used. Watson disregarded a number of safety precautions. As a result, neighboring buildings were damaged and Watson incurred personal injuries.

    a. H and M Contracting Corp. is liable to the owners of the damaged buildings, despite the fact that Watson disregarded the precautions and the fact that the corporation exercised reasonable care.

    b. H and M Contracting Corp. is not liable to the owners of the damaged buildings because Watson disregarded safety precautions and the corporation exercised reasonable care.

    c. H and M Contracting Corp. is not liable to Watson under the workers' compensation statutes.

    d. Watson is not liable for the damage to the neighboring buildings because he was acting on behalf of his employer.

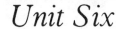

BUSINESS ORGANIZATIONS

As indicated in Chapter 34, various forms of organization may be utilized in order to engage in a business enterprise, the most common of which are the sole proprietorship, the partnership and the corporation. The formation, termination, management and rights and liabilities of partnerships and corporations and those associated with them are explored in the chapters in this unit.

Note that the law of contracts and agency form a foundation for your understanding of the material in this unit.

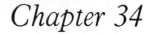

Chapter 34

Forms of
Business Organization

In this chapter the authors briefly explain and compare the basic forms of business organizations, the sole proprietorship, the partnership and the corporation, and describe some less frequently used types of business organizations.

THINGS TO KEEP IN MIND

The choice, as to which form of organization is most appropriate for a particular business enterprise, depends upon a number of considerations, some of which, such as capital needs, liability of participants and tax advantages, are referred to in this text. The type of organization selected in each case is a matter for sound business judgment, based in part upon knowledge of legal implications.

OUTLINE

I. Basic forms of business organization.

A. Sole proprietorship — A business owned by an individual, who is personally liable for the obligations of the business.

B. Partnership.

1. An association of two or more persons, who jointly control and carry on a business as co-owners for the purpose of making a profit. (Covered substantially by the Uniform Partnership Act — See Appendix C.)

2. A limited partnership is a partnership in which at least one partner is a general partner and at least one other is a limited partner, who does not participate in management and has limited liability. (See the Uniform

Limited Partnership Act in Appendix D and the Revised Uniform Limited Partnership Act in Appendix E.)

C. Business corporation.

  1. A separate legal entity, created by the state.

  2. The owners, the shareholders, have limited liability.

  3. Many states have adopted the Model Business Corporation Act or the Revised Model Business Corporation Act. (See Appendix F.)

II. Other forms of business organization.

A. Joint venture — A special type of association, formed to carry out a single transaction or a series of similar transactions, which for tax purposes is treated in the same manner as a partnership.

B. Syndicate or investment group — A number of persons agree to pool their resources in order to finance a business venture.

C. Joint stock company — An association, structurally resembling a corporation, but often treated as a partnership.

D. Business trust — Arises if a number of people turn over management and legal title to property to one or more trustees, who distribute the profits to the participants (the beneficiaries of the trust).

E. Cooperative — Association (that may be incorporated) organized in order to provide an economic service to its members (or shareholders).

III. Comparisons between different forms of organization.

A. Advantages and disadvantages of a sole proprietorship.

  1. Advantages.

    a. Receive all profits.

    b. Easier and less costly to initiate than other forms of organization.

    c. Possible tax benefits.

    d. Sole proprietor is his or her "own boss."

  2. Disadvantages.

    a. Bears entire risk of loss (unlimited liability).

    b. Difficult to raise large amounts of capital.

    c. Possible tax disadvantages.

B. Liability of owners.

    1. Sole proprietorship — Unlimited.

    2. Partnership — Usually unlimited.

    3. Corporation — Usually limited.

C. Ability to raise capital — Usually increases as organization changes from a sole proprietorship to partnership to corporation.

D. Comparison of partnership to corporate form of organization. See Exhibit 34-1 in text.

E. Tax considerations. See Exhibit 34-2 in text.

KEY WORDS AND PHRASES IN TEXT

Business organization
Sole proprietorship
Partnership
Limited partnership
Business corporation
Joint venture
Syndicate or investment group
Joint stock company
Business trust
Cooperative

Advantages and disadvantages of sole proprietorship form of business organization
Comparing a partnership with a corporation as to method of creation, legal position as an entity, liability of owners, duration, transferability of ownership interest, management, taxation, regulation by government and ease of raising financial capital

MULTIPLE CHOICE QUESTIONS

1. Simon Proper is the sole owner of SP Enterprises. He has filed the necessary forms with a government official in order to conduct his business under the trade name SP Enterprises. After paying taxes last year, Simon had profits of $182,000, $100,000 of which was used to make improvements in the plant and equipment of SP Enterprises and the balance personally retained, and subsequently spent, by Simon. AAAA Advertising, Inc. asserts that its bill for $90,000 for services rendered has not been paid and it has, therefore, sued Simon, doing business as SP Enterprises.

    a. Because Simon engaged in business as a sole proprietor, he is personally liable for payment of the $90,000 obligation.

    b. SP Enterprises is a corporation, and it alone is liable for the $90,000 obligation.

    c. Simon Proper and SP Enterprises are engaging in business as a general partnership and Simon, therefore, is individually liable as a partner for the $90,000 obligation.

    d. Simon Proper and SP Enterprises are engaging in business as a limited partnership; SP Enterprises is a general partner; and Simon is a limited partner. Simon, therefore, is not individually liable for the $90,000 obligation.

2. Warm and Tepid agree to pool their business property and talents in order to form and jointly operate a firm which will engage in the business of supplying computer

services.   They foresee that in the first two years the business will not be profitable.   Warm and Tepid, therefore, agree to make equal additional contributions of capital during that period.   They expect that after the two year "start up" period, the business will generate profits which they agree to share equally.   Warm and Tepid have formed:

a. a general partnership.
b. a limited partnershp.
c. a business corporation.
d. a joint venture.

3.   Hot and Cold agree to pool their computer programming talents in order to create a computer billing program for the Tri-County Water Company.   Hot and Cold agree that they will divide profits of the endeavor equally.   Hot and Cold have formed:

a. a limited partnership.
b. a business corporation.
c. a joint venture.
d. a joint stock company.

4.   In most states today, business corporations may be a member of:

a. a general partnership.
b. a limited partnership.
c. a joint venture.
d. All of the above.

Chapter 35

PARTNERSHIPS
Creation and
Termination

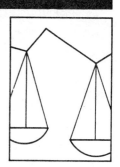

Much of the law relating to partnerships is codified in the Uniform Partnership Act (UPA), which defines a partnership as being "an association of two or more persons to carry on as co-owners a business for profit" (UPA Sec. 6). Persons means natural persons, other partnerships, associations and corporations (UPA Sec. 2). Business includes trades, occupations and professions (UPA Sec. 2).

THINGS TO KEEP IN MIND

Partnership law is based upon the law of agency, which is covered in Chapters 32 and 33. As a result, each partner is treated as an agent of his, her of its co-partners and, as shall be seen in Chapter 36, each partner may be liable as a principal to third persons if a partnership relationship exists.

Currently, consideration is being given to revision of the Uniform Partnership Act.

OUTLINE

I.   Characteristics of a partnership.

    A. Elements of a partnership.

        1. Common ownership interests in an ongoing business.

        2. Sharing of profits and losses of the business.

        3. Right to participate in the management of the operation of the business.

B. A partnership is treated as an entity, separate and apart from its individual members for limited purposes.

   1. The capacity of a partnership to sue and be sued in the name of the partnership varies from state to state.

   2. Judgments entered against a partnership in its partnership name may be collected from partnership property.

   3. Under the federal bankruptcy laws, a liquidation proceeding is effected against only the partnership itself if the petition specified the partnership in the firm name.

   4. With variation among the states, ownership to personal and real property may be transferred by and to a partnership in its firm name.

C. A partnership may be treated as an aggregate of the individual members.

   1. This is so under the law in some states.

   2. Under the federal tax laws, a partnership is treated as an aggregate.

II. Formation of a partnership.

A. No special formality is ordinarily necessary in order to create a partnership.

B. A partnership may be expressly created by contract.

   1. Partnership agreement may be oral or in writing.

      a. Because of the statute of frauds, a partnership agreement must be in writing in order to be enforceable, if it authorizes partners to deal in transfers of real property.

      b. If a partnership is formed for a term of more than one year but the agreement is oral, it will be treated as a partnership at will, which may be terminated by any party without liability, unlike a partnership for term, which requires the assent of all the partners for dissolution.

      c. Usual contents of articles of partnership.
         1) Name — State law may restrict use of certain names and/or words.
         2) Nature of business and duration.
         3) Contributions to be made by individual partners.
         4) Manner of dividing profits and losses — Unless otherwise specified, partners share profits equally; if no provision is made for the manner of sharing losses, losses are shared in the same proportion as are profits.
         5) Salaries and drawing accounts, if any.
         6) Restrictions on the authority of any partners.
         7) Conditions for withdrawal from partnership and provisions for the continuation of the business if the partnership is dissolved (partnership buy and sell agreement).

2. Capacity of partners.

    a. Minors — Partnership agreement is voidable by a partner who is a minor but, if rights of creditors are involved, the minor cannot withdraw his or her original investment in the partnership.

    b. If a partner is adjudicated to be mentally incompetent or insane after the partnership is formed, the partnership is not automatically dissolved.

    c. Corporations — State laws vary.
      1) Traditionally a corporation could not be a partner.
      2) If corporation's charter (certificate or articles of incorporation) so provides, it may be a partner.
      3) The Model Business Corporation Act, the Revised Model Business Corporation Act and the Uniform Partnership Act provide that a corporation may be a partner.

3. Consent to formation of partnership by all partners is necessary.

C. Partnership may be implied if parties intended to be co-owners of a business.

1. Factors to be considered are joint ownership of business property, sharing management responsibilities, contributing capital or investing jointly, and sharing profits or losses.

2. It does not, however, necessarily mean that a group of people have formed a partnership if they are co-owners of property or share gross income (UPA Sec. 7).

3. A person will not be treated as a partner merely because he or she receives a share of profits in payment of a debt, wages, interest on a loan, an annuity to a widow or representative of a deceased partner, or consideration for the sale of goodwill or other property.

D. Partner by estoppel.

1. A party, who is in fact not a partner, will be estopped from denying that he or she is a partner and, therefore, will be held liable as a partner to third persons, who reasonably relied and dealt with or advanced credit to the partnership if:

    a. He or she held himself or herself out as being a member of a partnership, or

    b. Consented to a misrepresentation of an alleged partnership relationship by another.

2. The purported partner does not become a partner, although he or she may be liable as one to third persons.

III. Partnership property includes:

A. Real and personal property contributed by individual partners, at the time of formation of the partnership or subsequently, for the permanent use of the partnership.

B. Property subsequently acquired with partnership funds on account of the partnership.

C. Any realized appreciation in the value of partnership property.

IV. Termination of partnership — Occurs following the dissolution and winding up (liquidation) of a partnership.

A. Dissolution — Occurs when a partner ceases to be associated with the partnership business, resulting in a change in the relations of the partners (UPA Sec. 29).

1. By acts of the partners (UPA Sec. 31).

a. If the partnership agreement provided for a partnership for term and the term has elapsed or the purpose for which it was formed has been accomplished, the partnership is dissolved.

b. Partners may mutually agree to dissolution.

c. If the partnership is a partnership at will, a partner's good faith withdrawal or expulsion dissolves the partnership without liability.

d. If the partnership was for a specified term, withdrawal of a partner, without cause, will subject withdrawing partner to liability; expulsion, without cause, subjects other partners to liability.

e. Admission of a new partner results in dissolution of the former partnership and the creation of a new one, which is liable for the obligations of the old partnership (UPA Sec. 41).

f. Voluntary or involuntary transfer of a partner's interest for the benefit of creditors does not automatically dissolve a partnership (UPA Secs. 27 and 28).
  1) Transferee acquires the right to receive transferring partner's share of profits.
  2) Transferee does not have the right to interfere with management or to inspect books of the partnership.
  3) A partner's interest in the partnership is subject to assignment, attachment or other charging orders.

2. Dissolution by operation of law.

a. Death of a partner.

b. Bankruptcy of the partnership or a partner (in most cases).

c. Illegality, which makes it unlawful to continue the business or to do so with one of the partners.

3. Dissolution by judicial decree (UPA Sec. 32).

    a. Upon application of a partner.
        1) A partner has been judicially declared mentally incompetent.
        2) A partner is permanently incapable of participating in management.
        3) The business of the partnership can only be operated at a loss.
        4) Improper conduct of a partner.
        5) Serious personal dissension among partners.

    b. Upon application of a third party.
        1) Assignee of a partner, if it was a partnership at will.
        2) Judgment creditor of a partner, who obtained a charge on the interest of his or her debtor in the partnership.

B. Notice of dissolution — Failure to give required notice results in liability.

1. A withdrawing partner must give notice to his or her co-partners.

2. Personal notice must be given to those who extended credit to the partnership and public notice must be given to those who dealt with the firm on a cash basis, if dissolution occurs because of acts of the parties or by operation of law, except for illegality or bankruptcy (UPA Sec. 35).

C. Winding up.

1. Dissolution terminates the authority of partners, except the authority to complete unfinished business and that which is necessary for winding up, including collecting, preserving and selling partnership assets, discharging liabilities, collecting debts owed to the partnership, allocating current income and accounting to each other for the value of their interests in the partnership.

2. Distribution of assets.

    a. Distribution is made out of partnership assets and any additional "contributions" by partners necessary to pay liabilities of the partnership.

    b. Order of payment.
        1) Payment to outside creditors.
        2) Payment to partners who have made advances or incurred liabilities on behalf of the partnership.
        3) Return of capital contributions to partners.
        4) Payment of any surplus to partners in accordance with ratios fixed by agreement or, if none, equally.

    c. Concept of marshalling of assets arises when the partnership and/or an individual partner is insolvent.
        1) Partnership is insolvent — Partnership creditors have priority over individual partner's creditors with respect to partnership assets and may then look to partners' assets.
        2) If a partner is insolvent, the order of payment is:
           a) His or her individual creditors.

b) Partnership creditors.

c) Other partners, who may be entitled to contribution.

KEY WORDS AND PHRASES IN TEXT

A partnership

The Uniform Partnership Act (UPA)

Partnership characteristics of common ownership interest in a business, sharing of profits, losses and management of business operations

Partnership as an entity

Legal capacity of partnership

Legal liability of partnership when judgment rendered against it in the name of the partnership

Doctrine of marshalling assets

Discharge in bankruptcy when adjudication applies only to partnership entity

Real and personal property may be held and conveyed in the partnership name

Aggregate theory of partnership

Formation of partnership based upon oral or written agreement

Duration of partnership

Partnership for term

Capacity of members of partnership

Corporation may be a partner (general view)

Prima facie inference that partnership formed if members jointly own business, have equal right of management and share profits or losses

Partner by estoppel

Partnership property

Termination of partnership

Dissolution by acts of the partners

Agreement to dissolve

Partner's power to withdraw, admission of new partners and transfer of a partner's interest

Dissolution by operation of law (death of partner, bankruptcy, illegality)

Dissolution by judicial decree (insanity, incapacity or improper conduct of a partner; business impracticability)

Notice of dissolution to partners and third parties

Winding up

Allocation of income and distribution of assets

Partnership buy and sell agreement

FILL-IN QUESTIONS

1. A partnership may be treated by state law as having the capacity to sue and be sued and to transfer property in its firm name, in which case it is considered to be _____. In other instances, such as the federal tax laws, it is treated as

_____.

2. A partnership is usually created by an _____ of those participating in it. A partnership may also be formed by the implied assent of its members, who agree to be co-owners of a business for profit and _____

_____

_____.

3. A partnership is dissolved by _____ if the partners mutually agree to its dissolution or the partnership agreement provides that the partnership will exist for a limited period and the period has expired.

4. A partnership is dissolved by operation of law upon the _____

_____.

5. A partnership will be terminated following dissolution and the completion of _____
    _____.

MULTIPLE CHOICE QUESTIONS

1. A and B, doing business as Able Co., a partnership, hold out to the public that C is also a partner and C, in his relations with third parties, acts as though he is a partner. Z enters into a contract with Able Co. through C. Able Co. now denies that C is, in fact, a partner.
    a. C is personally liable on the contract with Z.
    b. The partnership is not liable on the contract with Z.
    c. C is, in fact, a partner of A and B.
    d. C is a member of the partnership by operation of law.

2. Murray and Norton conducted a business in the name of Norton and Murray Associates. Their relationship was informal and neither one considered himself to be a partner of the other; stationery was printed with the name of Norton and Murray Associates. Loon loaned Murray $400 for and on behalf of the business. Murray informed Norton of this but Norton stated to Murray, "That's your responsibility. I've had nothing to do with it." Murray failed to pay the loan back and Loon seeks to hold both Murray and Norton liable on the debt. Under these circumstances:
    a. Loon cannot recover from Norton because Norton's statement to Murray was effective against Loon.
    b. Norton and Murray are partners by estoppel.
    c. since there was no signed, written partnership agreement, Loon cannot recover from Norton.
    d. the fact that neither Murray nor Norton considered their relationship to be a partnership precludes recovery against Norton.

3. A partnership is dissolved by operation of law when:
    a. one of the partners is bankrupt.
    b. one of the partners is imprisoned for a year.
    c. the purpose for which it was formed has been accomplished.
    d. a court enters a decree of dissolution.

Questions 4, 5 and 6 are based on the following fact situation: The partnership of Parnell and Quincy is being dissolved. The firm has assets of $100,000 and liabilities of $145,000, all owed to outside creditors. Parnell's total capital contribution was $10,000 and Quincy's was $5,000. The partnership agreement did not provide for sharing of profits or losses. The partnership and the two partners have all filed for voluntary liquidation under the Federal Bankruptcy Act. Parnell has personal assets of $200,000 and personal liabilities of $150,000. Quincy has personal assets of $85,000 and personal liabilities of $80,000. Neither is entitled to any exemptions.

4. The total amount due to be distributed from the partnership is:
    a. $100,000.
    b. $145,000.
    c. $160,000.
    d. none of the above.

5. The outside creditors of the firm will receive:
   a. $145,000.
   b. $135,000.
   c. $130,000.
   d. $100,000.

6. Parnell's share of the total firm deficiency is:
   a. $30,000, but the actual amount to be paid to firm creditors from his personal assets is $40,000.
   b. $30,000, but the actual amount to be paid to firm creditors from his personal assets is $20,000.
   c. $30,000, but the actual amount to be paid to firm creditors from his personal assets is $10,000.
   d. $40,000, but the partnership creditors cannot obtain anything from his personal assets.

7. R, S and T were equal partners in a partnership that engaged in the business of buying and selling real property for profit. Title to all property, purchased with partnership funds, was taken in the name of R. R died with partnership real estate and personal property standing in his name, valued at $100,000 and $10,000 respectively. The partnership had no debts. R's wife claims a dower right in the real property. R's children, to whom he had bequeathed all his personal property, claim a statutory right to one-third of the personal property. Under the circumstances:
   a. R's wife has a valid marital (or dower) right to all the real property held in her deceased husband's name.
   b. R's children are entitled to one-third of the personal property standing in their deceased father's name.
   c. R's wife is entitled to R's share of undistributed partnership profits.
   d. R's estate is entitled to settlement for the value of R's partnership interest, which is considered to be personal property.

8. Y and Z formed a partnership. Y contributed $1,000 and Z contributed $500. The firm has been dissolved and its creditors have been paid. There is $2,100 left.
   a. Y gets $1,300 and Z gets $800.
   b. Y gets $1,050 and Z gets $1,050.
   c. If Y had lent the firm an additional $1,000, he would get $2,000 and Z would get $100.
   d. Unless one of the partners died or became bankrupt, the partnership cannot be dissolved.

9. A, B and C, partners, have decided to call it a day and to dissolve their partnership, which has assets of $50,000 (all cash) and owes outside creditors $75,000. A has made a $5,000 loan to the partnership, which has not been repaid, and owns personal property worth $10,000. B has no assets but is a member of another partnership. The value of his interest in that partnership is $3,000. C has no personal assets. The capital balance of A, B and C in the partnership is $10,000 each.
   a. Creditors can receive no more than $50,000 of the partnership property and $10,000 from A.
   b. Creditors can only receive $50,000 of the partnership property.
   c. Creditors can receive no more than $50,000 of the partnership property, $10,000 from A and $3,000 from B.

    d. Creditors can receive no more than $45,000 of the partnership property and A can receive $5,000 of partnership property.

10. Kincaid, a member of the Joker Co., a partnership, wishes to retire as a partner. He, therefore, assigns his interest in the partnership to Lensing for $50,000 and assigns all his rights, title and interest in the partnership to Lensing, who he names as his successor partner in Joker Co.
    a. Absent any limitation, regarding the assignment of a partner's interest in the partnership agreement, Kincaid is free to assign it at his will.
    b. The assignment to Lensing effectively dissolves the partnership.
    c. Lensing is entitled to an equal voice in the management of the partnership.
    d. Although Lensing does not have the status of a partner, she can, upon proper demand, inspect the partnership books.

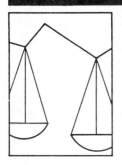

Chapter 36

PARTNERSHIPS
Operation and Duties

Partners usually have rights and duties to participate in the management of the affairs and business of the partnership and to share in the profits thereof. As each partner is an agent for his or her co-partners, a partner owes fiduciary duties to his or her partners as well as a duty to account. In addition, each partner may incur liability, as a principal, for contracts entered into and torts committed by co-partners, acting within the scope of their authority, or subsequently ratified. Knowledge received by one partner will be imputed to the other members of the partnership and representations, made by a partner, will be treated as having been made by all the partners.

THINGS TO KEEP IN MIND

Normally, partners include explicit provisions, relating to their respective rights and duties, in the partnership agreement, which provisions will be enforced as long as they are lawful. If the partners have not done so, the provisions of the Uniform Partnership Act will be controlling in those states which have adopted it. Provisions in a partnership agreement will be enforced as long as they are lawful.

OUTLINE

I.   Rights and duties of partners.

    A. Each partner has a right and a duty to share in the management of the partnership (UPA Sec. 18). Unless otherwise provided in the partnership agreement:

        1. Each partner has one vote, regardless of his interest in the firm.

        2. In connection with ordinary business decisions, majority vote controls.

3. Unanimous consent is required for changing the partnership agreement, the scope of the business or the capital structure and in matters significantly affecting the nature, liability or existence of the partnership (UPA Sec. 9).

4. Each partner is expected to devote full time and exclusive service to the partnership, absent a contrary agreement.

5. Unless otherwise agreed, partners do not receive remuneration for their partnership services, except that surviving partners are entitled to reasonable compensation for services rendered in winding up the affairs of a dissolved partnership.

6. Each partner has the right to examine the books and records of the partnership, which should be maintained at the place of business of the firm, and has the right to information concerning the partnership's business from his or her co-partners (UPA Secs. 19 and 20).

B. Accounting.

1. The purpose of accounting is to determine the value of each partner's proportionate share in the partnership.

2. An accounting may be rendered voluntarily.

3. A partner may bring an equitable action for an accounting.

   a. Usually accounting occurs in connection with dissolution proceedings.

   b. Accounting is available if:
      1) The partnership agreement so provides.
      2) A partner has been wrongfully excluded from the business.
      3) A partner is wrongfully withholding profits in violation of the fiduciary duty.
      4) Other circumstances "render it just and reasonable" (UPA Sec. 22).

C. Property rights.

1. Right with respect to specific partnership property (UPA Sec. 25).

   a. Partners are tenants in partnership — Co-owners of partnership property with the right to possession for partnership purposes.

   b. Upon the death of a partner, his or her rights in specific partnership property vest in the remaining partners.

   c. A partner may not assign rights to specific partnership property nor subject it to marital rights, such as dower, attachment or execution by his or her individual creditors, etc.

2. Rights to an interest in the partnership.

   a. Each partner has a right to his or her share of the profits and surplus, which is considered to be personal property (UPA Sec. 26).

      b. A partner's interest in the partnership is subject to assignment, attachment and other charging orders. An assignment does not dissolve the partnership or permit an assignee to interfere with management (UPA Secs. 27 and 28).

D. Fiduciary duties.

   1. Each partner is an agent for his or her co-partners and is, therefore, accountable as a fiduciary (UPA Sec. 21).

   2. A partner must act in good faith with loyalty and honesty for the benefit of the partnership and make full disclosure to his or her co-partners of matters relating to the partnership.

   3. A partner will be liable for any personal gain or profits, derived from using the partnership property or the exercise of power as a partner.

II. Relationship between partners and third persons.

A. In dealing with third persons on behalf of the partnership, each partner acts as an agent for the partnership and its members (UPA Sec. 9).

B. A partner's authority to bind the partnership contractually may be based upon:

   1. Express actual authority, provided for in the partnership agreement.

   2. Implied actual authority.

      a. Necessary for the conduct or the ordinary business of the partnership.

      b. Usually partners have broad implied authority, which will vary with the nature of the particular business of each partnership, unless limited by agreement.
         1) A partner of a trading partnership has authority to buy and sell commodities of the type in which the firm regularly deals, give warranties, borrow money and issue and indorse a negotiable instrument.
         2) A partner has the power to pay and collect debts, hire and discharge employees, give a security interest in personal property and lease or purchase property needed in the usual operation of the firm's business.
         3) Restrictions on partners' implied authority — Unanimous consent is required in order to:
            a) Convey or mortgage real property, other than in the ordinary course of the partnership's business.
            b) Make an assignment of property.
            c) Dispose of the firm's goodwill.
            d) Confess judgment or submit a controversy to arbitration.
            e) Do any act, which would make it impossible to continue the business of the partnership (UPA Sec. 9).

   3. Apparent authority.

    a. A third person, who deals with a partner, may assume that the partner has authority to bind the firm in a transaction relating to the usual business of the firm.

    b. Unless the third person knows that the partner lacks authority, the partnership and co-partners will be liable to him or her for any damage.

  4. Partners may ratify unauthorized acts of a partner.

C. Admissions and representations concerning partnership affairs, made by an authorized partner, bind the partnership, if they are made while conducting the ordinary business of the partnership (UPA Sec. 11).

D. Knowledge of or notice to a partner of facts, concerning matters relevant to the partnership's affairs, will be imputed to the partnership and other partners (UPA Sec. 12).

E. The partnership and the co-partners are liable for breaches of trust and torts committed by a partner or employee, while acting within the scope of his or her authority in the ordinary course of the business of the partnership.

F. Liability of partner to third persons.

  1. Partners are jointly liable in contract. In most states, actions based upon contract must be brought against all the partners jointly (together).

  2. Partners are jointly and severally liable for torts and breaches of trust. A third person may sue all the partners together or any one or more of them separately.

KEY WORDS AND PHRASES IN TEXT

Equal rights among partners to manage and conduct partnership business

Unanimous consent usually is not necessary except for matters which significantly affect the nature of the partnership

Partners' rights to compensation

Partners' rights to inspect books and records

Accounting

Partners' property rights

Partners' interests in the partnership

Partners are tenants in partnership of partnership property

Each partner is treated as an agent for co-partners

Partners' fiduciary duties

Joint contract liability

Liability of incoming partner

Joint and several liability

Distinction between trading and nontrading partnerships

Application of agency concepts of actual authority, apparent authority and ratification

FILL-IN QUESTIONS

1. Unless the partnership agreement provides otherwise, partners are presumed to have equal rights to possess partnership property for partnership purposes, to share in partnership profits and to _____.

2. Majority vote will be effective in connection with ordinary business decisions of a partnership. Unanimity is necessary, however, in order to _____ _____.

3. In a partnership, each partner has the right to _____, to have an interest in the partnership and to participate in management.

4. Partners' ownership rights with regard to specific partnership property are those of _____.

5. If a partner makes a contract on behalf of the partnership, the co-partners will be liable if he or she acted within the scope of _____ _____.

6. In addition to the usual implied actual authority of a partner, one, who is a partner in a trading partnership, has power to _____ _____.

7. Partners are _____ liable for a contract of the partnership, entered into by an authorized partner, and must in most states, therefore, all be included in a lawsuit based upon the contract. They are _____ liable for torts and may, therefore, be sued separately or together.

MULTIPLE CHOICE QUESTIONS

1. Able and Baker, doing business as Aber Co., a partnership, hold out to the public that Charlie is also a partner, and Charlie, in his relations with third persons, acts as though he were a partner. Frank enters into a contract with the firm through Charlie. Aber Co. now denies that Charlie is a partner.
    a. Charlie is not personally liable as a partner on the contract with Frank.
    b. The partnership of Aber Co. is liable on the contract with Frank.
    c. Charlie is, in fact, a partner of Aber Co.
    d. Charlie is, in fact, not a partner of Aber Co. but has some of the rights of a partner.

2. Unanimous consent is not required in order to:
    a. enlarge the scope of the business of a partnership.
    b. admit new partners.
    c. sell equipment of the partnership used in the ordinary operation of its business.
    d. purchase personal property needed in the ordinary operation of the business of the partnership.

3. Orange, Plum and Quince were general partners in the marmalade manufacturing business. Orange managed the partnership, Plum contributed her name and Quince contributed his capital. Absent an agreement to the contrary:
    a. Quince has the majority vote in respect to new business.
    b. Quince has assumed the responsibility of paying Plum's debts upon the insolvency of the partnership.
    c. Orange, Plum and Quince share profits and losses equally.
    d. Orange is entitled to a reasonable salary for his services.

*Questions 4 and 5 are based on the following fact situation: M, N and O operated a
pizza restaurant as a partnership.   All three partners worked in the restaurant.   The
partnership agreement provided that only M had authority to order beverages.*

4.   O ordered 100 cases of soda from the salesman for a bottling company. The sales-
      man knew that O was a partner but did not know that he was not the soda purchaser
      for the partnership.
      a. Only O is liable for the 100 cases of soda.
      b. O had apparent authority to make the purchase of soda.
      c. O had actual and apparent authority to make the purchase of soda.
      d. M, N and O are jointly and severally liable for the purchase of soda.

5.   One day N was mopping the floor, but he failed to clean up some anchovies that had
      fallen on the floor. H, a customer, slipped on the anchovies and broke a leg. H's
      damages total $5,000.
      a. H may sue each of the partners in separate actions for tort.
      b. H will have to sue the partnership in order to recover for his injury.
      c. H may sue and recover only from N.
      d. H may sue M, N and O in separate actions and recover $5,000 from each of
          them.

6.   D, a partner of the D E F partnership, engaged in the retail grocery business, gave
      X, a personal creditor (of D) a security interest in the inventory owned by the
      partnership. E also gave Y, a wholesaler, who supplied the firm with canned goods,
      a similar security interest in the inventory to secure the payment of the purchase
      price of canned goods delivered to the store.
      a. Y has no rights with respect to his security interest in the inventory.
      b. X has no rights with respect to his security interest in the inventory.
      c. E, but neither D nor F, will be personally liable for the purchase price of the
          canned goods purchased from Y.
      d. D, E and F are jointly and severally liable for the purchase price of the canned
          goods.

Chapter 37

PARTNERSHIPS
Limited Partnerships

A limited partnership is formed by complying with state statutory requirements, and consists of at least one general partner, who potentially has personal liability for all debts of the partnership, and one or more limited partners. A limited partner contributes capital, in the form of money or other property, owns an interest in the firm and shares in the profits of the partnership, but does not participate in management and is not personally liable for partnership obligations beyond the amount of his or her investment. This form of organization enables an investor to limit his or her liability and, in some instances, take advantage of certain tax benefits available to high risk enterprises.

THINGS TO KEEP IN MIND

If a limited partnership fails to comply with the statutory requirements or if a limited partner participates in management, the partnership will be treated as a general partnership and the limited partner will be liable as a general partner.

For a comparison between the provisions of the Uniform Partnership Act, the Uniform Limited Partnership Act and the Revised Uniform Limited Partnership Act, see Exhibit 37-1 in the text.

OUTLINE

I. Formation.

    A. Certificate, setting forth the firm name, nature and duration of business, location of principal place of business, names and addresses of members, capital contributions of limited partners, share of profits or other compensation that limited partners are entitled to receive, methods for changes in membership and subsequent continuation of the business, is signed by the partners.

B. Certificate is filed with a designated state or county official.

II. Liability of limited partner to creditors.

A. A limited partner is liable to creditors only to the extent of his or her contributed or promised capital.

B. A limited partner will be liable as a general partner if:

1. The surname of the limited partner is included in the partnership name.

2. The limited partner participates in management.

3. The limited partner learns that the firm is defectively formed and fails to withdraw from the partnership.

III. Rights of limited partner.

A. A limited partner (member) has no authority to bind the partnership.

B. A limited partner has the same rights as do partners in a general partnership with respect to suing, examining books, accounting, the return of his or her capital contribution, the assignments of rights to his or her interest, etc.

IV. Dissolution.

A. By acts of parties.

1. Expiration of term for which the partnership was formed.

2. If the partnership is not formed for a specified term, the will of a general partner.

3. Withdrawal or expulsion of a general partner, unless otherwise provided in the certificate or unless members consent to continuation.

B. By operation of law.

1. Death or insanity of a general partner, if the business cannot be continued in accordance with certificate or consent of other members.

2. Illegality.

3. Bankruptcy of firm or a general partner.

C. Limited partner's withdrawal, death, assignment of his or her interest or bankruptcy (unless it causes the bankruptcy of the firm) does not result in the dissolution of the firm.

D. Winding up and liquidation procedure, following dissolution, is the same as that for a general partnership, except for the priorities in distribution.

1. The Uniform Limited Partnership Act specifies the following order:

   a. Outside creditors.

   b. Limited partners' shares of profit and any other compensation.

   c. Limited partners' return of capital contributions.

   d. Advances, loans, etc., made by general partners.

   e. General partners' share of profits.

   f. General partners' return of capital contributions.

2. The Revised Uniform Limited Partnership Act changes the order by including claims of partners, who are creditors, with outside creditors and combining limited and general partners together.

KEY WORDS AND PHRASES IN TEXT

Limited partnership
General partner
Limited partner
Formation of limited partnership
Filing of signed certificate of limited partnership
Number of limited partners
Restrictions on limited partner's participation in management and use of limited partner's name

Role of the limited partner and liability of limited partner
Liability of general and limited partners to creditors of partnership
Rights of limited partner
Use of a limited partnership
Dissolution of limited partnership (causes and consequences)
Priorities in distribution of partnership assets
Limited partnership associations

FILL-IN QUESTIONS

1. In order to form a limited partnership, compliance with certain statutory requirements is necessary, including the filing of a certificate, stating _____ _____ _____ _____ _____ _____ .

   The certificate must also be _____ and _____ with the appropriate governmental official.

2. If the state limited partnership act is complied with in all respects, a limited partner is not liable to firm creditors except to the extent of _____ .

3. A limited partner will be liable to a creditor if the firm was defectively organized

and he or she failed to withdraw after receiving knowledge of the defect or if

_____ .

4. Assume that a limited partnership was formed for a term of ten years. Prior to the expiration of the ten-year period, the partnership may be dissolved if a general partner _____

_____

_____

or if the continuation of the firm will be illegal or if the firm is bankrupt. _____

_____
of a limited partner does not result in the dissolution of the firm.

MULTIPLE CHOICE

1. Angus is a limited partner in the Digby, Ernst and Friendly Ltd. partnership. Angus' existence and name is not disclosed to the public. Angus' liability will not be limited to the amount of his capital contribution because:
    a. his surname is not included in the name of the firm.
    b. his capital contribution is less than that of the general partners.
    c. he participates in decisions concerning the operation of the business.
    d. the government official with whom the partnership certificate was filed is not notified of Angus' change of address.

2. P, Q and R are active members of the P Q R Plumbing Co., a partnership. O is a limited partner thereof. P installed the plumbing system in G's new $150,000 home. G moved in and turned on the water, only to learn that the water lines had been negligently installed. The pipes burst and the entire house was flooded. Damage has been extensive.
    a. If G bases an action on tort, he must sue all the partners jointly.
    b. If G bases an action on contract, he may sue all the partners separately.
    c. G will not be able to recover from O if his action is based on contract.
    d. G will not be able to recover from P, Q or R if he sues them jointly but does not include O as a party.

3. The G H Limited Partnership, the partnership agreement of which provides for sharing of profits equally, is insolvent. F was a limited partner and is now solvent. G and H were general partners. G is now insolvent. He has no non-exempt property but owes $2,000 to personal creditors. H has a truck worth $1,000 and an interest in the H and R Co., another partnership, valued at $2,000. He has no individual debts. F's net worth is $500,000. The liabilities of the G H Limited Partnership amount to $3,000 all owed to V. No financial adjustments among the partners are necessary.
    a. Assume that F participated in management. V may collect only from F.
    b. Assume that F did not participate in management. V may collect only from H by attaching H's car and H's interest in the H and R partnership.
    c. Assume that F did not participate in management. V may collect only from F.
    d. Assume that F did not participate in management. V may collect $1,500 from F and $1,500 from H.

Questions 4 and 5 are based on the following fact situation: A certificate of limited partnership has been properly filed by a partnership, the books of which indicate the following:

The partnership consists of three partners, Manfred, Norstad and Oops, who share profits equally. The partnership agreement is silent as to the manner of sharing losses.

Manfred loaned the partnership $10,000, without interest, and made a capital contribution of $20,000; Norstad made a capital contribution of $10,000; Oops made no capital contribution but has devoted all his time to the partnership. Manfred, a general partner, and Norstad, a limited partner, have devoted no time to the management of the partnership.

4. Which of the following statements is false?
    a. Norstad will be liable as a general partner, if the name of the partnership is Manfred, Norstad and Oops, Ltd.
    b. Norstad will be liable as a general partner for willful, intentional torts, committed by Oops, while acting within the scope of his authority.
    c. The partnership will not be dissolved upon Norstad's death.
    d. The partnership will be dissolved upon the bankruptcy of Oops.

5. The partners have agreed to dissolve the partnership. Outside creditors are owed $50,000. The firm and each of the partners are solvent. Under the Uniform Limited Partnership Act, the order of distribution is:
    a. outside creditors ($50,000); Norstad for his share of the profits and capital contribution of $10,000; Manfred $10,000 for his loan; Manfred and Oops for their shares of the profits; Manfred $20,000 for his capital contribution.
    b. outside creditors ($50,000); Manfred $10,000 for his loan; Norstad $10,000 for his capital contribution; Manfred $20,000 for his capital contribution; Manfred, Norstad and Oops then share profits.
    c. the same as that of a general partnership.
    d. the same as that under the Revised Uniform Limited Partnership Act.

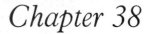

Chapter 38

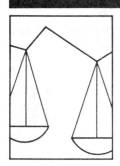

CORPORATIONS
Nature &
Classifications

A corporation is a legal entity, created by the state, under the terms of a general corporation statute. Important characteristics of a corporation include perpetual existence, centralized management, ease of transferability of ownership interests and limited liability for owners.

THINGS TO KEEP IN MIND

The formation, operation and rights and duties of corporations and those associated with them are regulated by state statutes which, with varying degrees, closely resemble the Model Business Corporation Act, which is referred to herein as MBCA. (See Appendix F in the text.) The Revised Model Business Corporation Act of 1984 is an internally consistent model for legislation. (See Appendix G.) It contains most of the provisions that are found in the MBCA but the order and numbering scheme of sections in the RMBCA differ from those in the MBCA.

OUTLINE

I.   Nature of corporations.

    A. Business corporations are artificial, legal entities whose creation and operations are controlled by state statutes.

    B. Corporations are regarded as "persons," separate from the shareholders, the owners of interests in corporations, for most purposes under federal and state constitutions and statutes, when application thereof is not restricted to natural persons.

        1. U.S. Constitution.

      a. A corporation is treated as a person under the due process clause of the Fifth Amendment and the equal protection clause of the Fourteenth.
        1) Corporation may sue and be sued; corporation is protected against unreasonable searches and seizures and double jeopardy.
        2) Corporation is not protected against self incrimination.

      b. A corporation is regarded as a citizen of the state in which it was incorporated for purposes of jurisdiction, but not necessarily entitled to all the privileges and immunities of citizens. (The states may impose burdens on corporations, incorporated in sister states, wishing to do intrastate business.)

    2. Criminal liability — A corporation may be prosecuted for a crime for which the penalty includes a fine.

    3. Licensing statutes — Corporations are excluded from some professions, which require personal qualifications.

C. Shareholders — As a general rule:

    1. Shareholders are holders of ownership interests in corporation, which are freely transferable.

    2. Death of a shareholder does not dissolve or otherwise affect the corporation.

    3. Shareholders are not personally liable for the debts of the corporation. Their liability is limited to the amount of their investments.

    4. Shareholders have equitable interests in but not legal title to corporate property.

    5. Shareholders do not represent the corporation, but vote for the board of directors, which determines corporate policy and appoints officers, who represent the corporation.

    6. Shareholders may sue and be sued by the corporation, and may deal with the corporation, in an arm's length transaction.

D. Tax considerations ("double taxation of profits").

    1. The profits of a corporation are taxed by the United States and the several states at special corporate rates.

    2. Distributions of profits, in the form of dividends, are treated and taxed as income to the recipients, the shareholders.

    3. Profits that are retained and invested by the corporation may result in capital gains. If a shareholder sells his or her shares, he or she is taxed but at a rate lower than the rate imposed on income.

II. Classifications of corporations.

  A. Based upon location.

1. Domestic corporation — One doing business in the state of its incorporation. See other chapters in this part of Unit VI.

2. Foreign corporation — One conducting business outside of the state of its incorporation.

   a. If a foreign corporation does intrastate (as contrasted with interstate) business in a state, it must comply with the laws of that state.
      1) Normally it must apply for and obtain a certificate to do business from a state official, such as the secretary of state (MBCA Secs. 106, 110 and 111; RMBCA Secs. 15.01 and 15.03) and will thereafter enjoy the same rights as domestic corporations (MBCA Secs. 107 and 112; RMBCA Sec. 15.05).
      2) It must maintain a local registered office and agent (MBCA Sec. 113; RMBCA Sec. 15.07), upon whom service of process may be made. If such service cannot be effected, the secretary of state will be an agent for this purpose (MBCA Sec. 115; RMBCA Sec. 15.01).

   b. Doing business within a state — Interpreted to mean some minimum contact, such as maintaining an office or factory, or conducting systematic commerce. It does not include holding meetings, maintaining or defending legal action, maintaining bank accounts, transfer agents, soliciting orders which are accepted outside the state, etc. (MBCA Sec. 106; RMBCA Sec. 15.01).

3. Alien corporation — A corporation incorporated in a country other than the United States.

B. Based upon sources of funds (or revenue), function and ownership arrangements.

   1. Public corporation — Formed by legislative bodies for governmental purposes.

   2. Private corporation — Created for private benefit.

      a. Issues shares of stock.

      b. May be a close corporation — Shares of stock are held by one individual or by a small group.

   3. Nonprofit corporation — Organized for charitable, religious, educational, social, etc., purpose, under special state statute.

   4. Professional corporation — Private corporation, the members of which engage in a profession, organized in order to gain advantages relating to taxes, pension and insurance plans, etc.

C. Chapter S corporation — A corporation that meets certain qualifications, provided for in Subchapter S of the Internal Revenue Code, may elect to be treated in a manner similar to a partnership for federal tax purposes. Corporate income is not taxed but is allocated among the shareholders for income tax purposes.

KEY WORDS AND PHRASES IN TEXT

The Model Business Corporation Act
The Revised Model Business Corporation
    Act
Corporation is a legal entity
Corporation as a "person"
Application of Bill of Rights to
    corporations (freedom of speech,
    equal protection, due process,
    unreasonable search and seizure,
    double jeopardy)
Nonapplicability of privileges and
    immunities clause and right against
    self-incrimination
Shareholders are not liable for
    corporation's debts
Shareholders do not have legal title to
    corporate property
Shareholders can sue and be sued by
    corporation
Derivative suit
Board of directors

Officers
Tax considerations
Double taxation
Domestic corporations
Foreign corporations must obtain
    certificate of authority to do
    intrastate business
Alien corporations
Private corporation
Public corporation
Nonprofit corporation
Close corporation (statutes, management,
    transfer of shares)
S Corporations (Subchapter S corporations)
Requirements for S Corporation
    qualification and benefits of electing
    S Corporation status
Professional corporations (liability of
    corporation and members for
    malpractice and torts)
Tax benefits of professional corporations

FILL-IN QUESTIONS

1. A corporation is an artificial being that is treated as a legal entity. It may conduct business, own property, and sue and be sued in its own _____.

2. The _____ of a corporation are the owners of the corporation and elect the _____, which oversees the general management of the corporation and appoints the corporate _____ who run the daily operations of the corporation.

3. A shareholder of a corporation may be distinguished from a partner in a general partnership because, unlike a partner, _____ _____.

4. A municipality (city) may have a charter and be created by statute for governmental purposes. It is a _____ rather than a _____ corporation.

5. A corporation, incorporated in one state but desiring to engage in business in another state, is required to obtain _____ in the other state and will have to maintain a _____ in that state. The purpose of this requirement is to protect residents of the state so that a state court can obtain jurisdiction over the corporation.

6. If a foreign corporation has complied with statutes relating to qualifying to do business and has received a _____ from the appropriate state official, it is empowered to do anything that a domestic corporation may do and those things which it is authorized to do in the state of its incorporation.

MULTIPLE CHOICE QUESTIONS

1. The United States Supreme Court has ruled that the protection afforded by the Fourth Amendment to the U.S. Constitution against unreasonable searches and seizures and by the Fifth Amendment against double jeopardy extends to:
    a. natural persons.
    b. corporate officers and employees.
    c. corporations.
    d. all of the above are correct.

2. The United States Supreme Court has ruled that the privilege against self-incrimination, which is protected by the Fifth Amendment, may be invoked by:
    a. natural persons.
    b. the Internal Revenue Service.
    c. corporations and other legal entities.
    d. all of the above are correct.

3. The concept of double taxation means that:
    a. the federal and state governments tax both the salaries of corporate officers and any dividends that have been paid to them.
    b. the federal and state governments tax both corporate earnings and dividends that are paid to corporate shareholders.
    c. the tax rate for corporations is double that for individuals.
    d. taxes are imposed upon corporations by both the federal and state governments.

4. A California corporation sells goods to residents of Illinois by mail, but has no employees or offices in Illinois.
    a. The California corporation is required to register or qualify as a foreign corporation in Illinois.
    b. The California corporation will not be able to sue an Illinois resident in Illinois, if the resident fails to pay for merchandise purchased from the California corporation.
    c. The California corporation will be required to qualify to do business in Illinois if it establishes a shipping office in Chicago, employing 40 people, and solicits and enters contracts from that office.
    d. An Illinois resident who has been injured by merchandise, purchased from the California corporation, can sue the corporation in Illinois by serving it with a complaint in California.

5. The certificate of incorporation of the Green and Red Corp., a New York corporation, states that it is formed for the purpose of manufacturing Christmas decorations in Rhode Island, where it maintains a plant and office.
    a. The corporation must qualify to do business in New York.
    b. The corporation must qualify to do business in Rhode Island.
    c. The corporation must qualify to do business in Utah, if it sends a traveling salesman there to solicit orders.
    d. The corporation must qualify to do business in Delaware, if it maintains a transfer agent there.
    e. All of the above.

Chapter 39

CORPORATIONS
Formation and
Corporate Financing

Preparatory groundwork for organizing a corporation is usually done by promoters prior to formal organization. During the preincorporation period, arrangements are made for assembling personnel, property and capital, by soliciting subscriptions for shares of stock to be issued by the corporation after it is ultimately formed. In addition, the necessary steps are taken in order to comply with the state statutory requisites for incorporation. The legal status of agreements made during the promotional period and the procedures for formal incorporation are subjects covered in this chapter.

After a corporation comes into existence, it issues securities in order to finance its operations. Corporate financing and various types of securities are the topics covered in the concluding section of the chapter.

THINGS TO KEEP IN MIND

1. The document prepared for purposes of incorporation may be referred to as a charter or articles of incorporation or certificate of incorporation or another similar word or phrase. The terms are used interchangeably in this book.

2. Typically corporations issue debt securities, which are evidences of obligations to pay money (bonds and debentures), and equity securities, representing ownership interests (shares of stock).

OUTLINE

I. Formation of a corporation.

   A. Promoters' activities before corporation comes into existence.

1. Analyze economic feasibility, find investors, assemble necessary personnel, property and capital, take preliminary steps for organization and incorporation.

2. Promoters are generally personally liable on pre-incorporation agreements.

   a. Liability during the promotion period.
      1) A promoter is a party to a contract and, therefore, bound as a party.
      2) The corporation is not in existence and, therefore, is not liable as a party to a contract.

   b. Liability after incorporation.
      1) Promoter remains liable to other contracting party, unless:
         a) Released by the contracting party.
         b) Contracting parties clearly indicated that the promoter would not be personally liable.
         c) Corporation is substituted as a party to the contract in a novation.
      2) Corporation becomes liable after incorporation if:
         a) It enters a novation.
         b) It adopts or becomes an assignee of the rights of the promoter, who remains secondarily liable.

3. Subscribers and subscriptions.

   a. A subscription is an agreement to purchase unissued shares of stock in a corporation that has not yet been formed.

   b. Subscription may be treated as:
      1) A continuing offer by the subscriber, which may be accepted by the corporation following incorporation.
      2) A contract among subscribers and, therefore, irrevocable.
      3) An irrevocable offer for the period specified in the statute, which typically is six months, unless all subscribers consent to revocation (MBCA Sec. 17; RMBCA Sec. 6.20).

B. Incorporation procedure.

   1. Charter, articles of incorporation or certificate of incorporation — Contents (MBCA Sec. 54; RMBCA Sec. 2.02).

      a. Corporate name (RMBCA Sec. 4.01).
         1) Must use word "corporation" or "incorporated" or abbreviation, such as "co.," "corp." or "inc."
         2) Name cannot be misleading or subject to confusion with the name of another organization.

      b. General nature and purpose.

      c. Duration — Usually perpetual.

      d. Capital structure.

    e. Internal organization — May be described in articles of incorporation or in bylaws.

    f. Location of registered office and agent to receive services of process within the state.

    g. Names, addresses and signatures of incorporators.
      1) Usually incorporators need not have any interest in the corporation, nor be subscribers.
      2) Number varies from one to three; statute may provide that incorporators need not be natural persons (MBCA Sec. 53; RMBCA Sec. 2.01).

2. Articles of incorporation are filed with the appropriate state official (typically the secretary of state), necessary fees are paid and notice of the filing given (MBCA Sec. 55; RMBCA Sec. 2.01).

3. Organizational meeting.

    a. Incorporators elect the board of directors, adopt bylaws, authorize the board to issue stock, etc.

    b. Board of directors adopts minutes of meeting of incorporators (if one was required), adopts pre-incorporation contracts, seal, form for stock certificate, accepts subscriptions, etc. (MBCA Sec. 57; RMBCA Sec. 2.05).

    c. Bylaws — Internal rules for governing and regulating the conduct of corporate affairs. Bylaws cannot conflict with articles of incorporation or statutes (MBCA Sec. 27; RMBCA Sec. 2.06).

C. Improper incorporation.

1. *De jure* corporation — Corporation organized in accordance with required mandatory conditions precedent to incorporation. The corporate status or existence cannot be attacked.

2. *De facto* corporation — Operates as a corporation but failed to comply with some statutory mandate so that the state may challenge its existence. Element:

    a. Statute exists, under which it could be validly incorporated.

    b. Good faith attempt to comply with the statute.

    c. Some exercise of the functions of a corporation.

3. Corporation by estoppel.

    a. Corporation has neither *de jure* nor *de facto* status.

    b. Associates (alleged shareholders, directors), who participated in holding the association out as a corporation, are precluded from denying that it was a corporation against third parties, who, in reliance upon the holding out, changed their positions and were, therefore, injured.

    c. Parties, who dealt with the association and entered into contracts with it in the belief that only the corporation would be liable, may be estopped from denying that it was a corporation.

    d. In general, if a corporation by estoppel cannot be established, the associates who took an active part in management will be liable as partners.

II. Disregarding the corporate entity.

  A. In unusual situations, a court may ignore the legal fiction of the corporation as an entity (pierce the corporate veil) when it is used to perpetuate fraud, circumvent law, accomplish an illegal purpose or otherwise evade law.

  B. Courts will disregard the corporate entity, even though technically a corporation exists, and hold directors, officers or shareholders personally liable for the transactions conducted in the corporate name.

  C. Courts will disregard corporate entity if a corporation is not maintained as an entity, separate from its shareholders, in order to prevent abuse of corporate privilege for personal benefit.

    1. Records and funds have been commingled and enterprise has not been established on an adequate financial basis (e.g., "thin capitalization").

    2. This arises occasionally in the case of a close corporation with only one or a few shareholders or in the case of parent-subsidiary corporations.

III. Corporate financing.

  A. Debt securities.

    1. In general, bonds are evidences of obligations to pay money. The term, "bond," is often used, although technically a particular obligation may be a debenture.

      a. Bonds — Secured by a lien or other security interest in assets.

      b. Debentures — Secured by the general credit of the borrower, rather than specific property.

      c. Issued by business firms, governments and others to investors, from whom they are borrowing funds, with a designated maturity date when the principal or face amount is to be paid.

      d. Bonds provide fixed income because interest is paid at specified times and at specified rates.

      e. Discount — Bonds may be sold for less than their face value.

      f. Premium — Bonds may be sold for more than their face value.

  2. Corporate bonds — Agreement is termed the bond indenture. Bondholders do not participate in corporate affairs.

      a. Debentures are unsecured obligations. If the issuing corporation defaults, holders of debentures can look only to assets in which other creditors or bondholders have no security interests.

      b. Mortgage bonds — Secured by real property.

      c. Equipment trust bonds — Secured by equipment, legal title to which is vested in a trustee.

      d. Collateral trust bonds — Secured by intangible corporate property, such as shares of stock in other corporations or accounts receivable.

      e. Convertible bonds — Bonds that may be exchanged for other bonds or stock at a specified rate.

      f. Callable bonds — The issuing corporation has the right to repay the principal prior to maturity.

B. Equity securities — Every corporation issues common stock and may be authorized to issue preferred stock.

  1. Terminology.

      a. Authorized shares — Stock which the corporation is empowered by its charter to issue.

      b. Issued shares — Authorized shares that have been sold.
         1) Outstanding shares — Shares that have been issued and are in the hands of shareholders.
         2) Treasury shares — Issued shares that have been reacquired by the corporation.

      c. Par value shares — Shares that have been assigned a stated, fixed dollar value.
         1) May be originally issued for an amount greater than par (premium).
         2) In most states, par value shares cannot be originally issued for less than par value (discounted).

      d. No par shares — Shares that are not assigned any specific fixed price. No par shares are usually issued for a price that is fixed by the board of directors.

      e. Stated capital.
         1) Sum of par value of all issued par value shares and consideration received for all no par value shares.
         2) Includes outstanding and treasury shares.

2. Classifications.

    a. Common stock.
       1) The owners of common stock are entitled to a pro rata share of properly declared dividends out of corporate profits, without any preferences and after payment of taxes, interest to lenders and bondholders, etc., and any specified dividends required to be paid to preferred shareholders, if any preferred stock has been issued.
       2) Common stock shareholders have right to vote.
       3) Common stock shareholders have rights to ultimate distribution of assets of corporation upon dissolution.

    b. Preferred stock — Holders of preferred stock have a preference that usually is in rights to receive dividends or distribution upon liquidation of the corporation. Corporations may issue different classes and/or series of preferred stock.
       1) Cumulative preferred — If the corporation fails to pay a dividend, the dividend is carried over and paid in a subsequent year, before the holders of common stock receive dividends.
       2) Participating preferred — Preferred shareholders share in distribution of additional dividends after payment of dividends to holders of preferred and common stock if there are additional distributions of corporate profits.
       3) Convertible preferred — Preferred shares may be exchanged for common stock or other preferred stock at a specified rate.
       4) Redeemable (callable) preferred — Corporation has the right to purchase, reacquire and cancel shares at a specified price.

KEY WORDS AND PHRASES IN TEXT

Incorporation
Promotion activities
Prospectus
Subscribers and subscriptions
Incorporation procedures
Articles of incorporation
Corporate name
General nature and purpose
Duration
Capital structure
Internal organization
Registered office and registered agent
Incorporators
Certificate of incorporation
First organizational meeting
Improper incorporation
De jure corporation
De facto corporation
Corporation by estoppel
Disregarding the corporate entity
    ("piercing the corporate veil")

Inadequate capitalization
Commingling personal and corporate
    interests
Corporate financing
Stocks (equity securities)
Bonds and debentures (debt securities)
Sale of bonds at discount or at a
    premium
Bond indenture
Debentures
Mortgage bonds
Equipment trust bonds
Collateral trust bonds
Convertible bonds
Callable bonds
Common stock
Authorized shares
Issued shares
Outstanding shares
Treasury shares
Par value and no par shares

Stated capital
Preferred stock (shares of stock with
  preferences)
Cumulative preferred stock

Participating preferred stock
Convertible preferred stock
Redeemable, or callable, preferred
  stock

FILL-IN QUESTIONS

1. A corporation, which has complied with all statutory requirements relating to incorporation, is considered to be a _____. A _____ corporation is one, which believed that it was properly organized, but whose organization was defective. The existence of such a corporation may normally only be challenged by _____.

2. Corporations obtain funds for their operations by issuing equity securities, or _____, and debt securities, such as _____, and by retaining some of their earnings and profits, rather than distributing them in the form of _____ to shareholders.

3. Debt securities include _____, which are secured by liens or other security interests in assets of a corporation, and _____, which are backed only by the general credit of a borrowing corporation.

4. Preferred stock refers to shares having some measure of preference in respect to priority rights associated with _____ or _____ or, in some instances, voting.

MULTIPLE CHOICE QUESTIONS

1. Piper, the promoter of the Atlas Corporation, made a contract for and on behalf of the Atlas Corporation with World Copy Inc. for the purchase of a copying machine. Piper failed to disclose that the corporation had not been created. Thereafter, the corporation was duly organized.
    a. Piper will not be liable on the contract if the corporation, after coming into existence, rejects the contract.
    b. Piper will not be liable on the contract if the corporation, after coming into existence, adopts the contract.
    c. Piper will not be liable on the contract, if the corporation, World Copy Inc. and Piper enter into a novation regarding the contract.
    d. Piper will not be liable on the contract if the corporation does not come into existence.

2. A written subscription, signed by a subscriber, to purchase shares of stock in a corporation to be formed in a state which has adopted the Model Business Corporation Act, is:
    a. unenforceable by the corporation when it comes into existence.
    b. revocable until the corporation comes into existence.
    c. irrevocable for six months after the corporation comes into existence.
    d. irrevocable for six months after it is signed by the subscriber.

3. Martin has determined that there is a large market for copper widgets. She, therefore, engaged in promotion activities for the purpose of organizing the Winking

Widget Co. Before filing articles of incorporation, she ordered a large quantity of copper from KK Koper Co. and leased office space in the name of the corporation. The copper was shipped to and used by Winking Widget Co. after its organization, but payment therefor has not been made. If at the first meeting of the board of directors, the board:

a. refused to accept the contract with KK Koper Co., the corporation will be required to pay for the copper.
b. declined to accept the lease of office space, the corporation will be liable for breach of contract.
c. accepted all the subscriptions for stock that Martin had obtained, the corporation may later revoke some of its acceptances.
d. refused to accept some of the subscriptions that Martin had obtained, the corporation will be obligated to all the subscribers.

4. Under the Model Business Corporation Act and the Revised Model Business Corporation Act, incorporators must:
a. be natural persons.
b. be residents of the state of incorporation.
c. subscribe to at least one share of stock.
d. none of the above.

5. U, V and W did business as Z Corporation but made no effort to incorporate. They never filed any documents with any state official. Arcus entered into a contract with Z Corporation to supply stationery to the corporation but did not know that it had not been formally incorporated. U, V and W breached the contract with Arcus by failing to pay for the stationery. Arcus is now suing Z Corporation and U, V and W jointly.
a. U, V and W are liable to Arcus as general partners, unless they are estopped from denying the existence of Z Corporation.
b. Z Corporation is a *de facto* corporation and, therefore, Arcus cannot dispute its existence.
c. U, V and W are liable to Arcus because the Z Corporation is a *de jure* corporation.
d. U, V and W are liable to Arcus because they are principals with relation to each other.

6. A, B and C represented to F that they are shareholders and directors of a corporation and persuade F to purchase stock in the corporation. There is, in fact, no corporation but A, B and C have been engaging in a business together. A, B and C manage the business and F participates in no way.
a. F will not be liable to a third party on a contract entered into by B in the name of the corporation.
b. A, B and C will be estopped to deny the existence of the corporation.
c. A third party, with whom the purported corporation contracted, will be estopped to deny the corporate existence because, when he or she contracted with the "association," his or her expectation was that only the corporation would have liability.
d. All of the above.

7. Jones paid $900 for a document that provided that ten years from the date of its issue the ABC Corporation promised to pay the holder $1,000, and until that date the corporation promised to pay the holder $40 on the first day of every March and September.

    a. Jones is a shareholder of the ABC Corporation.
    b. Jones has purchased a bond at a discount.
    c. Jones has a right to cumulative dividends.
    d. Jones has the right to vote at the annual shareholders' meeting.

Questions 8, 9 and 10 are based on the following fact situation: A corporation has issued 20,000 shares of common stock and 10,000 shares of nonparticipating, nonconvertible, redeemable, cumulative preferred stock.

8. Which of the following statements is correct?
    a. A preferred shareholder has a right to exchange his or her shares of preferred stock for common stock.
    b. A shareholder holding common stock has a right to exchange his or her shares for preferred stock.
    c. The corporation has the right to purchase, reacquire and cancel the preferred shares at a specified price.
    d. The corporation has the right to purchase and reacquire the preferred shares at a specified price and reissue the shares.

9. An owner of:
    a. common stock is entitled to vote at the annual meeting of the shareholders.
    b. common stock is entitled to receive a pro rata share of dividends before payment of dividends to preferred shareholders.
    c. either common or preferred stock is entitled to vote at the annual meeting of the shareholders, even though this right is not indicated on his or her share certificate.
    d. preferred stock has a right to share in the distribution of additional dividends, after payment of dividends to common shareholders.

10. If the corporation is dissolved and all taxes and other obligations are paid:
    a. the preferred shareholders must be paid the face amount of their respective shares before any distribution is made to common stock shareholders.
    b. each preferred and common shareholder shares pro rata in the distribution of remaining assets.
    c. the common shareholders must be paid the face amount of their respective shares before any distribution is made to the preferred shareholders.
    d. only the common shareholders share in the distribution of the corporate assets.

Chapter 40

CORPORATIONS
Corporate Powers and Management

Corporations have only those powers which are granted to them by the state of incorporation. Corporate powers are expressly provided for in statutes and corporate charters (articles or certificates of incorporation) and, generally, are quite broad. In addition, corporations have implied power to do those things that are necessary in order to execute their purposes and express powers.

A corporation is, in theory, owned by and for the benefit of its shareholders. Managerial policies are determined, however, by the board of directors, elected by the shareholders. Actual operation of a corporation is normally performed by officers, appointed and supervised by the directors.

THINGS TO KEEP IN MIND

Corporations usually are empowered to do almost anything, unless it is criminal or tortious, so that today it is rare that a corporation is found to have exceeded its powers.

OUTLINE

I.   Corporate purpose — Defines the nature of the business in which the corporation engages.

    A. The purpose must be legal and may be broadly stated in the charter (MBCA Sec. 3).

    B. The RMBCA (Sec. 3.01) provides that every corporation "has the purpose of engaging in any lawful business unless a more limited purpose is set forth in its articles of incorporation."

II. Corporate powers — Necessary to accomplish purpose for which the corporation is formed.

    A. Statutory, general powers apply to all corporations, organized under a state business corporation law, and usually include the power to have perpetual existence; to enter into contract; to sue and be sued; to lend and borrow money; to buy, hold, lease, receive, dispose of and sell real and personal property; etc. (MBCA Sec. 4; RMBCA Sec. 3.02).

    B. Express powers are those specifically enumerated in the corporate charter.

    C. Implied powers are those which are incidental or necessary in order to carry out the corporation's purpose and express powers.

    D. *Ultra vires* acts — Corporate exercise of power which it does not possess.

        1. While acting as an agent of the corporation, corporate director(s) or officer(s) does something that corporation is not authorized to do, because it is not in furtherance of the corporation's purpose.

        2. Illegal acts are *ultra vires*.

        3. An *ultra vires* act may be ratified by the shareholders.

            a. Act was one that could have been authorized by the shareholders when it was originally done.

            b. Unanimous ratification is necessary if there has been a gift or wasting of corporate assets.

        4. Judicial treatment of *ultra vires* — Approaches taken.

            a. Corporation has no capacity to perform the *ultra vires* act. An *ultra vires* contract that is executory or partially or completely executed is therefore void.

            b. An agent (corporate officer), acting without authority, does not bind his or her principal (the corporation).

            c. The defense of *ultra vires* can be raised in order to prevent enforcement of an executory contract, but not all courts allow the defense if the contract has been executed.

        5. Modern judicial and statutory approach (MBCA Sec. 7; RMBCA Sec. 3.04).

            a. The defense of *ultra vires* may not be raised in an action to enforce a contract (even if the contract is executory) by the corporation or the party with whom it contracted.

            b. The issue of *ultra vires* may only be asserted in an action brought by:
               1) Shareholders, in order to enjoin the carrying out of the act.
               2) The corporation (or shareholders in a derivative action), in order to

recover from officers or directors, who made an *ultra vires* contract or carried out the unauthorized act.

3) The state attorney general, in order to enjoin the *ultra vires* act or to dissolve the corporation.

E. Corporate liability for wrongful acts.

1. Torts — A corporation is liable for torts committed by its officers, directors, other agents and employees, acting within the scope of their employment in furtherance of the corporation's business. (See Chapter 33.)

2. Crimes — A corporation may be liable for a crime for which a fine is imposed as punishment.

   a. Some statutes expressly provide for corporate liability for crimes of commission and omission.

   b. The criminal act by the corporation's agent or employee was within the scope of his or her employment.

   c. If an element of the crime is wrongful intent, the intent of an agent or employee may be imputed to the corporation.

III. Corporate management—shareholders.

A. Shareholders' position in the corporation — Shareholders have limited powers.

1. The shareholders' approval is necessary in order to make fundamental changes affecting the corporation, such as amending the charter, merging with another corporation or dissolving.

2. The shareholders have power to elect and remove members of the board of directors for cause.

3. With some limitations, the shareholders have the right to inspect books, records and shareholders' lists.

4. The shareholders do not participate in the management of the corporation.

B. Meetings of the shareholders.

1. Annual meeting (MBCA Sec. 28; RMBCA Sec. 7.01).

   a. Usually the date and place is fixed in the bylaws.

   b. Written notice must be given within the specified statutory period of time, but may be waived (MBCA Sec. 29; RMBCA Sec. 7.05).

2. Special meetings may be called (MBCA Sec. 28; RMBCA Sec. 7.02).

3. Quorum (minimum number of shares that must be represented at a meeting) — Fixed in charter within specified statutory range.

4. Voting.

    a. List of record owners of shares as of a cutoff date is prepared by corporation (MBCA Secs. 30 and 31; RMBCA Secs. 7.07 and 7.20).

    b. Unless otherwise specified by statute or charter (MBCA Sec. 32; RMBCA Sec. 7.21), usual vote required for shareholder action:
       1) Election of members of board of directors — Plurality of those shares represented at meeting.
       2) Other non-extraordinary matters — Majority of those shares represented at meeting.
       3) Extraordinary matters.
          a) Statute or charter may require a specified proportion of all shares.
          b) Usually a greater than majority vote is required.

    c. Methods of voting (MBCA Sec. 33).
       1) Straight voting — One vote per share standing in the name of a record holder.
       2) Cumulative voting for election of directors.
          a) May be provided for in charter (RMBCA Sec. 7.28).
          b) In some states, cumulative voting is mandatory.
          c) A shareholder's vote is equal to the number of shares which he or she owns multiplied by the number of directors to be elected.
       3) Proxy voting (RMBCA Sec. 7.22).
          a) Shareholder may vote in person or by proxy.
          b) Written, revocable authorization to an agent to cast the vote of the shareholder.
       4) Voting agreements — Shareholders may agree to pool votes by casting them in a prescribed manner (MBCA Sec. 34; RMBCA Sec. 7.31).
       5) Voting trusts — Legal title to shares is transferred to a trustee, who then votes the shares, for the benefit of shareholders, who retain the rights to receive dividends and receive voting trust certificates (RMBCA Sec. 7.30).

IV. Corporate management—directors.

A. Qualifications, election and tenure.

1. There are few statutory requirements for qualification as a director (MBCA Sec. 35; RMBCA Sec. 8.02).

2. The number of directors is specified in the charter or bylaws (MBCA Sec. 36; RMBCA Sec. 8.03).

3. The initial board of directors is named in the charter or elected by the incorporators, and subsequent directors are elected by the shareholders (MBCA Sec. 36; RMBCA Secs. 2.05 and 8.05).

4. The term of a director is usually one year but may be longer; directors may be divided into classes with staggered terms (MBCA Sec. 37; RMBCA Sec. 8.06).

5. Provisions in the charter and/or statute determine method of filling vacancies (MBCA Sec. 38; RMBCA Sec. 8.10).

6. Shareholders have power to remove directors, with or without cause, in accordance with the charter or bylaws. Directors may have power to remove a director for cause (MBCA Sec. 39; RMBCA Sec. 8.08).

B. Functions of board of directors — Responsible for the management of the corporation.

1. The board must act as a body at a meeting (MBCA Sec. 43). The MBCA (Sec. 44; RMBCA Sec. 8.21) does, however, provide for signed, written unanimous consent in lieu of a meeting.

   a. Regular meetings are provided for in the bylaws. Notice is not necessary.

   b. Special meetings may be called, but notice is required.

   c. Quorum requirements vary from state to state (usually a majority) and are established by the bylaws (MBCA Sec. 40).

   d. Directors may not vote by proxy.

   e. Ordinarily a majority vote is necessary for board action.

   f. Directors may participate in meeting through conference telephone communications (MBCA Sec. 43; RMBCA Sec. 8.20).

2. Management responsibilities — Corporate powers are exercised by the board of directors (MBCA Sec. 35; RMBCA Sec. 8.01).

   a. Declares dividends.

   b. Makes policy decisions concerning the scope of business, initiates major changes in corporate financing, structure, etc.

   c. Appoints, supervises and removes officers.

   d. Fixes compensation of officers and directors.

3. Delegation of powers of board of directors.

   a. Functions, relating to ordinary, interim managerial decisions, may be delegated to an executive committee (MBCA Sec. 42; RMBCA Sec. 8.25).

   b. Functions relating to daily operations are normally delegated to officers, who as agents carry out the transactions on behalf of the corporation.

KEY WORDS AND PHRASES IN TEXT

Express corporate powers found in articles of incorporation

Implied corporate power in order to accomplish corporate purposes

Ultra vires doctrine and its modern statutory and judicial treatment

Corporate liability for tortious and criminal acts

Shareholders' power

The relationship between shareholders and the corporation

Shareholders' (forum) meetings

Notice of shareholders' meetings

Shareholder voting (quorum, voting lists)

Shareholders' resolutions

Voting techniques

Cumulative voting for election of directors

Proxy voting

Shareholder voting agreements and voting trusts

Board of directors

Removal of directors

Vacancy on board of directors

Fiduciary relationship of directors to corporation

Corporate management responsibilities of directors (declare dividends and other distributions to shareholders, authorize major corporate policy and financial decisions, and appoint, supervise and remove corporate officers and managerial agents)

Board of directors' forum (meetings)

Delegation of board of directors' powers

Executive committee of the board of directors

Corporate officers

FILL-IN QUESTIONS

1. _____ powers are those possessed by all corporations formed within a particular state. An example of such a power would be _____

    _____.

2. Corporations are empowered by corporation statutes to purchase real property but, if a corporation is not organized for the purpose of purchasing and selling real estate, it commits an _____ act if it buys land purely for speculative purposes. In most states today, however, the corporation _____ the defense that it lacked the power or capacity to make such a purchase in a lawsuit brought by the seller of the land for the unpaid purchase price.

3. A voting trustee is given _____ title to the shares of shareholders who are participating in a voting trust. The shareholders are considered to be the _____ owners of the shares.

4. _____ but not _____ may vote by proxy at their respective meetings.

5. Directors of a corporation are agents of and, therefore, owe a fiduciary duty to the _____.

MULTIPLE CHOICE QUESTIONS

1. The articles of incorporation of the Careful Chew Corporation state that it is formed for the purpose of manufacturing chewing gum. Even if there is no express authorization in the articles of incorporation to do so, the corporation has the implied power to:

a. purchase gum base, sugar and artificial flavoring.
b. purchase 50 acres of land which the board of directors, in good faith, believe will triple in value in one year.
c. manufacture razor blades.
d. purchase and use a factory in a state in which it is not incorporated without qualifying to do business in that state.

2. On March 2 an explosion and fire destroyed the Rubber Products Co. plant. The corporation filed an insurance claim with its insurer promptly. On April 15, the corporation, the president and two others were charged with arson (the intentional burning of any structure, punishable by imprisonment for up to 50 years) in connection with the March 2 fire. It was alleged that the president of the corporation paid $50,000 out of corporate funds to an "arson squad" which started the fire. Which of the following statements is false?
a. The corporation can escape criminal liability for the fire.
b. The president is liable for breach of duties owed to the shareholders.
c. The shareholders may bring a derivative action against the president for the *ultra vires* act.
d. The defense of *ultra vires* cannot be raised in a lawsuit instituted by the corporation against the insurer which refused to pay the claim.

3. The shareholders of the Unispol Corp. are to elect five directors. If there is cumulative voting, a shareholder with 100 shares may cast a maximum of:
a. five votes for one person.
b. 100 votes for one nominee.
c. 500 votes for one person.
d. 500 votes for one person and 500 in connection with other matters that are voted on at the meeting.

4. At a meeting of shareholders:
a. in order to amend the Articles of Incorporation, notice thereof must be given and a majority of the shareholders present must approve the amendment.
b. shares of a deceased shareholder may be voted only if the shares are transferred to and registered in the name of the representative of the decedent.
c. shareholders have the right to elect directors and to vote on any other business that may properly come before the meeting by cumulative voting.
d. a shareholder may vote by proxy only if he gives an irrevocable proxy.

5. The following is prohibited by statute:
a. A voting pool.
b. A voting trust.
c. The sale of a proxy.
d. The sale of property by a shareholder to the corporation in which he owns stock.

6. M and O Co. is incorporated in a state that has adopted the Model Business Corporation Act. It has a board of directors composed of nine people. Its charter and bylaws contain no provisions relative to quorum requirements for meetings of the board or the conduct of such meetings. The charter provides for cumulative voting by shareholders. Six members of the board of directors attended a meeting that had been called after due notice to ratify an important contract. Prior to the annual shareholders' meeting, P, a holder of 200 shares, gave A a proxy to vote her shares.

a. The board can ratify the contract by a vote of four to two.
b. The board can unanimously ratify the contract if two directors leave the meeting before the board acts on the contract.
c. A may not cast 1,800 votes for a single director.
d. A may vote P's shares if, on the day before the meeting, P gives her proxy to Z.

Chapter 41

CORPORATIONS
Rights and Duties of Directors, Managers, and Shareholders

In a corporation, the overall managerial responsibility rests with the board of directors, elected by the shareholders. The actual operation of a corporation is conducted by officers, elected or appointed and supervised by the board, other managers, agents and employees. The rights and duties of directors and officers and their potential liability to the corporation are discussed in the first part of this chapter.

Ultimately the risks and benefits of incorporation inure to the shareholders, the investors, who provide the funds which initially finance the corporate operations. Generally, they exercise no control over policies adopted by the corporation after participating in the election of the board of directors. Their rights and liabilities are treated in the latter section of the chapter.

THINGS TO KEEP IN MIND

Directors and officers are fiduciaries and have obligations to act in good faith, honestly and loyally. The trend has been to expand the nature and extent of their responsibilities to the corporation.

OUTLINE

I. Role of directors and officers.

    A. Directors manage the corporation and establish general policies and the scope of the business within the purposes and powers stated in the corporate charter (MBCA Sec. 35; RMBCA Sec. 8.01).

        1. Directors may not act individually; they must act convened as a board.

2. The board of directors has power to authorize actions which are legal exercises of the corporation's powers.

3. The board supervises and selects officers, defines their duties and authority and fixes their compensation, if not otherwise provided for in the bylaws.

4. Dividends are declared by the board of directors.

B. The business judgment rule.

1. Directors are normally not liable for poor business judgment or honest mistakes if they act in good faith, in what they consider to be the best interests of the corporation, and with the care that an ordinarily prudent person would exercise under similar circumstances.

2. The directors are not insurers of business success.

C. Duties of directors.

1. If there is a breach of these duties, directors are liable to the corporation — The corporation may sue in its own name, or a derivative suit may be brought by shareholders or a representative, such as a trustee in bankruptcy.

2. Standards of conduct for directors are set forth in RMBCA Secs. 8.30–8.33.

3. Fiduciary duties of directors are owed to the corporation.

   a. As fiduciaries directors are required to perform their duties in good faith, acting in the best interests of the corporation "and with such care as an ordinary prudent person in a like position would use under similar circumstances" (MBCA Sec. 35; RMBCA Sec. 8.30).

   b. Directors are required to be honest and loyal and to exercise reasonable diligence, care and skill.

   c. Directors are expected to be informed and attend meetings.
      1) If a director is present at a meeting, he or she is presumed to assent to action taken, unless he or she files a written dissent or has his or her dissent entered in the minutes (MBCA Sec. 35).
      2) A director, having a personal interest in a matter being considered by the board, should not vote thereon.

   d. Directors should supervise officers to whom they have delegated responsibilities.

   e. Directors should not use their positions to secure personal advantages.

   f. Directors, who deal with the corporation, must make full disclosure.

4. Directors are liable to the corporation if they:

   a. Compete with the corporation.

    b. Usurp a corporate opportunity.

    c. Fail to disclose an interest conflicting with that of the corporation (RMBCA Sec. 8.31).

    d. Engage in insider trading in buying or selling shares, by using confidential information that they possess because of their position.
      1) Liable to shareholder to whom they sold or from whom they purchased stock.
      2) See Chapter 43 with regard to liability under the securities laws.

    e. Improperly issue a dividend or other distribution (RMBCA Sec. 8.33).

    f. Make an improper stock issue.
      1) Shares may be issued for money, property or services actually performed.
      2) Par value shares cannot be issued for less than par value, unless bonus or discount issues are permitted by statute.
      3) No par shares cannot be issued for less than the consideration fixed by the board of directors or the shareholders (if the shareholders are so empowered by the charter).
      4) Directors are also liable if they overvalue the consideration (property or services) received for shares.

    g. Fail to comply with provisions of law, charter or bylaws of the corporation.

  5. Contracts between a corporation and a director of a corporation, having one or more common directors, may be scrutinized by the courts.

D. Rights of directors.

  1. Participate in meetings of the board of directors; notice of special meetings must be given (MBCA Sec. 43; RMBCA Sec. 8.22).

  2. Inspect books and records of the corporation.

  3. Indemnification for expenses, judgments, fines, costs, etc., incurred in corporate related criminal or civil actions, other than actions brought by or on behalf of the corporation (MBCA Sec. 5; RMBCA Secs. 8.50–8.58).

  4. Compensation may be fixed in charter or by the board of directors (MBCA Sec. 35; RMBCA Sec. 8.11).

E. Rights and duties of corporate officers and managers who deal with third persons as agents of and on behalf of corporation (MBCA Sec. 50; RMBCA Secs. 8.40 and 8.41).

  1. Usually officers include a president, one or more vice presidents, secretary and treasurer, selected by the board of directors.

  2. The board may also select other officers and agents.

3. Law of agency and employment applies. The authority of officers, other agents and employees may be express (in charter, bylaws or resolutions of board of directors) or implied (customary and incidental power of such officers) actual authority or apparent authority (because the corporation holds out that its officers have the usual power of similar officers of other corporations) or the board may ratify acts of its officers.

4. Officers have fiduciary duties similar to those of directors.

5. Standards of conduct for officers are set forth in RMBCA Sec. 8.42.

II. Shareholder rights.

A. Right to have a stock certificate, evidencing rights of an owner of a proportionate interest in the corporation according to the total number of shares issued.

1. Intangible personal property.

2. Shareholder, whose ownership interest is recorded, has right to:

a. Receive notice of meetings and participate in meetings.

b. Dividends when declared.

c. Participate in distribution of assets upon dissolution.

d. Receive operational and financial reports.

3. Certifies that the named person is the owner of the stated number of fully paid and nonassessable shares.

4. In some states, uncertificated shares of stock may be issued (MBCA Sec. 23; RMBCA Sec. 6.26).

B. Right to transfer shares. (See UCC, Article 8.)

1. Stock certificate is usually transferred by negotiation.

a. Physical delivery and indorsement on the certificate itself, so that a good faith purchaser for value is the owner of the shares represented by the certificate, free of adverse claims and entitled to be registered as a shareholder and to receive a new certificate.

b. Until the corporation is notified of the transfer, it recognizes the record holder (transferor) as entitled to all shareholder rights.

2. Restrictions on transferability are enforceable if noted on the certificate. Such limitations are usually provided for in the case of a small closely held corporation, in order to maintain ownership within the group.

a. Consent of group is necessary in order to transfer shares, or

b. Corporation or shareholders have the right of first refusal.

3. Provision has been made for transfers of uncertificated securities in the 1977 revisions of Article 8 of the UCC, which have been adopted in a few states.

C. Preemptive rights.

1. The right of current shareholders to purchase or subscribe to newly issued stock in proportion to the amount of stock currently owned before it is offered to the public.

2. Preserve prior relative power of each shareholder.

3. Statutes vary.

a. Right is denied, unless provided for in charter (MBCA Sec. 26; RMBCA Sec. 6.30).

b. Right is granted, unless denied in charter, but does not apply to certain issues (MBCA Alternate Sec. 26).

4. Stock warrants are issued to the shareholders of record so that they can purchase the shares in accordance with their preemptive rights.

D. Right to dividends and other distributions (MBCA Sec. 45; RMBCA Sec. 6.40).

1. Dividends are distributions of cash or other property, including shares of stock, to shareholders in proportion to their respective number of shares or interests in the corporation.

2. Dividends are payable to record holders on a specified record date.

3. Shareholders do not have rights to dividends (distributions of profits) until declared by the board of directors.

a. Cash — Once declared, dividends are corporate debts and cannot be rescinded.

b. Stock — May be revoked before actually issued to shareholders.

4. Statutes impose restrictions on issuance of dividends which will result in the corporation's insolvency or in impairment of its capital.

a. Dividends may only be paid out of legally available funds of a corporation, in accordance with state law.

b. Dividends cannot be declared if it will result in insolvency of the corporation or impair its capital. Directors may be liable to the corporation and/or shareholders for improper issuance of dividends, especially if they acted in bad faith.

5. Directors must act diligently, prudently and in good faith and may be liable civilly and criminally for improperly or illegally declaring dividends.

6. Ordinarily directors are not required to declare dividends unless a refusal to do so is an abuse of discretion.

E. Right to vote. (See Chapter 40.) Normally common and preferred shareholders have the right to vote, unless denied in the charter (MBCA Sec. 33; RMBCA Sec. 7.21).

   1. Usually preferred shareholders are denied the right to vote.

   2. Treasury shares cannot be voted.

F. Inspection right (MBCA Sec. 52; RMBCA Secs. 16.02 and 16.03).

   1. A shareholder has a right to obtain information and may examine and copy relevant books, records and minutes for proper purposes in person or by an agent, attorney, etc.

   2. A shareholder for more than six months or of more than five percent of the outstanding shares may so inspect.

   3. Written demand, stating the purpose, must be given.

   4. Shareholder must act in good faith and for a proper purpose.

G. Rights upon dissolution or an extraordinary change in the corporation. (See Chapter 42 herein.)

III. Shareholder liabilities — Shareholders are not normally personally liable to creditors of the corporation. They may, however, be liable in the following situations:

A. In some cases, majority shareholders are treated as also owing a fiduciary duty to the corporation and minority shareholders. See Chapter 39 herein with regard to disregarding the corporate entity.

B. A shareholder is liable for illegally or improperly paid dividends if he or she had knowledge that they were improper.

C. A shareholder is liable if he or she received shares that were issued for no consideration or consideration that did not satisfy the statutory requirements (watered stock).

D. A shareholder is liable for any unpaid stock subscriptions.

KEY WORDS AND PHRASES IN TEXT

The role of corporate directors and officers
Business judgment rule
Fiduciary duties

Duty of care and breach of duty of care
Duty of loyalty
Conflicts of interest

Contracts between directors and
    corporation
Contracts between corporations having
    common directors (interlocking
    directorates)
Rights of director to participate at
    meetings and inspect books and
    records
Right of director to indemnification
Right of director to be given compensation
Rights and duties of corporate officers
    and managers
Shareholder's right to a stock certificate
Shareholder's preemptive right
Stock warrants
Shareholder's right to dividends and other
    corporate distributions

Illegal dividends
Shareholder's right to vote and inspect
    books and records
Shareholder's right to transfer shares of
    stock
Limitations on right to transfer shares of
    stock
Right of first refusal
Record owner of shares
Shareholders' rights upon dissolution
Shareholders' right to compel receivership
Shareholder's liability based upon stock
    subscription (payment for shares,
    watered stock)
Shareholders' and directors' liability for
    illegal dividends
Duties and liabilities of major shareholders

FILL-IN QUESTIONS

1.   The directors of a corporation establish general policy for the corporation. In order to participate in meetings at which the board takes action, a director has a right to

    _____.
    Action taken by the board of directors must be taken by _____.

2.   A director is not liable to the corporation for action taken by the board of directors if _____
    or for losses caused by honest mistakes or_____
    and may have a right of indemnification for costs, expenses and judgments incurred as a result of defending in a lawsuit in an action _____.

3.   In general shareholders of a corporation are not liable for corporate indebtedness. They are, however, liable to creditors for the amounts of _____
    _____.

4.   Payment for stock subscriptions may be made in money, _____ or
    _____.

5.   Shareholders' _____ refers to the right to subscribe to newly issued stock in a corporation in proportion to the amount of stock currently owned before it is offered to the public.

MULTIPLE CHOICE QUESTIONS

1.   John was president and a director of the M Company, a manufacturing corporation. John learned that the corporation could probably obtain adequate, inexpensive electric power in the town of Electra, located near a nuclear power plant, due to be completed and operational in two years. John represented this information to the board of directors and recommended moving the corporation's operations to Electra. The board agreed and a new factory was constructed in Electra. Before

operations were begun the Electra Power Co., a public utility, advised M Company that it would be unable to provide electricity to the factory because its plant was denied a license to begin its operations by the Nuclear Regulatory Commission. As a result the corporation has sustained a considerable loss.

a. As John was a director of the corporation, he could not also serve as an officer.
b. John owed a fiduciary duty to the corporation, which he breached by recommending the move.
c. The directors are liable to the shareholders for the loss.
d. John is not liable for any loss sustained by the corporation.

2. Shares of stock may be issued without par value for such consideration as may be fixed by:
a. a corporation's board of directors.
b. a corporation's officers.
c. the bylaws of the corporation.
d. the statutes of the state of incorporation.

3. The Sell Wrong Corp. issued 1,000 shares of its $1 par value common stock to Mr. Rite, its vice president, for a price of $1,000. In consideration therefor, he gave the corporation $100 in cash, a note for $200, cancelled $400 salary owed to him for services rendered to the corporation in the past month and promised to render $300 worth of services in the following month. His shares are:
a. paid in full.
b. 70% paid for.
c. 50% paid for.
d. completely unpaid for.

4. An owner of common stock in a corporation, incorporated in a state in which the Model Business Corporation Act has been adopted, will not have liability beyond his actual investment, even though he:
a. purchased treasury shares for less than par value.
b. paid less than par value for stock purchased in connection with an original issue of shares.
c. failed to pay the full amount owed on a subscription contract.
d. was the sole shareholder and treated the corporation as a personally owned proprietorship.

5. DEF Corporation is authorized to issue 1,000 shares of $10 par value common stock and 1,000 shares of no par preferred stock. It has issued 1,200 shares of the common stock and 300 shares of the preferred stock at $10 per share. UCC Sec. 8-104 provides that:
a. the recipients of the 200 shares, representing an overissue, are entitled to receive 200 shares of the preferred stock.
b. the recipients of the 200 shares, representing an overissue, are entitled to the same rights of shareholders as the recipients of the 1,000 shares of properly issued common shares.
c. with regard to the preferred stock, stated capital would include the 300 authorized and issued shares only.
d. the preferred shares are considered to be a form of debt security.

6. Under the provisions of the UCC, a transfer of a share certificate in registered form may:

    a. not be made.
    b. be made by delivery alone.
    c. be made by delivery alone if indorsed in blank.
    d. be made by delivery if indorsed by an appropriate person.

7.   A dividend that may be revoked, unless actually distributed, is:
    a. a cash dividend.
    b. a stock dividend.
    c. a liquidating dividend.
    d. all of the above.

Chapter 42

CORPORATIONS
Merger, Consolidation, and Termination

As discussed in this chapter, a corporation, making a fundamental change in its structure or the nature of its business or terminating its existence, is required to comply with the laws of the state of incorporation. These fundamental or extraordinary changes may be accomplished by a merger or consolidation with another corporation, the sale of all or substantially all of the assets or stock of the corporation to another corporation, amendment of the articles of incorporation, or dissolution and termination.

THINGS TO KEEP IN MIND

A corporation cannot avoid compliance with statutory procedures, which are meant to safeguard the rights of corporate shareholders and creditors, by camouflaging an extraordinary fundamental corporate change as something else.

OUTLINE

I. Merger and consolidation — Exchange of shares of stock in one corporation for stock in another corporation.

    A. Merger — One corporation (the surviving corporation) acquires the assets of one or more other corporations (the merged or disappearing corporations).

        A Corporation ————————————— A Corporation (surviving corporation)

        B Corporation
        (merged corporation)

        1. The surviving corporation assumes the obligations and debts of the merged corporation and the existence of the merged corporation ceases.

2. The shareholders of the merged corporation become the shareholders of the surviving corporation.

    a. The surviving corporation exchanges its stock for the assets of merged corporation, which distributes the stock to its shareholders, or

    b. The surviving corporation exchanges its stock directly with the shareholders of the merged corporation.

B. Consolidation (exchange of shares of stock) — Two or more corporations combine so that each of them ceases to exist and a new successor corporation comes into existence. The new corporation acquires the assets and assumes the obligations and debts of the consolidated (disappearing) corporations.

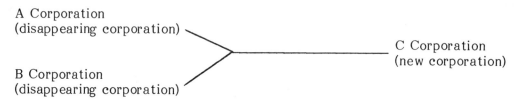

A Corporation
(disappearing corporation)

B Corporation
(disappearing corporation)

C Corporation
(new corporation)

C. Applicable legal principles, effect and procedure are basically the same for either merger or consolidation.

D. Procedure (RMBCA Chapter 11).

1. Board of directors of each corporation adopts a plan.   Contents of plan:

    a. Names of constituent merging or consolidating corporations and that of the surviving or new corporation.

    b. Terms of the merger or consolidation.

    c. Manner of converting shares of stock of constituent corporations into securities of the surviving or new corporation.

    d. In the case of a merger, the changes in the charter of the surviving corporation, and in the case of a consolidation, the appropriate provisions for the charter of the new corporation (MBCA Sec. 71 and 72).

2. Shareholder approval after notice to all (voting and nonvoting) shareholders of all corporations.

    a. Usually a two-thirds vote of voting shares is required (MBCA Sec. 73).

    b. The RMBCA requires a majority vote (Sec. 11.03).

3. Filing of Articles of Merger or Consolidation, which includes the plan, with the appropriate state official, who issues a certificate, and any local officials as required (MBCA Sec. 74; RMBCA Sec. 11.05).

E. If one or more of the corporations is a foreign corporation and the laws of each state permit merger or consolidation, each corporation complies with the laws of the state of its incorporation (MBCA Sec. 77; RMBCA Sec. 11.07).

F. Surviving corporation, in case of merger, or new corporation, in case of consolidation, acquires the assets, rights, liabilities and debts of the disappearing corporations (MBCA Sec. 76; RMBCA Sec. 11.06).

G. Short form (parent-subsidiary) merger — When the surviving (parent) corporation owns more than a stated proportion, such as 90% or 95%, of the outstanding shares of each class of stock of the subsidiary (merged) corporation, formal shareholder consent is not required (MBCA Sec. 75; RMBCA Sec. 11.04).

II. Sale of all or substantially all of the assets to another (acquiring or purchasing) corporation, other than in the regular course of business (MBCA Sec. 79; RMBCA Sec. 12.02).

A. Transaction may be a sale, lease, exchange or other disposition.

B. Acquiring corporation may pay cash, property or stock.

C. Each corporation remains in existence but the character of its assets and business change.

D. Procedure for corporation disposing of assets includes giving notice to all shareholders and vote of some prescribed proportion thereof.

E. Approval of shareholders of the acquiring corporation is not necessary unless payment is to be made in shares which are unauthorized or unavailable or if required by a stock exchange, upon which one or more of the corporations is listed.

F. Purchasing corporation is not liable for obligations of selling corporation unless:

1. Purchasing corporation expressly or impliedly assumes selling corporation's liabilities;

2. Sale of assets is in effect a merger or consolidation;

3. Purchasing corporation continues operation of business of selling corporation and retains its officers; or

4. Sale of assets is fraudulently executed in order to avoid selling corporation's liabilities.

III. Dissenting shareholders' rights to fair market value of shares (RMBCA Chapter 13).

A. Normally, if a shareholder disagrees with corporate policy or decisions, his or her recourse is to sell the stock.

B. A dissenting shareholder may have appraisal rights in cases of:

1. Disposition of all or substantially all of the assets of the corporation.

2. Consolidation and merger, including short form merger in some states (MBCA Sec. 80).

3. In some states only:

    a. Amendments of charter, affecting classifications of shares, when shareholders are adversely affected and not otherwise protected by preemptive rights.

    b. Acquisition of securities, to be distributed to shareholders, when disposing of assets of a dissolving corporation.

C. Dissenting shareholder must strictly adhere to statutory procedure (MBCA Sec. 81; RMBCA Secs. 13.20–13.28).

1. Vote against particular corporate action.

2. Give notice to corporation, which then makes offer to purchase shares.

3. Apply for appraisal of fair market value of shares by an appropriate court if offer of corporation is not accepted.

IV. Purchase of stock directly from shareholders by an "acquiring" corporation to acquire voting control of another (the "target") corporation.

A. "Tender offer" is publicly made and may be to exchange shares for cash or securities. Often the offer price is higher than the market value of the shares.

B. Today this method of gaining control is regulated by federal and state laws. (See Chapter 43.)

C. Responses of target corporation.

1. Board of directors of target corporation in exercise of its fiduciary duty makes a good faith recommendation to shareholders.

    a. Board of directors must disclose all material facts—those facts which it is likely reasonable shareholders will consider important in deciding whether to accept or reject tender offer.

    b. Board of directors may consider tender offer to be favorable and recommend acceptance by shareholders.

2. Board of directors may recommend rejection of tender offer and adopt a strategy directed at avoiding "takeover," such as:

    a. A corporate offer to buy stock from shareholders in order to retain control (a self tender).

    b. Solicit a merger with a different corporation (a white knight).

    c. Attempt to take over the acquiring corporation (Pac-man defense).

      d. A target corporation that adopts these defensive tactics is subject to the same federal and state statutes as acquiring corporation which makes a tender offer.

   3. Tactics of target corporation that are used in order to resist takeover.

      a. Scorched earth — Make a target corporation less attractive by selling off assets or divisions (the crown jewels) or taking out loans which are to be repaid if a takeover occurs.

      b. Shark repellant — Change articles of incorporation or bylaws of target corporation to require a greater shareholder vote for merger or other fundamental changes.

      c. Poison pill — Issue shares of target corporation that are to be redeemed for cash in the event of a takeover.

      d. Commence an action for an injunction against the acquiring corporation asserting that it is violating a statute (e.g., antitrust laws).

      e. Golden parachutes — Provide for payments to executive officers in the event that they are discharged or demoted.

      f. Greenmail — Purchase shares of target corporation's stock which had been acquired by the acquiring corporation.

  D. Insider trading — See Chapter 43.

V. Termination — Dissolution and liquidation.

  A. Nonjudicial dissolution.

   1. Act of the legislature in the state of incorporation.

   2. Expiration of duration provided for in charter, if not perpetual.

   3. Voluntary.

      a. By incorporators (MBCA Sec. 82; RMBCA Sec. 14.01).

      b. By unanimous action of all the shareholders (MBCA Sec. 83; RMBCA Sec. 7.04).

      c. By act of the corporation, after adoption of resolution by the board of directors and its approval by shareholders (MBCA Sec. 84; RMBCA Sec. 14.02).

   4. Procedure for liquidation and winding up (MBCA Secs. 86 and 87; RMBCA Chapter 14) — Corporation is required to:

      a. Cease conducting new business, notify creditors, pay debts and liabilities, including taxes, fulfill existing contracts, collect and sell assets.

  b. Distribute remaining assets among shareholders, according to their respective interests and preferences.

  c. Make any filings required by state law (MBCA Secs. 85, 92 and 93).

B. Involuntary judicial dissolution.

  1. Upon application of attorney general of state of incorporation for failure to comply with statutory, administrative or tax requirements, obtaining charter through fraud, abuse of corporate powers (see Chapter 40 herein), violation of state law or failure to commence or abandonment of business operations (MBCA Secs. 94, 95 and 96).

  2. In some states, petition for dissolution may be made by:

     a. Creditors (MBCA Sec. 97).

     b. Corporation, requesting court supervision of liquidation (MBCA Sec. 97).

     c. Majority of directors, if corporation is insolvent or if it will benefit shareholders.

  3. Upon application of shareholders, if directors or shareholders are deadlocked, or directors are acting illegally, oppressively, fraudulently or wasting or misapplying assets (MBCA Sec. 97).

  4. Involuntary dissolution is provided for in RMBCA.

     a. Administrative dissolution by secretary of state if corporation fails to pay franchise taxes, deliver annual report or give notification of change in registered office or agent or if period of duration of corporation expires (RMBCA Sec. 14.21).

     b. Judicial dissolution (RMBCA Sec. 14.30). Proceedings are instituted by:
        1) Attorney general if articles of incorporation obtained through fraud or corporation has exceeded or abused its authority.
        2) Shareholders.
           a) Deadlock in board of directors, which shareholders cannot break, as a result of which irreparable injury is threatened or being suffered by the corporation and business of the corporation cannot be conducted to the advantage of the shareholders.
           b) Actions of directors or those in control of corporation are illegal, fraudulent or oppressive.
           c) Shareholders are deadlocked and have failed to elect directors for two years.
           d) Corporate assets are being misapplied or wasted.
        3) Creditor when corporation is insolvent.
           a) Judgment creditor's execution on a judgment was returned unsatisfied.
           b) Corporation admitted in writing that the creditor's claim is due and owing.
        4) Corporation in order to have a voluntary dissolution continued under court supervision.

KEY WORDS AND PHRASES IN TEXT

Merger
Surviving corporation
Articles of merger
Consolidation
Newly formed corporation
Articles of consolidation
Procedure for merger or consolidation
    (approval of board of directors and
    shareholders of each corporation)
Short-form merger statutes for parent-
    subsidiary mergers
Dissenting shareholders' rights to be paid
    fair market value of shares and, if
    necessary, to have value of shares
    appraised
Amendments to articles of incorporation
Shareholder approval of extraordinary
    matters with dissenting shareholders'
    rights protected
Purchase of assets by acquiring corporation
Sale of all or substantially all of a
    corporation's assets
De facto merger
Purchase of stock in order to acquire
    control of another (target)
    corporation

Tender offer
Takeover statutes
Target corporation
Acquiring corporation
Target corporation's responses
Disclosure of material facts
Self tender
White knight
Pac-man defense
Scroched earth tactics
Shark repellant
Poison pill
Golden parachutes
Greenmail
Insider trading
Termination of corporations
Dissolution by act of legislature, expira-
    tion of specified time for duration of
    corporation, voluntary approval of
    board of directors and shareholders
    or unanimous action of shareholders
Involuntary dissolution
Deadlock in board of directors
Liquidation process (winding up affairs
    of corporation)
Freeze-out

FILL-IN QUESTIONS

1. A, B and C Corporations are planning to merge. Upon completion of the statutory requirements, C Corporation will continue to exist. A and B Corporations will _____ and C Corporation will acquire _____ and assume _____. The shareholders of A and B Corporations will receive _____.

2. E and F Corporations are planning to consolidate. Upon completion of the statutory requirements, E and F Corporations will _____. Their assets will be acquired and their liabilities assumed by G Corporation, _____ _____.

3. State corporation laws require _____ if a corporation is selling, leasing or otherwise disposing of all or substantially all of its assets, other than in the ordinary course of its business, even though the corporation's existence will _____ because it results in a fundamental change in _____ _____.

4. The objective of statutory provisions requiring shareholder approval for plans resulting in fundamental changes in the nature and structure of a corporation and filing with a state official is to protect the rights of _____. A

corporation _____ avoid compliance with the statutory procedures by characterizing or disguising a transaction in such a way as not to require such approval or filing.

5. A shareholder, who has voted against a merger, consolidation or disposition of all or substantially all of the assets of a corporation, may dissent. If so the shareholder has a right to be paid _____ by the corporation and, by adhering to the statutory provisions, may apply to an appropriate court for _____ .

MULTIPLE CHOICE QUESTIONS

1. Which of the following statements is incorrect?
    a. The surviving corporation in a merger assumes the liabilities of the corporation which merged into it.
    b. Assets of all consolidating corporations are acquired by the surviving corporation after consolidation.
    c. A shareholder, who dissents from a lease of all the assets of a corporation, is entitled to the fair market value of her shares.
    d. Bondholders have rights to corporate assets upon dissolution, superior to those of common shareholders.

2. C Co. was merged into D Co. C Co. had only issued common stock. Under the terms of the plan of merger, each share of common stock of C Co. received one share of 8% cumulative, nonvoting D Co. preferred stock. The directors and the required proportion of shareholders of both corporations voted in favor of the merger. The holders of 10% of the common stock of C Co. voted against the plan and have demanded that the corporation purchase their shares rather than give them D Co. stock.
    a. Creditors of C Co. are not entitled to payment from D Co. if D Co. did not agree to assume C Co.'s obligations.
    b. The merger is ineffective because the shareholders of C Co. are to receive nonvoting shares in exchange for their voting shares.
    c. Dissenting shareholders of C Co. are entitled to the fair market value of their shares.
    d. If the corporation refuses to pay the dissenting shareholders a price that they believe is adequate, a court will not substitute its judgment for that of the directors.

3. When a corporation acquires all or substantially all of the assets of another corporation (other than in the regular course of business):
    a. the selling corporation must have the approval of its shareholders but the acquiring corporation need not obtain shareholder approval.
    b. the acquiring corporation must have the approval of its shareholders but the selling corporation need not obtain shareholder approval.
    c. both the selling corporation and the acquiring corporation must have the approval of their shareholders.
    d. neither the selling corporation nor the acquiring corporation must have the approval of their shareholders.

Questions 4 and 5 are based on the following fact situation: The ABD Land Corp. has sold 98.3% of its assets, all of which is real property, to the FGH Land Corp.

4. Which of the following statements is correct?
   a. The board of directors of ABD may authorize the sale, if it is in the regular course of business.
   b. The sale must be approved by the shareholders of ABD, if it is in the regular course of business.
   c. The sale must be approved by the shareholders of FGH, if it is not in the regular course of business.
   d. The ABD Corp. will be dissolved by operation of law following the transfer of its assets to FGH.

5. If the sale is not in the regular course of business of ABD Land Corp:
   a. the sale must be approved by all the shareholders of ABD, including those without voting rights.
   b. the sale need not be approved by the shareholders of ABD, if the directors unanimously approved it.
   c. a dissenting shareholder of ABD has a right to be paid the fair market value of her shares, if she promptly notified and made a demand on the corporation.
   d. a dissenting shareholder of FGH has a right to be paid the fair market value of his shares, if he promptly notified and made a demand on the corporation.

6. A majority of the shareholders of a corporation may petition for dissolution, if the:
   a. assets of the corporation are insufficient to meet its liabilities.
   b. directors have failed to declare a dividend.
   c. directors are deadlocked in the management of the corporation.
   d. never.

7. A corporation's existence terminates when:
   a. the sole owner/shareholder dies.
   b. it becomes insolvent.
   c. all of its shares are purchased by another corporation.
   d. it legally consolidates with another corporation.

8. Under the provisions of the Revised Model Business Corporation Act, a business corporation may be administratively dissolved if:
   a. its sole shareholder has died.
   b. the corporation has failed to notify the Secretary of State of the change of address of its registered office.
   c. the articles of incorporation of the corporation have been obtained through fraud or the corporation has entered into *ultra vires* transactions.
   d. all of the shareholders of the corporation consent to its dissolution in writing.

Chapter 43

CORPORATIONS
Financial Regulation
and Investor Protection

The issuance and sale of corporate securities are extensively regulated by the Securities and Exchange Commission (the SEC), a federal agency, which administers the Securities Act of 1933, the Securities Exchange Act of 1934 and other federal statutes, relevant provisions of which are explained in this chapter. In addition, the states also regulate the offer and sale of securities. A major objective of securities regulation is to protect the investing public by requiring full and correct disclosure of relevant information.

THINGS TO KEEP IN MIND

As indicated in the text, the area of law relating to the issuance and regulation of investment securities is most complex. Should the occasion arise, consult an expert.

OUTLINE

I.   Federal securities regulation — Legislation is based on the power of Congress to regulate interstate commerce and the use of the mails.

    A. Federal regulatory statutes are administered by the Securities and Exchange Commission.

    B. Securities Act of 1933.

       1. The term "investment security" is broadly defined.

          a. "(A)ny note, stock, treasury stock, bond, debenture, evidence of indebtedness, certificate of interest or participation in any profit-sharing agreement . . . investment contract . . . or, in general, any interest or instrument commonly known as a 'security' or any certificate of interest or participation in ... receipt for ... or right to subscribe to or purchase, any of the foregoing." (Securities Act of 1933, Sec. 2.)

b. Includes those transactions in which:
  1) A person invests money or property in a common enterprise or venture, and
  2) Investor reasonably expects to make a profit primarily or substantially as a result of the managerial efforts of others.

2. The 1933 Act requires full disclosure of material information, which is relevant to investment decisions, and prohibits fraud and misstatements when securities are offered to the public through the mail and/or interstate commerce.

3. Registration statement, containing a thorough description of the securities, the financial structure, condition and management personnel of the issuing corporation and a description of material pending litigation against the issuing corporation, is filed with the SEC.

4. Prospectus, based upon the information in the registration statement, must be given to any prospective investor and purchaser.

5. After registration, there is a twenty day waiting period.

  a. During the waiting period, issuer can obtain underwriter and distribute red herring prospectus.

  b. Issuer may solicit revocable offers from prospective purchasers after filing registration statement but may not sell securities until the effective date of the statement.

6. After waiting period, the registered securities can be bought and sold and tombstone advertisements placed in newspapers and other publications.

7. Securities that are exempt from registration requirement:

  a. Intrastate offerings — All offerees and issuer are residents of state in which issuer performs substantially all of its operations.

  b. Issuer is a governmental body or nonprofit organization.

  c. Issuer is a bank, savings institution, common carrier or farmers' cooperative and subject to other regulatory legislation.

  d. Commercial paper having a maturity date of less than nine months.

  e. Stock dividends, stock splits and securities issued in connection with corporate reorganizations.

  f. Insurance, endowment and annuity contracts.

8. Regulation A — Less demanding disclosure and registration are required for small issues of less than $1,500,000.

9. Transactions that are exempt from registration requirement — Regulation D.

   a. Private, noninvestment company sales of less than $500,000 worth of securities in a twelve month period to investors who will not resell the securities within two years.

   b. Private, noninvestment company sales of less than $5,000,000 worth of securities in a twelve month period to:
      1) Accredited investors — Natural persons with annual income of more than $200,000 whose net worth exceeds $1,000,000, or
      2) Investors who are furnished with purchaser representatives, who are knowledgeable and experienced regarding finance and business, or
      3) Up to 35 unaccredited investors having financial and business knowledge and experience, who are furnished with the same information as would be contained in a full registration statement prospectus.

   c. Sale of any amount of securities to accredited investors or those furnished with independent purchaser representatives (private placement).

10. Civil liability for failure to register and for misstatements and omissions in a registration statement.

    a. Imposed upon the issuing corporation, its directors and anyone who signed or provided information that was incorporated in the registration statement, and underwriters.

    b. Liable to persons acquiring shares.

C. Securities Exchange Act of 1934.

   1. Regulates securities exchanges, those engaged in the markets in which securities are traded and corporations having assets of more than three million dollars and 500 shareholders.

   2. Insider trading (Sec. 10(b) and SEC Rule 10b-5).

      a. Liability is imposed upon directors and others (tippees) who, because of their positions, have access to information not available to the public which may affect the future market value of the corporation's securities.

      b. Liability is imposed when there have been misleading or deceptive omissions or misrepresentations of material facts in connection with the purchase or sale of securities.

      c. SEC, purchaser or seller of securities, who has been damaged, may bring action.

      d. An outsider who comes into possession of nonpublic market information does not have a duty to make a Rule 10b-5 disclosure.

3. Rule 10b-5 applies when the facilities of a stock exchange, the U.S. mail or an instrumentality of interstate commerce are used.

4. Insider reporting and trading (Sec. 16(b)) — Officers, directors and large shareholders are required to file reports with the SEC and may be liable to corporation for gains made in trading in securities.

5. The Insider Trading Sanctions Act of 1984 authorizes the SEC to bring a civil suit against a person who, while in possession of material nonpublic information, violates or aids in the violation of the 1934 Act or SEC rules.

6. Proxy statements (Sec. 14(a)) — Full disclosure is required of those soliciting proxies from shareholders.

II. Other federal laws.

A. Amendments and additions have been made to the Securities Exchange Act, some of which are referred to below.

B. Williams Act of 1968.

1. Applies to corporate takeovers and tender offers when a person or a corporation is seeking to acquire more than 5% of the stock of another (the target) corporation, whose stock is required to be registered under the Securities Exchange Act, by offering (making tender offers) to purchase shares held by shareholders of the target corporation.

2. Requires disclosure of material information to shareholders of target corporation and the SEC.

3. Prohibits misstatements and omissions of material facts, fraudulent, deceptive or manipulative acts or practices in connection with tender offers in order to protect the shareholders of the target corporation.

C. Foreign Corrupt Practices Act of 1977.

1. Administered by SEC and Justice Department.

2. Prohibited practices.

   a. Apply to corporations subject to registration and reporting provisions of Securities Exchange Act and any other person or business entity.

   b. Unlawful to use the mails or instrumentality of interstate commerce in order to corruptly offer or give anything of value to foreign officials or political parties for purposes of influencing decisions if the objective is to obtain or retain business.

3. SEC reporting corporations must develop and maintain strict systems of internal accounting controls that produce accurate financial statements which will alert them if prohibited payments are made.

D. Investment Company Act of 1940 requires registration with SEC and restricts activities of investment companies, including mutual funds.

III. State regulation of securities.

A. Article 8 of UCC deals with the transfer of investment securities.

B. Blue Sky Laws — State securities laws also regulate the offering and sale of securities in intrastate commerce.

1. Anti-fraud provisions similar to federal laws.

2. Regulation of brokers and dealers in securities.

3. Registration and disclosure are required before securities can be offered for sale.

4. Some state statutes impose standards of "fairness."

C. States have adopted legislation dealing with corporate takeovers and tender offers.

1. Some state statutes are more restrictive than the federal statute and SEC rules.

2. The constitutionality of some of these statutes has been questioned.

KEY WORDS AND PHRASES IN TEXT

The Securities and Exchange
   Commission (SEC)
Securities Act of 1933
A security
Registration statement (contents)
Prospectus
What the registering corporation can do
   before, during and after registration
Underwriter
Red herring prospectus
Tombstone ad
Exempt transactions
Exempt securities
Private noninvestment company offering
Accredited investor
Unaccredited investor
Private placement exemption

Intrastate transaction exemption
Securities Exchange Act of 1934
Section 12 companies
Stabilization
Insider trading
Tippees
Material omission or misrepresentation
SEC Rule 10b-5 (disclosure and
   application of Rule 10b-5)
Section 16(b) — insider reporting
   and trading
Insider Trading Sanctions Act of 1984
Proxy statements
Regulation of investment companies
Regulation of mutual fund activities
Foreign Corrupt Practices Act
State securities laws (Blue Sky Laws)

FILL-IN QUESTIONS

1. The regulation of securities is covered concurrently by state statutes, often termed _____, and federal legislation under the _____

and _____, administered by the _____. The basis for federal regulation is the power of Congress to regulate _____ and the use of the U.S. _____.

2. The Securities Act of 1933 relates to new issues of securities. It requires that an issuer of non-exempt securities register with _____. The registration statement must contain information such as _____

    _____

    and a copy of the prospectus that will be furnished to investors.

3. The _____ regulates the security markets in which securities are traded after they have been issued. Section 12 companies are those which have assets in excess of $1 million and _____ shareholders. Section 12 corporations are required to register their securities with _____.

MULTIPLE CHOICE QUESTIONS

1. The Securities Act of 1933 requires that the following securities be registered with the SEC:
    a. Securities issued by the XYZ Benevolent Society, a charitable organization.
    b. Securities issued by United Transportation Lines Inc., a common carrier.
    c. A stock dividend issued by General Motors Corporation.
    d. All of the above.
    e. None of the above.

2. The Securities Act of 1933 provides that firms that sell securities to the public furnish certain financial information to the SEC:
    a. after the sale of the securities.
    b. prior to the sale of the securities.
    c. prior to and after the sale of securities.
    d. if the purchasers of the securities are all financially sophisticated and were the three partners of a partnership that is changing its form of organization to a corporation.

3. Acme Canning Corporation has filed a registration statement with the SEC because it is planning to issue 600,000 shares of $10 par value preferred stock to the public.
    a. Acme Canning Corporation may not sell any of the stock but it may receive revocable offers from prospective investors who are furnished with a prospectus during the 20 day waiting period after the filing of the registration statement.
    b. Acme Canning Corporation may neither sell nor receive revocable or irrevocable offers for the purchase of securities during the 20 day waiting period after the filing of the registration statement.
    c. Acme Canning Corporation may sell shares of the stock to the public immediately after filing the registration statement only if it furnishes prospective investors with a prospectus.
    d. Acme Canning Corporation may sell shares of the stock to the public immediately after filing the registration statement because the stock issue is exempt from the requirements of the 1933 Act.

4. Which of the following is exempt from registration under the Securities Act of 1933?
    a. Interests in a limited partnership.

    b. Convertible preferred corporate stock.

    c. Corporate bonds secured by real property.

    d. An annuity contract issued by an insurer.

5.   Rule 10b-5 of the Securities Exchange Commission prohibits:

    a. short swing transactions by directors, officers and holders of more than 10% of any class of stock.

    b. trading on inside information by directors, officers and holders of more than 10% of any class of stock.

    c. trading on inside information by directors, officers, holders of more than 10% of any class of stock and those who receive "tips" from insiders.

    d. all of the above.

6.   The Z Corporation is planning to sell $2,000 worth of corporate debentures, which will mature in 25 years from the date of issue, to the public in the United States. The issue need not be registered with the SEC because:

    a. the federal securities acts apply only to the issuance of equity securities.

    b. bonds of this nature are not considered to be securities.

    c. Z Corporation is a municipal corporation.

    d. the amount of the issue is less than $5,000,000.

7.   A corporation, which desires to issue $2,000,000 worth of preferred shares, has complied with the appropriate state Blue Sky Laws and filed a registration statement with the SEC, but has omitted a material fact regarding the corporation's financing.

    a. An accountant, who certified a financial statement, made in conjunction with the registration statement, is liable to a purchaser of the new issue.

    b. The underwriter of the new issue is liable to a purchaser of the shares.

    c. A director of the corporation issuing the shares is liable to any person who acquires the shares of the new issue.

    d. All of the above.

8.   The Foreign Corrupt Practices Act prohibits bribery of officials of foreign countries. The Act:

    a. applies only to multinational corporations.

    b. applies to domestic corporations that engage in interstate commerce.

    c. applies only to corporations whose securities are required to be registered with the SEC under the Securities Exchange Act of 1934.

    d. provides that a person who has been injured may recover treble damages.

Chapter 44

Private Franchises

A franchise is an agreement or arrangement, in which the franchisor, the owner of a trademark, trade name, copyright or similar interest, grants the right to use the mark, name or other interest to another, the franchisee, in connection with selling, marketing or supplying goods and/or services.

The relationship between the franchisee and the franchisor may be one of agency, especially if the franchisor may exercise considerable control over the activities of the franchisee and derives substantial benefit from them. In other instances, the franchisee has a great deal of discretion and is subject to little control by the franchisor, in which case, the franchisee will be treated as an independent contractor. As you will recall from Unit Five, the nature of a relationship determines the respective liability of the parties.

THINGS TO KEEP IN MIND

There is considerable disparity in bargaining power in many franchise relationships. For this reason, a number of states have enacted statutes protecting franchisees, and courts have refused to enforce grossly unfair termination provisions in franchise agreements and have prevented franchisors from unconscionably refusing to renew franchise licenses without good cause.

OUTLINE

I.   The law of franchising.

   A. Some states have enacted statutes that deal specifically with franchising.

   B. The courts tend to apply general common law principles in cases involving franchising.

II. Types of franchises.

    A. Distributorship — A manufacturer licenses a dealer to sell its product.

    B. Chain-style business — A franchisee operates under a franchisor's name and is identified as a member of the group engaged in the franchisor's business.

    C. Manufacturing or processing plant arrangement — The franchisor furnishes ingredients or formula for making or processing a particular product and marketing it in accordance with the franchisor's standards.

III. Advantages.

    A. Franchisor.

        1. Furnishes aid, protection, goodwill, supportive services and customer acceptance.

        2. Gains rapid market expansion with minimal outlays of capital.

    B. Franchisee.

        1. The franchise system provides opportunities to individuals to own their own businesses.

        2. A legally independent business unit furnishes capital but is economically dependent upon the franchisor.

IV. The franchise agreement — Usually prepared by the franchisor.

    A. Payment for franchise — Initial fee for franchise license, a percentage of sales or profits and sometimes payment of a proportion of the franchisor's costs and expenses.

    B. Control by the franchisor over the franchisee's business location, organization and decisions.

        1. Franchisee may be required to lease or own the premises and/or supply equipment. In some cases, the franchisor supplies equipment and leases the premises.

        2. The franchisor may impose standards for the form of business organization, its capital structure, the operations, training of personnel and the price and quality of products or services.

        3. The franchisor may require that the franchisee purchase supplies and products at an established price, but may only suggest retail prices.

        4. Usually the agreement contains exclusive dealings provisions.

    C. Termination of the franchise arrangement.

        1. Initial duration may be limited to one year.

2. May be terminated by the franchisor for cause or because of death, disability or insolvency of the franchisee, breach of the agreement or failure to meet sales quota.

3. Notice of termination is generally necessary.

4. Courts have read good faith and commercial reasonableness into franchise contracts and will not enforce unconscionable provisions.

D. Legislation.

1. Federal Automobile Dealers' Franchise (Day in Court) Act and Petroleum Marketing Practices Act.

2. State statutes may be subject to constitutional challenges.

V. Regulation of the franchising industry in order to protect consumers and franchisees.

A. State statutes and case law are not uniform.

1. It is often difficult to prove the existence of the elements of fraud in the inducement and, even if proven, the remedies afforded by common law for fraud may be inadequate.

2. Some states have enacted franchise disclosure acts, which afford some protection to potential franchisees.

3. Some courts have attempted to apply state Blue Sky Laws to franchise agreements.

B. Federal regulation.

1. Franchise agreements have been held not to be investment securities, subject to regulation under the Securities Act of 1933.

2. Remedies available for mail fraud are generally unsatisfactory.

3. The FTC franchise rule imposes disclosure requirements to enable prospective franchisees to make informed decisions before entering into franchise arrangements.

   a. FTC Rule 436 (1979) requires that franchisors and franchise brokers furnish prospective franchisees with detailed information about the franchisor and its business in a Basic Disclosure Document.

   b. Registration, approval or filing with the FTC is not required.

   c. Failure to comply with Rule 436 is an unfair or deceptive act or practice under Section 5 of the Federal Trade Commission Act.

4. See also Chapter 48 dealing with antitrust.

KEY WORDS AND PHRASES IN TEXT

Franchise
Franchisee
Franchisor
The law of franchising
Distributorship franchises
Chain-style business franchises
Manufacturing or processing plant
    franchises
The franchise relationship and agreement
Payment for franchise
Franchisor's specifications as to location
    and business organization
Price and quality controls

Termination of the franchise arrangement
    (relief for franchisee, measure of
    damages)
Consumer and franchisee protection
    statutes
Regulation of the franchising industry
The franchise contract (disclosure
    protection)
The Federal Trade Commission (FTC)
    franchise rule
Franchisee's relationship to franchisor
    (agent or independent contractor)

Unit Seven

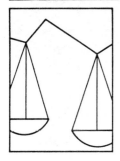

GOVERNMENT REGULATION

Government, at the federal, state and local level, has played an increasing role in regulating activities of individuals and businesses. The power to do so and to legislate in this area is derived, in general, from a governmental unit's power to protect and provide for the common defense, safety, health and welfare ("the police power") and, in the case of the federal government, Congress's authority to pass laws regulating interstate and foreign commerce (U.S. Constitution, Article I, Section 8). Evidence of regulation has been referred to in the preceding and subsequent units of the text and this material.

Chapter 45 provides an overview of such regulation and the agencies created to oversee them. Chapters 46 and 47 focus on consumer and environmental protection, areas about which each student, because of his or her own individual bias, will have varying personal interest. For this reason, extensive test materials concerning these matters have not been included in this Study Guide.

Chapter 48 deals with antitrust law and governmental efforts to regulate the economy in order to maintain the free private enterprise system. Legal issues relating to the employment relationship are discussed in Chapter 49.

Chapter 45

Introduction and Administrative Law

The objective of this chapter is to familiarize you with the federal regulatory process and the general scope of regulated activities. In the United States, there has been a trend away from market and common law or legislative controls, interpreted by the courts, to increasing regulation by governmental administrative agencies. Government agencies are created by legislative bodies and may be given legislative, judicial and/or executive authority. Federal agencies are established by the United States Congress and exercise their functions in accordance with the Administrative Procedure Act. Many federal agencies are part of the executive branch; others are independent agencies which are less subject to presidential influence and have been given broad legislative, judicial and executive powers.

THINGS TO KEEP IN MIND

The emphasis in the chapter is on federal agencies and their powers. Regulatory agencies (sometimes termed boards, departments, commissions, authorities, etc.) also exist in the states and at local levels of government.

OUTLINE

I.   Historical background.

   A. Creation of Interstate Commerce Commission (ICC) in 1887.

   B. At first, agencies were endowed with price setting and dispute resolution functions.

   C. 1930's—period of economic regulation during which the Securities and Exchange

Commission (SEC), Social Security Administration (SSA) and National Labor Relations Board (NLRB) were established.

D. 1960's and 1970's—period of social regulation during which the Consumer Product Safety Commission (CPSC), Environmental Protection Agency (EPA) and Occupational Safety and Health Administration (OSHA) were created.

E. Currently, there is a movement toward federal "deregulation."

II. Purposes of regulation.

A. Factors that have influenced growth of regulation by federal administrative agencies:

1. Recognition that a totally unregulated market may not best serve the nation's welfare.

2. Inability of Congress to specify detailed rules for regulating the market, which necessitate expertise in particular areas.

B. Control monopoly power and perceived excessive competition.

C. Ration scarce resources.

D. Correct unequal bargaining power.

E. Social regulation.

III. Methods of regulation.

A. Congress passes enabling statute creating an agency, setting forth a broad outline for regulation and giving the agency power to adopt specific rules.

B. Methods of regulation that may be employed.

1. Rate setting.

a. Agencies may control pricing by firms that have natural or legal monopolies in order to assure "fair" profits.

b. Profits may be controlled directly through taxation, or indirectly because of a regulatory board's power over rate making, particularly in industries in which participants have been given exclusive rights to produce a commodity or provide a service.

c. Price regulation may be effected by establishment of a maximum, minimum or uniform price.

2. Licensing and allocation of rights.

a. Some agencies may restrict entry into a market in which there are scarce resources or in order to protect health and safety.

b. A license may be conditioned on making a disclosure of information.

c. Establishment of quotas and imposition of duties or taxes may restrict levels of production, imports or sales.

d. Taxes may be imposed or subsidies granted in order to alter economic behavior.

3. Standard setting.

a. Agencies may be empowered to set specific standards that must be complied with by business firms.

b. Objective may be to protect health and safety or to provide information in the form of truthful disclosure to members of the public.

IV. Regulated activities — Virtually every economic activity is regulated to some extent. Often multiple agencies have regulatory power affecting a particular activity.

A. Transportation is regulated at the federal level chiefly by the Interstate Commerce Commission (ICC), which has extensive rate setting power.

B. Public utilities, which are granted monopolies, are traditionally regulated at the state and local level.

C. Energy is regulated by the federal Department of Energy and some independent agencies.

D. Communications — Licenses are granted by the Federal Communications Commission (FCC) in order to allocate limited air waves and air space.

E. Consumer protection — Direct regulation is imposed by the Consumer Product Safety Commission (CPSC) in order to protect the health and safety of the public. (See Chapter 46.)

F. Financing — Extensive regulation of banking, insurance, securities and other financial activities exists at the federal and state levels. (For example, see Chapter 43.)

G. General industry.

1. Employment and labor — See Chapter 49.

2. Patents and copyrights — Limited monopolies are given to inventors for 17 years (in most cases) in order to encourage innovation, development and production of new products, services and methods of production, and to authors and their estates for life plus 50 years. (See Chapter 5.)

3. Trademarks and trade names — Business firms that use words or symbols, which are associated with their products or services by the public, may register their trademarks and trade names and prevent infringement by others. (See Chapter 5.)

4. Environmental protection in order to control pollution — See Chapter 47.

V. Requirements of administrative law.

    A. Regulatory powers and procedures.

        1. Congress has delegated legislative, judicial and executive powers to government agencies, whose decisions may be reviewed by the courts.

        2. In general, a court will enforce an agency's decision and overturn its action only if it is clearly arbitrary, not supported by the record or contrary to law.

    B. Rulemaking — Legislative power.

        1. Following compilation of information, obtained through the exercise of investigatory power, hearings are held (after notification) and rules promulgated.

        2. Agencies adopt rules that broadly set prospective requirements for future activities.

        3. The Administrative Procedure Act (APA) establishes procedural and substantive requirements for regulatory actions.

            a. A rule is an agency "statement of general or particular applicability and future effect designed to implement, interpret or prescribe law or policy."

            b. Procedural requirements for rulemaking.
                1) Notice of a proposed rule is published in the *Federal Register.*
                2) Public comments may be submitted in writing within a specified period of time (e.g., 60 days).
                    a) Informal rulemaking — There may be no opportunity for oral comment.
                    b) Formal rulemaking — Public hearings, at which oral comment may be made, are held.
                3) The final rule is published in the *Federal Register.*
                4) *Ex parte* contacts are informal communications that are not part of the rulemaking record and cannot be the sole basis for adoption of a rule.

            c. Substantive requirements for rulemaking.
                1) A person who is adversely affected by a regulation has standing to challenge a new rule.
                2) Courts generally accept the findings of facts made by administrative agencies if they are based upon substantial evidence and are not arbitrary and capricious.

    C. Agency adjudication — Judicial power.

        1. Administrative law judges hear and adjudicate disputes.

        2. Administrative adjudicative procedures are similar to those used by courts and are initiated by the agency or, less frequently, private parties.

      a. Parties are represented by counsel at a hearing.

      b. There is, however, no jury and the rules for admission of relevant evidence are more liberal.

  3. Administrative court judge may render a final disposition in an initial order, from which an appeal can be taken to the agency, or a recommended order, which may be adopted by the agency. The agency's final order may provide for imposition of civil monetary penalties or a cease-and-desist order.

  4. Agency decisions may be reviewed by the courts.

      a. Ordinarily, a court defers to an agency with regard to fact finding and will not substitute its judgment for that of the agency.

      b. If procedures that are guaranteed by statute and the U.S. Constitution have not been complied with by an administrative agency, a court may conduct a *de novo* review.

D. Agency enforcement and administration — Executive power.

  1. Investigatory powers are necessary in order to obtain information.

      a. Agencies have power to issue subpoenas for production of documents and testimony, to inspect records and to request information.

      b. When exercising these powers, agencies must comply with the U.S. Constitution.

  2. Enforcement powers.

      a. Failure to comply with an order of an agency may result in the imposition of a civil remedy, such as money damages, an order to take some specific action or a cease and desist, or restraining, order.

      b. Violators of an agency's rules and orders may be prosecuted by the agency and subject to criminal penalties, such as a fine and/or imprisonment.

  3. Administrative powers.

      a. Agencies exercise internal management powers.

      b. Some agencies are empowered to disburse funds through grants and loans.

      c. An agency may be authorized to grant licenses in accordance with rules and guidelines that are fixed by Congress and/or formulated by the agency.

VI. Limitations on the powers of administrative agencies.

A. Major Constitutional limitations.

1. Freedom of speech protected by First Amendment.

2. Due process clause.

    a. Fifth Amendment provides that one cannot be deprived of life, liberty or property without due process of law.

    b. Fourteenth Amendment provides that no state shall deprive any person of life, liberty or property without due process of law.

3. Power of eminent domain — Fifth Amendment provides that if a governmental body takes private property for a public purpose, just compensation must be given.

4. The Fourth Amendment provides that persons cannot be subjected to unreasonable searches and seizures and that warrants must be obtained based upon probable cause.

5. The Fifth Amendment protection against self-incrimination applies to natural persons but not to corporations.

B. Statutes, such as the APA, passed by the Congress of the United States.

C. Judicial review.

1. The courts have the power to determine the constitutionality of Acts of Congress, to interpret statutes and to review administrative agencies' actions and procedures.

2. Courts generally accept the findings of administrative agencies if they are based upon substantial evidence and are not arbitrary or capricious.

3. In rare instances, a court may find that an agency's decision was not warranted by the facts and direct that the facts be tried again (*de novo*).

D. Other limitations.

1. In some instances in which federal statutes conflict with state statutes, the federal law preempts the field.

2. Public review.

VII. Public accountability.

A. Freedom of Information Act (FOIA).

1. Any person may request disclosure of records of the federal government.

2. Exempt information:

    a. Classified information related to national defense or foreign affairs.

    b. Information related solely to the internal personnel rules and practices of an agency.

    c. Information specifically exempted by other statutes.

    d. Trade secrets and privileged commercial information obtained by the government from private persons.

    e. Certain private intra-agency and inter-agency memoranda.

    f. Personnel and medical files.

    g. Information related to the supervision of financial institutions.

    h. Privileged geological data.

    i. Investigatory records that may be related to future prosecutions.

B. Government-in-the-Sunshine Act (the Sunshine Act or open meeting law).

    1. Meetings that are held by a group of agency officials for purposes of conducting deliberations or taking actions must be open to public observations.

    2. An agency must give notice of a planned meeting and its agenda.

    3. Exceptions include those which are covered in the FOIA. (See above at VII.A.2.)

    4. Meetings may also be closed when the following matters are under discussion:

        a. Accusations of crimes.

        b. Information that would frustrate implementation of a future agency action.

        c. Information that involves agency participation in future rulemaking or litigation.

C. Regulatory Flexibility Act.

    1. Purpose—reduce the burden of regulation on small business firms.

    2. An agency must conduct a regulatory flexibility analysis when a new rule will have a "significant impact upon a substantial number of small entities."

    3. In some cases, small business record keeping requirements are reduced.

KEY WORDS AND PHRASES IN TEXT

Administrative agencies
Independent regulatory agencies
Administrative law
Interstate Commerce Commission (ICC)
Securities and Exchange Commission (SEC)
National Labor Relations Board (NLRB)
Economic regulation
Consumer Product Safety Commission
   (CPSC)
Environmental Protection Agency (EPA)
Occupational Safety and Health
   Administration (OSHA)
Social regulation
Cost of compliance with agency rules
Deregulation
Nuclear Regulatory Commission (NRC)
Enabling statute
Controlling monopoly power
Excessive competition
Rationing scarce resources
Federal Communications Commission
   (FCC)
Correcting unequal bargaining power
Food and Drug Administration (FDA)
Rate setting
Licensing
Standard setting
Agency rulemaking—legislative power

Administrative Procedure Act (APA)
Procedural requirements for rulemaking
Notice of proposed rule
Federal Register
Public comment
Informal rulemaking
Rulemaking record
The final rule
Ex parte contacts
Substantive requirements for rulemaking
Standing of person who is adversely
   affected to challenge rule
Arbitrary and capricious action of agency
Substantial evidence test
Agency adjudication—judicial power
Administrative law judge (ALJ)
Civil Service Commission
Initial order
Recommended order
Cease and desist order
De nova review
Agency investigatory, enforcement and
   administration—executive power
Public accountability
Freedom of Information Act (FOIC)
Sunshine Act (Government-in-the-Sunshine
   or open meeting law)
Regulatory Flexibility Act

FILL-IN QUESTIONS

1. _____ administrative agencies are created in enabling statutes by Acts of _____ in which the agencies' powers are defined.

2. A decision or ruling made by a specialized regulatory body will be upheld by a reviewing court, unless it is _____.

3. An agency, authorized to grant licenses, has _____ power; one authorized to establish standards, with which firms must comply, has _____ power in order to obtain information, and _____ power so that it can promulgate appropriate standards.

4. Entry into a particular industry or business may be affected by a government agency through its power to regulate price, _____ _____ and to restrict private contracting rights and _____ as well as by taxation and subsidies.

5. The power of government to protect the health and safety of its citizens is the basis for regulation in the areas of _____.

6. Although our economic system is based on free competition, monopolies are granted to _____
in order to carry out strong public policies.

MULTIPLE CHOICE QUESTIONS

1. The Interstate Commerce Commission:
   a. regulates railroads, the trucking industry but not air carriers.
   b. may permit a merger of two railroads even if it is contrary to the objectives of the antitrust laws.
   c. has extensive rate making power.
   d. All of the above.

2. Regulations regarding safety, emissions controls and fuel economy of automobiles is regulated by:
   a. the Department of Energy.
   b. the Department of Transportation.
   c. the National Highway Traffic Safety Administration.
   d. the Department of Transportation and the National Highway Traffic Safety Administration.

3. In general, under statutes providing for the creation of administrative agencies, government agencies may be authorized to exercise:
   a. judicial powers.
   b. executive powers.
   c. legislative powers.
   d. All of the above are correct.

4. A federal administrative agency must comply with the procedural and substantive requirements of the United States Constitution and:
   a. the Administrative Procedure Act.
   b. the Federal Rules of Evidence.
   c. the National Labor Relations Board's rulings.
   d. the Association of Administrative Judges's rulings.

5. When a court reviews a decision made by an administrative law judge, the court:
   a. generally is bound by the factual conclusions reached by the administrative law judge.
   b. is guided by the "substantive evidence rule."
   c. generally will defer to the expertise of the administrative law judge.
   d. All of the above are correct.

6. Arrow Corporation was charged with having violated a provision of the Consumer Product Safety Act. Edwards, an examiner for the Consumer Product Safety Commission, concluded that Arrow Corporation had violated the statute and made adverse determinations on several issues. Arrow believes that Edwards had not based her decision upon substantial evidence and that her determinations were made in an arbitrary manner. Edwards has made her decision and submitted her opinion. Arrow Corporation does not wish to accept the determination. The corporation:
   a. is bound by the decision unless it was denied procedural due process.

b. should proceed in a state court in order to obtain injunctive relief ordering Edwards to reopen the case and make a new determination.
c. should appeal to the federal district court which may overturn Edwards' determination if it was not based upon substantial evidence or was arbitrary.
d. should not bother appealing to a court because a court will not substitute its judgment for that of the administrator.

(This question has been adapted from AICPA Examination, November 1983.)

right
Chapter 46

Consumer Protection

The distinct trend away from the *caveat emptor* (let the buyer beware) philosophy can be observed in judicial decisions, statutes and regulations issued by administrative agencies. The focus of this chapter is upon protection afforded to consumers engaging in sales and financing (credit) transactions. The emphasis of protective legislation and regulation has been upon preventing deceptive practices and assuring full disclosure of material information relating to sales of personal property, real property and services and credit transactions.

In this chapter, federal statutes relating to advertising, labeling, packaging, sales, credit, debt collection, health and safety and the ways in which federal administrative agencies carry on consumer protection activities are discussed. A section dealing with state consumer protection laws is found in the latter portion of the chapter.

The concept of consumer protection overlaps other areas of the law, with which you are already familiar. Recall, for example, discussions dealing with torts (Chapters 4 and 5), illegal bargains (Chapter 11), fraud and misrepresentation (Chapter 10), written agreements (Chapter 12), product warranties, safety and liability (Chapters 20 and 21), secured transactions (Chapter 29) and securities regulation (Chapter 43). See also material dealing with environmental protection (Chapter 47), the powers of the Federal Trade Commission (Chapter 48) and real property transactions (Chapter 52).

THINGS TO KEEP IN MIND

A consumer is usually considered to be a natural person, who obtains or tries to obtain personal property, real property, services, money or credit for personal, household or family use. In some cases too, small businesses and farmers or farm units are also afforded protection under legislation and regulation dealing with consumers.

center
397

OUTLINE

I.   Public policy issues.

    A. Balancing the potential benefits and costs of consumer protection judicial decisions, statutes and regulations.

    B. Existing and potential costs of compliance include increases in prices for consumer goods and services and fewer firms engaging in production and distribution of such goods and services.

II. Advertising.

    A. The Federal Trade Commission (FTC), an independent regulatory agency, administers a number of federal consumer protection statutes and is authorized to prevent "unfair or deceptive acts or practices in commerce," such as deceptive advertising.

    B. Procedures that are followed when the FTC believes that a deceptive advertisement is being used by a business firm.

        1. FTC conducts an investigation of a possible deceptive advertisement on its own initiative or following a consumer's or competitor's complaint.

        2. A hearing may be conducted by an administrative law judge, whose ruling may be appealed by the advertiser to the FTC.

        3. If the FTC upholds the decision against the advertiser, its decision can be appealed to a U.S. Court of Appeals, which normally will defer to the Commission unless its findings are not supported by substantial evidence.

    C. FTC may issue a cease and desist order requiring that an unfair or deceptive advertisement be discontinued and may initiate a "consumer redress" action for rescission or reformation of contracts that were entered into by consumers with the advertiser as a result of the misleading advertisement.

    D. Counter-advertising — FTC may require that advertiser correct misinformation in an advertisement.

    E. Unfair or deceptive acts or practices.

        1. Deceptive advertising refers to intentional misrepresentations of facts which are material factors in inducing purchasers' decisions to buy advertised products or services.

        2. Statements made in an advertisement are deceptive if they are scientifically untrue or contain false product differentiation.

        3. An advertisement is deceptive if a reasonable consumer would be misled. In general, puffing is not considered to be deceptive.

    F. "Bait and switch" advertising.

1. Advertisement relates to one item, which is offered for sale at a low price. When a consumer tries to purchase the item, a sales person tries to get the consumer to buy a more expensive item.

2. FTC guidelines are designed to prevent practices such as refusal to sell an advertised item, failure to have an adequate quantity of an advertised item available, failure to supply the advertised item within a reasonable time and discouraging employees from selling an advertised item.

III. Labeling and packaging laws.

   A. Fair Packaging Act — Labels on consumer goods must identify the product, the manufacturer, packer or distributor and its place of business, the net quantity of contents and the quantity of each serving if the number of servings is stated.

   B. Labeling and packaging of specific products, such as cigarettes, tobacco, cosmetics, drugs, food products and fabrics, are regulated by federal statutes.

IV. Sales practices.

   A. FTC regulates certain unfair practices engaged in by door-to-door salespersons.

      1. Regulations provide for a three day "cooling off" period, during which purchasers may cancel sales contracts that were solicited in the home.

      2. FTC issues cease and desist orders prohibiting particular unfair practices.

   B. FTC has issued regulations requiring truthful disclosures and prohibiting unfair sales practices engaged in by people in specific industries (e.g., dealers in used cars and funeral homes).

   C. Real estate sales.

      1. Interstate Land Sales Full Disclosure Act.

         a. Administered by the Department of Housing and Urban Development (HUD).

         b. Requires that there be a full disclosure of facts to assure that potential purchasers are able to make informed judgments concerning land purchases.

      2. Real Estate Settlement Procedures Act — Requires disclosure of necessary information about settlement process and costs to buyers of residential property.

V. Credit protection.

   A. Federal Truth-in-Lending Act (Consumer Credit Protection Act) is administered by the Federal Reserve Board, an independent agency.

      1. The Act applies when a debtor is a natural person; the creditor in the

ordinary course of its business is a lender, seller or provider of services; and the amount being financed is less than $25,000.

2. Regulation Z uniform disclosure requirements.

    a. The purpose of uniform disclosure requirements is to provide consumers with means of comparing the terms and costs of credit.

    b. Financing charges (including interest; charges for loans and insurance; and finders, credit report, appraisal, financing and service fees) must be stated in an annual percentage rate (APR).

    c. Consumer must be informed of the number of payments, dollar amount of each payment, dates upon which payments are due and prepayment provisions, including any prepayment penalties.

B. Credit cards.

1. Fair Credit Billing Act amends the Truth-in-Lending Act.

2. Credit cardholder is given limited right to withhold payment if there is a dispute concerning goods that were purchased with a credit card.

3. Billing disputes — If credit cardholder believes that an error has been made by issuer:

    a. Cardholder may suspend payment but must notify and give explanation to the card issuer concerning an error within sixty days of receipt of bill.

    b. Issuer of credit card must acknowledge receipt of notification within thirty days and has ninety days within which to resolve dispute.

4. Credit cardholder will not be liable for more than $50 if there was an unauthorized use of his or her card and notice thereof was given to card issuer.

5. Credit card issuer may not bill a cardholder for unauthorized charges if a credit card is improperly issued.

C. Fair Credit Reporting Act.

1. Upon request, one, who is refused credit or employment because of information in a credit bureau report, must be supplied with a summary of the information in the report, the sources and recipients of the information, and given an opportunity to correct errors.

2. Consumers have the right to be informed of the nature and scope of a credit investigation, the kind of information that is being compiled and the names of people who will receive a credit report.

3. Compiler of credit report must exercise reasonable care in preparing a credit report.

4. Inaccurate or misleading data must be removed from credit report and consumer has the right to add a statement regarding a disputed matter.

D. Equal Credit Opportunity Act prohibits discrimination based upon race, religion, national origin, color, sex, marital status, age or receipt of certain types of income.

VI. Debt collection.

A. Fair Debt Collection Practices Act prohibits debt collection agencies from engaging in certain practices:

1. Contacting a debtor at his or her place of employment, if employer objects.

2. Contacting debtor at unusual or inconvenient times or, if the debtor is represented by an attorney, at any time.

3. Contacting third parties about the payment of the debt without court authorization.

4. Harassing or intimidating debtor or using false and misleading approaches.

5. Communicating with the debtor after receipt of notice that the debtor is refusing to pay the debt, except to advise the debtor of action to be taken by the collection agency.

B. Garnishment.

1. A state court may issue an order for garnishment of a portion of a debtor's wages in order to satisfy a judgment that was obtained by a creditor.

2. TILA provides that a certain minimum income and no more than 25 percent of a judgment debtor's after-tax earnings can be garnisheed.

VII. Health and safety.

A. The Federal Food, Drug, and Cosmetic Act and amendments thereto.

1. The Food and Drug Administration (FDA) is authorized to establish standards and conduct inspections.

2. Adulteration and misbranding of food are prohibited, and standards for food and cosmetic products, including the levels of potentially dangerous additives, have been established.

3. Safety standards for automobiles, children's toys and fabric flammability have also been established.

B. Consumer Product Safety Act (CPSA).

1. The Consumer Product Safety Commission (CPSC) is authorized to regulate potentially hazardous consumer products; conducts research on product safety; and maintains a clearinghouse of information.

2. The CPSC may ban products that present an "unreasonable risk" to the user.

VIII. State laws.

    A. Common law — See Chapters 5, 10, 11, 12 and 30.

    B. Uniform Commercial Code (UCC).

        1. See chapters dealing with the sale of goods, commercial paper and secured transactions.

        2. Section 2-302 — State courts may refuse to enforce unconscionable clauses and contracts for the sale of goods.

    C. Uniform Consumer Credit Code (UCCC).

        1. The UCCC, which is similar to the federal TILA, has been adopted in eleven states, in some cases with variations; similar legislation has been enacted in other states.

        2. The UCCC is a comprehensive body of rules that apply to consumer credit. Its provisions cover maximum credit ceilings and interest rates; home solicitation and referral sales; required disclosure statements; and the form and contents of sales agreements.

    D. State consumer protection laws.

        1. Statutes, which vary from state to state, have codified, simplified and often expanded the protection afforded by the common law.

        2. Some state consumer protection legislation is stricter than comparable federal law.

KEY WORDS AND PHRASES IN TEXT

Caveat emptor
Caveat venditor
Federal Trade Commission Act
Federal Trade Commission (FTC)
Unfair or deceptive acts or practices
Deceptive advertisement
Counter-advertising
Puffing
Bait-and-switch advertising
Fair Packaging Act
Door-to-door sales
Cooling off period
Interstate Land Sales Full Disclosure Act
Department of Housing and Urban
    Development (HUD)
Real Estate Settlement Procedures Act

Truth-in-Lending Act (Consumer
    Credit Protection Act)
Regulation Z disclosure requirements
Private right of action
Fair Credit Billing Act
Fair Credit Reporting Act
Equal Credit Opportunity Act
Fair Debt Collection Practices Act
Garnishment
Federal Food, Drug, and Cosmetic Act
Federal auto safety laws
Consumer Product Safety Act
Consumer Product Safety Commission
Uniform Commercial Code
    unconscionability doctrine
Uniform Consumer Credit Code
State consumer protection statutes

FILL-IN QUESTIONS

1. The federal administrative agency that regulates deceptive acts and practices, including advertising, is the _____, an independent administrative agency. Federal consumer protection regulations relating to construction and safety standards for mobile homes and interstate land sales are enforced by the _____, an administrative agency that is part of the executive branch of the federal government.

2. Advertisements may be considered to be _____ if they include false statements or claims about the quality, effects, origins or availability of products or services or omit important material information. The _____ can issue cease and desist orders (which have the same effect as injunctive relief granted by a court) in order to prevent the use of such advertisements.

3. The _____, which is enforced by the Federal Trade Commission and the Department of Health and Human Services, requires that consumer goods have labels that identify the product, the manufacturer and the net quantity or weight of the contents.

4. The Federal Reserve Board administers the Consumer Credit Protection Act, which is commonly known as the _____. The Consumer Credit Protection Act is a disclosure law. It requires that credit or loan terms be disclosed by a seller of _____ goods or services, or a lender of money to be used in order to purchase _____ goods or services, to a debtor when the debtor is a natural person. It requires that the debtor be informed about the _____. The annual percentage rate of certain charges, including interest and finance, loan, appraisal, insurance, etc., fees must be stated. (It does not, however, regulate the rate of these charges.)

5. State statutes and the Postal Reorganization Act of 1970 provide that recipients of _____ will not be liable to senders for the purchase price of the goods if they do not return the merchandise.

MULTIPLE CHOICE QUESTIONS

1. The federal Consumer Protection Act (Truth-in-Lending Act):
    a. requires creditors to disclose all finance charges, including interest, in terms of annual percentage rates.
    b. establishes a maximum amount that may be charged by a lender or seller in a loan or credit transaction.
    c. is regarded as the federal usury law.
    d. applies to credit transactions between creditors and debtors without regard to the fact that they are natural persons or corporations.

2. Ordinary expenses incurred by a lender in a loan situation, which will be allowed in addition to the maximum contract rate of interest, are costs of:
    a. examining title to property, which is being given as collateral security.
    b. investigating the financial character of the borrower.
    c. drawing necessary documents.
    d. All of the above.

Chapter 47

Environmental Protection

Increased urbanization, economic growth and advanced methods of production have accentuated the conflict between freedom of contracting and the right to use one's own property, on the one hand, and the needs of society to be protected against harm, caused by pollution to the environment, on the other.

The federal Congress and the state legislatures have responded to the increased awareness of the presence and harmful effects of pollution by enacting statutes aimed at reducing contamination and improving the quality of the air, water and land.

OUTLINE

I.   Compliance with federal regulations.

    A. Many of the environmental protection statutes are administered by the Environmental Protection Agency (EPA), which has been empowered to promulgate rules in order to control emissions of pollutants.

    B. Air pollution — Clean Air Act of 1963, as amended.

       1. The establishment of quality standards is delegated to the EPA.

       2. Automobile pollution — The objective of the statute and EPA regulations is to reduce certain automobile emissions which are a source of pollution.

       3. Stationary sources of pollution (utilities and industrial plants).

    C. Water pollution — Clean Water Act (Water Pollution Control Act), as amended, and Safe Drinking Water Act.

D. Hazardous waste disposal — Resource Conservation and Recovery Act.

E. Toxic chemicals — Toxic Substances Control Act.

F. Wildlife preservation — Endangered Species Act.

G. National Environmental Policy Act (NEPA).

  1. A statement, analyzing the environmental impact of proposed federal action (including legislation), or a statement explaining why an impact statement is not required, must be prepared.

  2. Statement indicates the social benefits, risks and costs of the proposed action.

  3. Environmental impact statements are prepared by the agencies responsible for carrying out proposed actions and, in some cases, private companies which enter into contracts for major federal actions.

II. Liability for damages.

A. Common law remedies, available to people who are injured by pollution in actions based upon tort theories of negligence, strict liability and nuisance, include money damages and injunctive relief, but frequently are not successful or the relief granted inadequate.

B. Some statutes authorize private lawsuits, based upon violations or noncompliance with mandated standards.

C. Superfund — Comprehensive Environmental Response, Compensation and Liability Act (CERCLA).

  1. A federal fund to be used by the EPA for cleaning up hazardous waste disposal sites has been established.

  2. Clean-up costs may be recovered from the people who generated, transported, owned or operated the site when the waste was disposed, and/or currently own or operate the site and are jointly and severally liable.

KEY WORDS AND PHRASES IN TEXT

Pollutants
Air pollution
Clean Air Act
Environmental Protection Agency
Automobile pollution
Stationary sources of pollution
Ambient standards for common pollutants
New Source Performance Standards (NSPSs)
Best available technology
National Emission Standards for Hazardous
    Air Pollutants (NESHAPs)

Water pollution
Clean Water Act (Federal Water Pollution
    Control Act)
Hazardous waste
National Pollutant Discharge Elimination
    System (NPDES)
Resource Conservation and Recovery Act
    (RCRA)
Uniform Hazardous Waste Manifest
Toxic Substances Control Act
Safe Drinking Water Act

Endangered Species Act
National Environmental Policy Act (NEPA)
Common law liability for injuries caused by pollution (negligence, strict liability and nuisance)
Superfund (Comprehensive Environmental Response, Compensation and Liability Act)

MULTIPLE CHOICE QUESTIONS

1. The Clean Air Act as amended:
   a. establishes a national standard for air pollutants that are emitted by industrial plants.
   b. provides that each state is to develop a state implementation plan.
   c. requires that the EPA develop emission standards for hazardous air pollutants, such as sulfur dioxide and lead.
   d. All of the above are correct.

2. The major purpose of the Resource Conservation and Recovery Act's manifest (tracking) system is to:
   a. provide a framework for documenting cases in which natural persons have been injured by dangerous chemical wastes.
   b. provide a regulatory framework for the tracking of hazardous chemical wastes from the generator to the storage or disposal site.
   c. provide for a recording system in order to document the natural resources that have been adversely affected by hazardous wastes.
   d. provide a systematic record of the effect of pollutants on endangered species in the United States.

3. The National Environmental Policy Act requires that an environmental impact statement must be filed whenever:
   a. any person is going to construct a building that will affect the environment.
   b. a state is going to take action that will affect the environment.
   c. any federal governmental activity, which will affect the environment, is to be conducted.
   d. All of the above are correct.

Chapter 48

Antitrust

In the United States strong public policies, that are predicated upon the premise that economic concentration is harmful, favor the maintenance of business competition. For this reason, restraints of trade and other unfair methods of competition have long been discouraged and, in some cases, prohibited by judicial decisions and statutes. The Sherman Act of 1890 was the first major federal legislation adopted in order to deal with anticompetitive practices. It was followed by the Clayton Act in 1914. Both statutes have since been amended.

As discussed in the beginning of the chapter, the Sherman Act prohibits contracts, combinations, conspiracies and other joint actions to restrain, or limit, trade and monopolization and attempts to monopolize trade or commerce. The Clayton Act and subsequent legislation has been directed at particular types of business behavior that have the effect of reducing competition. The prohibitions, which are set forth in the Clayton Act (as amended), against price discrimination, exclusionary practices and certain mergers and acquisitions, "when their effect might be to substantially lessen competition or increase monopoly," are discussed in the second section of the chapter.

THINGS TO KEEP IN MIND

At this time, antitrust policies are undergoing critical examination and reevaluation by economists, lawyers, administrators, jurists and others. Substantial changes in federal enforcement policies appear to be occurring particularly in the area of corporate mergers and other combinations. In the early 1980s, for example, long standing, prominent antitrust litigation involving large corporations that had been initiated, in some instances, by the Department of Justice and, in other cases, by the FTC, was discontinued by the government. New Merger Guidelines have since been issued by the Department of Justice. The new Guidelines appear to indicate that there will be changes in the enforcement policies of the government.

OUTLINE

I. Introduction.

    A. Common law antecedents of antitrust statutes.

        1. General restraints of trade (agreements or promises not to compete) are against public policy and will not be enforced, but reasonable ancillary, partial restraints, which are necessary to protect a property interest (such as goodwill) may be enforced. (See Chapter 11.)

        2. Formation of "trusts" in the late nineteenth century — The trust device was used in order to engage in monopolistic and predatory tactics, the objective being to drive out small competitors in a number of industries.

    B. Enforcement of the federal antitrust laws is conferred upon both the Department of Justice and the Federal Trade Commission. In addition, persons who have been or may be injured because of violations of the provisions of antitrust laws may seek civil legal (damages) or equitable (specific performance, injunction, reformation or rescission) relief.

    C. The federal antitrust laws provide for the following exemptions:

        1. Labor organizations.

        2. Public utilities.

        3. Insurance, banking and other regulated industries.

        4. Agricultural, livestock and fishing cooperatives.

        5. Professional baseball organizations.

        6. Governmental bodies that are pursuing legitimate state interests.

        7. Firms engaging in foreign trade.

        8. Certain cooperative research ventures.

II. The Sherman Act — Prohibits unilateral and group attempts or actions to restrain trade or monopolize an area of business.

    A. Section 1 focuses on agreements that are restrictive and have a wrongful purpose.

    B. Section 2 is directed at misuses of monopoly power by one person or several people.

    C. Proscriptive nature of the Sherman Act — Tells people how they should *not* act rather than how they should act (prescriptive or regulatory).

    D. Jurisdiction.

1. In cases brought under the Sherman Act, courts have jurisdiction over natural persons, corporations and other firms that engage in interstate commerce.

2. Interstate commerce has been given a broad interpretation. The Act applies to activities that have significant anticompetitive effects on interstate commerce.

E. Who has standing, or the right, to sue in order to enforce provisions of the Act?

1. The Department of Justice.

2. State governments.

3. Private parties, who can show that:

   a. Antitrust violation was a substantial factor in an injury that was incurred, and

   b. The unlawful action of the defendant affected a business activity of the plaintiff that was intended to be protected.

F. Sanctions and remedies.

1. Criminal penalties for violations — Fine and/or imprisonment.

2. Civil remedies.

   a. Obtained by Department of Justice — Injunction, divestiture or seizure of property.

   b. Obtained by a plaintiff in a civil action — Treble damages.

G. Prohibited conduct — *Per se* violations versus the rule of reason.

1. *Per se* violations.

   a. As a matter of law, certain conduct violates the Sherman Act, without regard to proof of injury to the public, the reasonableness of the action or worthiness of motives.

   b. *Per se* violations include price fixing, horizontal market divisions, limitations on production and joint refusals to deal or coercive group boycotts.

2. The rule of reason — Unreasonable general restraints of trade are violations of the Sherman Act.

H. Section 1 and horizontal agreements among competitors.

1. Section 1 of the Sherman Act provides that: "Every contract, combination in the form of trust or otherwise, or conspiracy, in restraint of trade or commerce among the several states or with foreign nations is declared to be illegal."

2. Express agreements and conspiracies among competitors to fix prices, allocate markets and boycott competitors are *per se* violations of this section.

3. Agreements and other concerted activities, the objective of which is to restrict competition, may be implied.

   a. Concerted action aimed at fixing prices.
      1) The exchange of information among competitors or the collection and dissemination of information by a trade association, even if it results in stabilizing prices, is not alone sufficient to establish a violation of Sec. 1 of the Sherman Act.
      2) The defendant's state of mind or intent is also an element of a criminal antitrust offense.

   b. Horizontal market division — Allocating or dividing the territory in which a product is sold among competitors.

   c. Joint refusals to sell or to deal with a buyer or class of buyers, and group boycotts.

   d. Non-traditional, hidden methods of restraining competition include provisions in shopping center leases giving a major tenant the right to disapprove of other prospective tenants.

4. The rule of reason is applied to activities of trade associations, which are composed of competitors who wish to promote their common interests.

5. The rule of reason is applied to joint ventures, in which two or more firms participate for a specific purpose by pooling their resources.

I. Section 1 and vertical agreements among firms in different industries at successive stages or levels in the chain of production and/or distribution.

   1. Resale price maintenance (fair trade agreements).

      a. An agreement between a seller (manufacturer) and buyer (retailer who sells to the public), establishing a minimum or maximum price for a product, is illegal *per se*.

      b. A seller may, however, suggest a price at which its products may be sold by a retailer.

   2. Vertical market division — Territorial and customer restrictions are not violative of antitrust laws if they are reasonable.

   3. Consignment through agents — A seller who retains title to goods and bears risks associated with ownership may specify the price at which the goods are to be sold.

J. Section 2 and monopolization.

   1. Section 2 of the Sherman Act provides that: "Every person who shall monopolize or attempt to monopolize, or combine or conspire with any other

person or persons to monopolize any part of the trade or commerce among the several states, or with foreign nations shall be deemed guilty . . . "

2. The literal meaning of "monopoly" — There is only one seller of a particular product.

3. For purposes of the antitrust laws, a monopoly, or monopolization, exists when one firm controls such a high proportion of the market for a product that it is able to dictate the price and exclude competition.

4. In order to establish that a defendant has violated Section 2, the following elements must be proven:

    a. Possession of monopoly power in the relevant product (or service) market.
       1) Relevant market depends upon the character of the product or services, the availability of substitutes and the geographic area in which they are sold.
       2) Defendant's share of the market is substantial.

    b. Intentional, willful, purposeful acquisition or maintenance of monopoly power.

III. The Clayton Act.

A. Prohibits certain anticompetitive practices "where the effect" of the practice "may be to substantially lessen competition or tend to create a monopoly in any line of commerce."

B. Sanctions and remedies.

1. Criminal sanctions (Sec. 14).

    a. If a corporation is found to be guilty of a violation of a criminal provision, the corporation is criminally liable and the officers, directors and agents, who have been found to have committed or authorized the unlawful acts, are also subject to the penalties of imprisonment and/or fine.

    b. FTC and alleged violator of the Clayton Act may enter into a settlement agreement for entry of a "consent decree," in which case the violator accepts certain penalties but does not admit guilt.

2. Government initiated civil cases.

    a. FTC may issue cease and desist orders.

    b. The government may bring actions for divestiture, dissolution or divorcement.

    c. The U.S. may recover actual damages for injuries resulting from violations.

3. Private civil remedies.

   a. A civil action may be brought in order to recover damages (Sec. 4).

   b. Equitable relief may be granted if damages are inadequate and "danger of irreparable loss is immediate" (Sec. 16).

   c. A final judgment or decree rendered in a litigated criminal or civil action brought by the U.S. is *prima facie* evidence of violation of the Act (Sec. 5).

C. Section 2, as amended by the Robinson-Patman Act of 1936 — Price discrimination.

   1. It is unlawful for a seller to discriminate in price for goods or other commodities between different purchasers when the effect would be to lessen competition or tend toward monopoly, except when the difference is due to grade, quality, quantity or cost of transportation or if done, in good faith, to meet competition; nor may a seller perform services for purchasers which are not available on equal terms to all customers.

   2. It is also unlawful for any person "knowingly" to induce or receive a discriminatory price for goods.

D. Section 3 — Exclusionary practices.

   1. It is unlawful to sell, lease or fix the price of commodities on condition that the purchaser or lessee agrees not to deal in the goods of a competitor of the seller or lessor, when the effect would be to reduce competition or tend to create a monopoly.

   2. Exclusionary practices may also be violations of Section 1 of the Sherman Act, in which case the rule of reason applies and the tying arrangement may involve tying purchase of a commodity with services. (Clayton Act violations only relate to tying sale of one product with sale of another product.)

   3. Tying arrangements ("bundling").

      a. A seller, who has substantial market power, requires that a buyer of one product also agrees to buy a second, different commodity.

      b. The tying arrangement violates the Act if it will have a significant effect in the market for either product.

   4. Exclusive dealings contracts.

      a. A seller promises to supply a buyer with certain goods (and services, such as advertising) and the buyer agrees to buy products only from the seller. (See Chapter 44 regarding franchising.)

      b. Courts apply a modified rule of reason in cases involving exclusive dealings arrangements.

5. Requirements (and output) contracts.

    a. In a requirements contract, the seller agrees to furnish and the buyer promises to purchase all of a particular product that the buyer might need over a specified period of time. (See Chapter 9.)

    b. Requirements contracts violate the Act only if they substantially lessen competition in the relevant markets for the goods.

E. Section 7 — Mergers and other acquisitions.

1. Section 7, as amended by the Celler-Kefauver Act, prohibits acquisitions of stock or assets of another corporation, when the effect might be to substantially lessen competition or tend to create a monopoly in any line of business in any geographic area of the country. The purpose is to preserve competition.

2. Horizontal mergers.

    a. Horizontal combinations involve competitors in the same market.

    b. In determining whether or not a merger will tend to result in anticompetitive effects, the FTC has relied upon the degree of existing and potential concentration (market shares) of the merging firms, as well as the capital requirements and economies of scale in the industry.

    c. Courts have examined the effect of the merger on potential collusion, entry into the market and increases in efficiency, which will result in benefits to consumers.

    d. The Department of Justice Guidelines indicate that it will oppose mergers which result in the creation or expansion of "market power" — "the ability of one or more firms profitably to maintain prices above competitive levels for a significant period of time."

       1) Quantitative tests that are based upon the Herfindahl-Hirshman Index (HHI) of market concentration are set forth in the Guidelines.

       2) The HHI is calculated by adding the sum of the squares of the market shares of all the firms in a particular industry or market. HHI = $\Sigma[(\text{market share of firm A})^2 + (\text{market share of firm B})^2 + (\text{market share of firm C})^2 + \ldots (\text{market share of firm N})^2]$.

          a) If HHI is below 1,000, the industry is unconcentrated and the Justice Department will not object to a merger.

          b) If HHI is between 1,000 and 1,800, the industry is moderately concentrated. The merger may be challenged if the HHI will increase by more than 100 and if other factors are present.

          c) If HHI exceeds 1,800, the industry is highly concentrated. If, as a result of the merger, the HHI will increase by less than 50, the merger will not be challenged. If, as a result of the merger, the HHI will increase between 50 and 100, the merger may be challenged if other factors are present. If, as a result of the merger, the HHI will increase by more than 100, it is likely that the merger will be challenged.

3. Vertical mergers and acquisitions.

    a. Vertical combinations involve control over firms in industries at successive stages of production and/or distribution.

    b. Vertical mergers may result in restrictions in supply of resources or inputs to competitors (backward acquisitions) or blocking or foreclosing competitors from part of a market for the product or service.
       1) Such vertical combinations result in barriers to entry into the industry itself or the market and sale of a product.
       2) Factors considered by the FTC and courts include definitions of the relevant product (and the amount of product differentiation), the degree of concentration and the market for the product.

    c. The Department of Justice Guidelines appear to deemphasize the distinction between horizontal and vertical mergers.

4. Conglomerate mergers which increase the diversification of multi-product or multi-industry firm.

    a. It is often difficult to measure latent changes in market structure, firms' market shares and concentration ratios and indexes.

    b. Potential exists for offsetting a loss in one product (caused possibly by price cutting or extensive advertising to drive out competitors) by profitable operations in other products.

5. Industry-wide conditions may be investigated by the FTC in order to identify reasons for reduced performance, evidenced by high prices and profits, lack of product innovation or absence of entry by new firms.

6. State statutes set forth formal procedures for mergers and acquisitions. See Chapter 42.

F. Section 8 — Interlocking directorates.

1. An interlocking directorate exists when one person serves as a director of two or more corporations.

2. Section 8 prohibits interlocking directorates if one of the corporations has capital, surplus and undistributed profits exceeding one million dollars, when elimination of competition between the corporations would violate the antitrust laws.

IV. Administration of Sherman and Clayton Acts.

A. Federal antitrust laws are enforced by the antitrust division of the Justice Department, which is part of the executive branch of government, and the Federal Trade Commission (FTC), an independent agency, both of which have issued Guidelines.

B. Current Justice Department Guidelines set forth enforcement policies relating to opposing mergers based upon Section 1 of the Sherman Act and Section 7 of the Clayton Act.

C. The FTC has power to prevent "unfair methods of competition in commerce and unfair or deceptive acts or practices in commerce" (Section 5 of the Federal Trade Commission Act as amended), including:

    1. Investigatory power relative to alleged antitrust violations.

    2. Authority to make recommendations and report to Congress.

    3. Power to promulgate rules, policy statement and regulations defining particular acceptable or unacceptable acts or practices.

V. State-action defense.

A. Government entities are not automatically exempt from the antitrust laws.

B. State-action doctrine — Exemption is given to restraints of trade which are "clearly articulated and affirmatively expressed as state policy" and "actively supervised" by the state or other governmental unit.

KEY WORDS AND PHRASES IN TEXT

Antitrust laws
Monopoly
Monopoly power
Trusts
Sherman Act
Agreements that restrain trade or
    commerce
Exemptions from antitrust laws
Standing to sue
Department of Justice
Divestiture
Per se violation
Rule of reason
Sherman Act—Section 1
Horizontal agreements which violate
    Section 1
Price fixing
Group boycotts
Horizontal market division
Trade associations
Joint ventures
Vertical agreements which violate
    Section 1
Resale price maintenance

Fair trade laws not authorized
Consumer Goods Pricing Act
Vertical market division
Sherman Act—Section 2
Monopolization
Market share test
Intent requirement
Attempted monopolization
Clayton Act
Federal Trade Commission
Consent decree
Price discrimination—Section 2 of
    Clayton Act
Exclusionary practices—Section 3 of
    Clayton Act
Tying arrangements
Exclusive dealings contracts
Requirement contracts
Mergers—Section 7 of Clayton Act
Horizontal mergers
Herfindahl index of concentration
Vertical mergers
Conglomerate mergers
State-action defense

FILL-IN QUESTIONS

1. A contract of employment contains a provision to the effect that the employee agrees that, while employed and for ten years thereafter, he will not engage in the same business in competition with his employer anywhere in the U.S. This is a _____ restraint of trade and will not be enforced. If the employee promises not to compete with the employer while employed by him or her and for one year thereafter in a limited geographic area, the provision will be enforced because it is a _____ restraint.

2. A voting trust is a legal arrangement whereby shareholders give the right to vote their shares to a trustee. Under Section 1 of the Sherman Act, it is not illegal to create a voting trust, unless it is a _____.

3. Labor and agricultural organizations are _____ from the federal antitrust laws. Unlike other professional sports, _____ is also _____ from the antitrust laws.

4. The U.S. (Department of Justice) can bring a _____ action against an individual or corporation, which violates the Sherman Act. An individual or corporation, which has been injured as a result of a violation of the Sherman Act, may recover _____ in a _____ action against the violator.

5. As a matter of law, certain forms of restraints of trade are treated as violations of the Sherman Act, even if they are reasonable and cannot be shown to have been injurious. They are referred to as _____ illegal activities and include _____.

6. The Sherman Act is _____ rather than prescriptive because it tells businesses how they should act. The effect is _____ rather than regulating business conduct.

7. The Clayton Act declares that certain activities are unlawful. Section 2 prohibits _____; Section 3 prohibits certain tying and _____ contracts, and Section 8 prohibits certain corporate purchases and acquisitions of stock or assets of other corporations when the effect is to _____ or tend to create a monopoly.

8. With regard to its authority to enforce the provisions of the antitrust laws, the Federal Trade Commission has power to issue _____ orders. It also has power to _____.

9. The term, monopolize, is not defined in the antitrust laws. Any person, however, who _____, violates Section 2 of the Sherman Act. The Clayton Act prohibits certain monopolistic practices, such as _____, when the effect might be to reduce competition or tend to create a monopoly, and interlocking directorates.

10. A and B Corporations both manufacture the same product and are planning to merge. The merger will be a _____ merger or combination. If the effect of the merger will be _____, it is prohibited by the antitrust laws.

11. C Corporation manufactures a particular product, which is sold by D Corporation in its chain of retail stores. C and D Corporations enter into a contract providing that C will supply all of D's requirements for 20 years and will not sell the product to stores, with which D competes, and D agrees that it will sell the product at a price to be determined by C. This is _____ restraint of trade.

MULTIPLE CHOICE QUESTIONS

1. Strawberry, Coffee and Vanilla are operators of ice cream manufacturing plants in a metropolitan area. They meet informally to compare prices and production and have agreed to divide the market into three equal shares. They have not, however, agreed to sell their comparable ice cream at the same prices.
   a. As they are not fixing prices, this is not illegal *per se.*
   b. The arrangement is an illegal vertical restraint of trade.
   c. The arrangement is an illegal tying agreement under the Clayton Act.
   d. The division of the market is an illegal restraint of trade.

2. A trade association engages in compiling data about an industry and supplying the firms participating in the industry with the collected information. The trade association:
   a. has engaged in an activity that is a *per se* violation of the Sherman Act.
   b. and its members have engaged in an activity that is a *per se* violation of the Sherman Act.
   c. violated the Sherman Act, if its activities go beyond information gathering and supplying and are a facade for price fixing or dividing the market.
   d. does not violate the Sherman Act, if its activities go beyond information gathering and supplying, when the members of the association represent a minority group in the industry.

3. The impact of antitrust legislation is felt directly and most heavily by:
   a. sellers of a commodity in a market in which few firms compete.
   b. sellers of a commodity in a market in which many firms compete.
   c. consumers, who purchase a commodity, which is produced by only a few manufacturers.
   d. the U.S. government to which fines, imposed for violations of the antitrust laws, are payable.

4. The following organizations are *not* exempt from the provisions of the antitrust laws:
   a. an American firm that engages in exporting goods to foreign countries.
   b. an American manufacturing firm that sells its products in three states.
   c. a labor union which represents workers in three states.
   d. an agricultural cooperative which sells the products of farmers in 20 states.

5. Resale price maintenance is:
   a. a form of vertical price fixing.
   b. a form of horizontal price fixing.
   c. a means of territorial allocation.
   d. never a *per se* violation of the antitrust laws.

6. P Corp., a large national manufacturer of paper products, acquires more than 50% of the outstanding shares of common stock of L Co., a national producer of paper.

P Corp. had previously purchased its paper needs from competitors of L Co. but now obtains all of its requirements from L Co. alone.

a. The acquisition of the stock of L Co. does not violate the Clayton Act because it was not a purchase of the assets of L Co.

b. Competitors of L Co. have standing to sue P Corp. under the Clayton Act and may recover damages for the actual harm incurred.

c. Competitors of P Corp. have standing to sue P Corp. under the Clayton Act and may recover treble damages.

d. This is an example of a horizontal combination, which is prohibited by the Clayton Act.

Questions 7, 8 and 9 are based on the following data:

		Alpha Industry				*Beta Industry*	
Firm	*% of sales revenue*	*Minimum efficient scale as a % of the total market*	*Capital required for minimum efficient scale, in millions*	*Firm*	*% of sales revenue*	*Minimum efficient scale as a % of the total market*	*Capital required for minimum efficient scale, in millions*
1	40	20	$100	1	15	2.5	$ 2
2	20	5	70	2	15	2.5	2
3	20	5	70	3	15	2.0	3
4	10	2	50	4	15	2.0	3
5	10	2	55	5	10	1.0	2
				6	10	1.0	2
				7	10	1.0	2
				8	10	0.5	2
5	100%	34%	$345	8	100%	12.5%	$18

7. A consolidation is being considered by firms 4 and 5 in Alpha industry.

a. A consolidation is different than a merger and is not within the purview of the Clayton Act.

b. Firm 3 cannot bring an action in order to obtain an injunction.

c. The FTC will issue a cease and desist order because the consolidation will reduce competition in the industry, even though firms 3 and 4 will be forced out of the industry if they do not consolidate.

d. The FTC may not issue a cease and desist order, even though the consolidation will result in fewer firms in the industry, if it is established that firms 3 and 4 will be forced out of the industry if they do not consolidate.

8. Which of the following statements is *incorrect*?

a. The opportunity for collusion is greater in Alpha industry than it is in Beta industry.

b. The degree of concentration is higher in Beta industry than it is in Alpha industry.

c. A new firm will be more likely to enter Beta industry than Alpha industry.

d. Firm 1 in Alpha industry has a more dominant position than firms 1 and 2 combined in Beta industry.

9. Assume that there is no evidence of direct agreement among the firms in Beta industry but that they all charge the same price. They are being prosecuted by the U.S. Department of Justice. The prosecution will:
   a. not be successful because there is no evidence of a conspiracy.
   b. be successful because the fact that they all charge a uniform price is sufficient evidence of a conspiracy.
   c. be successful because proof of evidence of a conspiracy may be implied from the fact that the firms simultaneously had changed their previously varying prices to the uniform price.
   d. none of the above.

10. An agreement between a manufacturer of gidgets and a wholesaler dealer not to sell any parts used to repair the gidgets to a particular retail seller is an illegal:
    a. joint boycott or tying contract.
    b. exclusive dealings and tying contract.
    c. vertical price fixing agreement.
    d. monopolization.

11. An agreement between a manufacturer of photocopy machines and a lessee, to whom the manufacturer leases a machine, whereby the lessee agrees not to purchase its paper from any supplier other than the machine lessor, is an example of:
    a. a joint boycott and price fixing contract.
    b. price fixing and an exclusive dealings contract.
    c. exclusive dealings or tying contract.
    d. a fair trade agreement.

Chapter 49

Employment and Labor Relations Law

The objectives of government regulatory legislation affecting the employment relationship are to protect the health, safety and general welfare of the nation's workforce and to promote an environment that is relatively free from industrial strife and discriminatory practices. The major focus in this chapter is upon areas of employment law that are currently of concern. Topics included, therefore, are unions and collective bargaining, discrimination in employment, wrongful discharge of at will employees, workers' health and safety protection and employees' income security.

THINGS TO KEEP IN MIND

1. States as well as the federal government have enacted statutes dealing with employment. For example, workers' compensation laws, providing for payments in case of employment related death, injury or disease, are state statutes. In some cases, such as the regulation of minimum wages and maximum hours or work, state laws often duplicate the federal statutes and apply to employees who may not be covered by the Fair Labor Standards Act.

2. The applicability of many of the laws referred to in this chapter is limited to people who are classified as being employees. You may, therefore, wish to refer to Chapter 32, in which the criteria for distinguishing agency relationships from those of employment are discussed.

OUTLINE

I. Unions and collective bargaining.

    A. The purposes of early regulation of the employment relationship was to protect workers' rights to organize and collectively bargain with employers.

B. Federal statutes.

    1. Norris-La Guardia Act (1932) — Recognition was given to rights of employees to organize and engage in peaceful strikes, picketing and boycotts.

    2. National Labor Relations Act or Wagner Act (1935).

        a. Provides for creation of the National Labor Relations Board (NLRB).

        b. Sets forth certain unfair management practices.

    3. Labor-Management Relations Act or Taft-Hartley Act (1947).

        a. Sets forth certain unfair union practices.

        b. Prohibits closed shops.
          1) Union membership may not be required in order to obtain employment.
          2) Union shops are permitted so that employees may be required to become union members within a specified period of time after obtaining employment.

        c. Empowers the President to obtain an injunction against a strike for an eighty-day cooling off period if the strike would result in a national emergency.

    4. Labor-Management Reporting and Disclosure Act — Landrum-Griffin Act (1959).

        a. Establishes a bill of rights for employees.

        b. Regulates internal operations of labor organizations.
          1) Regulates union elections in order to assure union democracy.
          2) Requires that officers be bonded and prohibits certain loans to officers and members.
          3) Requires filing of reports with the Secretary of Labor.

        c. Prohibits hot cargo contracts — Agreements between union and employers that employer will not handle, use, sell, etc. goods of other employers.

C. The right to organize — Employees have the right to form and join unions.

    1. If 30 percent of the workers in a job category sign authorization cards supporting a union election, the election may be voluntarily initiated by the employer or required by the NLRB.

    2. NLRB oversees election procedures in order to assure fairness.

D. Unfair labor practices.

    1. Employer practices that are treated as unfair to labor because of the Wagner Act.

    a. Interfering with efforts of employees to form, join or assist labor organizations (unions).

    b. Dominating or contributing to labor unions.

    c. Discriminating against employees because of their union activities.

    d. Discriminating against employees who file charges or give testimony to the NLRB.

    e. Refusing to bargain in good faith with representatives of employees (NLRB certified union).

2. Union practices that are treated as being unfair because of the Taft-Hartley Act:

    a. Refusing to bargain in good faith with employer.

    b. Charging excessive or discriminatory initiation fees or dues.

    c. Causing an employer to pay for work that was not performed (featherbedding).

    d. Coercing or restraining employees from exercising their rights to join a union.

    e. Causing or attempting to cause an employer to discriminate against employees or to encourage (or discourage) membership in a particular union.

    f. Striking, picketing or engaging in secondary boycotts for illegal purposes.

E. Collective bargaining.

1. After election, the union is the exclusive bargaining representative for employees.

2. The employer and legally recognized union are required to engage in collective bargaining in good faith when negotiating wages, benefits, working conditions and other terms of employment contract.

F. Strikes may be called by union if collective bargaining process breaks down.

1. Employer may hire replacement employees.

2. Illegal strikes.

    a. Secondary boycott—striking or picketing against firms that do business with the primary employer is illegal.

    b. Hot cargo contract, in which employer agrees with union that the employer will not deal with nonunion firms, is illegal.

  c. Wildcat strikes by a minority of the employees, violent strikes and sitdown strikes, in which workers refuse to leave the place of employment, are illegal.

II. Employment discrimination.

  A. General requirements of Title VII of the Civil Rights Act (1964) as amended by the Equal Employment Opportunity Act (1972), which is administered by the Equal Employment Opportunity Commission (EEOC).

   1. Coverage — Title VII applies to employers employing more than 15 workers, labor unions having more than 15 members, employment agencies, federal, state and local governments and government agencies.

   2. Protected classes — Title VII prohibits discrimination in hiring, discharging, terms of employment, compensation, promotion and granting of privileges based upon religion, sex, race, color or national origin unless there is a bona fide occupational qualification for employment.

   3. Procedures and remedies.

    a. Person who alleges that he or she has been injured because of discrimination files claim with the EEOC.

    b. EEOC investigates and seeks a voluntary conciliation, a settlement between the employer and employee.

    c. EEOC may sue the employer; only if EEOC decides not to sue may employee sue employer.

    d. Remedies — Damages for back pay, retroactive promotion, injunction (prohibiting future discrimination) and other corrective relief.

  B. Disparate treatment discrimination.

   1. *Prima facie* case of discrimination is established by showing:

    a. Plaintiff is a member of a protected class.

    b. Plaintiff applied and was qualified for the position in question.

    c. Plaintiff was rejected by the employer.

    d. Employer continued to seek applicants for the position and filled the position with a person who was not a member of a protected class.

   2. If a *prima facie* case is established, there is a presumption of discrimination that can be rebutted by the employer (defendant) showing that a legitimate nondiscriminatory reason existed for its employment decision; the plaintiff then has an opportunity to show that the reason given was not the true reason for the employer's decision.

  C. Disparate impact discrimination.

1. An apparently neutral and fair employment practice may have a discriminatory effect.

2. A plaintiff can establish a *prima facie* case and, therefore, does not have to prove the existence of discriminatory intent by showing:

    a. The employer employs a smaller percentage of people who are members of a protected class than would be expected when compared to the number of applicants or the percentage of members of the protected class in the local population.

    b. The low percentage of such employees is the result of an employer practice that has the effect of excluding large numbers of members of the protected class.

D. Defenses that may be asserted by an employer who allegedly discriminated.

   1. Business necessity — Job related tests and educational requirements.

   2. Bona fide occupational qualifications — Religion or gender goes to essence of the employment position.

   3. Bona fide fair seniority system.

E. Affirmative action.

   1. Executive orders issued by Presidents and regulations of the Department of Labor have required that government contractors must undertake affirmative recruitment efforts and ensure nondiscriminatory treatment of employees and applicants for positions.

   2. Title VII does not prohibit an employer or union from adopting a voluntary affirmative action hiring or promotion plan in an attempt to remedy racial or gender imbalances.

   3. Affirmative action programs which result in discharging employees who have more seniority than employees who are retained may violate the Fourteenth Amendment, and possibly Title VII.

F. Sexual harassment.

   1. *Quid pro quo* harrassment — Hiring, promotion or granting of employment is dependent upon the giving of sexual favors.

   2. Harassing environment discrimination — Continual offensive sexual jokes, comments, advances create an uncomfortable work environment.

   3. Employer is liable for sexual harassment engaged in by supervisory employees but not for harassment engaged in by lower level employees unless the employer knew or should have known about the harassment and failed to take corrective action.

G. Other types of discrimination.

    1. Religious discrimination.

    2. Age discrimination — Age Discrimination in Employment Act.

III. Wrongful discharge.

A. Common law at will employment doctrine — An at will employee may be discharged by his or her employer for a good reason, no reason or even a bad reason.

B. There has been a trend in the states to recognize exceptions to this rule in statutes and judicial decisions.

    1. Public policy exception.

        a. Employee may not be discharged for reasons that violate public policies such as serving on a jury or refusing to commit an illegal act.

        b. Under federal law and in some states, whistle blowers are protected from being discharged under certain circumstances.

    2. Contract theories.

        a. Statements of employer's policy in handbook or other oral or written communications to the effect that employees will be discharged only for good and sufficient cause are part of the contract of employment, for breach of which some courts will award damages.

        b. In a few states, courts have held that there is an implied covenant of good faith in all employment contracts, which is violated when an employer arbitrarily and without justification discharges an employee.

    3. Tort theory — In some states, in extreme cases, courts recognize a tort cause of action for intentional infliction of emotional harm or defamation because of abusive employer discharge procedures.

IV. Worker safety and health — Statutes dealing with working conditions.

A. State Workers' Compensation Acts.

    1. Employers are strictly liable to employees for accidental death, injury and disease arising out of or during the course of their employment.

    2. The amount of compensation is limited to statutory scheduled benefits, which vary from state to state.

    3. Common law defenses, such as the fellow servant rule, assumption of the risk and comparative (or contributory) negligence are eliminated.

    4. Rulings made by state agencies that administer Workers' Compensation Acts are subject to judicial review.

5. In order to recover workers' compensation, a worker must establish:

    a. He or she is an employee and not an independent contractor.

    b. The injury or illness arose out of or in the course of employment.

B. Occupational Safety and Health Act (1970).

    1. Employees must have a place of employment that is "free from recognized hazards" that may result in death or serious harm.

    2. Employees are required to comply with safety and health rules.

    3. Occupational Safety and Health Administration promulgates rules, establishes safety and health standards and may conduct investigations and inspections.

    4. Employers are required to keep detailed records relating to accidents, injuries and illnesses of employees.

V. Statutes relating to income and retirement security.

A. Social Security Act (1935) as amended.

    1. Provides income when families' income ceases or is reduced because of death, disability or retirement.

    2. Federal Insurance Contributions Act (FICA) requires that employers deduct a specified percentage (scheduled to increase in steps to 7.65% in 1990) of employees' wages and pay a matching sum on all earnings up to a statutory maximum amount.

    3. Employers are required to maintain accurate records, file quarterly reports and, in most cases, make monthly deposits.

    4. Medicare.

        a. Federal health insurance available to those who are 65 or older and others who are disabled covering inpatient hospital care, skilled nursing home and home health care and some other medical costs.

        b. Additional optional insurance is available to cover physician services.

        c. Medicaid — Program for additional hospital insurance.

B. Employee Retirement Income Security Act (ERISA).

    1. Protects private pensions by establishing standards which require that pension plans be adequately funded.

    2. Applies to private pension plans provided by employers or unions covering 25 or more employees or members.

3. Tax deferred individual retirement income accounts may also be established by employees and those who are self employed.

4. Legislation is administered by the Labor Management Service Administration of the Department of Labor. Regulations have also been promulgated by the Internal Revenue Service.

C. Unemployment compensation.

1. Joint federal-state program.

2. Tax is imposed upon employers in covered businesses and paid into unemployment insurance plans.

3. Workers, who have been discharged without cause, are entitled to draw payments for a specified period of time (which varies from state to state) if:

   a. They have been employed in a covered industry.

   b. They worked for at least a minimum period of time or earned at least a minimum amount of wages. The time periods and minimum earned wages vary from state to state.

   c. They are ready, willing and able to accept another position.

VI. Fair Labor Standards Act, as amended — Wage and Hour Law (1938).

A. Child labor provisions.

1. With some exceptions, children under the age of 14 may not be employed.

2. Children between the ages of 14 and 16 may be employed in nonhazardous occupations, but only during nonschool hours.

3. Children, who are less than 18, may not be employed in hazardous occupations.

B. Minimum wage to be paid by covered employers is established periodically by Congress.

C. Employees, who work more than 40 hours per week, are required to be paid time and a half for the overtime.

D. Exempt employees include executives, administrators, professionals and outside sales personnel.

E. Employees working on government construction projects are required to be paid at the prevailing wage rate in the geographic area (Davis-Bacon Act—1931).

F. Manufacturers or suppliers, who have entered into contracts with agencies of the federal government, are required to pay employees a minimum wage and time and a half for overtime (Walsh-Healy Public Contract Act—1936).

KEY WORDS AND PHRASES IN TEXT

Right to organize and bargain collectively
Norris-LaGuardia Act
National Labor Relations Act (Wagner Act)
National Labor Relations Board (NLRB)
Taft-Hartley Act
Landrum Griffin Act
Right of employees to organize (form
    and join unions)
Unfair labor practices
Collective bargaining
Strikes (legal or illegal)
Secondary boycott
"Hot cargo" agreement
"Wildcat" strike
"Sitdown" strike
"Cooling-off" period
Title VII of the Civil Rights Act of 1964
Equal Employment Opportunity Commission
Protected classes
Title VII voluntary conciliation
Disparate treatment discrimination
Prima facie case of illegal disparate
    treatment discrimination
Disparate impact discrimination
Prima facie case of illegal disparate
    impact discrimination
Business necessity defense
Bona fide occupational qualification
Bona fide seniority system defense
Affirmative action
Sexual harassment

Quid pro quo harassment
Harassing environment discrimination
Religious discrimination
Age discrimination
Age Discrimination in Employment Act
    (ADEA)
Wrongful discharge
At will employment
Exceptions to at will employment
    discharge doctrine
Public policy exceptions to at will
    employment doctrine
Whistle-blowing
Contract theory exceptions to at will
    employment doctrine
Implied (in fact) employment contract
Implied covenant of good faith
Tort theory of wrongful discharge
State Workers' Compensation Laws
Occupational Safety and Health Act
Occupational Safety and Health
    Administration (OSHA)
OSHA safety standards
General duty clause
Employee Retirement Income Security
    Act (ERISA)
Vesting of right to pension benefits
Investment guarantees
Rehabilitation Act of 1973
Social Security Act of 1935
Fair Labor Standards Act of 1935

FILL-IN QUESTIONS

1. Recognition of the rights of employees to organize was first accorded in the
    _____ Act of 1932. The public policy encouraging
    collective bargaining is supported by provisions in federal labor relations laws, such
    as the _____ Act of 1935, which provides that the
    refusal to bargain collectively with designated representatives of labor organi-
    zations is an unfair labor practice, and the _____ Act
    of 1947, which provides that the refusal to bargain collectively with represen-
    tatives of employers is an unfair labor practice.

2. Today, _____ shops (requiring that union membership be a prerequisite
    to employment) are prohibited. _____ shops are, however, legal in
    states which do not have _____ laws. In order to have
    continued employment, employees may, therefore, be required to become members
    of a labor organization within a specified period of time.

3. Title VII of the Civil Rights Act as amended prohibits discrimination in employment based upon race, color, _____. The statute is administered by the _____ Commission.

4. If an employee is not hired for a specified term, he or she is considered to be an _____ employee. The common law rule has been that an _____ employee can be discharged at any time by an employer without liability. The employer, therefore, can discharge the employee with "good cause, no cause or even bad cause." The trend has been to recognize exceptions to this rule. Some states rely upon _____ theories, others upon _____ theories and a few upon tort theories in order to provide remedies to _____ employees who have been wrongfully discharged.

5. In general, employees, who incur accidental injuries or diseases or die as a result of or in the course of their employment, have a right to recover under the terms of state _____ laws and the federal _____ _____ Act, which provides for survivors and disability insurance.

6. Because of common law principles, employers are required to provide their employees with a safe place of employment. This common law principle has been reinforced by state statutes and by the federal _____ Act.

7. _____ is a joint federal-state plan, which requires that _____ pay a tax on their payrolls to the _____ Insurance Fund, and provides that eligible employees, who have been discharged without cause, may receive periodic payments from the _____ Insurance Fund while they are unemployed.

MULTIPLE CHOICE QUESTIONS

1. The employees at the PQ Manufacturing Company plant have elected the LMW Union as their representative for collective bargaining purposes. The president of the local chapter of the LMW Union is Smith.
    a. If PQ Manufacturing Company demotes Smith because she filed a complaint with the NLRB, it has committed an unfair labor practice.
    b. If PQ Manufacturing Company gives Smith $3,000 to be used for union purposes, it has committed an unfair labor practice.
    c. If PQ Manufacturing Company agrees with the LMW Union that Smith will continue to be paid her regular wages but will not be expected to work for PQ Manufacturing Company for more than four hours a week, it has committed an unfair labor practice.
    d. If PQ Manufacturing Company engages in any of these activities, it has committed an unfair labor practice.

2. Title VII of the Civil Rights Act of 1964 prohibits certain employers that engage in interstate commerce from discriminating against potential and existing employees because of their race, color, sex, religion or national origin. Title VII:
    a. is administered by the Department of Labor.
    b. has been interpreted as prohibiting discrimination based upon the sexual preference of an applicant for a job.

    c. prohibits unions and employment agencies from discriminating because of sex, race, color, religion or national origin.

    d. also prohibits employment discrimination based upon age.

3. Title VII of the Civil Rights Act of 1964 prohibits certain employers that engage in interstate commerce from discriminating against potential and existing employees because of their race, color, sex, religion or national origin. Title VII:

    a. prohibits employers from establishing educational criteria for different jobs.

    b. does not prohibit such discrimination if the employer can show that it is based upon a bona fide occupational qualification for a position.

    c. requires that every covered employer adopt an affirmative action plan.

    d. provides that a person, who believes that he or she is a victim of discrimination, may directly and immediately sue the employer and, if successful, recover treble damages.

4. Emeree, an at will employee, worked for Rogue for five years but was discharged yesterday. Emeree will probably be successful in a lawsuit against Rogue for wrongful discharge if Rogue fired Emeree for the following reason:

    a. After notifying Rogue that he had been called for jury duty, Emeree served on a jury for one week.

    b. Emeree refused to follow Rogue's instructions to make repairs at the place of employment.

    c. Emeree assaulted one of Rogue's customers.

    d. Rogue's business has not been profitable for the past year and she has made a business decision to reduce the staff.

5. Workers' compensation laws are:

    a. governed by federal regulation.

    b. designed to eliminate some common law defenses, such as the fellow servant rule, when an employee is injured.

    c. not applicable if an employee's negligence contributed to his own injury.

    d. applicable to all employees and agents.

6. While driving an automobile, Davidson was injured in an automobile accident. Davidson will not be able to recover workers' compensation if it is proven that at the time of the accident:

    a. Davidson was on his employer's business but was negligent in the operation of the vehicle.

    b. Davidson was driving from home to his place of employment.

    c. Davidson was using his personal automobile in order to call on a client of his employer.

    d. All of the above answers are correct.

Questions 7 and 8 are based on the following fact situation: The ABC Co. is a medium sized manufacturing firm. Its only factory is located in Pennsylvania, where it employs 100, including eight women above the age of 16 and five children, who are 15 years of age. All employees work a minimum of 38 hours per week and are paid a minimum of $5.00 per hour. Sales of its product in Pennsylvania account for 90% of ABC Co.'s business.

7. Under the general rules of the Federal Fair Labors Standards Act, ABC Co.:

    a. violated the statute because it employed children under the age of 16 and did not fall under an exemption.

b. violated that statute because its employees worked less than 40 hours a week.
c. did not violate the statute by employing children if the work they did was non-hazardous.
d. did not violate the statute because it paid more than minimum wage.

8.   ABC Co.:
a. is exempt from the Federal Occupational Safety and Health Act because all of its employees are working in the state of Pennsylvania.
b. is exempt from the Federal Occupational Safety and Health Act only if Pennsylvania has equivalent legislation.
c. is subject to the Federal Equal Opportunity Act because it engages in interstate commerce.
d. is not subject to the Federal Equal Pay Act if it pays its female workers less than it pays its male workers because less than 10% of its work force is female.

Unit Eight

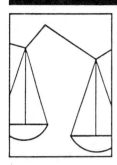

PROPERTY AND
ITS PROTECTION

Property refers to the collection of rights and interests associated with the ownership of things. Traditionally, real property (rights and interests relating to land and those things growing on the land or affixed to it or contained above or below it) has been accorded special status by the law. All other things, which are capable of being owned, are treated as personal property. Note that contracts, the topic of Unit One, frequently affect the rights of owners of property and that, if the property is personal property, it may be the subject matter of commercial transactions, which are covered in Unit Two.

The nature of personal property, how it may be acquired and transferred and the bailment relationship, which is created when one, who has possession of personal property, transfers possession of it to another, are discussed in Chapters 50 and 51.

The nature of real property, the various forms of present and future interests that may exist in such property, the manner of its transfer and restrictions on its use are presented in Chapter 52. The subject matter of Chapter 53 is the landlord-tenant relationship that exists when a tenant is given possessory rights in real property.

Owners and others, having interests in real and personal property, will incur financial or economic loss if their property is destroyed or damaged. In such case, in order to provide funds so that their property can be replaced, they may obtain insurance, the subject matter of Chapter 54. Other forms of insurance, such as life insurance and automobile insurance, are also covered in Chapter 54.

Chapter 50

Personal Property

Personal property includes rights and interests in things, other than real property, which are capable of being possessed. Personal property may be tangible or intangible. The chapter deals mainly with the ways in which such property may be acquired and transferred.

THINGS TO KEEP IN MIND

Property is not an object itself. Rather, it is the collection of rights and interests, associated with ownership, that are protected by law.

OUTLINE

I. The nature of personal property — The rights and interests in things, other than real property, which are moveable and capable of being possessed and controlled (chattels).

    A. Tangible personal property — Rights in moveable property that is subject to physical possession.

    B. Intangible personal property — Rights in a thing that lacks physical substance, e.g., contract rights, ideas, stocks, bonds, computer programs, utility services.

    C. Fixtures — Personal property that is attached to real property.

II. Property rights and ownership title.

    A. Personal property rights include:

    1. Right to possession.

    2. Right to make disposition by sale, gift, rental, lease, etc.

B. Ways in which title to property may be held.

    1. Fee simple — Entire collection of ownership rights held by one person.

    2. Concurrent ownership by two or more persons.

        a. Tenancy in common — Two or more persons own undivided shares, which may be unequal, in property, transferable during their lifetimes and by inheritance, without rights of survivorship among the co-tenants.

        b. Joint tenancy with right of survivorship.
            1) Two or more persons own equal undivided interests, which were acquired simultaneously, and have equal rights to use, enjoy, etc. and rights of survivorship.
            2) The transferor must have clearly indicated an intention to create a joint tenancy.
            3) A joint tenant may sever and transfer his or her interest during his or her lifetime (partition).

        c. There is a presumption that a cotenancy is a tenancy in common.

        d. Tenancy by the entirety — A joint tenancy existing between spouses, which cannot be transferred by either spouse without the consent of the other.

        e. Community property — Undivided interests held by spouses in property acquired during the course of marriage in Arizona, California, Idaho, Louisiana, Nevada, New Mexico, Texas, Washington, Wisconsin and Puerto Rico.

III. Acquisition and transfer of ownership of personal property.

A. Possession or occupation.

    1. Possession, with intent to control and exclude others, gives one rights with respect to personal property.

    2. One may take possession of unowned property, such as wild animals, fish in their native state and personal property that has been voluntarily abandoned.

B. Purchase — Subject of Uniform Commercial Code and Chapters 16 to 19.

C. Gift — Voluntary transfer of ownership rights without receipt of consideration.

    1. Requirements for effective gift.

        a. Delivery by donor.
            1) Actual physical transfer of possession to donee.

2) Constructive delivery by transferring symbol, such as key to safe deposit box or stock certificate, to donee without retention of control or dominion.

3) Constructive delivery to a third person with unconditional and absolute instructions to deliver to donee. (Gifts to minors by delivery to a custodian are covered by a Uniform Act.)

b. Donative intent — Donor intends to presently transfer rights of ownership and relinquishes control.

c. Acceptance by donee.

2. Types of gifts.

a. *Inter vivos* — Absolute, present, irrevocable transfer during donor's lifetime.

b. *Causa mortis* -- Transfer given in contemplation of imminent death as a result of illness or peril. Revocable:
1) Expressly by donor while living.
2) If and when donor recovers or survives peril.
3) Upon death of donee before donor.

D. Accession — Annexation or addition of new value through labor or materials to existing personal property.

1. Without consent of owner.

a. If innocent accession is not severable and the identity of the original object is changed or the value added exceeds the prior value of the property, improver has ownership rights, but original owner recovers value of lost property.

b. If accession is willful, original owner is usually entitled to the property with the improvements.

2. Annexation pursuant to contract, with owner's consent.

a. Owner retains rights to property with the improvements.

b. If owner fails to pay for contracted improvements, the improver may exercise possessory artisan's or mechanic's lien by selling property, retaining part of the price to reimburse himself or herself and giving balance to owner.

E. Confusion.

1. Goods, owned by a number of people, may be commingled so that they cannot be identified.

2. Fungible goods — Every unit is exactly the same as every other unit, e.g., grain, oil, livestock, steel, logs, money.

3. If confusion occurs because of an agreement, an innocent mistake or an act of a third person:

   a. If proportionate ownership shares are known, all parties have rights to their proportionate shares.

   b. If amounts owned are unknown, each party shares equally in ownership.

4. If confusion is caused intentionally or because of negligence of a party:

   a. If there has been no loss, each party shares as in 3 above.

   b. If there has been a loss, only the innocent parties share in the manner set forth in 3 above.

F. Lost, abandoned and mislaid property.

1. Mislaid or misplaced — Owner intentionally left property at a location that was inadvertently forgotten. Owner of premises, where property has been found, is entrusted with holding property as a bailee for owner. (See Chapter 51.)

2. Lost — Property is accidentally, involuntarily left by owner.

   a. Finder's right of possession is good against all but true owner.

   b. In many states, if found on private property by one who is trespassing, owner of the premises holds lost property as bailee for true owners.

   c. If found by an employee, employer holds lost property as bailee.

3. Abandoned — Owner discarded property without intending to reclaim it. Property belongs to first person who takes possession with intention of owning it.

4. Treasure trove — Nontrespassing finder has right to possession of money, which has been hidden so long in the past that it is unlikely owner will return.

5. Estray statutes — Finder of lost property becomes owner after publication of notice, if property is not reclaimed by true owner within statutory period.

G. Inheritance — Discussed in Chapter 56.

H. Creation or production — Property created through mental or physical labor belongs to producer or creator.

1. Patents — Federal statute gives inventors monopolies or exclusive right to use their inventions for 17 years in exchange for full disclosure.

2. Trademarks — (Federal Statute) — Perpetual protection from infringement is given to one who first adopts and uses a distinctive symbol, design or mark.

3. Copyright — Federal statute prohibits reproduction of literary or other creative works, without permission, for the life of the creator plus fifty years. This is subject to some exceptions, such as "fair use," library reproduction and works created prior to 1978.

4. These rights are protected because of the law of torts. See Chapter 5.

KEY WORDS AND PHRASES IN TEXT

Property
Real property (realty or real estate)
Personal property (personalty or chattels)
Tangible property
Intangible property
Rights to possess and dispose of property
Ownership title (such as fee simple)
Concurrent ownership
Tenancy in common
Joint tenancy with right of survivorship
Partition
Tenancy by the entirety and community property (ownership by spouses)

Acquiring ownership of personal property by possession, purchase and production
Acquiring ownership of personal property by gift
Effective gift requires delivery by donor, who has donative intent, and acceptance by donee
Gifts *inter vivos* and gifts *causa mortis*
Acquiring ownership by accession, confusion, will or inheritance
Mislaid, lost and abandoned property
Estray statutes

FILL-IN QUESTIONS

1. Property is a concept that deals with _____ in things. Those things, which are not real property, which are moveable and _____ _____, are considered to be personal property.

2. Usually personal property is transferred by purchase, but it may also be acquired by _____.

3. In order to transfer ownership of personal property by gift, it is necessary that three things occur. They are _____, _____ and _____.

4. Personal property is mislaid if the owner _____, but it is considered to be lost if the owner _____.

MULTIPLE CHOICE QUESTIONS

1. When a judge refers to personal property, he or she means:
   a. rights associated with ownership of things other than real property.
   b. rights associated with ownership of physical objects.
   c. tangible physical things that are not part of real property.
   d. property that is privately owned.

2. A United States Treasury Bond is considered to be:
   a. intangible personal property.

    b. intangible real property.
    c. tangible personal property.
    d. public property.

3. Peg will acquire ownership of a rabbit by occupation if:
    a. the rabbit was previously wild and she took possession of it when it came on her land.
    b. the rabbit was previously wild and she took possession of it when she went to visit a wildlife preserve owned by the state.
    c. the rabbit had run away two years before from its owner, who had not been able to find it.
    d. all of the above.

4. Sara had never flown in a plane because of her fear of flying. She had a great desire to see Disneyland and, despite her fear, she decided to fly there. Before leaving, she signed over title to her automobile and gave the car keys to Fred, her dear friend, saying, "I'll probably never make it back alive and I don't want my relatives to have my car, so it's yours." Fred drove off. Later, he opened the glove compartment and found a box, inside of which was a ring and a note to Gloria, Fred's ex-girlfriend, in which Sara stated that the ring was for Gloria.
    a. Gloria becomes the owner of the ring by accession.
    b. When Sara safely returns, she may not reclaim the car from Fred, because she made an irrevocable *inter vivos* gift.
    c. When Sara safely returns, she may reclaim the car from Fred because she made a revocable gift *causa mortis.*
    d. Sara has made a valid *inter vivos* gift of the ring to Gloria by constructive delivery.

5. Pat has received a gift of the contents of a safe deposit box by constructive delivery if her father put the key to the box in an envelope with Pat's name on it and:
    a. placed it in a drawer in his desk.
    b. left it in Pat's desk, with instructions to keep it for him.
    c. gave it to his attorney with instructions to give it to Pat in three years if he (father) did not reclaim it.
    d. mailed it to Pat, who received it.

6. Martha left her watch with a jeweler in order to be cleaned and repaired. The charges were $20.
    a. The jeweler may sell the watch and retain the proceeds because Martha has failed to reclaim the watch within one year.
    b. The jeweler may retain possession of the watch and use it because Martha has failed to pay the $20.
    c. The jeweler acquires ownership rights in the watch by occupation.
    d. The jeweler may sell the watch, retain $20 and hold the balance for Martha.

7. R, S and T stored varying quantities of grain in M's silo. Half of the grain and M have disappeared. R can prove that he stored 100 bushels of grain in the silo, and S and T are able to prove that they stored 200 bushels each. M had stored 100 bushels of his own grain in the silo.
    a. R is entitled to 60 bushels and S and T are each entitled to 120 bushels.
    b. R is entitled to 50 bushels and S and T are each entitled to 100 bushels.

    c. R is entitled to 50 bushels and S and T are each entitled to 100 bushels. R, S and T then share equally in M's share.

    d. R, S and T share equally in the grain.

8. Johnson has invented a device which enables the user to produce gasoline from walnut shells. If he obtains a patent, he can prevent others from using his idea:
    a. for as long as he uses the idea.
    b. for his lifetime, even if he does not use the idea.
    c. for a statutory period of 17 years, even if he does not use the idea.
    d. for a statutory period of 28 years, if the patent was obtained before 1978.

9. Harry dumped an old painting, which he no longer wanted, in a street waste container and Tom found and kept it.
    a. Tom will be treated as a bailee of the painting, which was mislaid.
    b. Tom's right to possession is good against all but Harry who is the true owner.
    c. The painting is now Tom's property because he found it after it was abandoned.
    d. If Tom paints over the picture, Harry is still entitled to reclaim the painting.

Chapter 51

Bailments

A bailment is a legal relationship that is created when one person, the bailor, delivers temporary possession of personal property to another, the bailee, who has a duty to return the property to the bailor or deliver it or dispose of it as directed by the bailor.

THINGS TO KEEP IN MIND

1. Usually, but not always, bailments are created by contract.

2. In most instances, problems involving bailment relate to the contract or tort liability of a bailee, who has not carried out his or her duty of returning or correctly disposing of the bailed property.

OUTLINE

I. Elements of a bailment.

   A. Subject matter of bailment is personal property, in which the bailor has a possessory interest.

   B. Actual physical or constructive delivery of possession to the bailee.

   1. In a voluntary bailment, the bailee must be given exclusive possession and control over the property.

   2. The bailee must knowingly accept possession.

   3. Constructive delivery.

        a. Bailee may be given some symbol, which evidences right to possession.

        b. Bailee may have possession of property belonging to another under circumstances which obligate the bailee to deliver property to rightful owner (involuntary bailment).
            1) Finder of lost property.
            2) Bailee to whom stolen property was delivered or who has knowledge of an adverse claim to the property.
            3) One who has absolute control over area in which property is deposited.
            4) One to whom a container is delivered has sufficient contol over contents to be considered a bailee of objects, which normally would be expected to be in the container.

C. Bailment agreement may be express or implied. Generally it need not be in writing.

D. Duty of bailee to return specific property to bailor or dispose of it in manner which bailor directs.

    1. Bailee receives possession only. Bailee does not receive ownership interests, such as title to the property.

    2. Duty of bailee is to deliver identical property, unless the bailed property consists of fungible goods, in which case only the same quantity is to be returned to the bailor.

    3. Bailment with option to purchase — Prospective purchaser must either return property at termination of agreed period or agree to purchase goods.

II. Types of bailments — Liability of bailee is determined to some extent by the type of bailment.

A. Ordinary bailments — Bailee must exercise reasonable care. What is reasonable depends upon the type of bailment.

    1. Bailment for the sole benefit of the bailor (gratuitous) — No consideration is given to the bailee.

    2. Bailment for the sole benefit of the bailee (gratuitous) — No consideration is given to the bailor.

    3. Bailment for mutual benefit (contractual) — Most bailments envision that consideration be given to each party. (Usually a fee or other compensation is given.)

B. Special bailments — Carriers, warehouses and innkeepers are covered at VII herein.

III. Rights and duties of bailee.

A. Rights of bailee.

1. Temporary control and possession of bailed property. Bailee can, therefore, recover from a third party, who interferes with bailee's possession.

2. Use the property in accomplishing purpose of the bailment.

3. Receive compensation for a nonrental bailment, if bailment is not gratuitous.

B. Duties of bailee.

1. Exercise reasonable care of the property in his or her possession. What is proper care depends upon:

   a. Time and place of bailment.

   b. Facilities of bailee.

   c. Nature of property and bailee's knowledge of its nature.

   d. Type of bailment:
      1) For benefit of bailor — Slight care.
      2) For benefit of bailee — Great care.
      3) Mutual benefit — Ordinary care.

2. Contractual duty to relinquish property at end of bailment in same condition in which it was when received, unless the property has been lost, stolen or damaged through no fault of bailee.

   a. Allowance is made for normal wear, depreciation and deterioration.

   b. If bailee was to perform services in order to repair or improve the property, he is required to do so.

   c. There is a presumption that a bailee was negligent if the property is not in correct condition or not relinquished at end of bailment.

IV. Rights and duties of bailor.

A. Rights of bailor — Bailor has right to expect that bailee will:

1. Use reasonable care to protect bailed property.

2. Correctly relinquish property at end of bailment.

3. Perform in accordance with contract of bailment.

   a. If the bailee has the right to use the property, bailee does so in the agreed manner.

   b. If bailee is to compensate bailor, bailee makes agreed upon payment.

   c. If bailee is to render services on the property, he does so correctly.

B. Duties of bailor.

1. Tort liability — Bailor has duty to furnish property that is free from certain defects.

   a. Mutual benefit bailment — Bailor must notify bailee of known and latent defects (hidden and not ordinarily discoverable).

   b. Bailment for sole benefit of bailee — Bailor must inform bailee of defects of which he or she has actual knowledge.

2. Contract liability — Bailor warrants that property is fit for intended purpose of the bailment.

V. Contractual limitations on liability of bailee — If bailor knows of the limitations on liability or if bailee's attention is called to them, they will be enforced. Absolute disclaimers and exculpatory clauses, however, are rarely enforced.

VI. Termination of bailments.

A. If bailment is for a specified term, it ends at expiration of term.

B. If bailment is not for a specified period, it may be terminated by demand of either party or completion of the purpose of the bailment.

C. A bailment may also be terminated by:

1. Mutual agreement,

2. Act of a party which is inconsistent with the terms of the bailment, or

3. Operation of law.

VII. Some specific types of bailments.

A. Article 7 of the Uniform Commercial Code (UCC).

1. Documents of title.

   a. Bill of lading is "a document evidencing receipt of goods for shipment issued by a person engaged in the business of transporting or forwarding goods, and includes an airbill" (Sec. 1-201(6)).

   b. Warehouse receipt is "a receipt issued by a person engaged in the business of storing goods for hire" (Sec. 1-201(45)).

   c. Delivery order is "a written order to deliver goods directed to a warehouseman, carrier or other person who in the ordinary course of business issues warehouse receipts or bills of lading" (Sec. 7-102(d)).

2. Functions of a document of title:

   a. Receipt for property bailed.

b. Represents the goods so that the person holding it has right to the property represented by it.

c. Contract for shipment or storage.

3. Negotiable documents of title.

  a. Document of title is negotiable if it provides that "goods are to be delivered to bearer or to the order of a named person" (Sec. 7-104(1)(a)).

  b. A holder is one who "purchased document of title for value, in good faith and without notice of any defenses against or claims to it" (Sec. 7-501(4)).

  c. Holder of negotiable document of title has right to receive, hold and dispose of the documents and the goods covered by it and may acquire greater rights to the document of title and the goods than his, her or its transferor.

4. Transfer of documents of title.

  a. Negotiable document of title is "duly negotiated":
     1) By indorsement and delivery if document of title runs to the order of a named person or has been indorsed to a specified person.
     2) By delivery alone if document of title runs to bearer or is indorsed in blank or to bearer. (Sec. 7-501.)

  b. Nonnegotiable document of title may be transferred by assignment.

5. Possessory liens of common carriers and public warehouses.

6. Other federal and state regulatory statutes.

B. Carriers — Transport goods.

1. Contract carrier — Provides transportation services under individual contracts to selected users.

2. Private carrier — Maintains transportation facilities that are privately owned and operated for the sole benefit of the owner and not for hire.

3. Common carrier — Holds self out to furnish transportation to the public for compensation, without discrimination, as long as it has available facilities. Usually it has a definite route and/or schedule.

  a. Mutual benefit bailment.

  b. Extraordinary liability approaches that of an insurer. Carrier is absolutely liable for loss, destruction or damage to property carried, without regard to fault, unless due to:
     1) Act of God.
     2) Act of war or public enemy.

3) Order of public authority.
4) Act of the shipper.
5) Inherent nature of the goods.

   c. Carriers issue documents of title, bills of lading.

   d. Carrier may limit its liability by contract to:
     1) Stated losses but may not relieve itself of liability based on intentional wrongful acts or negligence.
     2) Some maximum dollar amount, but must afford shipper an opportunity to obtain a higher limit by paying a higher charge.

C. Warehouse companies — Engage in business of storing personal property of others for compensation, without discrimination. Their rights and duties are those of bailees for mutual benefit, modified by statutes.

  1. A public warehouse is liable for its failure to exercise reasonable care.

  2. If property is lost, damaged or destroyed, while in the possession of the warehouse, it has the burden of proving its nonliability.

  3. Warehouses issue documents of title, warehouse receipts.

D. Innkeepers, hotels, motels, etc.

  1. At common law, one, who offered living accommodations to transients, was practically an insurer with respect to the personal property of guests.

  2. Statutes limit liability or provide methods by which liability may be limited by a hotel, etc.

   a. Typically a hotel will not be liable for valuables unless they are deposited in a safe provided by the hotel, notice of which is given to guests.

   b. Hotel will be liable for ordinary negligence, resulting in the loss of property of guests, which are necessary or part of usual wearing apparel and not put in safe.

KEY WORDS AND PHRASES IN TEXT

Bailment
Bailor
Bailee
Elements of a bailment (subject matter
   is personal property, possession of
   the property is given to the bailee
   and parties have an agreement)
Delivery of possession
Actual physical delivery
Constructive delivery
Bailment agreement may be express or
   implied

Fungible goods
Ordinary bailments
Bailment for the sole benefit of the
   bailor
Bailment for the sole benefit of the
   bailee
Bailment for the mutual benefit of the
   bailee and the bailor (contractual
   bailments)
Artisan's lien
Standard of care owed by party in
   possession

Rights of the bailee (possession, use of
bailed property, compensation and
limit liability)
Duties of the bailee (exercise care and
return bailed property to the
correct person)
Presumption of negligence
Rights and duties of bailor
Warranty liability of bailor
Termination of a bailment
Documents of title

Bill of lading
Warehouse receipt
Delivery order
Negotiable document of title
Negotiation of document of title
Common carriers
Shipper's loss
Connecting carriers
Warehouse companies
Innkeepers, hotel owners and similar
operators

FILL-IN QUESTIONS

1. A bailment arises when one person, called the _____, delivers temporary possession of _____ property to another, called the _____, who is obligated to _____ the property to the person who delivered it or dispose of it in the manner which he or she directed.

2. Property may be actually or _____ delivered to a bailee. If the bailee is given some symbol, evidencing a right to possession, or has possession involuntarily, under circumstances which obligate him or her to deliver it to the rightful owner, there has been _____ delivery of the property.

3. A bailee owes a duty of reasonable care with respect to bailed property. If a bailment is for the sole benefit of the bailee, the bailee must exercise _____ care; if it is for the sole benefit of the bailor, the bailee will be liable if he or she fails to exercise _____ care. Most bailments are _____ _____, in which case bailees owe a duty of _____ care.

MULTIPLE CHOICE QUESTIONS

1. In a bailment relationship:
   a. the bailee has temporary title to the bailed personal property.
   b. consideration is necessary to form the relationship.
   c. the bailee has temporary possession of the bailed property.
   d. the property is returned to the bailor or one who the bailee believes has valid title to the property.

2. Which of the following statements is *not* true?
   a. One, who is not an owner of personal property, may be a bailor of the property.
   b. One, in possession of personal property, may not avoid liability to the owner of the property, if he or she sells it to a third person.
   c. One need not be given actual physical possession of personal property in order to be considered a bailee.
   d. One, in possession of personal property, is not a bailee unless the owner of the property entered into an express bailment agreement.

3. Jackson brought his car to a local garage for a tune-up and a number of repairs.
   a. The garage will be liable to Jackson for the value of the car, if it was stolen because the mechanic left the keys in the ignition.

    b. The garage will be liable to Jackson for the value of the golf clubs that had been in the trunk but are now missing.

    c. The garage will be liable to Jackson, if it refuses to deliver the car to him because he has not paid for the repairs.

    d. The garage will be liable to Jackson for damage done to the car while on its premises a month after it notified Jackson that the work on the car was completed.

4.   A parking lot is liable to the owner of an automobile:

    a. who had parked and locked his own car, retaining the keys, if the car is stolen.

    b. who had parked and locked his own car, delivering the keys to an attendant, if the car is stolen.

    c. whose car was parked by an attendant, even if there is a large sign stating that it will not be liable for cars which are damaged by persons other than its employees, if the car is damaged by another user of the parking lot.

    d. whose car was parked by an attendant, if his briefcase, containing business papers and securities worth $3,000, was stolen from the car while it was parked in the lot.

5.   Lukins placed a suitcase, containing clothing, in a self-service locker at an airport. He put a quarter in the slot, locked the door and took the key. Marlin checked his suitcase, containing clothing, in a checkroom at the same airport. In this case an attendant took the case from him and put it in a rack in full view of all the attendants in the checkroom. The attendant charged $1 for the storage and gave Marlin a claim check with nothing but a number printed on it. Both the lockers and the checkroom were owned and maintained by the airport.

    a. The airport will be liable to Lukins, if his suitcase is missing when he returns to reclaim it.

    b. The airport will be liable to Marlin, if the suitcase is missing when he returns to reclaim it.

    c. The airport will be liable to Lukins, if the suitcase cannot be returned because an explosion wrecked the checkroom, if the explosion was caused by a bomb left by terrorists and in no way due to the fault of the airport.

    d. The airport will be liable to Marlin, if the suitcase cannot be returned because an explosion wrecked the lockers, if the explosion was caused by terrorists and in no way due to the fault of the airport.

6.   A common carrier is:

    a. liable for damage, caused to food carried by it, which is harmed by unseasonably warm temperatures.

    b. not liable for livestock destroyed by a mentally deranged railroad engineer.

    c. not a contract carrier.

    d. not liable for injuries to its passengers.

7.   A common carrier is *not* liable for damage to property being shipped, if the damage is caused by:

    a. theft.

    b. a tornado.

    c. rioters.

    d. negligence of a trespasser.

8.   A public warehouse may limit its liability for loss, destruction or damage to goods it stores, in the contract with an owner, who delivers goods to it for storage:

a. but it is required to offer the owner higher limits of liability at increased rates.
b. by using exculpatory clauses.
c. but must obtain a release from the owner in the warehouse receipt which functions as the contract of bailment.
d. by calling the owner's attention to the limitation on its liability following the delivery of the goods.

9. The common law liability of hotels has been changed by statute so that, if a hotel provides a safe and posts notices of its availability and a guest has been robbed, the hotel will be:
   a. liable for a $200 gold watch, even if it is not deposited in the safe by a guest.
   b. not liable for a $300 gold watch, even if it is not deposited in the safe by the guest.
   c. liable for $400 worth of uncut diamonds if they were not deposited in the safe by the guest.
   d. never be liable for the property of guests.

10. Traveler was staying at the Buena Vista Motel in a state which permits innkeepers to limit their liability by providing safes for valuables belonging to their guests and notifying them of its availability. Traveler did not use the safe. Among his belongings were a rare 1882 inverted stamp worth $10,000, diamond cuff links worth $5,000, which he wears a few times a week, and dirty laundry of uncertain value. All of these items have disappeared from Traveler's motel room. The motel is:
    a. liable for the loss of the rare 1882 stamp.
    b. not liable for the dirty laundry.
    c. liable for the cuff links.
    d. liable for the loss of the 1882 stamp, the dirty laundry and the cuff links.

11. Which of the following is **not** a warranty made by the seller of a negotiable warehouse receipt or bill of lading to the purchaser of the document under the provisions in UCC Sec. 7-507?
    a. The negotiation or transfer of the document is fully effective with respect to the goods that it represents.
    b. The issuer of the document will honor the document.
    c. The seller has no knowledge of any facts that would impair the document's validity.
    d. The document is genuine.

(This question has been adapted from the AICPA Examination, November 1988.)

Chapter 52

Nature and Ownership of Real Property

Real property refers to rights associated with ownership or possessory interests in land and things of a permanent nature growing on or affixed to the land or contained above or below the surface. Most of the material in this chapter relates to the nature of real property, the types of present ownership and present possessory interests in land and the manner in which they may be acquired or transferred.

Nonpossessory interests in land may also be created. For example, the right to possession of real property may be deferred. If so, one may have a future interest in the property—a reversion, possibility of reverter, power of termination, remainder or executory interest—the subject matter of a later section in this chapter. It is also possible to grant nonpossessory interests or rights to other persons in the form of easements, profits and licenses, all of which may restrict the present and future rights of owners of land.

As indicated in the last section of the chapter, additional limitations on the use of land may be imposed, privately with restrictive covenants (in conveyances) and equitable servitudes (in separate, recorded agreements), and by state zoning statutes or local zoning ordinances.

THINGS TO KEEP IN MIND

1. The rights to possession and enjoyment of land are protected by law. Typically, if there is an interference with the use and enjoyment of real property, a tort action may be brought based upon trespass. If one has acquired title to real property by conveyance and there is a defect in the title, the transferee may sue the grantor because of a breach of a convenant or a warranty contained in the deed.

2. The terminology and concepts used and explained in this chapter are probably unfamiliar to most readers. For this reason, it may be necessary to devote con-

siderable time to studying this topic in order to gain understanding of the relevant legal principles. A number of fill-in questions are provided, with which you can test your comprehension of the concepts and terminology used in the chapter.

OUTLINE

I.   Nature of real property.

    A. The land or soil itself, bodies of water contained on the land, natural and artificial structures attached to it and plant life and vegetation growing on it.

    B. Subsurface and air rights.

        1. Today one has rights to the air immediately above the land sufficient to have a cause of action, based upon trespass, for a direct interference with the use and enjoyment of the land.

        2. A property owner has the exclusive right to minerals, oil and other matter found beneath the surface, and may transfer this right to another.

    C. Plant life and vegetation — Includes trees, natural vegetation and cultivated crops. (See Chapter 16.)

    D. Fixtures — Personal property affixed to real property.

        1. Fixtures that are attached or affixed to real property are included in the sale of the realty unless the contract for sale provides otherwise.

        2. Objective intention of the party, who placed the item, determines whether or not the item is a fixture.

        3. Trade fixtures.

            a. Items attached to rented premises by a tenant (who pursues a trade or business) in connection with the business, are treated as personal property of the tenant and usually intended to be removed by the tenant. If their removal causes harm to the premises, the tenant is required to reimburse the landlord.

            b. If fixtures are not trade fixtures, they are usually treated as part of the real property and are not removable by a tenant.

II.   Ownership interests in real property — Estates in land.

    A. Estates are collections of rights associated with ownership.

    B. Freehold estates — Estates for indefinite time (possessory interests in land).

        1. Estates in fee — Transferable during owner's lifetime or as an inheritance.

            a. Fee simple absolute — The owner possesses all the rights which one may possess in land and which may be conveyed or inherited.

2. Multiple Insurance Coverage
3. Insurable Interest"[2]

The AICPA specifications do not indicate the relative emphasis that may be placed upon the various topics within the seven major areas of business law. This is expected to fluctuate on future examinations as it has in the past.

SOME CONCLUSIONS

The importance of contract law to accountants and, therefore, Unit II in *West's Business Law: Alternate UCC Comprehensive Edition,* Fourth Edition and this Study Guide, can not be overstressed. Approximately 15% of the CPA Business Law Examination is devoted to specific topics relating to contracts. One must also realize that contract law provides the foundation for what are normally treated as other areas of business law.

With regard to the area referred to as the CPA and the law, information relating to this subject is presented in Chapter 57 of the Text and this Study Guide. (In addition, see material dealing with torts in Chapter 4, contracts in Unit II and security regulations in Chapter 43.) This subject is usually also covered in accounting courses, such as auditing and taxation.

In addition to contracts and the CPA and the law, topics that have received significant treatment on past CPA examinations have included commercial paper, federal securities legislation,[3] corporations, partnerships, sales and secured transactions.

---

[2]The Revised Business Law Content Specification Outline for the Uniform Certified Public Accountant Examination (Effective May 1986), Copyright © 1986 by the American Institute of Certified Public Accountants, Inc. Reprinted with permission.

[3]Knowledge concerning the Federal Securities Acts is tested specifically and also in conjunction with a CPA's statutory liability.

1. Two or more persons own undivided shares (which may be equal or unequal) in property.

2. Each tenant may transfer his or her interest during his or her lifetime or by will or by inheritance, without rights of survivorship among the other co-tenants.

B. Joint tenancy with right of survivorship.

1. Two or more persons own equal undivided shares of an entire estate, which they acquire simultaneously, and have equal rights of enjoyment and rights of survivorship.

2. The transferor must have clearly indicated an intention to create a joint tenancy.

3. A joint tenant may sever and transfer his or her interest during his or her lifetime.

4. Today, there is a presumption that a co-tenancy is a tenancy in common unless there is a clear intention to create a joint tenancy.

C. Tenancy by the entirety — A joint tenancy existing between spouses, which cannot be severed by either spouse without the consent of the other.

D. Community property — In some states spouses own undivided half interests in property acquired during the period of their marriage (other than by gift or inheritance).

E. Condominium ownership — Each owner owns the unit that he or she occupies and is a tenant in common with others with respect to common areas.

IV. Transfer of ownership.

A. Conveyance by deed.

1. In order to transfer an interest in land by sale or gift, a conveyance is made by delivery of an instrument called a deed.

   a. Signed by the grantor (the person conveying the real property).

   b. States the names of the grantor (seller or donor) and the grantee (buyer or donee).

   c. Describes the property and the interest conveyed.

   d. Indicates the grantor's intention to make a present transfer of title to real property.

2. Covenants of title that may be included in a deed.

   a. *Seizen* — Grantor has title and the right to convey the particular estate.

FUTURE CPA EXAMINATIONS

Uniform CPA Examinations are scheduled as follows:

1990	May 2, 3, 4		1993	May 5, 6, 7
	November 7, 8, 9			November 3, 4, 5
1991	May 8, 9, 10		1994	May 4, 5, 6
	November 6, 7, 8			November 2, 3, 4
1992	May 6, 7, 8		1995	May 3, 4, 5
	November 4, 5, 6			November 1, 2, 3

Students who plan to sit for the examinations are encouraged to obtain copies of *Information for CPA Candidates* issued by AICPA.[4] In their preparation, CPA candidates will, no doubt, find the outlines and other materials in this book useful for review purposes. For this reason, cross references to the *Study Guide to Accompany West's Business Law: Alternate UCC Comprehensive Edition,* Fourth Edition are provided in a Cross Reference Table for the traditional business law subjects covered on the CPA Examination.

---

[4]Copies may be obtained by writing to:

The American Institute of Certified Public Accountants
1211 Avenue of the Americas
New York, New York 10036

3. Upon the death of the owner of the reversionary interest, the interest vests in his or her heirs or devisees, named in the grantor's will (if it has not been otherwise disposed of during his or her lifetime).

4. Reversion.

   a. The interest retained by a grantor, who transfers a life estate to another, without making a disposition of the interest remaining after the death of the person, who is the measuring life.

   b. A reversion is a vested future interest.

5. Possibility of reverter.

   a. The interest retained by a grantor, who has conveyed a fee simple determinable.

   b. It is contingent upon the happening of the event specified in the conveyance, which terminates the grantee's interest automatically.

6. Power of termination.

   a. The interest retained by a grantor, who has conveyed a fee simple subject to a condition subsequent, which is not automatically terminated upon the happening of the condition.

   b. The grantor (or his or her heirs or devisees) must affirmatively exercise his or her right of entry.

B. Remainders and executory interests.

   1. Created by the same instrument that conveyed a present possessory interest.

   2. May be conveyed and inherited.

   3. Vested remainder — An absolute right to possession, existing at the end of a prior life estate or leasehold.

   4. Contingent remainder — The right to possession depends upon the termination of a preceding estate and the occurrence of a contingency or the existence and identification of some person.

   5. Executory interest — The right to possession takes effect either before the natural termination of a preceding estate, upon the happening of some contingency (a shifting executory interest), or after the termination of the preceding estate (a springing executory interest).

VI. Nonpossessory interests.

A. Easements and profits.

   1. Easement — The limited right to make use of property of another person without taking anything from it.

2. Profit — The limited right to go onto the property of another person and remove something from it.

3. Easement (or profit) appurtenant — The right to go onto and/or remove something from the land of another person (the subservient parcel), which is created for the benefit of the owner of an adjacent parcel of land (the dominant parcel).

   a. If the dominant parcel is sold, the easement may also be transferred.

   b. If the easement is recorded, a subsequent owner of the subservient parcel must recognize the easement or profit.

4. Easement (or profit) in gross — The right to use or remove something from the land of another (which need not be adjacent to the property of the party given the right) for a specific personal or commercial purpose.

5. Creation of an easement or profit.

   a. By deed or will.

   b. By implication, when circumstances surrounding a division of property infer the creation of an easement (or profit) and the use of the property is apparent, necessary and continuous.

   c. By necessity, when circumstances, other than a division of property, are such that it is clearly necessary that one person use another's property.

   d. By prescription, when one person, without permission, openly, adversely, notoriously and continually uses or takes something from the land of another for the period of time provided by statute.

6. Termination of easement (or profit) may be by:

   a. Deed, expiration of agreed duration or fulfillment of the purpose for which the easement (or profit) was created.

   b. Intentional abandonment.

   c. Merger of the dominant and subservient parcels.

   d. Destruction of the subservient property.

   e. Prescription, when the owner of the subservient property prevents the use of the easement (or profit) for a statutory period.

B. License — Revocable, nontransferable right to use property of another with consent, created by contract.

VII. Land use control — Limitations placed upon property owners' rights to use or convey property.

A. Private agreements.

1. Restrictive covenant running with the land — An agreement made by an owner of land which binds subsequent owners of the land to a restriction or limitation on some ownership right. Requisites:

   a. Written agreement, usually contained in a conveyance.

   b. Clear intention that the covenant is to bind subsequent owners. Use of words, "successors, heirs and assigns" is usually sufficient.

   c. The subject matter of the covenant has some connection with the land.

   d. The original parties were in privity of estate at the time the covenant was created.

2. Equitable servitude.

   a. A restriction on some ownership right, created by a written instrument, other than a conveyance.

   b. Constructive notice of the restriction is given by recording.

3. Restrictive covenants and equitable servitudes, which provide for discrimination, are unconstitutional and prohibited by statute, and will not be enforced.

B. Zoning.

1. State and local governmental control of land use may be effected by exercises of the power of eminent domain (requiring payment of compensation for the taking of property) or the police power, in order to protect the public health, safety, morals and general welfare (without payment of compensation).

2. Limitations on the power of the states to restrict land use.

   a. If regulation is confiscatory, compensation must be paid to the owner.

   b. If a restriction is arbitrary, unreasonable, discriminatory or without a rational basis, it will be deemed to be a taking of property without due process or a denial of the equal protections of the laws, which are prohibited by the Fourteenth Amendment.

3. Existing nonconforming uses will be permitted for a reasonable period of time.

4. Floating zones — The amount of land designated for a particular purpose is determined initially but none of the land is preassigned.

5. Variances.

   a. Obtained by owner, whose use of land is limited by existing zoning regulation, in order to use it for an alternative purpose.

b. Granted upon showing:
    1) As zoned, the land will not produce a reasonable return.
    2) Adverse effect of zoning is peculiar to the applicant rather than all land owners in the zone.
    3) Variance will not substantially alter the essential character of the zoned area.

KEY WORDS AND PHRASES IN TEXT

Real property (real estate or realty)
Land
Subsurface and air rights
Plant life and vegetation
Fixtures
Ownership interests in real property
Estates in land
Freehold estates
Fee simple absolute
Fee simple defeasible
Life estate
Waste
Nonfreehold estates (leasehold estates)
Tenancy for years
Periodic tenancy
Tenancy at will
Tenancy at sufferance
Termination of leasehold
Transfer of ownership by will or inheritance
Power of eminent domain
Adverse possession
Conveyance by deed
Deed
Grantor
Grantee
Warranty deed (with covenants of *seisin*, right to convey, against encumbrances and quiet enjoyment)
Special warranty deed (deed with covenants against grantor's acts)

Quitclaim deed
Grant deed (bargain and sale deed)
Recording statutes (race statutes, pure notice statutes and notice-race statutes)
Warranty of habitability
Future interests (nonpossessory future estates)
Reversionary interests and powers of termination
Possibility of reverter
Remainders and executory interest
Vested or contingent remainder
Springing executory interest (or use)
Shifting executory interest
Nonpossessory interests
Easements and profits (appurtenant or in gross)
Effect of sale of property on easement or profit
Creation of an easement or profit by deed or will, by implication, by necessity or by prescription
Licenses
Land use control
Covenants running with the land
Equitable servitudes
Zoning
Floating zones
Spot zoning
Variances

FILL-IN QUESTIONS

1. Real property includes rights associated with land and things of a permanent nature _____.

2. Fixtures are items that are personal property until they are _____ _____. If such items are affixed to a business premises by a tenant with the understanding that they may be removed, they are referred to as _____.

3.   Ownership interests in land are referred to as _____, which may be
     for an indefinite period of time, in which case they are called _____,
     or may be for determinable periods, in which case they are _____.

4.   If A and B concurrently own equal undivided shares of an entire estate in real
     property, they will be considered to be _____ only if the grantor
     clearly indicated an intention to create such a tenancy. Upon A's death, his
     interest passes to _____. If A and B are spouses, in most states
     they will be considered as having a _____.

5.   A _____ is created when two or more persons own undivided
     shares of an entire estate in real property, which may not be equal, and which may
     be transferred separately during the lifetimes of the co-tenants and, upon death of
     a co-tenant, by will or inheritance. A surviving co-tenant has no rights to a
     deceased co-tenant's interest in the property.

6.   Real property may be transferred by the owner during his or her lifetime by _____
     _____. If the grantor is transferring merely the interest,
     which he or she had, the document of conveyance is called a _____
     deed. It is used frequently to remove _____ in the title to the
     property.

7.   A future interest is not created if a grantor makes a conveyance in fee _____
     _____.

8.   If a grantor conveys a fee simple determinable, the estate terminates automatically
     upon the happening of some event and possession of the property will revert to the
     grantor, who has retained a _____ or pass to another person, to
     whom the grantor gave a _____.

9.   A _____ is created in the same instrument by which a grantor
     conveys a fee simple determinable.

10. If a grantor conveys a fee simple determinable, without naming a remainderman,
     the grantor may subsequently transfer his or her future interest to another person.
     The transferee will then be the owner of the _____. If the grantor
     does not transfer the future interest during his or her lifetime, it passes to the
     grantor's heirs or devisees, who will then be the owners of the _____.

11. A possibility of reverter and _____ may never vest, if the condi-
     tioning event, which terminates the fee simple determinable, does not occur.

12. Upon the death of the person, whose life determines or measures a life estate, the
     possessory interest reverts to the grantor, who has a vested interest, which is
     referred to as a _____, or passes to another person, to whom the
     grantor gave a _____ when he or she conveyed the life estate.

13. If a grantor conveys a life estate, without naming a remainderman, the grantor may
     subsequently transfer his or her future reversionary interest to another person. The
     transferee will then be the owner of _____. If a grantor does not
     transfer his or her reversionary interest during his or her lifetime, it passes to the
     grantor's heirs or devisees, who will then be the owners of the _____.

14. A _____ is created in the same instrument by which a grantor conveys a life estate.

15. A conveyance of a fee simple, subject to a condition subsequent, does not terminate automatically upon the happening of the conditioning event. The grantor of such an estate retains a _____, which he or she must affirmatively exercise, or the person, to whom the grantor has given _____ must exercise his or her right to possession.

16. The right to use property of another in a specified manner, without removing anything from it, is referred to as _____. The right to go onto the property of another and remove something from it is called _____. These rights are _____ interests in land and may be given to owners of adjacent property, in which case they are called _____.

17. A grantor may restrict the right to use or further transfer land by making a conveyance containing _____. The use or right to make future transfers of land may also be restricted by recording a separate instrument. This is referred to as _____.

MULTIPLE CHOICE QUESTIONS

Unless otherwise indicated, assume that there are no relevant statutes and that common law rules are applicable.

1. The greatest ownership interest a person may have in real property is a:
    a. fee simple absolute.
    b. fee simple defeasible.
    c. tenancy by the entirety.
    d. less than freehold estate.

2. The least amount of protection is given to a grantee who receives:
    a. a warranty deed.
    b. a grant deed.
    c. a quitclaim deed.
    d. a special warranty deed.
    (This question has been adapted from the AICPA Examination, November 1988.)

3. The greatest amount of protection is given to a grantee who receives:
    a. a warranty deed.
    b. a special warranty deed.
    c. a bargain and sale deed.
    d. a quitclaim deed.
    (This question has been adapted from the AICPA Examination, November 1988.)

4. Jacob's land was sold to pay his delinquent taxes. The purchaser at the sheriff's sale would acquire title by:
    a. adverse possession.
    b. full warranty deed.
    c. right of eminent domain.
    d. none of the above.

5.   Margaret owned real property in fee simple absolute. She made a conveyance to Ann and Betty, with rights of survivorship, as long as the land was used for agricultural purposes.
   a. Ann and Betty are tenants in common of a fee simple absolute.
   b. Ann and Betty are joint tenants of a fee simple defeasible.
   c. If Ann dies, her interest in the property passes in accordance with her will.
   d. If Ann and Betty use the property for industrial purposes, Margaret's remedy is to sue for breach of warranty.

Questions 6 and 7 are based on the following fact situation: Teasdale had no living relatives but died leaving a will, by which he granted a life estate to certain real property to McCormick, with remainder to Nesbett and Owens, as joint tenants with right of survivorship.

6.   The following statement is true:
   a. McCormick has a present possessory freehold interest.
   b. McCormick may neither transfer his interest during his lifetime nor, upon his death, by will.
   c. The gift to McCormick will fail because the devise to McCormick violates the rule against perpetuities.
   d. As a life tenant, McCormick has the right to remove improvements and mineral deposits from the land.

7.   With regard to Nesbett and Owens:
   a. during the lifetime of McCormick, their interests are not subject to being inherited.
   b. during the lifetime of McCormick, their interests may not be transferred.
   c. they have vested remainders.
   d. they are tenants in common.

8.   Abrams owned 100 acres of land, only ten of which bordered on a road. Abrams sold and conveyed 25 acres to Bennett and, because the 25 acres did not border on any road, granted the right to Bennett, in his deed, to go over a described strip of his (Abrams') land in order to reach Bennett's land.
   a. Bennett has an easement by prescription.
   b. If Bennett later conveys the land to Calahan, Calahan does not have the right to go over Abrams' land.
   c. Bennett has an easement in gross.
   d. Bennett has an appurtenant easement.

9.   A municipal ordinance requiring that pet animals be restrained from leaving their owners' property is:
   a. unconstitutional because it interferes with an owner's rights with respect to his real property.
   b. not a valid exercise of governmental power because an owner of property has an absolute right to use his own property.
   c. a valid interference with owners' rights with respect to property.
   d. an invalid interference with the use of both personal and real property.

Chapter 53

Landlord-Tenant Relationships

A landlord-tenant relationship exists when the owner of real property transfers temporary, exclusive possession of the property to another person. The owner of the real property is referred to as the landlord or lessor. The person to whom possession is transferred is called the tenant or lessee. Their agreement is referred to as a lease and provides for the payment of rent by the tenant. Leases are contracts to which common law principles apply. In addition, state statutes, including the Uniform Residential Landlord and Tenant Act (URLTA), and local ordinances that relate to landlord-tenant relationships have been enacted.

THINGS TO KEEP IN MIND

1. Statutes relating to the landlord-tenant relationship vary from state to state.

2. Often, the form of the lease and the rights and duties of the landlord and tenant depend upon the use to be made of the leased property. It may, therefore, be necessary to distinguish commercial from residential property.

OUTLINE

I. Creation of the landlord-tenant relationship.

   A. Statutes provide that some leases (typically, those for more than one year) be written.

   B. The lease may cover residential or commercial property.

   C. Lease form—contents:

      1. Expression of intent to establish a landlord-tenant relationship.

2. Provision for transfer of possession of the property to the tenant at the beginning of the term.

3. Provision for the reversionary interest of the landlord, entitling the landlord to retake possession at the end of the term.

4. Description of the property.

5. Statements indicating the length of the term, the amount of the rent and the manner and time for payment of the rent.

D. Statutory and public policy prohibitions.

1. Discrimination based upon race, color, religion, sex and national origin.

   a. Owners of property cannot discriminate against prospective tenants.

   b. Commercial tenants cannot agree to discriminate against members of a protected class.

2. Statutes may prohibit a provision that tenant agrees to pay attorneys' fees in a suit to enforce lease.

3. Statutes and public policy prohibit lease or use of property for illegal purposes.

4. Local building codes and zoning ordinances may restrict leasing of property that is not in compliance with their provisions.

5. A lease or clause in the lease may be found to be unconscionable and, therefore, unenforceable because of the circumstances surrounding the transaction and/or the relative bargaining power of the parties.

II. Rights and duties of landlord and tenant.

A. Possession.

1. Landlord has obligation to deliver possession of the property to the tenant at the beginning of the term.

   a. English and URLTA rule — Lessor must give lessee actual physical possession, which includes removal of previous tenant who has remained in possession.

   b. American rule — Lessor gives lessee right to possession, in which case lessee has responsibility of removing previous tenant who has remained in possession.

2. Tenant has right to retain exclusive possession until expiration of lease term.

   a. This right is lost if tenant defaults under the terms of the lease.

b. Usually, landlord has right to come onto the property in order to inspect, make repairs or to show property to prospective buyers or tenants.

3. Covenant of quiet enjoyment.

    a. Landlord will not evict or dispossess tenant from the premises.

    b. Landlord will not interfere with the tenant's right to use and possess the premises. If landlord interferes with the tenant's rights, it is a constructive eviction.

4. Wrongful eviction by landlord.

    a. Eviction occurs if landlord deprives tenant of possession or enjoyment of property.

    b. Partial eviction — If tenant is deprived of use of a portion of the premises, tenant may cease paying rent, terminate the lease or sue for damages or possession.

    c. Constructive eviction — If tenant's use and enjoyment of the premises is made difficult or impossible because of landlord's failure to correctly carry out obligations, tenant, after notifying landlord, may vacate premises and cease paying rent.

    d. Retaliatory eviction — If landlord evicts or attempts to evict tenant as retaliation for reporting violations of codes to government agency, statutes give tenant remedies.

B. Tenant's right to use premises for purposes that do not injure landlord's interest and are legal and reasonably related to the purpose for which the property is adapted or ordinarily used.

1. Tenant should not create a nuisance by interfering with rights of others.

2. Tenant has duty not to commit waste by abusive or destructive use of the property and will be liable for damage that he or she causes but not for ordinary wear and tear.

3. Alteration to the premises by tenant — Improvements or changes that substantially affect the property.

    a. In most states, tenants cannot make alteration without landlord's consent.

    b. Fixtures are items of personal property that are affixed to the real property.
        1) In some states, fixtures in residential property become part of the landlord's property and may not be removed by tenant.
        2) In other states, residential tenants can remove fixtures if it can be done without damage to the premises.

C. Maintenance of the premises.

    1. Landlord must comply with statutory construction and maintenance standards.

    2. Common areas must be maintained by landlord, who is required to repair known defects and those about which he, she or it should reasonably know.

    3. Lease may expressly designate party who is to maintain premises; tenant has duty to make repairs that are necessitated as a result of tenant's intentional or negligent acts.

    4. In most states, landlord makes an implied warranty of habitability.

       a. The premises are safe and suitable for people to live in when lease term begins and during entire term.

       b. Warranty applies to substantial physical defects about which landlord knows or should know and has reasonable time within which to repair.

    5. Tenant's remedies for landlord's failure to maintain premises.

       a. Tenant may have statutory right to withhold all or a portion of the rent or to pay rent into an escrow account or to an escrow agent.

       b. Tenant, who makes necessary repairs, may deduct their cost from rent.

       c. Tenant may cancel lease or sue for damages when there has been a constructive eviction or a breach of warranty of habitability.

D. Tenant has a duty to pay the agreed upon rent or, if none is provided for, reasonable rent.

    1. Landlord may require a security deposit which will be subject to forfeiture, in whole or in part, if tenant fails to pay rent or damages the property; and may impose late charges if tenant fails to pay rent when it is due.

    2. Unless there is a rent escalation clause in the lease, the rent cannot be increased during the lease term.

    3. Usually, landlord has the duty to pay assessments and taxes on leased property.

    4. Landlord's remedies for tenant's failure to pay rent.

       a. If tenant vacates premises without justification, tenant remains liable to pay the rent for the remainder of the term of the lease and may be sued for unpaid rent; landlord, however, may be required to mitigate the damages by making a reasonable attempt to lease the property to another person.

       b. Statutes in some states provide that a landlord may have a landlord's lien on a tenant's personal property if rent is not paid.

    c. If there is a breach of the lease by a tenant, the landlord has a right of entry in order to peaceably retake possession and evict the tenant.
      1) Common law action for ejectment.
      2) Summary procedure for unlawful detainer.

III. Liability for injuries on the premises.

  A. The party who controls an area of the property owes a duty to exercise reasonable care in order to avoid foreseeable risks which might cause injuries to others. What is reasonable care depends upon the circumstances, including the status of an injured person.

    1. Invitee — A person, such as a guest or customer, who has been invited onto the premises by the tenant for the benefit of the tenant.

    2. Licensee — A person, such as a salesperson, who is invited or allowed onto the premises by the tenant for the benefit of the licensee.

    3. Trespasser — An uninvited person who has no right to be on the premises.

  B. Landlord's liability to injured parties.

    1. Landlord is liable for injuries occurring on part of property over which landlord has control; landlord has duty to inspect and properly maintain common areas.

    2. Landlord is liable for injuries caused by his, her or its failure to make repairs or negligence in making repairs when landlord has an obligation or has undertaken to make repairs.

    3. Landlord's liability may result from a dangerous condition about which landlord knew, should have known or failed to inform tenant.

    4. Landlord has a duty to inspect and make repairs to commercial property before tenant takes possession in order to prevent unreasonable risks to members of the public.

    5. Landlord may be liable for injuries that were caused by criminal acts of third persons when the crimes are reasonably foreseeable and the landlord has taken no steps to prevent them.

    6. Exculpatory clauses, relieving landlord of liability, are unenforceable if they relieve the landlord of liability for injury or damage caused by the landlord's failure to comply with a statute or by the landlord's own negligence or intentional acts.

  C. Tenant's liability to injured parties.

    1. Tenant is liable for injuries occurring on part of the premises over which tenant has control and which he, she or it has a duty to reasonably maintain.

    2. A commercial tenant owes a duty of exercising reasonable care, including warning invitees of any latent dangerous condition on areas of approach to

the tenant's premises and areas used in common with other tenants as well as on the premises which are leased by the tenant; in some cases, both the landlord and the commercial tenant may be liable to an injured party.

IV. Transferring rights to leased property.

    A. Transfer of the landlord's interest.

        1. The landlord, as a property owner, can sell or otherwise transfer the interests in real property which he, she or it owns (see Chapter 52), including the reversionary interest.

        2. When the landlord transfers title to the leased property, an existing tenant becomes the tenant of the transferee.

    B. Transfer of the tenant's interest.

        1. A lease may prohibit assignment and/or subleasing; a statute or a clause in a lease may require the landlord's consent to a tenant's assignment of the tenant's interest in the lease or subleasing of the premises.

        2. If a tenant makes an assignment of all the remaining rights under the terms of the lease, the assignee assumes the tenant's obligations. If the assignee fails to pay the rent, the original tenant (assignor) is liable for payment of the rent to the landlord.

        3. If a tenant transfers less than all the remaining rights (a sublease), the transferee is liable to the tenant and the tenant remains liable to the landlord for payment of the rent.

V. Termination or renewal of the lease.

    A. Termination of lease and obligation to pay rent.

        1. A lease terminates at the expiration of the specified term or in accordance with a provision of the lease.

        2. A statute or a lease may provide that notice of termination is required to be given by the landlord.

        3. A periodic tenancy (e.g., from month to month) is renewed automatically; it can be terminated by giving one period's notice or as provided by statute.

        4. If a landlord conveys his, her or its interest in the real property to a tenant, the transfer is a release and the tenant's interest in the property is merged into the title to the property.

        5. The tenant and landlord may agree to terminate a lease prior to the end of the term, in which case the tenant surrenders possession of the property.

        6. A tenant may abandon the property by completely moving off the premises with no intention to return. Abandonment may be treated as an offer of

surrender so that if the landlord retakes possession, the obligation of the tenant to pay rent may cease.

7. A statute or lease may provide that when the landlord or tenant fails to comply with a lease provision, there is a forfeiture and the lease is terminated.

8. Destruction of the premises by a cause that was beyond the control of the landlord may terminate a residential lease; if there is no relevant provision in a commercial lease, the destruction of an entire building may relieve a commercial tenant of the responsibility for paying rent.

B. Renewal — A lease may provide for renewal, in which case, the tenant must comply with provision for timely notification, or the landlord and tenant may agree to renew a lease.

KEY WORDS AND PHRASES IN TEXT

Landlord-tenant relationships
Uniform Residential Landlord and Tenant
    Act (URLTA)
Landlord (lessor)
Tenant (lessee)
Lease
Exclusivity of possession
Lease form
Reversionary interest of landlord
Prohibitions against discrimination
Compliance with building codes and
    zoning ordinances
Unconscionability
Landlord's duty to deliver possession
    to tenant
Tenant's right to retain possession
Covenant of quiet enjoyment
Eviction (depriving tenant of possession
    or enjoyment)
Partial eviction
Constructive eviction
Retaliatory eviction
Duty of tenant not to create nuisance or
    commit waste
Alteration of the premises
Fixtures
Maintenance of the premises
Common areas
Implied warranty of habitability
Tenant's remedies for landlord's failure
    to maintain leased premises
Withholding rent
Deposit of withheld rent in escrow
    account or with escrow agent

Repair and deduct statutes
Canceling the lease
Rent
Security deposits
Late charges
Rent escalation
Payment of property taxes
Landlord's remedies for tenant's failure
    to pay rent
Landlord's lien
Recovery of possession by landlord
Right of entry
Remedies of ejectment and unlawful
    detainer procedure
Invitees, licensees and trespassers
Attractive nuisance doctrine
Duty to exercise reasonable care to avoid
    foreseeable risks
Landlord's liability for injuries occurring
    on the property
Landlord's duty to make repairs
Exculpatory clauses
Tenant liability for to maintain safe
    conditions
Effect of transfer of landlord's interest
Effect of transfer of the tenant's interest
    by assignment or sublease
Termination of lease by notice of by
    release and merger
Surrender of premises by agreement
Abandonment of premises by tenant
Forfeiture of lease
Effect of destruction of the property
Renewal of lease

FILL-IN QUESTIONS

1. A landlord-tenant relationship arises when an owner of real property transfers temporary exclusive _____ of the property to another person in exchange for the payment of _____. The owner of the real property is referred to as the _____ or lessor. The party who is given the right to assume temporary _____ of the property is called the tenant or lessee.

2. In order to create a landlord-tenant relationship, the parties enter into a contract, that is referred to as a _____, in which their intent to agree to the transfer of possession of real property is expressed. The _____ is a document which contains a description of the property and indicates the period of time during which the tenant is entitled to have possession of the property and the amount of consideration, or _____, which the tenant will pay to the landlord. The lease also provides for the landlord's _____, which entitles the landlord to regain possession of the property at the end of the term specified in the lease.

3. It is implied, if not expressed, that a landlord promises that the tenant's use and enjoyment of the leased property will not be disturbed or interfered with by the landlord or another person having superior title during the term of the lease because of the covenant of _____. In addition, today, the landlord also makes an implied warranty of _____ to the effect that the premises are _____ and, therefore, fit for human occupancy.

4. Because of state statutes and local ordinances, a _____ is required to meet certain standards relating to construction and maintenance of a residential building. In addition, the landlord is required to maintain _____, such as hallways, stairways, elevators which are used by tenants, so that they are free from defects of which the landlord has actual knowledge and those about which the landlord reasonably should know.

5. If a tenant makes an assignment of his or her rights under a lease, the assignee pays rent to the _____; if the tenant subleases his or her rights, the sublessee pays rent to the _____. In either event, if the assignee or sublessee fails to pay the rent, the _____ is liable for the unpaid rent to the landlord.

MULTIPLE CHOICE QUESTIONS

1. A tenant must exercise reasonable care in maintaining leased property over which the tenant has control; a landlord must exercise reasonable care in maintaining leased property over which the landlord has control. If another person is injured because repairs have not been made to an area over which both the landlord and tenant have control:
    a. only the landlord will be liable to the injured person, who may recover damages because of the landlord's negligence.
    b. only the tenant will be liable to the injured person, who may recover damages because the tenant has created a nuisance.
    c. both the landlord and tenant will be liable to the injured person, who may be awarded damages against both.

d. the injured person may not recover from the landlord if the landlord is able to prove that the repairs were not made to correct a latent condition.

2. A tenant is required to exercise reasonable care in order to prevent harm to people who foreseeably may be in the area over which the tenant exercises control. Similarly, the landlord is required to exercise reasonable care in order to prevent harm to people who foreseeably may be in the area over which the landlord exercises control. What is reasonable care depends upon the circumstances, including whether an injured party was an invitee, licensee or trespasser.
   a. An invitee is one whom a tenant invites onto the premises for the tenant's benefit.
   b. A licensee is one whom the tenant allows on the premises for the benefit of the landlord.
   c. An invitee is one whom the tenant allows on the premises for the benefit of the invitee.
   d. Because a trespasser is one who has no right to be on the premises, no duty to exercise care is owed to a trespasser by either a tenant or landlord.

3. Luxor Realty Co. is the owner of an apartment house in which there are 88 units. Tucker has leased one of the apartments. Tucker, Friendley (a friend of Tucker's), Charity (who was soliciting contributions to the United Way), and Burgler (a thief) were injured when a cable for the elevator in which they were riding broke.
   a. Luxor Realty Co. owes a greater degree of care in order to prevent harm to Charity than it does to Tucker.
   b. Luxor Realty Co. owes a greater degree of care in order to prevent harm to Charity than it does to Friendley.
   c. Luxor Realty Co. owes a greater degree of care in order to prevent harm to Burgler than it does to Friendley.
   d. Luxor Realty Co. owes a greater degree of care in order to prevent harm to Friendley than it does to Burgler.

Questions 4 and 5 are based upon the following fact situation: Tennent leased a building under a five year written lease at a monthly rental of $600. The premises were used as a restaurant and Tennent, therefore, installed an air conditioning system, a counter and stools. Six months after the commencement of the lease, the landlord turned off the water and has since refused to reconnect the water pipes. Tennent moved out and wishes to remove the counter and stools without damage to the premises and the air conditioning system, which will inflict considerable damage to the premises.

4. By turning off the water, the landlord has:
   a. violated the implied terms of the year to year lease.
   b. actually evicted Tennent by breaching the covenant of possession.
   c. constructively evicted Tennent by breaching the covenant of quiet enjoyment.
   d. not terminated the lease and has a right to receive the monthly rent of $600 from Tennent.

5. The counter, stools and air conditioning system are:
   a. part of the real property and their removal by Tennent is wrongful.
   b. fixtures. They became part of the real property and can be removed only by the owner of the premises.
   c. trade fixtures. Tennent may remove the counter and stools because their removal does not damage the premises but he may not remove the air conditioning system.

d. trade fixtures. Tennent may remove the counter, stools and air conditioning system but will be required to reimburse the landlord for damage caused by the removal of the air conditioning.

6. In January, Great Records Inc. rented a store in a building from Hamilton Realty Corp. under a three year written lease at a rental of $1,000 per month. Great Records Inc. operated a record store on the premises. In May, the structure was badly damaged, when a helicopter lost one of its rotors and crashed into the building. The record store cannot be used without substantial repairs. If Great Records Inc. leased:

   a. only the store, the lease is terminated and Great Records Inc. need not continue to pay rent.
   b. only the store, the lease is not terminated until the expiration of the three year period.
   c. the entire building, the lease is terminated and Great Records Inc. need not continue to pay rent.
   d. the entire building, Great Records Inc. will be required to make the necessary repairs and Great Records Inc., but not Hamilton Realty Corp., may recover damages from the operator of the helicopter.

Chapter 54

Insurance

The objective of insurance is to transfer and allocate risk—an existing contingency, over which one has little control, but which will result in an economic loss. In order to obtain insurance, one enters into a particular kind of contract, called an insurance policy. For it to be valid and enforceable, all the requisites of a contract must be present and, in addition, the person obtaining the insurance must have an insurable interest in the subject matter (life, health or property) which is insured.

The first part of the chapter is devoted to general principles of insurance law. Characteristics of particular types of insurance are discussed in the last segment of the material.

THINGS TO KEEP IN MIND

Insurance companies, insurance agents and brokers, the contents of insurance policies, the rates charged as premiums, etc., are subject to regulation by the several states.

OUTLINE

I.   The nature of insurance.

   A. The concept of risk pooling.

      1. An insurance company is able to spread certain risks among a large group of people based upon the estimated amount of benefits that it will have to pay in case certain contingencies occur.

      2. An insurance company establishes premium rates which it will charge each

member in the group based upon its predictions as to the total benefit payments that it will have to pay and to assure that it will receive a profit.

B. Terminology.

    1. Policy — Instrument by which a contract of insurance is made.

    2. Parties.

        a. Insurer — Insurance company which issues a policy.

        b. Insured — The person obtaining property insurance or the person, whose life is insured under the terms of a life insurance policy.

        c. Insurance agent — Employed by the insurer, for which he or she is an agent. (See Chapters 32 and 33.)

        d. Insurance broker — An independent contractor, who is treated as an agent for the person for whom he or she is obtaining insurance, except when otherwise provided by state statute.

    3. Premium — The consideration paid to the insurer by the party obtaining insurance.

II. Insurable interest — A legal or equitable interest in the subject matter of insurance (a life or property), such that one will benefit from its preservation or incur a direct, pecuniary or monetary loss if it is destroyed or damaged.

A. Life insurance.

    1. An insurable interest must exist at the time the policy is obtained.

    2. Every person has an insurable interest in his or her own life.

    3. A spouse, child or parent has an insurable interest in the life of his or her spouse, parent or child.

    4. A creditor has an insurable interest in the life of a debtor.

    5. Partners have insurable interests in the lives of co-partners, and shareholders in close corporations have insurable interests in the lives of the other shareholders.

    6. Business units have insurable interests in the lives of "key" personnel.

    7. A beneficiary or assignee need not have an insurable interest in the life of the person whose life is insured.

B. Property (real or personal) insurance.

    1. An insurable interest must exist at the time when the insured-against loss occurs.

2. The following people have insurable interests in property — owners, including life tenants, joint tenants, tenants in common and remaindermen, lessees, mortgagees, bailees, pledgees, trustees and buyers and sellers, who have made executory contracts for the sale of property.

III. The insurance contract.

A. General principles of contract law are applicable.

B. When an insurance policy is effective.

1. Application made to an insurance broker — Customer is not insured until the broker procures a policy.

2. Application made to an agent of an insurer.

a. Life insurance — Insurance is effective after application is accepted and premium is paid. A binder may result in earlier coverage upon payment of a premium.

b. Property insurance is effective when agreement is reached as to coverage. A binder may be given.

C. Important provisions in insurance policies.

1. State statutes mandate inclusion of certain provisions.

2. Incontestability clause in life or health insurance policy.

a. An insurance company may not contest or refuse payment, after a stated period of time.

b. Incontestability clause does not prevent insurance company from refusing to pay benefits or reduction in the amount of benefits because of lack of insurable interest, failure to pay premiums or failure to file proof of loss within a specified period.

3. Coinsurance clauses — The insured is required to insure property at a stated percent of its full replacement value in order to recover the face amount of the policy in case of a total loss or the replacement cost when there has been a partial loss.

$$\text{Loss} \times \frac{\text{Amount of insurance carried}}{\substack{\text{Amount of insurance required} \\ \text{(\% x replacement value)}}} = \text{Amount of recovery}$$

4. Appraisal and arbitration clause — Value of property will be determined by appraisal or arbitration when the insured and the insurer disagree as to value of a loss.

5. Multiple insurance coverage ("other insurance," "*pro rata*," etc., clauses) — If there are multiple policies covering the same property or health risk, the loss is apportioned among the several insurers.

6. Antilapse clause.

    a. Most life insurance policies contain provisions for grace periods, during which delinquent payments can be made in order to prevent lapse of insurance coverage.

    b. Statutes often require that a smaller paid up policy be issued or extended insurance coverage be given or the cash surrender value be paid to the owner of the policy.

7. Cancellation of insurance policies.

    a. Written notice of cancellation must be given and unearned premiums that were paid in advance refunded by insurance company.

    b. Property and automobile insurance may be cancelled by either party upon giving required notice.

    c. Life and health insurance can be cancelled by insurer prior to effective incontestability date.

    d. Life insurance antilapse provisions are an alternative to cancellation.

8. Subrogation.

    a. If an insurer of property pays an insured for a loss, caused by another's intentional or negligent act, it is subrogated to (or "stands in the shoes" of) the insured.

    b. An insurer has no right of subrogation against a third person, who caused the death of one covered by life insurance.

D. Interpretation of provisions when terms of policy are ambiguous.

    1. Words are given their ordinary meaning unless it is clear that a technical or unusual meaning has been intended.

    2. Provisions are interpreted most strongly against the insurer which prepared the contract.

E. Property insurance is treated as an indemnity contract because the insurer agrees to pay the amount of loss upon the occurrence of a contingency that may or may not happen.

F. Duties and rights of parties.

    1. Applicant must disclose all material facts that are necessary in order for the insurer to evaluate risk (e.g., those facts that would influence the insurance company's decision to refuse to insure against a risk or to charge a higher premium).

    2. After a claim is filed, insurer is required to conduct an investigation, make

reasonable efforts to settle third party claims and defend an insured in any suits that are brought against the insured.

G. Payment by an insurer may be denied or a policy rescinded.

    1. Failure to comply with reasonable requirements as to notice and proof of loss.

    2. Acts that are illegal or against public policy.

    3. Lack of insurable interest.

    4. Policy procured through use of fraud, misrepresentation, etc.

    5. An insurance company may not contest or refuse payment, after a stated period of time, if the insurance policy contained an incontestability clause.

IV. Types of insurance.

    A. Life insurance.

        1. Types of life insurance.

            a. Whole (straight or ordinary) life insurance — Stated premiums are paid during the lifetime of the insured.
               1) Investment feature — Cash value increases over time and may be borrowed.
               2) May provide for retirement income (annuity or living benefit program).

            b. Limited payment whole life insurance — Premiums are paid for a specified number of years, after which the policy is paid up and fully effective.

            c. Term insurance — Provides temporary coverage during a stated period, but may be renewable after the period or convertible into whole life insurance. Does not have savings features.
               1) Level term insurance.
               2) Decreasing term insurance.
               3) Mortgage term insurance.

            d. Endowment insurance — Premiums are paid for a specified term, at the end of which fixed periodic payments are made to the insured (an annuity) or, upon the death of the insured, to a beneficiary.

            e. "Universal" life insurance.
               1) Permanent life insurance that provides for investment by insurer of premiums after expenses in interest bearing government securities and payment of the proceeds to policyholders.
               2) Proceeds, which are tax free, increase the cash value of the policy and may be used for payment of premiums or withdrawn.
               3) The amounts of death protection and premiums may be adjusted up or down.

2. Some provisions in life insurance policies.

    a. Exclusions from insurer's liability—death due to suicide, service in military action during war, execution for a crime, etc.

    b. If the age of the insured was misstated, the premium payments and/or benefits will be adjusted.

    c. The owner of the policy designates one or more beneficiaries to whom the death benefits are to be paid and, unless the beneficiaries' rights are vested, the policy owner may change the beneficiaries and assign the rights to the policy upon giving notice to the insurer.

    d. Creditors' rights.
        1) Creditors can reach insurance proceeds that are payable to the estate of the insured or payable to a beneficiary if the payment of premiums constituted a fraud on creditors.
        2) Creditors cannot usually reach the cash surrender value of a policy or compel changing the name of a beneficiary to that of a creditor.
        3) In most states, at least part of the proceeds of life insurance are exempt from creditors' claims.

    e. Termination occurs upon default in premium payments (see III.C.6. above); death of the insured and payment of benefits; expiration of the term of the policy; and cancellation by the policy owner.

B. Home, property and liability insurance.

    1. Standard fire insurance policy.

        a. The insurer's liability extends to losses caused by hostile fires, but not by friendly fires unless there is extended coverage.

        b. Liability of insurer when there is a total loss.
            1) Valued policy — Insurer is liable for amount specified in policy.
            2) Open policy — Insurer is liable for the lesser of the fair market value of property or a maximum specified amount.

        c. When there is a partial loss, insurer is liable for the actual loss.

        d. Proof of loss must be filed by the insured within a specified period of time or immediately (which is interpreted as meaning within a reasonable period of time after a loss).

        e. Most policies provide that coverage is suspended if the premises are unoccupied for a stated period of time.

        f. Property insurance is nonassignable before there is a loss.

    2. A homeowner's, renter's or condominium owner's policy may include property coverage and liability coverage in case someone is injured on the insured property.

3. An insured may obtain a floater policy on specific personal articles that are located at the insured property or on personal effects when they are taken off the property.

C. Automobile insurance.

1. Insurance to cover liability for property damage and bodily injury to others.

2. Collision insurance covers damage to the insured's auto.

3. Comprehensive insurance covers loss, damage and destruction caused by fire, hurricane, hail and vandalism.

4. Other forms of coverage.

   a. Uninsured motorists.

   b. Accidental death benefits.

   c. Medical payments.

   d. No-fault auto insurance.

D. Some forms of business liability insurance.

1. General liability insurance.

2. Product liability insurance.

3. Professional malpractice insurance.

4. Workers' compensation insurance.

KEY WORDS AND PHRASES IN TEXT

Insurance
Risk
Risk management
Risk pooling
Insurance policy (the insurance contract)
Premium
Insurance company (insurer/underwriter)
The insured
Insurance agents and brokers
Insurable interest
Beneficiary of life insurance
Key-person insurance (business insurance)
Application for insurance
Binder
Incontestability clause
Coinsurance clause

Appraisal and arbitration clause
Multiple insurance coverage
Antilapse clause
Grace period
Cash surrender value
Cancellation of insurance policy
Disclosure of material facts by applicant
    for insurance
Defenses against payment that can be
    raised by insurance companies
Rebuttal of insurance company's defenses
Life insurance
Whole (straight, ordinary) life insurance
Limited payment life insurance
Term life insurance
Endowment life insurance

Annuity
Universal life insurance
Liability of life insurer
Exclusions from liability
Adjustment due to misstatement of age
Assignment and change of beneficiary
Creditors' rights to benefits
Standard fire insurance policy
Personal theft insurance
Comprehensive liability insurance policy
Hostile as opposed to friendly fires
Valued property insurance policy
Open property insurance policy
Proof of loss
Occupancy clause
Assignment of insurance policy
Homeowners policy
Renters and condominium owners policies

Personal articles and personal effects floaters
Automobile insurance
Automobile liability insurance
Umbrella policy
Collision and comprehensive automobile insurance
Uninsured motorist coverage
Accidental death benefits
Double indemnity clause
Medical payment coverage
Other-driver (omnibus) clause
No-fault insurance
Business liability insurance
Comprehensive general liability insurance
Product liability insurance
Professional malpractice insurance
Workers' compensation insurance

FILL-IN QUESTIONS

1. In general, wagering bargains are illegal, because they are agreements based upon _____ risks, and are distinguishable from contracts of insurance, which provide for _____ existing risks.

2. With regard to property insurance, any person, who has a legal or equitable interest in real or personal property, is treated as having an _____ interest because he or she will benefit if the property is not damaged or destroyed or will _____.

3. In order to recover under a policy providing for property insurance, the insured must have an _____ interest at the time that _____.

4. With regard to life insurance, the owner of a life insurance policy must have an _____ interest in the life of the person whose life is insured. One can obtain a life insurance policy covering his or her own life or the life of another if he or she will benefit economically from the continued life of the person whose life is insured or will _____.

5. In order to recover under a life insurance policy, the owner of the policy must have had an _____ interest at the time _____.

MULTIPLE CHOICE QUESTIONS

1. John, an insured, is fifty years of age. In applying for life insurance, he misstated his age as being 47. The amount of insurance on his life will be adjusted to the sum that the premiums paid by John would have purchased:
    a. at age 47.
    b. at age 50.
    c. at a reasonable age.
    d. at no age because the policy is unenforceable.

2. Carol and Nan were business partners. They agreed that each would insure the life of the other for her own benefit. On the application for insurance, Nan stated that she had never had any heart trouble. She had, in fact, suffered a heart attack three years before. Carol's policy on Nan's life contained the usual two year incontestability clause. Four years later, after the dissolution of the partnership but while the policy on her life was still in force, Nan was killed when struck by a car driven by Marcia.
   a. Carol cannot recover from the insurer because of the misrepresentation in the application.
   b. Carol cannot recover because the partnership has been dissolved and she, therefore, lacks an insurable interest.
   c. Carol can recover if the insurance company refuses to pay the proceeds of the life insurance on Nan's life to her.
   d. If the insurance company has to pay the proceeds of the life insurance on Nan's life to Carol, it will be subrogated to Nan's rights against Marcia.

3. An insurance company paid Zandarski for a loss due to fire. The insurance company has a right to recover from Frazer, who caused the fire. Such right is known as:
   a. insurable interest.
   b. subrogation.
   c. subordination.
   d. contribution.

4. The Smart Corp. obtained a fire insurance policy on its factory from the ABC Insurance Company. The policy was for $500,000 which was the value of the property insured. The policy was the standard fire insurance policy sold in the United States. A fire occurred and resulted in a $100,000 loss. Which of the following will prevent Smart Corp. from recovering the full amount of its loss from the insurance company?
   a. The coinsurance clause.
   b. Smart Corp. had a similar policy with another company for $300,000.
   c. $200,000 worth of the loss was caused by smoke and water damage.
   d. Smart Corp. did not notify ABC Insurance Company of the fire until the day after the fire.

Questions 5 and 6 are based on the following fact situation: Young was the owner of a warehouse that was insured by the Ivy Fire Insurance Co. The face value of the fire insurance policy was $600,000. The policy covered the warehouse itself and the contents and contained a 90% coinsurance clause. Careless, an employee of Young, negligently dropped a lighted cigarette on some packing material which caught fire.

5. Assume that the fire totally destroyed the warehouse and the goods stored therein and that the loss was subsequently appraised at $1 million. Young is entitled to a payment of:
   a. $600,000, the face amount of the policy, from Ivy Fire Insurance Co. because there was a total loss.
   b. $900,000 from Ivy Fire Insurance Co. because of the coinsurance clause.
   c. $540,000 from Ivy Fire Insurance Co. because of the coinsurance clause.
   d. Nothing because the fire was caused by the negligence of an employee of Young.

6. Assume that the fire damaged the warehouse and destroyed goods, valued at $100,000. Repairs to the warehouse will cost $80,000. At the time of the fire loss,

the replacement value of the warehouse was $900,000.

a. Young is entitled to a payment of $120,000 because of the coinsurance clause.
b. Young is entitled to a payment of $162,000 because of the coinsurance clause.
c. Young is entitled to a payment of $20,000 and the insurance company will be required to pay $100,000 to the people who had stored the goods that were destroyed in the fire.
d. Young is entitled to a payment of $72,000 from the insurance company. The owners of the goods stored (and destroyed) in the warehouse are entitled to a payment of $90,000 from the insurance company and $10,000 from Young.

Unit Nine

SPECIAL TOPICS

The four chapters in this unit, the final portion of the Fourth Edition of *West's Business Law*, deal with topics that may be of interest to a limited number of students and that ordinarily are not included in the legal studies curriculum at some colleges and universities.

For example, Chapter 57 includes information about the common law and statutory duties that accountants owe to their clients and, in some cases, third parties who foreseeably may rely upon statements and other documents that are prepared by accountants. The subject matter covered in Chapter 56 is also of particular interest to accounting students. The chapter deals with transfers of ownership interests in real and personal property by the creation of trusts and, upon death, by will or in accordance with inheritance statutes. For those of you who are preparing to sit for the CPA Examination, there are series of multiple choice questions in Chapters 56 and 57, some of which have been adapted from past CPA Exams, that may be helpful in your review. Note too, that following the materials in this *Study Guide to Accompany West's Business Law*, which are coordinated with the text, is a section containing information about the Uniform CPA Business Law Examination.

Chapters 55 and 58 deal with topics of increasing concern to business people. Because of the difficulty in making generalizations as to the relevant legal principles and lack of unanimity, review test questions are not provided in these chapters. These chapters are illustrative of a theme in this book—the evolving nature of business and law that results from changes in the general environment in which both business and law exist and function—for, over time, both law and business have adapted to gradual, and revolutionary, changes that have occurred in society. Most recently, accommodations by lawmakers have been necessitated by concomitant dynamic technological transformations in the ways in which we conduct business.

Today, data maintenance and a substantial proportion of business transactions are conducted through the facilities that have been made available because of computers.

How the law has dealt and is dealing with the computer age are discussed in Chapter 55. (You may also wish to refer to Chapter 28.) In addition, because of technology, the work has shrunk. Business people recognize that they must be more sensitive to the law that is relevant when they engage in international business transactions. Chapter 59 contains information about the internationalization of business and some of the germane legal doctrines and problems that one may encounter when conducting business in the global economy.

Chapter 55

Computers and
the Law

Law evolves over time and adapts to changing conditions brought about by new technologies. In recent years, the computer has revolutionized the way in which business is conducted and a body of law, now known as "computer law," has been developing in order to keep pace with the ever increasing utilization of computer technology. Among the concerns that are being dealt with are computer crime and torts, protection of computer hardware and software developers from infringement, and privacy. In some instances, existing statutory and case law have been applied to legal disputes regarding computers and their use. In other cases, new legislation has been enacted particularly in order to specify that certain forms of computer abuse, which fall outside the traditional definitions of particular existing crimes, are criminal wrongs.

OUTLINE

I.   Computer crime.

    A. Many states have adopted specific statutes that define as crimes certain wrongful acts relating to computers and their use. In other states, existing criminal laws have been applied to such acts.

    B. A computer crime refers to a wrongful act directed against a computer and/or its parts or a wrongful use of a computer as an instrument of a crime (computer assisted crime) or an abusive use of a computer.

    C. Types of computer crime.

        1. Financial crimes — Altering computer records and/or conducting unauthorized financial transactions by accessing a computer.

2. Theft of computer equipment (hardware) or goods that are controlled and accounted for by means of a computer applications program.

3. Theft of data, computer time and services.

   a. Unauthorized use of another person's computer system or data stored in another person's computer system may not be larceny, which encompasses a physical taking and carrying away of property from the possession of another person (i.e., theft of tangible property).

   b. A person who, without authorization, uses another person's computer system or data stored in another person's computer system may be prosecuted for the crime of theft of services or the crime of larceny in states which broadly construe criminal statutes.

   c. Computer hacking — Breaking a computer security code (password) or system and perusing information in the computer records.

4. Software piracy — In some states and under federal law, the unauthorized decoding and making copies of software programs may be criminal.

5. Vandalism and destructive programming (disseminating a computer virus).

D. Preventing and controlling computer crime.

   1. Private protective measures — Limiting access to data.

      a. Computer security may take the form of restricting usage only to those with special clearance.

      b. Passwords may be required but should be frequently changed.

      c. In order to protect data, data may be encoded before it is stored and when it is communicated using a secret code.

      d. Off-site backup storage of data should be constantly maintained so that lost or destroyed records can be reconstructed.

   2. Federal computer crime control legislation.

      a. Federal statutes relating to theft, transportation of stolen property, wire fraud and mail fraud have been the bases for some prosecutions for computer related crimes.

      b. The Counterfeit Access Device and Computer Fraud and Abuse Act (1984) makes it a crime to knowingly access a computer in order to:
         1) Obtain restricted government information with the intent of using the information to injure the United States or aid a foreign nation.
         2) Obtain information contained in a financial institution's financial records or in a consumer reporting agency's files relating to consumers.
         3) Use, modify, destroy or prevent the authorized use of a computer

operated for or on behalf of the federal government or to disclose the information that it contains.

    c. The Electronic Fund Transfer Act (EFTA, which is discussed in Chapter 28) makes it a crime to use, sell, furnish or transport in interstate commerce any counterfeit, fictitious, altered, forged, lost, stolen or fraudulently obtained device (e.g., an ATM card or personal identification number) which is used to conduct an electronic fund transfer in order to obtain money, goods, services or anything else of value.

  3. State computer crime control legislation.

II. Intellectual property protection for software.

  A. Intellectual property resulting from intellectual creative processes may be protected by the patent and copyright laws; in addition, the trademark act prohibits the unauthorized reproduction of marks, words, symbols or pictures which are used to distinguish goods in a market from those of competitors.

  B. Patent protection.

    1. A patent applicant must show that an invention or process is genuine, novel, useful and not obvious. A patent protects the application of an idea.

    2. It is difficult to obtain a patent for software because the product simply automates procedures that can be manually performed or because the basis for software is often a mathematical equation or formula, which is not patentable. In addition, there is a waiting period for a patent.

  C. Copyright protection.

    1. A copyright protects the expression of an idea. Thus the U.S. copyright law provides that literary works, which include expressions in words, "numbers, or other. . . numerical symbols or indicia," are copyrightable subject matters.

    2. In order to be copyrightable, the subject matter must be an 'original work of authorship and fixed in a tangible medium of expression.'

    3. A copyright extends to works that are in a tangible means of expression 'from which they can be perceived, reproduced, or otherwise communicated, either directly or with the aid of a machine or device.'

    4. The Computer Software Copyright Act of 1980.

      a. A computer program is defined as a "set of statements or instructions to be used directly or indirectly in a computer in order to bring about a certain result."

      b. The statute provides that computer programs are among the kinds of creative works that can be protected by the copyright laws.

      c. Both a computer program's source code and object code may be copyrighted.

      d. Based upon case law, copyright protection has been expanded to cover the overall concept of a program, including its structure, sequence and organization.

  D. Computer hardware and software trademarks may be registered with the U.S. Patent and Trademark Office.

  E. The Semiconductor Chip Protection Act (1984) — The owner of a mask work, which is registered with the U.S. Copyright Office, obtains the exclusive right to reproduce, import or distribute the mask work or a semiconductor chip product containing it for ten years.

  F. A firm may protect trade secrets—information or a process that is not commonly known and which gives it an advantage over its competitors.

III. The privacy issue.

  A. The U.S. Constitution does not expressly guarantee a right to privacy but, based upon constitutional protections, it is implied that an individual's privacy is protected against government intrusion.

  B. At common law it is tortious to wrongfully invade another person's privacy; an injured party can recover for an unauthorized intrusion into private records and for the public disclosure of private facts when the nature of the disclosure is such that it would be objectionable to a reasonable person.

  C. In some cases, it is difficult to apply the common law doctrine of privacy to possible computer invasions and disclosures.

  D. Relevant federal privacy legislation.

     1. Crime Control Act (1973) — Protects confidentiality of certain computerized criminal records.

     2. Family Education Rights and Privacy Act (1974) — Limits access to computerized records of education related evaluations and grades in colleges and universities.

     3. Privacy Act (1974) — Protects the privacy of individuals about whom the federal government has information.

     4. Tax Reform Act (1976) — Protects the privacy of personal financial information.

     5. Right to Financial Privacy Act (1978) — Prohibits financial institutions from providing the federal government with access to customers' records.

     6. Electronic Fund Transfer Act (1980) — Financial institutions must notify an individual if a third party gained access to his or her account.

     7. Counterfeit Access Device and Computer Fraud and Abuse Act (1984) — Prohibits unauthorized use of a computer in order to retrieve information in a financial institution's or consumer reporting agency's file.

8. Cable Communications Policy Act (1984) — Regulates access to data collected by cable service operations relating to subscribers.

9. Electronic Communications Privacy Act (1986) — Prohibits the interception of information that is communicated by electronic means.

IV. Computer assisted legal research — WESTLAW (West Publishing Company) and LEXIS (Mead Data Control, Inc.) provide data base systems for accessing law related materials, including cases, statutes and regulations, that can be accessed through data delivery systems.

KEY WORDS AND PHRASES IN TEXT

Computer crime
Financial crimes involving the use of
    computers
Theft of computer property (equipment)
Theft of property by using a computer
Theft of computer data or services
Larceny
Computer security
Passwords
Hacking
Software piracy
Vandalism and destructive programming
Private protective measures to control
    and prevent computer crime

Federal computer crime control laws
Counterfeit Access Device and Computer
    Fraud and Abuse Act
Electronic Fund Transfer Act
State computer crime control legislation
Intellectual property protection
Patents, copyrights, trademarks and
    trade secrets
Computer Software Copyright Act
Source code and object code protection
Program structure protection
Semiconductor Chip Protection Act
Common law privacy doctrine
Federal and state privacy legislation

Chapter 56

Wills, Trusts, and Estates

As indicated in Chapters 51 and 53, a person may transfer ownership rights with respect to personal and real property by sale or gift during his or her lifetime. A person may also provide for the disposition of his or her property upon his or her death. Compliance with certain formalities, however, is required.

The concept of private ownership of property, the effectuation of a natural person's testamentary intent, and the public policy of protecting the family underlie inheritance laws which exist in all states. These statutes regulate the disposition of decedents' estates by will, by descent and distribution and by establishment of trusts. These topics, as well as the taxation of inheritances and estates, are discussed in this chapter.

THINGS TO KEEP IN MIND

Although the purposes of inheritance laws are similar among the states, the manner in which these objectives are achieved varies. Some states have recently revised their statutes and the legislatures in other jurisdictions are considering revisions.

OUTLINE

I.   Wills — Final, formal declaration by persons concerning the manner in which their property is to be disposed of after their death; during one's lifetime, one may change and/or revoke his or her will.

A. Terminology.

1.   Testator (male) or testatrix (female) — Person who has made a will.

2. Probate court — Court which administers the law relating to wills and estates of decedents.

3. Executor (male) or executrix (female) — Personal representative, named in a will, to settle the affairs of a decedent.

4. Administrator or administratrix — Personal representative, appointed by a court to settle the affairs of a decedent, who did not leave a will or who left a will but failed to name an executor or named an executor, who is unable or unwilling to serve.

5. Devise — Gift of real property by will. Title vests in devisee.

6. Bequest (legacy) — Gift of personal property by will. Title vests initially in personal representative.

7. Specific devise or bequest — Gift of identified, particular, described property.

8. General devise or bequest — Gift of a quantity of real property or personal property (usually a sum of money) without a specific identification or description of it.

9. Residuary clause — Provision for a disposition of remaining property, not otherwise effectively disposed of by devise and bequest, after payment of decedent's obligations.

10. Uniform Probate Act has been adopted in a few states.

B. Testamentary capacity.

1. Age — In most states, 18 is the minimum age for executing a will.

2. "Being of sound mind."

   a. Able to formulate and comprehend a personal plan for the disposition of one's property.

   b. Document intended to be a will.

   c. Not necessarily the same as contractual capacity.

C. Formal requirements.

1. A will must be in writing.

   a. Holographic will — Handwritten, dated and signed by testator. Some statutes do not require witnessing and publication.

   b. Nuncupative will — A few states permit oral wills under special circumstances.

2. A will must be signed by the testator.

3. A will must be attested by two or more witnesses. Some statutes require that they be disinterested (not benefit from the will), witness the signing of the will by the testator and/or sign in each other's presence.

4. Testator is required to orally declare that the will is his last will and testament in some states (publication).

D. The validity of a will may be challenged if it was executed because of fraud in the execution, fraud in the inducement, mistake, duress or undue influence.

E. Revocation by act of the testator.

1. Intentional, deliberate burning, tearing, cancellation, obliteration or destruction by the testator or another person, in the presence of and at the direction of the testator, in compliance with statute.

2. Codicil — Separate writing which revokes, amends or supplements a prior will.

a. Executed with same formality as a will.

b. Refers to testator's will.

c. If a codicil, or a later will, does not expressly revoke a prior will, the codicil or later will controls when it is inconsistent with a provision in an earlier will.

F. Revocation by operation of law (varies from state to state) — Subsequent marriage, divorce, annulment, birth or adoption of children.

G. Renunciation of rights under a will.

1. A surviving spouse often has a right to take a statutory marital intestate (forced, elective or widow's) share, rather than take under will of deceased spouse.

2. A beneficiary may renounce a devise or legacy and elect instead to take his or her intestate share.

II. Intestacy statutes of descent and distribution.

A. Provide for inheritance of property by intestate succession if a decedent failed to execute a valid will or omitted a provision for the disposition of some property.

B. Statutory rules vary from state to state.

C. Descent — Real property vests in heirs upon the death of the owner of land.

D. Title to personal property vests in the personal representative of a decedent, who makes distributions in accordance with statute, after paying obligations of the decedent and the estate.

E. General statutory pattern for distribution of decedent's property, if decedent is survived by:

1. Spouse and no descendants (children, grandchildren, etc.) — Spouse inherits entire estate.

2. Spouse and one or more descendants — Spouse takes one-third (elective, marital share) and children share remaining two-thirds equally.

    a. In some states, if there is only one child, the spouse takes one-half and the child one-half.

    b. If a child predeceased the decedent, his or her children share equally the share his or her parent would have taken (*per stirpes*).

    c. A statute may also provide that a spouse is entitled to homestead, household and other allowances.

3. Surviving children or descendants, but no surviving spouse — Children share equally and descendants of children, who died before the decedent, share *per stirpes*.

4. No spouse or lineal descendants.

    a. Parents and/or siblings (and lineal descendants of deceased brothers and sisters *per stirpes*).

    b. Grandparents.

    c. Collateral heirs, such as aunts, uncles, nieces and nephews.

5. If no relatives survive decedent, property escheats to the state or county.

III. Trusts.

A. A trust is created when one person (the settlor) transfers legal title to property to another (the trustee) to administer the property (the *res* or *corpus*) for the benefit of another person or persons (the beneficiaries).

1. The settlor must have an interest in the property that becomes the trust *corpus* and an intention to create a trust.

2. The beneficiary must be an identified, existing natural person or entity.

3. The trustee owes fiduciary duties to the beneficiaries.

B. Express trust — Intentionally created by the settlor.

1. *Inter vivos* trust.

    a. Comes into existence during the lifetime of the settlor.

   b. May be orally created unless subject to a provision of the statute of frauds.

2. Testamentary trust.

   a. Comes into existence upon the death of the settlor.

   b. Formalities required in order to execute a will must be complied with.

C. Implied trust created by operation of law.

   1. Resulting trust is implied when a settlor makes a disposition of property under circumstances from which it can be inferred that the settlor's intention was to create a trust and not to transfer a beneficial interest.

   2. Constructive trust may be imposed as a remedy, without regard to the intention of the parties, in order to prevent unjust enrichment.

D. Other kinds of trusts.

   1. Charitable trust — One that is created for charitable (eleemosynary or philanthropic), educational, religious, scientific or general social purposes.

   2. Spendthrift trust — One that provides for maintenance of the beneficiary and secures the corpus against his or her improvidence by bestowing periodic payments and prohibiting creditors from reaching the beneficiary's interest in future distributions.

   3. Totten trust — A tentative trust that is created when a person deposits money in his or her own name as trustee for a beneficiary.

E. The trustee.

   1. Duties.

      a. Trustee must act with honesty, good faith, loyalty and prudence in administering the trust.

      b. Trustee must maintain accurate accounts, keep trust assets separate from his or her own assets, furnish complete accurate information to the beneficiary, pay an income beneficiary net income at reasonable intervals and distribute the risk of loss from investments by diversification and disposal of assets that do not represent prudent investments.

   2. Powers.

      a. The powers of the trustee may be prescribed by the settlor.

      b. State statutes typically restrict investments to conservative debt securities and apply if settlor has not otherwise defined trustee's investment power.

3. Allocation between principal and income — To the extent that the trust instrument does not provide instructions, ordinary receipts and expenses are to be allocated to the income beneficiaries and extraordinary receipts and expenses are allocated to the principal beneficiaries.

F. Termination of trusts.

1. Trust instrument usually specifies termination date or provides that it will end upon accomplishment of a specific purpose.

2. Unless otherwise provided in the trust instrument, a trust is not terminated by death of trustee or beneficiary.

3. A trust terminates if the purpose for which it was created becomes illegal or impossible.

IV. Estate administration.

A. The personal representative (the executor or appointed administrator) is supervised by the court (usually a probate court).

1. Collects and preserves the decedent's property.

2. Receives and pays valid claims of creditors and taxes.

3. Required to post a bond to insure the honest and faithful performance of his or her duties.

4. Distributes the estate pursuant to court order.

B. Some statutes may permit distribution of assets of a decedent without probate proceedings, and/or in accordance with family settlement agreements.

V. Estate taxes.

A. Federal estate tax is levied upon the total value of the estate after payment of debts and expenses and after allowance for exemptions.

B. Some states impose inheritance taxes on the recipient of a bequest; others impose an estate tax that is similar to the federal estate tax; typically, the tax rates are graduated based upon the relationship between the decedent and the beneficiary.

KEY WORDS AND PHRASES IN TEXT

Principles underlying inheritance law (private property, effectuating an individual's testamentary intent, policy favoring the family and societal interests)

A will

Testamentary disposition of property

Testator or testatrix

Probate court

Personal representative (executor or executrix and administrator or administratrix)

Devise (of real property)
Bequest or legacy of personal property
Specific devise or bequest (or legacy)
General devise or bequest (or legacy)
Ademption by extinction
Ademption by satisfaction
Abatement
Demonstrative bequest
Lapsed legacy
Residual clause
Uniform Probate Code
Testamentary capacity
Formal requirements of a will (writing, signed by testator or testatrix, witnessed and in some cases published)
Holographic handwritten will
Nuncupative will
Effect of undue influence
Revocation of will (by testator or testatrix) by a physical act or another writing (codicil or new will)
Revocation by operation of law
Effect of marriage, divorce, annulment or children born after will is executed
Rights under a will
Spouse's elective or forced share
Renunciation by a beneficiary

Statutes of descent and distribution (intestacy laws)
Lineal descendants
Collateral heirs
Pattern of intestate distribution for children (*per stirpes* or *per capita*)
Trust
Express trust
Settlor (grantor)
Trustee
Beneficiary
Trust deed
Duties and powers of trustee
Allocations between principal and income
Termination of trusts
Inter vivos trust
Testamentary trust
Implied trusts (constructive and resulting trusts)
Charitable trust
Spendthrift trust
Totten trust
Duties of the personal representative
Process of probate
Family settlement agreements
Summary procedures
Federal estate taxes
State inheritance taxes

FILL-IN QUESTIONS

1. A personal representative of a decedent is referred to as an _____ if he or she has been named by the decedent in a properly executed and witnessed _____. If a personal representative is appointed by a _____ court to settle the affairs of a decedent, he or she is referred to as an _____ _____.

2. In general, in order to be effective, a will, executed by one having _____ capacity, must be _____ _____.

3. Statutes of descent and distribution provide for inheritance of property if a decedent _____. Such statutes usually provide that, if a decedent died leaving a spouse and children, the _____ may take an elective one-third share and the remaining share is divided _____. Grandchildren, whose parents died before the decedent, divide _____.

4. An express trust is created when a person (_____) transfers title to real property or personal property to another person (_____) for the benefit of _____.

5. An *inter vivos* trust is a trust that comes into existence _____
    _____; a testamentary trust is one that comes into existence _____
    _____ of the settlor and will be effective if the settlor has complied
    with statutes _____.

MULTIPLE CHOICE QUESTIONS

Questions 1 and 2 are based on the following fact situation: At the time of his death, John Doe, a widower, was the owner of a farm, $20,000 worth of General Motors Corporation stock and $30,000 worth of miscellaneous personal property. His properly executed and witnessed will provided that the farm be left to his only son, the stock in General Motors to his only daughter, and, after payment of taxes and debts, the remaining personal property be divided equally between the son and daughter.

1. Upon John Doe's death:
    a. title to the farm vested in John Doe's son.
    b. title to the stock vested in John Doe's daughter.
    c. title to the miscellaneous personal property vested in an executor appointed by a court to administer the estate, if none was named in the will by John Doe.
    d. title to the miscellaneous personal property vested in the testator, named in the will by John Doe, to administer the estate.

2. The gift:
    a. of the farm to the son was a general bequest.
    b. of the stock to the daughter was a general bequest.
    c. of the stock to the daughter was a specific devise.
    d. of the miscellaneous personal property was a general bequest.

Questions 3 and 4 are based on the following fact situation: In 1970 Mary executed a will which provided that, upon her death, her estate was to be equally divided among her children, August, April and May. Mary died in 1985.

3. If Mary:
    a. was declared judicially insane in 1975, the will was revoked by operation of law.
    b. was divorced from her husband in 1976, the will was revoked by operation of law.
    c. crossed out May's name in the will in 1978, Mary has effectively amended the will.
    d. signed a writing in 1975, stating that her daughter, June, was to share in her estate with her other children, in the presence of two neighbors, who witnessed the writing, Mary has made an effective codicil.

4. Mary's husband:
    a. is not entitled to any share in her estate if he married Mary in 1977.
    b. is not entitled to any share in her estate if they were separated in 1978.
    c. is entitled to take his statutory intestate share.
    d. is entitled to share equally with the named children.

Questions 5, 6 and 7 are based on the following fact situation: H, the husband of W, and father of A and B, died without leaving a will. Before the death of H, H's son, S, who had two children, and H's daughter, D, who had four children, died.

5. Under the statutes of descent and distribution in most states:
   a. W inherits the entire estate.
   b. W takes a life estate in all of H's property.
   c. W, A and B share the entire estate equally.
   d. W may renounce her right to take any share in H's estate.

6. After W has taken her elective share, the rest of the estate is divided:
   a. equally among A and B.
   b. A takes a one-quarter share, B takes a one-quarter share, D's four children and S's two children share equally in the remaining one-half.
   c. A takes a one-quarter share, B takes a one-quarter share, D's children share D's one-quarter share equally and S's children share S's one-quarter share equally.
   d. equally among A, B and the six grandchildren.

7. Assume that H left $18,000 worth of property that has all been reduced to cash. The distribution will be as follows:
   a. W receives $6,000; A receives $3,000; B receives $3,000; S's two children each receive $1,500; D's children each receive $750.
   b. W receives $6,000; A receives $3,000; B receives $3,000; S's children each receive $1,000; D's children each receive $1,000.
   c. W receives $6,000 and A, B, each of S's children and each of D's children receive $1,500.
   d. W, A, B, S's children and D's children each receive $2,000.

8. In her will, Settling conveyed real property to the Orphans' Foundation, a charitable organization, for use in benefiting orphans.
   a. This is an *inter vivos* trust.
   b. The Orphans' Foundation holds legal and equitable title to the property.
   c. A resulting trust arises for the benefit of orphans.
   d. The Orphans' Foundation is a fiduciary and has power to sell the property in order to carry out the purposes of the trust.

9. A person has acquired property under circumstances which make it unjust for him to retain it.
   a. An implied resulting trust will arise by operation of law.
   b. A constructive trust may be imposed by a court.
   c. A probate court will administer the distribution of the property.
   d. None of the above is correct.

Questions 10 and 11, which have been adapted from AICPA Examination, May 1987, are based upon the following fact situation: Ralston established an inter vivos trust on January 1, 1988. The written trust instrument was signed by Ralston and provided that income be paid to her son for his life with the remainder to her granddaughter. Ralston transferred rental property and securities to Central Bank, which was designated as the trustee. Assume that a calendar year has been selected as the accounting period and that the trust instrument is silent as to the allocation of trust receipts and disbursements to principal and income.

10. Which of the following allocations of annual receipts and disbursements would be proper?
    a. The allocation of rental receipts of $35,000 to income and the payment of a fire insurance premium of $2,000 charged to principal.

b. The allocation of mortgage interest payments of $8,000 charged to income and the allocation of mortgage principal payments of $10,000 charged to principal.

c. The allocation to income of insurance proceeds of $16,000 for the destruction of two rental units as a result of a fire.

d. The allocation of a street assessment of $1,000 charged to principal and the allocation of half of forfeited rental security deposits of $1,000 to principal and half to income.

11. Which of the following allocations of receipts and disbursements would be improper?

a. The allocation to income of bond interest received.

b. The allocation to income of cash dividends on stock.

c. The allocation to income of dividends of additional shares of stock.

d. The allocation to principal of the proceeds of the sale of rights to receive additional shares of stock in the distributing corporation.

12. Kramer's will provided for the creation of a trust, to which all of Kramer's securities were to be transferred. The will named Kramer's wife as both the trustee of the trust and executrix of the estate and his children as beneficiaries of the trust.

a. Kramer has created an *inter vivos* trust.

b. Kramer has created a testamentary trust.

c. Kramer's wife may not serve as both the trustee and personal representative of Kramer's estate.

d. The trust is invalid because it will not become effective until Kramer's death.

(This question has been adapted from AICPA Examination, November 1988.)

Chapter 57

Liability of Accountants

As members of the accounting profession, accountants are expected to comply with standards of ethics and perform their services in accordance with generally accepted accounting principles (GAAP) and generally accepted auditing standards (GAAS). As discussed in this chapter, duties are also imposed upon accountants because of statutes and past court decisions. Accountants, who fail to carry out these duties, may be civilly liable to clients, for whom they have agreed to provide services, and third persons, who may have relied upon financial statements, audits, etc. prepared by them. In addition, sometimes civil and criminal liability may be imposed upon accountants because of statutes, such as the federal securities laws.

THINGS TO KEEP IN MIND

Much of the material in this chapter involves applications of principles of law, which relate to contracts, torts and the federal securities acts (topics that are presented in earlier chapters), to situations dealing with accountants. Cross references to other relevant units and chapters in the text and Study Guide are, therefore, supplied in the following chapter outline.

OUTLINE

I. Potential common law liability to clients.

    A. Liability based upon breach of contract. (See Unit II.)

        1. The failure to perform one's contractual duties is a breach of contract, for which one is liable to the party to whom the performance was to be rendered.

2. Thus, if an accountant has agreed to perform certain services for a client and fails to honestly, properly and completely carry out his, her or its contractual duties, the accountant will be civilly liable to the client for breach of contract.

3. In most cases, if there has been a breach of contract by an accountant, courts will award compensatory damages as a remedy to the client.

    a. The measure of damages will be equal to the foreseeable losses that the client incurs as a result of the breach.

    b. Damages may include expenses that are incurred by a client in order to secure the services of another accountant and penalties that are imposed upon the client, who failed to meet statutory deadlines.

4. In an action that is based upon breach of contract, liability is not imposed because of breach of a duty that exists as a result of tort law. It is, therefore, not a defense that:

    a. The accountant exercised reasonable care and conformed to generally accepted accounting principles and auditing standards.

    b. The client's own negligence contributed to his, her or its injury.

B. Liability based upon the tort of negligence. (See Chapter 4.)

    1. An accountant has a duty to exercise the same standard of care which a reasonably prudent and skillful accountant in the community would exercise under the same or similar circumstances.

    2. A violation of generally accepted accounting principles and auditing standards is *prima facie* evidence of negligence.

    3. Although an accountant may have complied with GAAP and GAAS, he, she or it may still be considered as not having acted with reasonable care.

    4. An accountant is not liable for errors of judgment.

    5. An accountant is liable for his, her or its negligence in failing to discover improprieties, defalcations or fraud.

    6. If an accountant is found to be liable for negligence, damages may be awarded in order to compensate the client for any reasonable, foreseeable injuries which were incurred.

    7. Defenses that may be asserted by an accountant in an action that is based upon negligence.

        a. Lack of negligence.

        b. Lack of proximate cause between the breach of the duty that was owed by the accountant and the injury that was incurred by the client.

       c. The client's own negligence (or intentional acts) contributed to his, her or its loss.

    8. Liability based upon negligence in preparation of unaudited financial statements ("write up" work).

C. Accountant's liability based upon fraud. (See Chapters 4 and 10.) In an action based upon fraud, the client must establish that:

    1. The accountant made a false representation of a material fact.

    2. The representation was made by the accountant with knowledge that it was false (actual fraud) or with reckless disregard for its truth or falsity (constructive fraud).

    3. The accountant intentionally made the misrepresentation in order to induce the client to act.

    4. As a result of the client's reasonable reliance on the misrepresentation, the client was injured.

II. Potential common law liability to third persons (people who were not clients of the accountant but who had knowledge of statements, audits, etc. that were prepared by the accountant).

A. Contract liability.

    1. Traditionally, at common law, an accountant does not owe contractual duties to people unless they are direct parties to or third party beneficiaries of a contract for the services of the accountant.

    2. This is so because there is lack of privity of contract between the accountant and the other person.

B. Tort liability based upon negligence in failing to exercise ordinary, reasonable care in the preparation of financial statements, audits, etc.

    1. An accountant owes a duty of exercising care to the parties with whom the accountant has privity of contract.

    2. Strict *Ultramares* rule — Accountants are not liable for negligence to persons with whom they are not in privity.

    3. *Restatement of Torts (Second)* position — An accountant may be liable to a third person, with whom there is no privity of contract, but who reasonably and foreseeably relies upon the statements, audits, etc. that were prepared by the accountant.

    4. Variations on the *Ultramares* rule.

        a. Accountants' liability for negligence to third persons extends only to those for whose primary benefit accounting statements are prepared.

    b. Accountants may be liable to third persons when the accountants are aware of the existence of the third persons, the purpose of the report, and that an "end and aim" of the preparation of statements and/or audits is to also provide information to the third persons.   [*Glanzer v. Shepard*, 233 N.Y. 236, 135 N.E. 275 (1922); *Credit Alliance Corp. v. Arthur Anderson and Co.* and *European American Bank and Trust Company v. Strauhs & Kay*, 65 N.Y.2d 536, 483 N.E.2d 110, 493 N.Y.S.2d 435 (1985).]

III. Potential statutory liability.

  A. Liability under Section 11 of the Securities Act of 1933. (See Chapter 43.)

    1. Securities Act of 1933 relates to new issues of investment securities (i.e., "going public").

    2. Registration statements, including financial statements, must be filed with the SEC before investment securities can be offered for sale by issuer.

    3. An accountant, who prepares a financial statement, which is included in a registration statement, is liable for misstatements and omissions of material facts in the registration statement.

    4. An accountant's liability extends to those who acquire the securities, which are covered by a registration statement (i.e., purchasers of the securities who incur losses).

      a. Purchaser need not show that he, she or it relied upon the misrepresentation or omission.

      b. Privity of contract between the accountant and the purchaser is not a requisite.

    5. The accountant has the burden of proving that he, she or it exercised "due diligence" in preparation of financial statements.

      a. The failure to follow GAAP and GAAS is proof of lack of due diligence.

      b. An accountant must establish that, after reasonable investigation, he, she or it had a reasonable basis to believe that the statements in the registration statement were true and that there was no omission of material facts, which were required or necessary in order to prevent the statements from being misleading.

      c. Other defenses:
        1) There were no misstatements or omissions in the registration statement.
        2) If there were misrepresentations or omissions of facts, they were not material.
        3) There was no causal connection between the misstatements or omissions and the purchaser's loss.
        4) The purchaser bought the securities with knowledge of the misstatement or omission.

d. Purchaser may recover the difference between the amount paid for the security and either:
  1) The value of the security at the time that the suit was brought.
  2) The price at which the security was disposed of in the market prior to commencing the suit.
  3) The price at which the security was disposed of after the suit was commenced (but prior to judgment) if the amount is less than the difference between the amount paid for the security and the value of the security at the time that the suit was commenced (Securities Act, Section 11(e)).

B. Liability under the Securities Exchange Act of 1934. (See Chapter 43.)

1. The Securities Exchange Act of 1934 relates to the purchase and sale of investment securities in the market (i.e., "being public").

2. Section 18 — An accountant is liable for false and/or misleading statements of material facts that are made in applications, reports, documents and registrations statements, which are prepared by the accountant and filed with the SEC.

   a. An accountant is liable to purchasers or sellers of securities:
     1) When false or misleading statements have affected the price of the securities.
     2) When the purchasers or sellers of the securities have relied upon the statements and were not aware of their inaccuracy.

   b. An accountant, who exercised "good faith" and did not have intent to deceive ("scienter"), is not liable to purchasers or sellers of the securities.

3. Section 10(b) and SEC Rule 10b-5.

   a. Liability is imposed upon those (including accountants) who, because of their "inside" positions, have access to material information (which is not available to the public and which may affect the value of securities) and trade in the securities without making a disclosure.

   b. Section 10(b) provides that it is unlawful to use any manipulative or deceptive device in connection with the sale or purchase of securities.

   c. Rule 10b-5 provides that, "in connection with the purchase or sale of any security," it is unlawful:
     1) To "employ any device, scheme, or artifice to defraud."
     2) To "make any untrue statement of a material fact or to omit to state a material fact necessary in order to make the statements made, in the light of the circumstances under which they were made, not misleading."
     3) To "engage in any act, practice, or course of business which operates or would operate as a fraud or deceit upon any person."

   d. An accountant may be liable to a person, who purchased or sold securities, when it can be established that:

1) The statement or omission was material.
2) The accountant intended to deceive or defraud others.
3) As a result of his, her or its reliance upon the misrepresentation, the purchaser or seller incurred a loss.

C. Criminal liability for willful conduct is imposed by the Securities Act of 1933, the Securities Exchange Act of 1934, the Internal Revenue Act, other federal statutes and state criminal codes.

IV. Working papers and accountant-client communications.

A. Working papers are documents used and developed during an audit.

1. Unless there is an agreement or statute that provides otherwise, working papers are the property of the accountant.

2. Information in working papers is confidential.

a. The client has a right of access to working papers; contents of working papers cannot be disclosed without the consent of the client or in response to a subpoena.

b. Working papers cannot be transferred to another accountant without the consent of the client.

B. Communications between the accountant and client.

1. Under the AICPA Code of Professional Ethics, accountant-client communications are considered to be confidential and cannot be disclosed without the consent of the client, or in accordance with GAAP or GAAS, or in response to a subpoena.

2. The majority of states and the federal courts do not treat accountant-client communications as privileged. An accountant, therefore, cannot refuse to testify or reveal information in response to a subpoena.

3. In those states that recognize the accountant-client relationship as privileged, an accountant may refuse to testify concerning the contents of communications with clients.

C. The Internal Revenue Service has investigatory powers and can obtain subpoenas directing people to testify and/or produce relevant books, records, etc.

KEY WORDS AND PHRASES IN TEXT

Generally accepted accounting principles (GAAP)
Generally accepted auditing standards (GAAS)
Common law liability of accountants to clients
Liability to clients for breach of contract
Liability to clients for negligence
Defenses that can be raised by accountant in action based upon negligence
Liability to clients for fraud
Actual fraud

Constructive fraud
Common law liability of accountants to
    third persons
Liability to third persons for negligence
The *Ultramares* rule
Liability to third persons for fraud
Section 11 of the Securities Act of 1933
Registration statement for new issues of
    investment securities
Misstatements and omissions of material
    facts in registration statement
Liability of accountant to purchasers of
    securities

Accountants' duty to exercise due diligence
    in preparation of financial statements
Accountants' defenses in actions based
    upon misstatements and omissions
Sections 18 and 10(b) of the Securities
    Exchange Act of 1934
Securities Exchange Commission
    Rule 10b-5
Confidentiality of working papers
Confidentiality of accountant-client
    communications

MULTIPLE CHOICE QUESTIONS

1. In an action against a CPA based upon negligence, "the custom of the profession"
    standard is used to some extent in order to determine whether or not the CPA was
    negligent. Which of the following statements best describes how this standard is
    applied?
    a. If the CPA proves that she literally followed GAAP and GAAS, it will be
        conclusively presumed that the CPA was not negligent.
    b. The "custom of the profession" argument may only be raised by the defendant.
    c. Despite a CPA's adherence to the custom of the profession, negligence may
        nevertheless be present.
    d. The failure to satisfy the "custom of the profession" standard is equivalent to
        gross negligence.
    (This question has been adapted from AICPA Examination, November 1983.)

2. Arthur, CPA, was engaged by Alpha Corp. in order to audit Beta Inc. Alpha Corp.
    purchased Beta Inc. after receiving Beta Inc.'s audited financial statements, which
    included Arthur's unqualified auditor's opinion. Arthur was negligent in the perfor-
    mance of the Beta Inc. audit. As a result of Arthur's negligence, Alpha Corp.
    incurred damages of $50,000. Alpha Corp. appears to have grounds to sue Arthur
    for:
    a. breach of contract and negligence.
    b. breach of contract but not negligence.
    c. negligence but not breach of contract.
    d. neither breach of contract nor negligence.
    (This question has been adapted from AICPA Examination, November 1983.)

3. In which of the following situations concerning a CPA firm's action is scienter or
    its equivalent absent?
    a. The CPA firm has actual knowledge of fraud.
    b. The CPA firm has made a statement with reckless disregard for its truth or
        falsity.
    c. The CPA firm intended to gain a financial benefit by concealing fraud.
    d. The CPA firm used substandard auditing procedures.
    (This question has been adapted from AICPA Examination, November 1983.)

4. EFG Enterprises, Inc. engaged an accounting firm in order to perform its annual
    audit. The firm performed the audit in a competent, nonnegligent manner and

billed EFG Enterprises, Inc. for $15,000, the agreed fee. Shortly after delivery of the audited financial statements, EFG Enterprises' comptroller disappeared, taking with him $50,000 of EFG Enterprises' funds. It was then discovered that the comptroller had been engaged in a highly sophisticated, novel defalcation scheme for a number of months, during which he had embezzled $60,000 from EFG Enterprises. EFG Enterprises, Inc. has refused to pay the accounting firm's fee and is seeking to recover the $110,000 that was taken by the comptroller. Which of the following statements is correct?

a. The accounting firm cannot recover its fee and is liable for the $110,000.
b. The accounting firm is entitled to collect its fee and is not liable for the $110,000.
c. EFG Enterprises, Inc. is entitled to rescind the audit contract and thus is not liable for the $15,000 fee, but it cannot recover damages.
d. EFG Enterprises, Inc. is entitled to recover the $60,000 defalcation and is not liable for the $15,000 fee.

(This question has been adapted from AICPA Examination, May 1981.)

5. Garrison loaned money to Lilly & Company relying upon Lilly's financial statements which were audited by Moore & Co., CPAs. When it conducted the audit, Moore & Co. knew that the statements were to be supplied to Garrison. If Garrison brings a common law action based upon fraud against Moore & Co., the action will probably be unsuccessful if:

a. Garrison is only able to show that Moore & Co. failed to meticulously follow GAAP.
b. Moore & Co. can establish that it fully complied with the statute of frauds.
c. the alleged fraud was based in part upon oral misrepresentations and Moore & Co. pleads the parol evidence rule.
d. Garrison is not a third party beneficiary in light of the absence of privity between Garrison and Moore & Co.

(This question has been adapted from AICPA Examination, November 1983.)

6. Caesar and Napoleon, CPAs, rendered an unqualified opinion on the financial statements of a corporation that sold common stock in a public offering subject to the Securities Act of 1933. Based upon a false statement in the financial statements, Caesar and Napoleon are being sued by an investor who purchased shares of this public offering. The following represents a viable defense:

a. The investor has not met the burden of proving fraud or negligence by Caesar and Napoleon.
b. The investor did not actually rely upon the false statement.
c. Detection of the false statement by Caesar and Napoleon occurred after the date of their examination.
d. The false statement related to a fact that was immaterial.

(This question has been adapted from AICPA Examination, November 1983.)

7. Gibson is suing Carter, Prito & Adams, CPAs, in order to recover losses that were incurred in connection with Gibson's transactions in Zebra Corporation securities. Zebra's Annual Form 10-K Report contained false and misleading statements relating to material facts in financial statements, which had been audited by Carter, Prito & Adams. In order to recover from Carter, Prito & Adams under the Securities and Exchange Act of 1934, Gibson must, among other things, establish that:

a. all of his past transactions in Zebra Corporation securities, both before and after the auditors' report date, resulted in a net loss.

b. the transaction in Zebra Corporation securities that resulted in a loss occurred within 30 days of the auditors' report date.

c. he relied upon the financial statements in his decision to purchase or sell Zebra Corporation securities.

d. the market price of the stock dropped significantly after corrected financial statements were issued by Zebra Corporation.

(This question has been adapted from AICPA Examination, November 1983.)

8. The Internal Revenue Code provisions dealing with tax return preparation:
   a. require tax return preparers, who are neither attorneys nor CPAs, to pass a basic qualifying examination.
   b. apply to a CPA who prepares the tax returns of the president of a corporation, for which the CPA conducts audits, without charging the president.
   c. apply to all tax preparers whether they are compensated or uncompensated.
   d. only apply to preparers of individual income tax returns.

(This question has been adapted from AICPA Examination, November 1983.)

9. An accountant has prepared a tax return for a client in a fraudulent manner. With regard to the accountant's potential liability to various parties, which of the following actions would be dismissed?
   a. A federal criminal action.
   b. A federal action for civil penalties.
   c. A federal action to revoke the accountant's CPA certificate.
   d. A malpractice action brought by the client.

(This question has been adapted from AICPA Examination, November 1983.)

10. Working papers that are prepared by a CPA in connection with an audit engagement are owned by the CPA, subject to certain limitations. The rationale for this rule is to:
    a. protect the working papers from being subpoenaed.
    b. provide the basis for excluding admission of the working papers as evidence because of the privileged communication rule.
    c. provide the CPA with evidence and documentation which may be helpful in the event of a lawsuit.
    d. establish a continuity of relationship with the client whereby indiscriminate replacement of CPAs is discouraged.

(This question has been adapted from AICPA Examination, November 1983.)

Chapter 58

The Effect of International Law in a Global Economy

With the increasing internationalization of business, business people often need to be aware of important principles of international law and relevant federal statutes. A number of legal doctrines and statutes, which are relevant to international business transactions and trade, are introduced in this chapter.

OUTLINE

I.   The context of international law.

A. Sources of international law.

1. International organizations (e.g., the United Nations) and conferences.

a. Resolutions, declarations and standards for behavior of nations have been adopted by international bodies and conferences.

b. Legal disputes between nations may voluntarily be submitted to and resolved by the United Nations International Court of Justice.

2. Regional multilateral agreements among countries in geographic proximity to each other.

a. The European Economic Community (EEC, which is also known as the Common Market) has eliminated public tariffs and private restrictive agreements among its members and promotes free trade and competition and the free movement of workers, goods and capital among the member nations. Belgium, Denmark, France, Greece, Ireland, Italy, Luxembourg, the Netherlands, Portugal, Spain, West Germany and the United Kingdom are members of EEC.

      b. The Association of Southeast Asian Nations (ASEAN) promotes economic cooperation and has established trade rules for Brunei, Indonesia, Malaysia, the Philippines, Singapore and Thailand.

   3. Bilateral trade agreements created by treaties.

      a. A treaty is an agreement between two or more nations that has been authorized and ratified by the appropriate person or group within each nation's government.

      b. Article II Section 2 of the United States Constitution confers the power to enter into treaties upon the President with the consent of two-thirds of the Senate.

   4. International customs — General practices that have evolved over time and are accepted as law.

B. Act of state doctrine.

   1. The courts of one country will not examine the validity of acts, which are engaged in by a foreign government, when the acts take place within the territory of the foreign nation.

   2. Comity — The courts in one jurisdiction will defer and give effect to the laws and judicial decrees of another jurisdiction because of mutual respect.

C. Doctrine of sovereign immunity.

   1. A foreign nation is not subject to the jurisdiction of courts of another country and is, therefore, immunized against law suits.

   2. Foreign Sovereign Immunities Act of 1976 (FSIA) provides for exceptions to sovereign immunity of foreign countries.

      a. Actions may be brought against a foreign government in a United States District Court.

      b. Courts, rather than the Department of State, determine claims of sovereign immunity.

      c. United States courts have jurisdiction:
         1) When a foreign nation has waived immunity explicitly or by implication.
         2) When the action is "based upon a commercial activity carried on in the United States by the foreign state."
           a) A foreign state includes political subdivisions and instrumentalities of the foreign nation.
           b) Commercial activity means business (rather than governmental) transactions engaged in by a foreign nation.

II. Transacting business abroad.

A. Letters of credit are used in order to facilitate international business transactions.

   1. A letter of credit is a written instrument which contains "an engagement by a bank or other person made at the request of a customer" of the bank or other person whereby "the issuer will honor drafts or other demands for payment upon compliance with the conditions specified in the" letter of credit (UCC Sec. 5-103).

   2. Parties to a letter of credit. (See UCC Sec. 5-103.)

      a. Issuer — The bank or other person who issues a letter of credit.

      b. Beneficiary — The person (e.g., the seller of goods) who is entitled to draw or demand payment under the terms of a letter of credit.

      c. Account party (e.g., the buyer of goods) — The customer of a bank (which issues a letter of credit), who promises to reimburse the issuer.

      d. Advising bank — The bank which gives notification of the issuance of a letter of credit by another bank and transmits information.

      e. Confirming (paying) bank — The bank which engages that it will honor a letter of credit which has been issued by another bank or that a letter of credit will be honored by the issuer or a third bank.

   3. Documentary letter of credit — A letter of credit may be conditioned upon presentation of a document, such as a document of title (bill of lading), security, invoice, certificate, etc.

   4. Use of a letter of credit assures seller (beneficiary of letter of credit) of payment and assures buyer (account party) that payment will not be made until the seller has complied with the terms and conditions of the letter of credit.

   5. Letter of credit is independent of the transaction for the sale of goods and the transaction between the issuer and the account party (buyer).

   6. Compliance with terms of letter of credit.

      a. Issuer has duty to determine that documents presented by beneficiary (seller) comply with terms of letter of credit.

      b. Traditionally, courts have required strict compliance.

      c. Some courts require substantial or reasonable compliance.

B. Technology transfer.

   1. There are restrictions on the export of certain technologies, particularly those relating to national security.

2. International protection of proprietary rights to intellectual property.

    a. Inventors may obtain patents in foreign countries. The Paris Convention guarantees nondiscriminatory treatment in countries which adhere to the convention.

    b. International copyright and trademark protection is covered in the Berne Convention.

C. The Convention on Contracts for the International Sale of Goods.

    1. Similar to the Uniform Commercial Code (UCC) with the following differences:

        a. There is no requirement that certain contracts be reduced to a writing.

        b. An acceptance must conform exactly to offer. If it does not, it will be treated as a counteroffer.

        c. A contract is formed when an acceptance is received, not when it is sent by a reasonable means of communication.

        d. The Convention does not apply to sales of goods to consumers.

    2. The Convention applies when the parties are residents in countries which have ratified it.

    3. The parties may specify that the terms of the Convention will (or will not) apply to their transactions.

III. Dispute resolution.

A. Judicial resolution.

    1. If parties to an international transaction enter into a contract, they may in their agreement specify what nation's courts will have jurisdiction over a dispute and what nation's laws will apply should a dispute arise, etc.

    2. Even if there is a judicial resolution of a dispute in a court in one country, remedies may not be available in other nations. Usually, if a decision or judgment is rendered in a foreign country, courts in the United States will presume that the judgment is valid and enforce it because of the policy of comity.

B. Arbitration.

    1. Frequently, parties include arbitration clauses in the agreements.

    2. Court enforcement of arbitration is governed by the Convention on the Recognition and Enforcement of Foreign Arbitral Awards.

IV. Extraterritorial application of U.S. antitrust laws.

A. Section 1 of the Sherman Act applies to foreign governments and foreign nationals.

B. Antitrust laws apply to acts which occur outside of the United States that have a substantial effect on commerce in the United States.

C. A *per se* violation may occur if a domestic firm joins a foreign cartel which controls production, price or distribution of goods and there is a substantial restraining effect on commerce in the United States.

D. People in foreign nations may be sued because of violations and may sue if they have been injured as a result of a violation of the United States antitrust laws.

E. Relevant amendments to the antitrust laws — A violation of the Sherman Act or Federal Trade Commission Act is actionable if it has a direct, substantial, and reasonably foreseeable effect upon domestic trade within the United States, or import trade, or export trade of a United States exporter.

V. Import restrictions.

A. Quotas limiting the number of certain imports into a country and tariffs, taxes on imports, may be imposed.

B. The General Agreement on Tariffs and Trade (GATT) is designed to minimize trade barriers among nations.

C. The U.S. government has tried to control the practice of dumping, the selling of foreign goods in the U.S. at a price below the price at which they are sold in the country from which they are exported.

VI. The Foreign Corrupt Practices Act — See Chapter 43.

KEY WORDS AND PHRASES IN TEXT

International Court of Justice
International organizations, such as the
  United Nations
International conferences
Regional multilateral agreements
European Economic Community (EEC)
  or Common Market
Association of Southeast Asian Nations
  (ASEAN)
Tariffs
Bilateral trade agreements (treaties)
International customs
Act of state doctrine
Doctrine of sovereign immunity
Foreign Sovereign Immunities Act (FSIA)
Exceptions to jurisdictional immunity of
  a foreign country

Commercial activities of foreign states
Force majeure clause
Letter of credit
Parties to letter of credit transaction
  (issuer, beneficiary and account
  party)
Bill of lading
Compliance with terms and conditions of
  letter of credit
Technology transfer
Paris Convention (International Convention
  for Protection of Industrial Property)
Berne Convention (copyright protection)
Judicial resolution of international
  business disputes
Policy of comity
International arbitration clauses

United Nations Convention on the
Recognition and Enforcement of
Foreign Arbitral Awards
Convention on Contracts for the
International Sale of Goods
Extraterritorial application of U.S.
antitrust laws
Quota

General Agreement on Tariffs and Trade
(GATT)
Dumping of foreign products in U.S.
market
Antidumping Act
International Trade Commission (ITC)
Foreign Corrupt Practices Act (FCPA)

Uniform CPA Business Law Examination Information

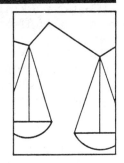

Public accountants must fulfill certain requisites, which are prescribed by state examining boards, in order to be certified. A prerequisite in every state is successfully passing the Uniform Certified Public Accountant Examination, that is prepared and graded by the American Institute of Certified Public Accountants (AICPA). The Uniform CPA Examination is administered twice a year (in May and November) and contains four sections—accounting practice, accounting theory, auditing and business law.

The business law portion of the CPA Examination is a three and a half hour test composed of objective and essay questions. It is administered on the third day of the examination (Friday) from 8:30 a.m. until noon. Since November 1980, the format has been a series of sixty one point multiple choice questions and four essay questions, each given a value of ten points.[1] Usually, essay questions have two or more parts which test candidates' knowledge of different business law topics. A typical essay question includes a statement of a fact situation involving a number of legal issues. Candidates are expected to discuss these issues in determining the liability of the parties. The multiple choice questions are similar to those in this Study Guide. Occasionally, correctly answering a multiple choice question also requires knowledge of more than one area of law.

Extensive in-depth knowledge of business law is necessary in order to pass the test. Detailed information about the subject matter content and the approximate percentage

---

[1] AICPA contemplates making changes in the CPA Examination format. If the proposed changes are adopted, they would go into effect with the May 1990 Examination. Proposals include making all questions objective ones and reducing the time allocations. For example, the business law section would be a two and a half hour objective test administered on the first morning of the CPA Examination.

of the examination devoted to each of seven broad areas of law is provided in specifications adopted by the Board of Examiners of AICPA. The revised content specifications (effective in May 1986) state:

"The Business Law section tests the candidates' knowledge of the legal implications of business transactions, particularly as they relate to accounting and auditing. The section includes the CPA and the law, business organizations, contracts, debtor-creditor relationships, government regulation of business, Uniform Commercial Code, and property. Many of the subjects on the examination are normally covered in standard textbooks on business law, auditing, taxation, and accounting; however, some subjects either are not included in such texts or are not covered in adequate depth. Important recent developments with which candidates are expected to be familiar may not yet be reflected in some texts. Candidates are expected to recognize the existence of legal implications and applicable basic legal principles, and they are usually asked to indicate the probable result of the application of such basic principles.

"The Business Law section is chiefly conceptual in nature and is broad in scope. It is not intended to test competence to practice law or expertise in legal matters, but to determine that the candidates' knowledge is sufficient (1) to recognize relevant legal issues, (2) to recognize the legal implications of business situations, (3) to apply the underlying principles of law to accounting and auditing situations, and (4) to seek legal counsel or recommend that it be sought.

"This section deals with federal and widely adopted uniform laws. Where there is no federal or appropriate uniform law on a subject, the questions are intended to test knowledge of the majority rules. Federal tax elements may be covered where appropriate in the overall context of a question.

"Business Law — Content Specification Outline

I. The CPA and the Law (10 percent).

   A. Common Law Liability to Clients and Third Persons
   B. Federal Statutory Liability

      1. Securities Acts
      2. Internal Revenue Code

   C. Workpapers, Privileged Communication, and Confidentiality

II. Business Organizations (20 percent).

   A. Agency

      1. Formation and Termination
      2. Liabilities of Principal
      3. Disclosed and Undisclosed Principals
      4. Agent's Authority and Liability

   B. Partnerships and Joint Ventures

  1. Formation and Existence
  2. Liabilities and Authority of Partners and Joint Owners
  3. Allocation of Profit or Loss
  4. Transfer of Interest
  5. Termination, Winding Up, and Dissolution

C. Corporations

  1. Formation, Purposes, and Powers
  2. Stockholders, Directors, and Officers
  3. Financial Structure, Capital, and Dividends
  4. Merger, Consolidation, and Dissolution

D. Estates and Trusts

  1. Formation and Purposes
  2. Allocation Between Principal and Income
  3. Fiduciary Responsibilities
  4. Distributions and Termination

III. Contracts (15 percent).

A. Offer and Acceptance
B. Consideration
C. Capacity, Legality, and Public Policy
D. Statute of Frauds
E. Statute of Limitations
F. Fraud, Duress, and Undue Influence
G. Mistake and Misrepresentation
H. Parol Evidence Rule
I. Third Party Rights
J. Assignments
K. Discharge, Breach, and Remedies

IV. Debtor-Creditor Relationships (10 percent).

A. Suretyship

  1. Liabilities and Defenses
  2. Release of Parties
  3. Remedies of Parties

B. Bankruptcy

  1. Voluntary and Involuntary Bankruptcy
  2. Effects of Bankruptcy on Debtors and Creditors
  3. Reorganizations

V. Government Regulation of Business (10 percent).

A. Regulation of Employment

      1. Federal Insurance Contributions Act
      2. Federal Unemployment Tax Act
      3. Worker's Compensation Acts

  B. Federal Securities Acts

      1. Securities Registration
      2. Reporting Requirements
      3. Exempt Securities and Transactions

VI. Uniform Commercial Code (25 percent).

  A. Commercial Paper

      1. Types of Negotiable Instruments
      2. Requisites for Negotiability
      3. Transfer and Negotiation
      4. Holders and Holders in Due Course
      5. Liabilities, Defenses, and Rights
      6. Discharge

  B. Documents of Title and Investment Securities

      1. Warehouse Receipts
      2. Bills of Lading
      3. Issuance, Transfer, and Registration of Securities

  C. Sales

      1. Contracts Covering Goods
      2. Warranties
      3. Product Liability
      4. Risk of Loss
      5. Performance and Obligations
      6. Remedies and Defenses

  D. Secured Transactions

      1. Attachment of Security Interests
      2. Perfection of Security Interests
      3. Priorities
      4. Rights of Debtors, Creditors, and Third Parties

VII. Property (10 percent).

  A. Real and Personal Property

      1. Distinctions Between Realty and Personalty
      2. Types of Ownership
      3. Lessor-Lessee
      4. Deeds, Recording, Title Defects, and Title Insurance

B. Mortgages

1. Characteristics
2. Recording Requirements
3. Priorities
4. Foreclosure

C. Fire and Casualty Insurance

1. Coinsurance
2. Multiple Insurance Coverage
3. Insurable Interest"[2]

The AICPA specifications do not indicate the relative emphasis that may be placed upon the various topics within the seven major areas of business law. This is expected to fluctuate on future examinations as it has in the past.

SOME CONCLUSIONS

The importance of contract law to accountants and, therefore, Unit II in *West's Business Law: Text, Cases, Legal Environment, Fourth Edition* and this *Study Guide,* cannot be overstressed. Approximately 15% of the CPA Business Law Examination is devoted to specific topics relating to contracts. One must also realize that contract law provides the foundation for what are normally treated as other areas of business law.

With regard to the area referred to as the CPA and the law, information relating to this subject is presented in Chapter 57 of the Text and this Study Guide. (In addition, see material dealing with torts in Chapter 4, contracts in Unit II and security regulations in Chapter 43.) Usually, this subject is also covered in accounting courses, such as auditing and taxation.

In addition to contracts and the CPA and the law, topics that have received significant treatment on past CPA examinations have included commercial paper, federal securities legislation,[3] corporations, partnerships, sales and secured transactions.

---

[2]The Revised Business Law Content Specification Outline for the Uniform Certified Public Accountant Examination (Effective May 1986), Copyright © 1986 by the American Institute of Certified Public Accountants, Inc. Reprinted with permission.

[3]Knowledge concerning the Federal Securities Acts is tested specifically and also in conjunction with a CPA's statutory liability.

TABLE

CROSS REFERENCES:

Business Law Subjects Covered on CPA Examination —

Chapters in Study Guide

AREA, APPROXIMATE AICPA PERCENTAGE & GROUP	STUDY GUIDE CHAPTERS
THE CPA AND THE LAW (10%)	57
BUSINESS ORGANIZATIONS (20%)	
A. Agency	32 and 33
B. Partnerships and Joint Ventures	34, 35, 36 and 37
C. Corporations	38, 39, 40, 41, 42 and 43
D. Estates and Trusts	56
CONTRACTS (15%)	
A. Offer and Acceptance	8
B. Consideration	9
C. Capacity, Legality, and Public Policy	10 and 11
D. Statute of Frauds	12
E. Statute of Limitations	9 and 14
F. Fraud, Duress, and Undue Influence	10
G. Mistake and Misrepresentation	10
H. Parol Evidence Rule	12
I. Third Party Rights	13
J. Assignments	13
K. Discharge, Breach, and Remedies	14 and 15
DEBTOR-CREDITOR RELATIONSHIPS (10%)	
A. Suretyship	30
B. Bankruptcy	31
GOVERNMENT REGULATION OF BUSINESS (10%)	
A. Regulation of Employment	49
B. Federal Securities Acts	43
UNIFORM COMMERCIAL CODE (25%)	
A. Commercial Paper	22, 23, 24, 25, 26, 27 and 28
B. Documents of Title and Investment Securities	39, 41, 43 and 51
C. Sales	16, 17, 18, 19, 20 and 21
D. Secured Transactions	29
PROPERTY (10%)	
A. Real and Personal Property	50, 51, 52 and 53
B. Mortgages	30 and 53
C. Fire and Casualty Insurance	54

FUTURE CPA EXAMINATIONS

Uniform CPA Examinations are scheduled as follows:

1989	May 3, 4, 5 November 1, 2, 3	1992	May 6, 7, 8 November 4, 5, 6
1990	May 2, 3, 4 November 7, 8, 9	1993	May 5, 6, 7 November 3, 4, 5
1991	May 8, 9, 10 November 6, 7, 8	1994	May 4, 5, 6 November 2, 3, 4

Students who plan to sit for the examinations are encouraged to obtain copies of *Information for CPA Candidates* issued by AICPA.[4] In their preparation, CPA candidates will, no doubt, find the outlines and other materials in this book useful for review purposes. For this reason, cross references to the *Study Guide to Accompany West's Business Law: Text, Cases, Legal Environment, Fourth Edition* are provided in a Cross Reference Table for the traditional business law subjects covered on the CPA Examination.

---

[4]Copies may be obtained by writing to:

The American Institute of Certified Public Accountants
1211 Avenue of the Americas
New York, New York 10036

Answer Section

CHAPTER 1 — Introduction to Law and Legal Reasoning

Fill-In Questions

1. traditional; sociological.
2. judges in deciding cases based on general principles of law established in previously decided cases.
3. *stare decisis.*
4. Judicial; administrative process.
5. Uniform Commercial Code; all.
6. private law; public law.
7. the federal and state constitutions, statutes enacted by the United States Congress, state legislative bodies, local ordinances, administrative agency rules and case law.

Multiple Choice Questions

1. c
2. b
3. d
4. e
5. d
6. b
7. b
8. a
9. c
10. d
11. c
12. b

CHAPTER 2 — Courts and Civil Dispute Resolution

Fill-In Questions

1. jurisdiction.
2. *in personam* (jurisdiction over the person).
3. general; United States District Court; United States Supreme Court or United States Court of Appeals for the Federal Circuit or Tax Court or Claims Court or Bankruptcy Court or Customs Court, etc.; special.
4. appellate; the Supreme Court or the Circuit Court of Appeals; District Court.
5. legislative; judicial review.
6. plaintiff; filing a complaint with the clerk of the court and serving a copy on the defendant.
7. complaint; complaint; answer.
8. to dismiss; a deposition be taken.
9. alternative dispute resolution; mediator; arbitration; arbitrator.

Multiple Choice Questions

1. d
2. d (Note—Appellate courts usually have little or no original jurisdiction.)
3. c
4. b
5. c
6. a
7. d
8. a

CHAPTER 3 — Constitutional Authority to Regulate Business

Fill-In Questions

1. powers; states.
2. states.
3. legislative; House of Representatives; President; judicial branch.
4. Bill of Rights.
5. commerce; states, uniform.
6. unreasonable; probable; person; thing or property.
7. natural person; corporations, partnerships. (Other entities, which are beyond the scope of this chapter, include associations, nonprofit organizations, etc.)

Multiple Choice Questions

1. d   6. c
2. d   7. a
3. a   8. b
4. c   9. a
5. d

CHAPTER 4 — Torts

Fill-In Questions

1. defendant breached a duty, that was owed, which breach of duty was the proximate cause of the injury incurred by the plaintiff.
2. tort.
3. person; property.
4. assault; battery; consent; defense of others; defense of property.
5. False imprisonment; reasonable manner; reasonable.
6. in writing; orally; truth.
7. supervening or intervening, unforeseen force, assumption of the risk, contributory or comparative negligence. (Do you know whether or not the legislature or courts of the state in which you reside have adopted the doctrine of comparative negligence?)

Multiple Choice Questions

1.	d	7.	c
2.	a	8.	a
3.	b	9.	a
4.	b	10.	b
5.	d	11.	d
6.	a		

CHAPTER 5 — Torts Related to Business

Fill-In Questions

1. that the defendant has published false statements concerning the product or business of the plaintiff; malicious injury to business or combination to divert trade.
2. tort, intentionally.
3. wrongful interference with a contractual relationship; contract; IT Corp.
4. predatory; interference with business relationships.
5. infringement of trademark.
6. the United States Patent Office; 17.
7. theft of trade secrets.
8. disparagement of product or slander of quality or trade libel; disparagement of reputation (slander, if statements were oral; libel, if statements were written).

Multiple Choice Questions

1. c   Note that a tort arises because of a breach of duty by a defendant other than an obligation arising out of a contract.
2. b
3. d
4. c
5. d
6. a

CHAPTER 6 — Criminal Law

Fill-In Questions

1. wrong; the state.
2. committed a specified wrongful act (or, in some cases, failed to perform a required act); purpose, knowledge and awareness, recklessness or negligence or implied.
3. defense.
4. innocent; guilty.
5. unreasonable searches and seizures; cruel and unusual punishment and excessive bail or fine.
6. self-incrimination and double jeopardy.
7. a speedy, public trial by jury and the right to be informed of the charges against him or her, to be confronted with the person accusing him or her of committing a crime, to subpoena witnesses and to the assistance of an attorney.
8. forceful, unlawful taking of property; larceny.

Multiple Choice Questions

1. b
2. b
3. a
4. d
5. a
6. c
7. a
8. c
9. d
10. d

CHAPTER 7 — Contracts: Nature and Terminology

Fill-In Questions

1. two or more.
2. an agreement by two or more competent parties, whose apparent assent to the same terms is real and genuine, supported by valid, legal consideration, in the form required by law (if one is required) and having a legal purpose and subject matter.
3. an express; an implied-in-fact.
4. bilateral; performance of or forbearance from an act.
5. formal; informal; informal contracts.
6. executed; executory.

Multiple Choice Questions

1. c
2. c
3. c
4. a
5. b
6. d
7. b
8. d
9. c
10. b

CHAPTER 8 — Contracts: Agreement

Fill-In Questions

1. an offer; accepts.
2. identification of parties, the sum of money being borrowed, personal services to be performed or real or personal property being sold. (Notes—(1) Under certain circumstances the price and quantity need not be specified with certainty if a method is provided by which they can be made certain; (2) If no specified time for performance is stated or otherwise indicated in the offer, it is implied that performance is to be rendered within a reasonable period of time.)
3. revocation.
4. rejection or counteroffer.
5. reasonable period of time has elapsed; one of the parties has died or been adjudicated incompetent, the subject matter has been destroyed, or a statute has been enacted which makes performance of the contract illegal.

Multiple Choice Questions

1.	a	6.	b
2.	e	7.	b
3.	c	8.	d
4.	c	9.	b
5.	a	10.	d

CHAPTER 9 — Contracts: Consideration

Fill-In Questions

1. benefit; detriment.
2. mature, liquidated, undisputed
3. illusory; consideration; consideration; requirements.
4. Forbearance; consideration.
5. sufficient, forbear or refrain.
6. modifications of existing contracts under Sec. 2-209 of the U.C.C.; a signed writing which complies with the Model Written Obligations Act or other state statute; a new promise to pay a debt barred by the statute of limitations or a written affirmation to pay a debt that is to be discharged in bankruptcy which is filed with the Bankruptcy Court.

Multiple Choice Questions

1.	a	7.	a
2.	c	8.	c
3.	d	9.	b
4.	b	10.	c
5.	c	11.	d
6.	d	12.	a

CHAPTER 10 — Contracts: Capacity and Genuineness of Assent

Fill-In Questions

1. voidable; disaffirm, avoid or rescind.
2. disaffirm, avoid or rescind.
3. food, shelter, clothing, necessary medical or dental care; the reasonable value.
4. majority.
5. he or she cannot appreciate, understand or comprehend the nature and effect of a particular transaction; void.
6. disaffirm or avoid; voidable.
7. mutual or bilateral; unilateral.
8. injury; reliance.
9. opinion.
10. undue influence.

Multiple Choice Questions

1.	c	8.	d	15.	a
2.	a	9.	a	16.	d
3.	c	10.	b	17.	c
4.	d	11.	b	18.	b
5.	b	12.	c	19.	a
6.	c	13.	b	20.	a
7.	d	14.	a		

CHAPTER 11 — Contracts: Legality

Fill-In Questions

1. statutes; public policy.
2. Usury.
3. $0 in those states which treat the entire transaction as tainted with illegality because of the usurious interest. $100 in those states which treat only the interest as being illegal because of usury. $110 in those states which treat only the excess interest as being usurious.
4. wagering or gambling; transferring or shifting.
5. restraint of trade; reasonable.
6. exculpatory.

Multiple Choice Questions

1.	a	5.	b
2.	a	6.	c
3.	d	7.	a
4.	d	8.	c

CHAPTER 12 — Contracts: Writing and Form

Fill-In Questions

1. not performable within one year; to answer for the debt, default or miscarriage of another; for the sale of an interest in real property; for the sale of goods when the price is $500 or more; for the sale of securities; for the sale of miscellaneous personal property when the price is greater than $5000; in consideration of marriage; of an administrator or executor to pay a debt of the estate out of his own property.
2. to pay the debt or answer for the miscarriage or obligation of another; the leading object or main purpose was to benefit the promisor.
3. 500.
4. inadmissible.
5. void; voidable.
6. the meaning of ambiguous or vague terms; a modification; that the contract was void or voidable or otherwise terminated; that the writing was incomplete; gross errors contained in the writing.
7. plain meaning; intent; valid/legal/lawful/enforceable.

Multiple Choice Questions

1.	c	7.	c
2.	d	8.	c
3.	a	9.	b
4.	c	10.	a
5.	a	11.	c
6.	a		

CHAPTER 13 — Contracts: Third Party Rights

Fill-In Questions

1. privity.
2. third party donee; third party creditor.
3. donee; creditor; incidental.
4. assignment; assignor; assignee.
5. delegated.
6. statutory prohibition; materially increased or altered.

Multiple Choice Questions

1.	d	6.	c
2.	b	7.	a
3.	a	8.	c
4.	c	9.	c
5.	c		

CHAPTER 14 — Contracts: Performance and Discharge

Fill-In Questions

1. precedent; subsequent.
2. precedent; discharged.
3. subsequent; discharged; breach.
4. full, complete performance.
5. discharged; discharged; discharged; discharged.
6. discharged; discharged; discharged; discharged; breach.
7. mutual rescission, substituted agreement; novation.
8. the statute of limitations has run or a decree in bankruptcy has been issued.
9. impossibility.

Multiple Choice Questions

1.	c	5.	c
2.	d	6.	b
3.	d	7.	a
4.	a	8.	d

CHAPTER 15 — Contracts: Breach of Contract and Remedies

Fill-In Questions

1. compensatory money.
2. the contract price; the market price.
3. compensatory; 6,000; market price or value.
4. special; breach of contract.
5. liquidated damages; is not excessive but bears a reasonable relationship to the foreseeable, expected damages that would be incurred if the contract were breached.
6. Rescission and restitution.
7. rescission and restitution, specific performance, injunction, reformation and quasi contract; inadequate.
8. voidable; rescission; restitution.

Multiple Choice Questions

1.	b	6.	b
2.	c	7.	a
3.	a	8.	d
4.	c	9.	c
5.	a	10.	d

CHAPTER 16 — Sales: Introduction to Sales Contracts and Their Formation

Fill-In Questions

1. transfer; goods or tangible personal property; price.
2. merchants; deal in goods of the kind involved in the sales transaction.
3. price; quantity.
4. new consideration; the contract, as modified, provided for the sale of goods for a price of $500 or more.
5. irrevocable; reasonable.
6. merchant; merchants; the additional or changed terms materially alter the offer.
7. $500 or more.

Multiple Choice Questions

1.	b	6.	a
2.	d	7.	a
3.	d	8.	b
4.	d	9.	d
5.	c		

CHAPTER 17 — Sales: Title, Risk, and Insurable Interest

Fill-In Questions

1. a contract to sell goods in the future.
2. the sales contract is formed; marked, shipped.
3. on approval; or return.
4. seller's place of business.
5. of contracting; the buyer receives the goods from the merchant.
6. free on board; free alongside; seller; risk of loss.
7. insurance and freight charges; freight charges.
8. shipment; delivered to the carrier; an insurable interest.

Multiple Choice Questions

1. c
2. b
3. a
4. b
5. b
6. d
7. a

CHAPTER 18 — Sales: Performance and Obligation

Fill-In Questions

1. that conform to the contract; pay for; concurrent.
2. put the goods into the possession of the carrier.
3. delivered to the dock "alongside" of the ship; unloaded.
4. insurance during transit; transportation charges or freight charges; cost of the goods and transportation charges or freight charges; buyer or purchaser or consignee.
5. accept all of the goods; reject all of the goods; accept some of the goods and reject others that do not conform to the contract.
6. received by the buyer; any other commercially acceptable method.
7. anticipatory breach.

Multiple Choice Questions

1.	d	5.	a
2.	b	6.	c
3.	c	7.	b
4.	b	8.	a

CHAPTER 19 — Sales: Remedies of Buyer and Seller for Breach

Fill-In Questions

1. withhold delivery of the goods; stop delivery of the goods in the possession of a bailee.
2. recover the purchase price; sue for damages; identify the goods to the contract; resell goods, of which he or she rightfully has possession; cancel the contract.
3. reclaim the goods from the buyer.
4. recover identified goods, if the seller becomes insolvent (within ten days after receiving first payment); effect cover by contracting for the purchase of substitute goods; replevin the goods; obtain an order for specific performance; sue for damages; cancel the contract; resell properly rejected goods in his or her possession, if he or she had a security interest in the goods.
5. accepted; rejected.
6. the contract price; incidental.
7. reasonable.

Multiple Choice Questions

1.	a	5.	b
2.	c	6.	c
3.	d	7.	d
4.	a		

CHAPTER 20 — Sales: Introduction to Sales Warranties

Fill-In Questions

1. free from any liens, security interests or other encumbrances; free from adverse claims based upon patents, trademark, trade name, copyright, etc., infringement.
2. express; factual.
3. merchantable; fit for the particular purpose for which they are intended.
4. reasonably fit for the normal or ordinary purpose for which such goods are usually used; of average or usual quality existing in the market; merchantability.
5. fitness for a particular purpose; express; express; implied warranty of merchantability or title.
6. third party beneficiary; use, consume or be affected.

Multiple Choice Questions

1.	c	6.	c
2.	b	7.	d
3.	b	8.	a
4.	b	9.	c
5.	a	10.	d

CHAPTER 21 — Sales: Product Liability

Fill-In Questions

1. Products liability.
2. warranty; negligent.
3. express warranty; reasonably relied upon the representation; injured.
4. privity of contract; negligence; failed to exercise reasonable care.
5. the defect resulted in the product being unreasonably dangerous, while in ordinary use, and that the defect was the proximate cause of his or her injury.

Multiple Choice Questions

1. a
2. d
3. c
4. c
5. b
6. b
7. d
8. a
9. d
10. a

CHAPTER 22 — Commercial Paper: Basic Concepts of Commercial Paper

Fill-In Questions

1. commercial paper.
2. order; bank; demand.
3. drawee; acceptor; drawer (or payee); payee (or drawer).
4. promise; maker; payee.
5. on demand (or at sight); time paper (or time instruments).
6. note; maker; John Jones; demand or sight.
7. draft; David Duke; Ben Beier; bearer; time.

Multiple Choice Questions

1.	d	5.	a
2.	c	6.	b
3.	c	7.	d
4.	a	8.	d

CHAPTER 23 — Commercial Paper: The Negotiable Instrument

Fill-In Questions

1. maker; drawer; order; money; definite time; bearer; drawee.
2. It is in writing, signed by the drawer of the draft, contains an unconditional order to pay a sum certain in money on demand; it is not payable to the order of a named payee or bearer.
3. It is in writing, signed by the maker of the note, to pay a sum certain in money at a definite fixed future time, to the order of a named payee; single, unconditional promise to pay, because payment will depend upon the existence and sufficiency of a particular source of funds.
4. It is in writing, signed by the maker, containing a single, absolute promise to pay a sum certain in money, to a named payee, and payable to the order of the payee; it is not payable on demand or at a definite fixed or determinable future time.

Multiple Choice Questions

1. a
2. d
3. a
4. d
5. c
6. b
7. d
8. a
9. b
10. b

CHAPTER 24 — Commercial Paper: Transferability and Negotiation

Fill-In Questions

1. negotiation; indorsement; signature.
2. holder.
3. signature; delivery.
4. special; signature; delivery; delivery plus indorsement of the person to whom instrument was made payable.
5. s/s Lucy Low, Pay to the order of Tom Trustee for the benefit of Benny Fishiary; s/s Tom Trustee, as trustee for Benny Fishiary; s/s Henry Hunt, for deposit only (or for collection).

Multiple Choice Questions

1.	b	6.	b
2.	d	7.	d
3.	c	8.	a
4.	c	9.	a
5.	b	10.	a

CHAPTER 25 — Commercial Paper: Holder in Due Course

Fill-In Questions

1. bearer; in blank.
2. in good faith, for value; overdue; dishonored; any defenses against it.
3. actually given or performed; performance of services, delivery or sale of property or payment of money; under legal process; not in the ordinary course of business.
4. holder; there are defenses against the instrument or that there are claims to it.

Multiple Choice Questions

1. d
2. b
3. a
4. b
5. a
6. c
7. c
8. d
9. a

CHAPTER 26 — Commercial Paper: Defenses, Liability, and Discharge

Fill-In Questions

1. signature; the contract that is implied in the negotiable instrument.
2. the maker of a note and the acceptor of a draft; the drawer of a draft, unqualified indorsers and accommodation parties, other than accommodation makers.
3. notice of dishonor.
4. good title; no knowledge that the signature of the maker or drawer is not authorized; the instrument has not been materially altered.
5. breach of contract, lack or failure of consideration, lack of real, genuine assent (fraud in the inducement, misrepresentation, mistake, undue influence, duress that is not extreme), illegality or incapacity, which renders a contract voidable (rather than void), discharge by payment or other satisfaction or discharge by cancellation or renunciation when the instrument is not removed from circulation or some evidence of the discharge indicated on the instrument itself; unauthorized completion of an incomplete instrument, conditional delivery or nondelivery; any holder, including a holder in due course.

Multiple Choice Questions

1.	a	4.	a	7.	d
2.	d	5.	c	8.	b
3.	b	6.	c	9.	b

CHAPTER 27 — Commercial Paper: Checks and the Banking System

Fill-In Questions

1. Customer; payor (or in Federal Reserve System Regulations parlance, paying).
2. cashier's check; certified check.
3. the drawer; a holder; prior indorsers.
4. (2) a stale check (an uncertified check dated more than six months before) is presented; (3) the depositor has died or become otherwise incompetent; (4) the depositor has given the bank a stop payment order; (5) there is a forgery, alteration or irregularity on the instrument.

Multiple Choice Questions

1. b
2. a
3. c
4. b
5. a
6. d
7. d (This question requires application of the temporary funds availability schedule set forth in the Expedited Funds Availability Act.)
8. c (This question requires application of the permanent funds availability schedule set forth in the Expedited Funds Availability Act.)

CHAPTER 28 — Electronic Fund Transfers

Fill-In Questions

1. cashless; electronic fund transfer.
2. Float time (or Float); transfer.
3. automated teller machine (or customer-bank communication terminal or remote service unit); access card; personal identification number.
4. personal, family or household; commercial (nonconsumer).
5. the customer's liability for unauthorized transfers, resulting from the loss or theft of the access card, code or other access device; whom and what telephone number to call in order to report a loss or theft; the customer's right to have written evidence of electronic fund transactions; the manner in which errors can be corrected; the customer's right to stop payment.
6. receipt; location (site); monthly.
7. two (2); 500; sixty (60).

Multiple Choice Questions

1. b   5. b
2. a   6. c
3. c   7. c
4. a   8. d

CHAPTER 29 — Secured Transactions

Fill-In Questions

1. security interest; secured party.
2. collateral.
3. consumer goods; inventory.
4. attached; perfected.
5. rights in the collateral; given value.
6. after acquired property of the debtor; future advances to be given by the secured party.
7. persons who have perfected their security interests in the same collateral; or who have become lien creditors; or who have purchased the collateral from the debtor in the ordinary course of business; or who are buyers or other transferees in bulk, not in the ordinary course of business, to the extent that they give value and receive delivery of the collateral without knowledge of the security interest; or who are transferees of accounts and general intangibles to the extent that they give value without knowledge of the security interest.
8. in the ordinary course of business. (See Chapter 30 for information dealing with possessory liens.)
9. whose security interest attached first or the one who perfected first.
10. dispose of it by sale or other commercially reasonable means and apply the proceeds to the satisfaction of the underlying obligation.

Multiple Choice Questions

1.	b	5.	c	9.	d
2.	a	6.	d	10.	d
3.	c	7.	c	11.	b
4.	d	8.	b	12.	a

CHAPTER 30 — Rights of Debtors and Creditors

Fill-In Questions

1. surety; guarantor.
2. mechanic's.
3. artisan's.
4. directing the sheriff to seize specified property of the debtor, sell it and deliver the proceeds to the judgment creditor.
5. Garnishment.
6. mortgagor/debtor.
7. the family home and furniture or household furnishings; pensions on account of military service and a proportion of disposable income paid as wages.

Multiple Choice Questions

1.	a	6.	b
2.	a	7.	d
3.	d	8.	b
4.	d	9.	c
5.	a	10.	d

CHAPTER 31 — Bankruptcy and Reorganization

Fill-In Questions

1. U.S. Constitution; Congress.
2. creditors of the debtor.
3. reorganization; automatic stay.
4. including individuals, partnerships or corporations; $5,000; involuntary liquidation.
5. the Bankruptcy Court; six months.
6. the debtor.
7. that creditor being favored over other creditors; the trustee of the debtor's estate.
8. reorganization; an adjustment of debts.

Multiple Choice Questions

1.	c	4.	a	7.	a
2.	d	5.	a	8.	d
3.	d	6.	d	9.	a
				10.	b

CHAPTER 32 — Agency Relationships

Fill-In Questions

1. employee or servant; agent.
2. independent contractor.
3. ratification, estoppel or operation of law.
4. coupled with an interest.
5. follow lawful instructions without deviation, use reasonable skills and diligence in acting on behalf of his principal and use special skills which he or she possesses, relating to the agency.
6. loyally, in good faith in furthering the interests of his or her principal, without benefiting himself or herself or a third person in conflict with the interests of his or her principal; voidable.
7. reasonable compensation for his or her services.
8. indemnification; indemnification.
9. revoking; the agency was an agency at will (not created for a stated period of time or purpose) or for cause.
10. the bankruptcy of the principal, impossibility (destruction of the subject matter, outbreak of war, change in law making the agency illegal), unforeseen circumstances.

Multiple Choice Questions

1.	c	6.	b	11.	c
2.	d	7.	c	12.	b
3.	a	8.	a	13.	b
4.	c	9.	b	14.	d
5.	b	10.	d	15.	c
				16.	d

CHAPTER 33 — Liability to Third Parties and Employer-Employee Relationships

Fill-In Questions

1. scope of authority.
2. express; generally known custom or usage or an emergency situation.
3. estopped; apparent.
4. ratified; not; breach of an implied warranty of authority.
5. identity; undisclosed principal.
6. torts; the scope of their authority or employment in furtherance of the business of the superior.

Multiple Choice Questions

1.	d	5.	a	9.	a
2.	c	6.	a	10.	c
3.	c	7.	b	11.	a
4.	a	8.	d	12.	a

CHAPTER 34 — Forms of Business Organization

Multiple Choice Questions

1. a
2. a
3. c
4. d

CHAPTER 35 — Partnerships: Creation and Termination

Fill-In Questions

1. an entity; an aggregate of its individual members or partners.
2. express agreement; contribute capital or make joint investments, are co-owners of property that is used for partnership purposes and share profits of the business.
3. act of the parties or partners.
4. death of a partner, its bankruptcy or that of a partner or illegality.
5. its winding up by the partners (or liquidation by distribution of partnership property in accordance with law).

Multiple Choice Questions

1. a
2. b
3. a
4. c
5. a
6. a
7. d
8. a
9. c
10. a

Solutions for 4, 5 and 6:

4. The amount that is due = $145,000 owed to creditors + $10,000, return of capital to P, + $5,000, return of capital to Q = $160,000.

5. The outside creditors get paid in full. $100,000 is available from the partnership assets and the deficiency of $60,000 is theoretically met by equal contributions from P and Q. Of this, $45,000 is paid to creditors and the balance to P and Q.

6. Each partner's share of the total firm deficiency of $60,000 is half, or $30,000. Q, however, only has $5,000 of personal assets that can be reached by creditors of the partnership under the principle of marshalling of assets. The creditors can reach up to $50,000 of P's personal assets but only need $40,000 to satisfy claims of the $45,000 deficiency.

CHAPTER 36 — Partnerships: Operation and Duties

Fill-In Questions

1. manage the affairs of the partnership.
2. change the scope or nature of the partnership business; alter the capital structure; admit new partners; assign partnership property for the benefit of creditors; dispose of the partnership goodwill; confess judgment; submit a dispute, involving the partnership, to arbitration; or undertake any act that would make the further conduct of the partnership business impossible.
3. possess partnership property for partnership purposes.
4. a tenant in partnership.
5. his or her actual or apparent authority or the co-partners ratified the contract.
6. buy and sell goods of the kind in which the partnership regularly deals, give warranties, borrow money and issue and negotiate commercial paper on behalf of the other partners.
7. jointly; jointly and severally.

Multiple Choice Questions

1.	b	4.	b
2.	d	5.	a
3.	c	6.	b

CHAPTER 37 — Partnerships: Limited Partnerships

Fill-In Questions

1. the partnership name, its duration, the nature of its business, the location of its place of business, the names and addresses of members, the capital contributions of limited partners and their share of profits and other compensation, methods for changes in membership and subsequent continuation of the business; signed by the members of the partnership; filed.
2. his or her capital contribution.
3. the limited partner participated in management or his or her surname is used in the name of the firm.
4. dies, retires, withdraws or is expelled for cause, becomes insane or bankrupt, unless otherwise provided in its certificate or unless the other members consent to its continuation; The death, retirement or bankruptcy (unless it results in the bankruptcy of the firm).

Multiple Choice Questions

1.	c	4.	b
2.	c	5.	a
3.	b		

CHAPTER 38 — Corporations: Nature and Classifications

Fill-In Questions

1. name.
2. shareholders; board of directors; officers.
3. shareholders are not personally liable for obligations of the corporation; share-holders do not have the right to possess corporate property (they are not tenants in partnership, tenants in common or joint tenants with other shareholders with respect to corporate property); death of a shareholder does not dissolve the corporation; shareholders are not representatives of the corporation nor agents for other shareholders nor fiduciaries of the corporation or the other shareholders.
4. public; private.
5. a certificate or license to do business; registered office and registered agent.
6. certificate or license to do business as a foreign corporation.

Multiple Choice Questions

1. d
2. a
3. b
4. c
5. b

CHAPTER 39 — Corporations: Formation and Corporate Financing

Fill-In Questions

1. *de jure*; *de facto*; the state.
2. shares of stock; bonds and debentures; dividends.
3. bonds; debentures.
4. rights to dividends; liquidation rights.

Multiple Choice Questions

1. c
2. d
3. a
4. d
5. a
6. d
7. b
8. c
9. a
10. d

CHAPTER 40 — Corporations: Corporate Powers and Management

Fill-In Questions

1. Statutory, general; the power to have and use a corporate seal; to have perpetual existence; to enter into contracts; to sue and be sued; to issue shares of stock; to borrow and lend money; to acquire by purchase or otherwise real and personal property; to dispose of by sale or otherwise real or personal property; to conduct its business and carry on its operations; to elect or appoint officers and agents and define their duties and fix their compensation; to make and alter bylaws, not inconsistent with its charter (articles or certificate of incorporation) or the laws of the state of incorporation; to transact lawful business.
2. *ultra vires*; cannot assert or raise.
3. legal; equitable.
4. Shareholders; directors.
5. corporation (not the shareholders).

Multiple Choice Questions

1. a   4. a
2. b   5. c
3. c   6. a

CHAPTER 41 — Corporations: Rights & Duties of Directors, Managers & Shareholders

Fill-In Questions

1. inspect the books and records of the corporation (and to receive notice of special meetings of the board of directors); the directors convened as a board.
2. his or her dissent is entered in the minutes of the meeting of the board of directors or a written dissent filed with the minutes; poor business judgment; relating to the corporation, not brought by or on behalf of the corporation.
3. unpaid stock subscriptions; improperly or illegally declared dividends, when they had knowledge thereof; deficiencies caused by failure to pay satisfactory consideration for shares of stock issued by the corporation.
4. property; services actually performed.
5. preemptive rights.

Multiple Choice Questions

1. d
2. a
3. c
4. a
5. c
6. d
7. b

CHAPTER 42 — Corporations: Merger, Consolidation, and Termination

Fill-In Questions

1. cease to exist and disappear; the assets of A and B Corporations; the liabilities, debts and obligations of A and B Corporations; shares of C Corporation stock.
2. cease to exist and disappear; a new corporation, which comes into existence because of the consolidation.
3. shareholder approval; not cease; the character of the corporation's assets and business.
4. shareholders and creditors of the corporation; cannot.
5. the fair market value of his or her shares; an appraisal of the fair market value of his or her shares. (The court may appoint appraisers "to receive evidence and recommend a decision on the question of fair market value." MBCA Sec. 81; RMBCA Sec. 13.30.)

Multiple Choice Questions

1.	b	5.	c
2.	c	6.	c
3.	a	7.	d
4.	a	8.	b

CHAPTER 43 — Corporations: Financial Regulation and Investor Protection

Fill-In Questions

1. Blue Sky Laws; Securities Act of 1933; Securities Exchange Act of 1934; Securities and Exchange Commission (SEC); interstate commerce; mails.
2. the Securities and Exchange Commission (the SEC); descriptions of the securities being offered for sale, including the relationship between the securities and other capital securities of the issuer and the manner in which the issuer intends to use the proceeds of the sale, descriptions of the issuer's business and properties, its management, its security holdings, remuneration, and other benefits (such as pensions and stock options) inuring to directors and officers, a financial statement certified by an independent public accounting firm, and a description of pending or threatened lawsuits.
3. Securities Exchange Act of 1934; 500 or more; the SEC.

Multiple Choice Questions

1.	e	5.	c
2.	b	6.	c
3.	a	7.	d
4.	d	8.	b

CHAPTER 45 — Government Regulation: Introduction and Administrative Law

Fill-In Questions

1. Federal; Congress.
2. arbitrary, capricious, not supported by the record or contrary to law.
3. executive (or ministerial); investigatory; rulemaking (or legislative).
4. profits, advertising, quotas, licensing, allocation rights, standards and disclosures; use of certain materials and processes in production.
5. consumer products, working conditions and employment.
6. utilities, some carriers, those engaged in communications, inventors and authors.

Multiple Choice Questions

1. d   4. a
2. d   5. d
3. d   6. c

CHAPTER 46 — Consumer Protection

Fill-In Questions

1. Federal Trade Commission; Department of Housing and Urban Development.
2. deceptive; Federal Trade Commission.
3. Fair Packaging Act.
4. Truth-in-Lending Act; consumer; consumer; cost of credit.
5. unsolicited merchandise.

Multiple Choice Questions

1. a
2. d

CHAPTER 47 — Environmental Protection

Multiple Choice Questions

1. d
2. b
3. c

CHAPTER 48 — Antitrust

Fill-In Questions

1. unreasonable, general; reasonable, partial, ancillary.
2. restraint of interstate or foreign trade or commerce.
3. exempt; baseball; exempt.
4. criminal or civil (equitable); treble damages; civil.
5. *per se*; price fixing (setting minimum or maximum prices), horizontal market division (dividing a market among competitors), agreements limiting production or establishing quotas, joint refusals to deal or coercive group boycotts.
6. proscriptive; policing.
7. price discrimination; exclusive dealings; lessen monopoly.
8. cease and desist; initiate investigations and promulgate interpretative rules, policy statements and regulations.
9. monopolizes or attempts to monopolize interstate commerce; price discrimination, exclusive dealings and tying contracts and acquisition of stock or assets of another corporation.
10. horizontal; anticompetitive (or to lessen competition or tend to create a monopoly).
11. a vertical, illegal.

Multiple Choice Questions

1. d	5. a	9. c
2. c	6. b	10. a
3. a	7. d	11. c
4. b	8. b	

CHAPTER 49 — Employment and Labor Relations Law

Fill-In Questions

1. Norris-La Guardia; National Labor Relations or Wagner; Labor-Management or Taft-Hartley.
2. closed; Union; right-to-work.
3. religion, country of national origin and sex; Equal Employment Opportunity.
4. at will; at will; public policy; contract; at will.
5. workers' compensation; Social Security.
6. Occupational Safety and Health.
7. Unemployment compensation; employers; Unemployment; Unemployment.

Multiple Choice Questions

1. d	5. b
2. c	6. b
3. b	7. a
4. a	8. c

CHAPTER 50 — Personal Property

Fill-In Questions

1. rights and interests; capable of being possessed.
2. occupation, gift, accession, confusion, inheritance and creation.
3. donative intent, delivery by donor; acceptance by donee.
4. inadvertently left or misplaced it; accidentally and involuntarily left it.

Multiple Choice Questions

1. a
2. a
3. a
4. c
5. d
6. d
7. a
8. c
9. c

CHAPTER 51 — Bailments

Fill-In Questions

1. bailor; personal; bailee; return.
2. constructively; constructive.
3. great; slight; bailments for mutual benefit; ordinary.

Multiple Choice Questions

1. c
2. d
3. a
4. b
5. b
6. c
7. b
8. a
9. a
10. c
11. b

CHAPTER 52 — Nature and Ownership of Real Property

Fill-In Questions

1. growing on or affixed to the land or contained above or below the surface of the land.
2. affixed to the real property; trade fixtures.
3. estates; estates in fee or life estates (or freehold estates); estates less than freehold or leaseholds.
4. joint tenants; B, the surviving joint tenant; tenancy by the entirety.
5. tenancy in common.
6. delivery of a deed of conveyance; quitclaim; clouds or defects.
7. simple absolute.
8. possibility of reverter; contingent remainder.
9. contingent remainder.
10. possibility of reverter; possibility of reverter.
11. contingent remainder.
12. reversion; vested remainder.
13. reversion; reversion.
14. vested remainder.
15. power of termination or entry; executory interest.
16. an easement; profit; nonpossessory; easements or profits appurtenant.
17. a restrictive convenant running with the land; equitable servitude.

Multiple Choice Questions

1. a   6. a
2. c   7. c
3. a   8. d
4. d   9. c
5. b

CHAPTER 53 — Landlord-Tenant Relationships

Fill-In Questions

1. possession; rent; landlord; possession.
2. lease; lease; rent; reversionary interest.
3. quiet enjoyment; habitability; habitable.
4. landlord; common areas.
5. landlord (or lessor); tenant (or lessee) from whom the sublease was obtained; original tenant (or lessee).

Multiple Choice Questions

1. c   4. c
2. a   5. d
3. d   6. a

CHAPTER 54 — Insurance

Fill-In Questions

1. creating; transferring and allocating.
2. insurable; incur a financial or pecuniary loss if the property is damaged or destroyed.
3. insurable; the loss is incurred.
4. insurable; incur a pecuniary of financial detriment or loss if that person dies.
5. insurable; the insurance policy was obtained.

Multiple Choice Questions

1. b
2. c
3. b
4. b
5. a
6. a   Solution:

$$\text{Loss} \times \frac{\text{Amount of Insurance Carried}}{\text{Amount of Insurance Required}} = \text{Amount of Recovery}$$

$$\$80,000 + \$100,000 \times \frac{\$600,000}{90\%(\$900,000 + \$100,000)}$$

$$\$180,000 \times \frac{2}{3} = \$120,000.$$

CHAPTER 56 — Wills, Trusts and Estates

Fill-In Questions

1. executor or executrix; will; probate; administrator or administratrix.
2. testamentary; in writing, signed by the testator or testatrix, attested by two or more witnesses (who may be required to be disinterested, to witness the signing of the will by the testator and to sign in the presence of each other) and, in some states, published and declared by the testator to be his or her last will and testament.
3. failed to execute a valid will or to provide for the disposition of some property in his or her will; spouse; equally among the children; equally the share their parent would have received (*per stirpes*).
4. the settlor; the trustee; another person, a beneficiary, or other persons, beneficiaries.
5. during the lifetime of the settlor; upon the death; prescribing formalities for the execution of wills.

Multiple Choice Questions

1.   a
2.   d
3.   d
4.   c
5.   d
6.   c
7.   a
8.   d
9.   b
10. b
11. c
12. b

CHAPTER 57 — Liability of Accountants

Multiple Choice Questions

1.   c
2.   a
3.   d
4.   b
5.   a
6.   d
7.   c
8.   b
9.   c
10. c

†